AS/400 Client/ Server Systems

Business Applications and Solutions

Tony Baritz

McGraw-Hill, Inc.

New York San Francisco Washington, D.C. Auckland Bogotá
Caracas Lisbon London Madrid Mexico City Milan
Montreal New Delhi San Juan Singapore
Sydney Tokyo Toronto

McGraw-Hill

*A Division of The **McGraw·Hill** Companies*

Library of Congress Cataloging-in-Publication Data

Baritz, Tony.
   AS/400 client/server systems : business applications and solutions
/ by Tony Baritz.
     p. cm.
   Includes index.
   ISBN 0-07-018311-2 (hc)
   1. Client/server computing. 2. IBM AS/400 (Computer)   I. Title.
QA76.9.C55B37 1995
004'.36—dc20   95-32900
                                                        CIP

hc 1 2 3 4 5 6 7 8 9 DOC/DOC 9 0 0 9 8 7 6 5

ISBN 0-07-018311-2

*The sponsoring editor of this book was Gerald Papke and the supervising
editor was Susan W. Kagey. The book editor was Theresa Cuningham.
The production supervisor was Katherine G. Brown. This book was set in
ITC Century Light. It was composed in Blue Ridge Summit, Pa.*

Printed and bound by R.R. Donnelley & Sons Company, Crawfordsville, Indiana.

McGraw-Hill books are available at special quantity discounts to use as
premiums and sales promotions, or for use in corporate training programs.
For more information, please write to the Director of Special Sales, McGraw-
Hill, 11 West 19th Street, New York, NY 10011. Or contact your local
bookstore.

MH96
0183112

For Mom and Dad

Contents

Introduction

This book is a comprehensive discussion of major client/server concepts and techniques for the AS/400 computer and personal computers (PCs) and includes examples of how to set up various client/server systems, as well as actual solutions for business problems. This single volume is a fast-entry path into AS/400 client/server application development for programmers, analysts, managers, and users. Those who learn about client/server systems can increase their own value and marketability in addition to helping their companies gain a competitive edge.

The AS/400 is a versatile, powerful, and intelligent node on the network. It combines a powerful database with automatic network configuration and integration. PCs, with their easy user interfaces and feature-rich software packages, have become the de-facto standard for desktop business packages. Combining the best features of these two systems on networks provides a very productive and attractive environment in which to develop total business systems and is known as the *client/server environment*. The AS/400 is increasingly being used as the database server engine integrated with a user-friendly PC front-end, such as Windows. It is then possible for users to access the corporate database without knowing commands or keyboard layouts or even how to sign on. The exciting new field of client/server solutions enables businesses to combine the best features of the midrange computer and the PC to provide a long-awaited productivity boost.

It is difficult for programmers to maintain current skills in this fast-changing field. The necessity to be knowledgeable quickly in a new and diverse environment is a serious problem. When a company takes a new direction, such as toward client/server systems, it immediately needs skilled professionals to develop its systems, and in an evolving environment like the client/server, it is difficult to achieve these skills. The ease of use enjoyed by the end user is implemented through the complex configurations and multiple features of various platforms developed by skilled professionals. This hands-on book facilitates creating these client/server applications. This book contains the results of a careful distillation and compilation of the latest topics necessary to begin working with AS/400-to-PC system development. Windows, OS/2, DB2, PowerBuilder, ODBC, and Visual Basic, as well as many more packages, are discussed. Visual controls, screen design, event-handling, database connectivity, and user interfaces are also included. The process of setting up Client Access/400 for terminal emulation, shared printers, and all its other features is explained, along with how to bind controls on the PC screen to the AS/400 database, process remote requests, and run reports and queries from the PC to the AS/400 databases. All these features are the components of the client/server paradigm.

The Client/Server Environment

The client/server environment consists of many parts; it is one solution to the problem of integrating multiple computer platforms and services into a simple interface. Generally, a PC is used as the front-end for a larger database server on the back-end. The server described in this book is the AS/400. PC programs, running in Windows, OS/2, or even DOS, can access information from the AS/400 and present it to the user as if it were local data. This approach greatly eases the process of getting information from computers for the user. It also greatly increases the integration complexity for the developer. It is not possible to implement these systems solely with the tools available on the AS/400, like RPG or COBOL. Nor can the PC do it alone. To create a client/server system, it is necessary to understand and implement tools on various platforms. A typical client/server system might include CL, RPG, DDS, Data Queues, PC Support (Client Access), DOS, Windows, and PowerBuilder. In addition, the computers involved in this interchange are tied together by some type of network. These elements represent a whole range of skills and languages not always found in one person.

The client/server concept is a broad way of thinking about user information needs and solutions. Often, several methods exist for providing a solution to the same problem. For example, you can use Query or RPG or COBOL to collect data from the AS/400. File transfer could be used to bring the data down to the PC for presentation or further processing, or an ODBC connection could be used to view the data directly from the server. The mechanism of viewing or manipulating data originating on the server is on the PC in the form of Visual Basic, PowerBuilder, VISTA, or Lotus. Many interchangeable parts exist for the developer, who is trying to provide an elegant and seamless integration for a specific purpose.

The graphical user interface (GUI) is usually used as the front-end for the client/server system because Windows (the most popular GUI) has become the de-facto standard for both home and office computing. Users who have no need to learn how to navigate and use the AS/400 expect to be able to point and click their way to timely information from the database. This expectation is now reasonable, and those who can satisfy this user expectation will find themselves more and more useful to their organizations. The main point of client/server development is to bring server data to the GUI desktop.

To bring data from the server to the desktop, multiple platforms and operating systems need to be understood. The more one knows about platforms and operating systems, the better. For example, a perfect solution might be available in OS/2, while Windows simply cannot do the job. Can you use the Apple Macintosh already on the vice president's desk, or is a PC necessary? Which aspects of the client/server application are best performed on the server, and which on the client? Should you use a third-party gateway or IBM's Client Access to access the AS/400? When is Lotus a better client tool than Visual Basic? All of these questions come up when developing a client/server application.

Many different applications are conceivable with all these pieces, as you might imagine:

- *You could use PowerBuilder to present the user with various menus and pushbuttons. Some of these could submit jobs to batch queues on the AS/400 and inform the user when they are finished running.*

- *You could initiate an automatic download of the data to the PC or PC network.*

- *You could present data windows for changing or manipulating the resulting data.*

- *You could use another menu choice or pushbutton to generate reports, using a PC Windows report writer.*

All these functions happen as easily as pushing buttons with the mouse, and these processes are explained in later chapters on these tools.

Another approach might be to design a system that uses a DOS program like Clipper or dBASE to send a remote command to the AS/400. It could wait for the command to complete and then download the data, just like the Windows PowerBuilder application. It could also present the data for editing and running reports, all from the menu. This approach is not as appealing or fully featured as the Windows example, but it does provide client/server functionality in the DOS environment.

The development paradigm for systems is changing. The client/server platform both offers and demands a sophistication, elegance, and level of knowledge beyond that of the single platform idiom. We have many more building blocks with which to fashion the appropriate solution. It is necessary to think the project through all the implications of each component or link to determine which are best used. It is also to consider which components can best perform the necessary processing inherent to the task. If you need to process the data from the AS/400 beyond its natural state in the physical files, do you, for example, process the data in RPG, Query, download it, and then use Visual Basic or Lotus, or do you wait until the end and use calculated fields in your report writer, such as R&R? These questions can only be answered through familiarity with the associated products. That is the goal of this book—to provide that familiarity.

To understand client/server development, it is necessary to understand the graphical user interface (GUI). Most people are quite familiar with GUI from using Windows. Some issues, however, are not immediately apparent to the casual GUI user. Windows is an operating system as well as an interface, and its features are critical to the conception and execution of client/server systems. The mouse is the most obvious attribute of GUIs. It points to what are known as controls on the desktop. Controls are menu items or pushbuttons.

Our task as client/server developers is to present these controls to the user and manage what they do in response to them. This process is known as event-handling. What the user does with the mouse or the keyboard triggers what the program does next. Object-oriented programming is very helpful to us in this endeavor because it gives us many encapsulated tools, or black boxes, we can place on the desktop, like pushbuttons. They know when they are clicked and can institute further processing automatically. Different types of windows can be used in putting client/server interfaces on the desktop. Multiple-document-interface windows as well as response windows and data windows contain the various controls that constitute the application's functionality.

Windows, although by far the most prevalent interface, is not the only GUI platform for client/server: OS/2 has its presentation manager, Apple has System 7, and UNIX offers X-Windows. All of these can work in client/server systems.

Client/server technology is at the core of these developments. Without the network connections and software interfaces or middleware, none of these applications would be possible. We no longer think what we can do with a software package, but of what we can do between cooperating packages on remote platforms. Obviously, some standards must be applied to this task to develop consistent tools.

Open Systems Interconnect (OSI) is a worldwide standard for distributed systems. The Open Software Foundation (OSF) offers the Distributed Computing Environment (DCE) as a standard of interconnection. While DCE is a well-known standard and the basis of many college textbooks, it is not the de-facto method of interconnecting computers with the AS/400. In the AS/400 world, various bridges, routers, and gateways use their own protocols to connect the AS/400 to remote clients. System Application Architecture (SAA) is IBM's overall plan for applications, and common communications support is SAA's standard for interconnections. System Network Architecture (SNA) is a group of protocols that constitute the IBM world of networking. Advanced peer-to-peer networking (APPN) is key to this approach. It provides routing services and auto-configuration of devices to ease the building of networks. Advanced program-to-program communication (APPC) provides services that allow programs to talk to each other over the SNA network.

Application program interfaces (API) are hooks that can be used in one program to access functions from another program or remote system. APIs really form the core of cooperative distributed processing. One program can call a function of another, even on a different system. Sophisticated application services thus become available as a result of these APIs. Client Access, for instance, is really an implementation of APIs between the PC and the AS/400. Remote SQL is a standard that provides data access between programs and systems. An SQL statement in PowerBuilder can be sent to the AS/400 for execution and return a data subset. Open database connectivity (ODBC), implemented as a driver, is a pipeline for data access between two programs, using SQL as the access method. You load the driver to enable access from the PC program to native data on the AS/400. Remote procedure calls (RPC) enable a PC program to run a program on the AS/400. Taken together, these functions provide a powerful group of tools with which to design client/server applications.

Concept of Client/Server

1.1 The Client/Server Concept

Client/server computing is a form of distributed processing. The client computer requests a service from the server on the network. The server responds by returning data. The response can take many forms, including a database extract, a file transfer, a display screen (terminal emulation), or a remote printer function. This interaction has existed in the form of terminal emulation for a few years. Other forms, such as using a PC spreadsheet graph as a query viewer into the AS/400 database, are more recent. Client/server systems rely on the theory that different types of processing should be performed on the computer platform most suited to them. The larger machine, in our case an AS/400, excels in database functionality, maintaining access paths and security, and providing data to remote SQL calls quite efficiently. The PC surpasses the AS/400 in ease of use, presentation platforms, and user productivity features such as spreadsheets and graphical user interfaces (GUI).

Client/server computing integrates these different platforms, using the best features of each and attempting to avoid the lesser features. It would make little sense to use the green and black character-based screen of the AS/400 to display data requests served by a PC. Allowing corporate executives to access AS/400 data effortlessly and transparently from a PC screen, however, does make sense. The executives can point at a little picture (or icon) on their screens of the United States divided into regions, click a button, and receive a color bar chart of regional sales. Pushing another button with the picture of a printer on it could send the file to the printer. This printer could be connected to the PC, the AS/400, or even be in a different city. The user does not need to manage these things; they are built into functions that underlie the pictures.

These systems provide a new functionality in the workplace. They allow users increased access to the corporate database but do not require users to know arcane codes or different keyboard layouts. Imagine trying to explain to the CEO that the PC Ctrl key is really the Enter key on the AS/400 but the PC Enter key is really Field Exit. Why should the CEO need to know these things? Client/server systems provide the information needed from computers without requiring data processing skills. With client/servers, typing becomes much less important, and objects and processes are found and invoked much more easily. Information can be retrieved without directly involving computer programmers. End users become empowered, relieving the backlog of the computer department.

Although client/server relationships can take many forms, the following are the strengths of the platforms in the client/server environment:

- Client (PC)
  ~Presentation features (GUI)
  ~Spreadsheets
  ~Word processing
  ~User's projects
  ~Drawing and graphics
  ~Multimedia
  ~Data entry and validation
- Server (AS/400)
  ~Database services
  ~Network management
  ~Batch processing
  ~Centralized repository
  ~Shared resources

Intricate presentation methods, such as Windows-based exploding pie charts from a remote AS/400 SQL call, are a very appealing and useful client/server application. Services much more humble, however, also qualify as client/server. A process that executes quietly in the middle of the night, refreshing a local mirror image of a remote database, invisibly and unnoticed, is a client/server function, too. PC Support (now Client Access) is another client/server application that provides many features and functions, such as terminal emulation and file transfer. Some client/server processes require a live hot-link to the AS/400, while others can rely on batch downloads or file transfers at periodic intervals.

It is clear that the client/server can take on many forms and shapes involving divergent hardware platforms, operating systems, network connections, and application services. No single platform can provide the richness and power available through the hybrid forms of client/server systems. A clear understanding of the facets and components of the client/server environment can lead to applications that are elegant and incisive.

1.2 Graphical User Interface

Computers have a new face. Not so long ago, when you wanted a computer to do something, you had to punch little holes in cards and then stand in line to feed them to the computer. After a while, results would appear in a relatively decipherable format. Today, you simply point at a little picture or icon of what you want to do, on a color screen, and click the mouse button. A customized graphical format then appears to show you the result of your inquiry or process in meaningful human terms. It's easier, more productive, and more enjoyable. This type of interface, known as a *graphical user interface (GUI),* has become the norm for home computing and is becoming the standard for office desktop systems. In addition, it is being used in client/server systems to provide an easy, friendly front-end for the enterprise-wide database. While not all client/server functions incorporate a GUI front-end, an increasing number do. Vendors cannot afford to ignore this trend, and coming years will see more GUI screens and fewer character-based screens.

Several systems offer the GUI look, characterized by icons on the screen and a mouse-driven, point-and-click interface. The Apple Macintosh computer was the first to standardize this approach. GUI, however, is very inefficient in terms of processor overhead. A lot of CPU cycles are burned just in maintaining the pixels and monitoring where the mouse pointer is, but exponential leaps in PC processing power make GUI feasible. Apple users raved about its ease of use, and it wasn't long before the IBM world wanted to institute this new look as well. They offered Windows and OS/2, both derived from the Apple interface with mouse and icons. The popularity of Windows has by far outstripped that of OS/2.

While DOS waits for the user to type a command and parameters at the command line (the C:> prompt), the GUI interface shows you pictures and waits for you to pick one by pointing and clicking. With GUI, you don't need to know the commands of the operating system or even the names of programs you want to invoke. In the GUI environment, the developer has attached the functions and features of the system to intuitive pictures that a child can understand and execute. I have seen a three-year old get into the Paintbrush program in Windows and draw a picture, unaided. In DOS, this entire procedure would be inconceivable. The mouse can in fact be used in some DOS programs, but they lack the easy elegance and environmental integration of the GUI approach. The GUI interface provides a seamless desktop approach to computing (Figure 1.1).

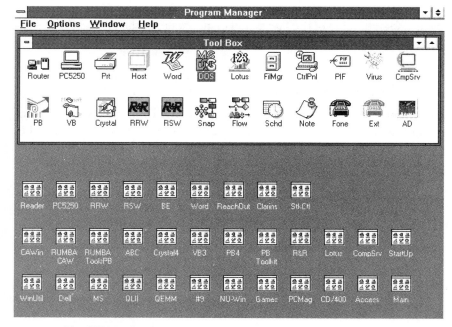

Figure 1.1 The GUI interface provides a seamless desktop approach to computing.

Menus, pop-up windows, and icons guide the GUI user through the available options toward the desired function. Extensive online help is a feature of GUIs and the messages to the user tend to be more understandable, extensive, and cross-referenced than in DOS or certainly OS/400. GUIs provide pictures such as a shredder or garbage can for deleting files. You don't need to remember commands. A picture of the directory tree of your disks helps navigate the disk drives without remembering the directories on a drive or the drives themselves; they are all visible as pictures in a window. Of course, many complicated configurations and programs lie under the surface of these easy operations, but they are the province of the computer people, not the end users. This distinction is central to the client/server concept: give end users easy access to the services they require and leave the bits and bytes to programmers and systems people. Users can then take a large step toward information systems, rather than mere data retrieval.

1.3 Platforms and Operating Systems

Many machines, operating systems, and application packages can participate in client/server relationships. Even limiting the discussion to the AS/400 world of client/server development involves numerous hardware and software options. As the AS/400 becomes more open in architecture and connectivity options, many more systems can be connected to the AS/400 to share data. These systems can be combined with others in an impressive, if initially somewhat bewildering, array of configurations. It is important to keep in mind that the client/server world is similar to a French menu: you don't order the whole thing at one time, but make careful selections from various categories. Some of the items included in these categories for client/servers are the following:

- Hardware
  ~AS/400
  ~IBM PCs
  ~RS/6000
  ~Sun
  ~HP
  ~Apple Macintosh
  ~Networks

- Operating systems
  ~OS/400
  ~DOS
  ~Windows
  ~OS/2
  ~UNIX
  ~X-Windows
  ~System 7
  ~Networks

- Client/server application software
  ~Client Access/400
  ~DB2/400
  ~Remote SQL
  ~PowerBuilder
  ~Visual Basic
  ~Rumba
  ~Vista
  ~Visual C++

Various routers and software application program interfaces (APIs) enable client/server systems at the communications level. These programs handle the intricacies of communications between divergent hardware platforms and operating systems. They operate over the physical layer of the communications network (cards, cables, etc.) to establish a conversation between two or more machines. In the IBM scheme, these conversations take advantage of the services and features of advanced peer-to-peer networking (APPN) and advanced program-to-program communications (APPC). (The chapter on client/server technology discusses these in more detail.) In this way, the routers set up a data highway between different machines, which wait for distributed processes or client/server applications to be invoked.

Routing programs is crucial to the ultimate performance and features of your system. For example, when you start up PC Support or Client Access, a router program is loaded on the PC in communication with the AS/400. This router provides many communications services between the intelligent workstation (which is the PC) and the AS/400 (which is the server) across the network. Using the functions of this router, application programs on the PC can address requests to the AS/400 and receive responses. For example, Visual Basic, running in Windows on a PC, could use its open database connectivity (ODBC) driver to send a request out of Windows, through the router, to the AS/400. The AS/400 receives the request and services it with perhaps an SQL/400 extract of a database. The data is then sent back through the router to the PC whose address on the network requested it. When the data comes back through the PC router, ODBC intercepts it, and it is displayed in Windows using the Visual Basic display formats.

1.4   Sample Applications

A few sample client/server application descriptions can help show the diversity and potential of this environment.

Vista showing query results. In many cases, executives and other end users need to access up-to-the-minute data and information from the AS/400 database. Unfamiliarity with navigating the network and the AS/400 does not prevent them from accessing the information. Using Vista, they can work in the Windows environment to design a query that can go to the AS/400 database. Using the mouse, they choose fields from a list and define sort orders and headings. When the query is finished, they can run it right from the Windows environment. The configurations behind the scenes submit the request to the AS/400's DB2/400 (formerly called the database manager), and receive the data back over the network. Then Vista takes over and presents the results in a spreadsheet of your choice (Excel, Lotus, etc.), as a column of numbers, or even a color chart (Figure 1.2). These online queries can be very useful in meetings or for presentations.

Rumba terminal emulation with cut and paste. Working in Rumba's 5250 terminal emulator is a good way to take advantage of the features of GUI while still accessing the screens and displays of the AS/400. Actually, the AS/400 displays are embedded within Windows or other GUI context (Figure 1.3). Using this facility enables the user to cut and paste between the AS/400 screens and other GUI applications. For instance, a programmer could cut out sections of AS/400 screens and paste them into documentation for the users. Any AS/400 screen that can be displayed can be cut and pasted into other formats at the PC end. Word processors and spreadsheets

	A	B	C	D	E	F	G	H
1	QWRETL	QWXSLS	QWPSLS	MO04	MO05	MO06	QW2SLS	QWLSLS
2	26	1587	1548	0	0	0	1482	882
3	2	0	0	9409	9410	9411	0	0
4	28.5	0	0	9409	9410	9411	0	12
5	28.5	0	0	9409	9410	9411	0	0
6	28.5	0	0	9409	9410	9411	0	0
7	28.5	0	0	9409	9410	9411	0	0
8	28.5	0	0	9409	9410	9411	0	0
9	28.5	0	0	9409	9410	9411	0	0
10	40	0	0	9409	9410	9411	0	0
11	21	1863	1896	0	0	0	1557	1041
12	21	1275	1614	0	0	0	1323	585
13	21	2172	2715	0	0	0	2367	1321
14	21	792	1146	0	0	0	738	414
15	21	897	1155	0	0	0	660	441
16	21	1242	1628	0	0	0	1221	714

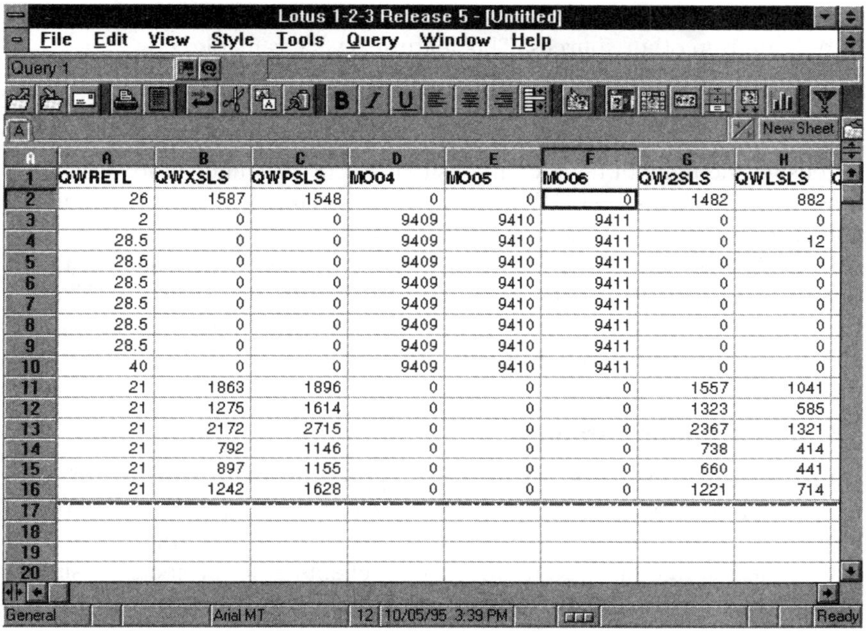

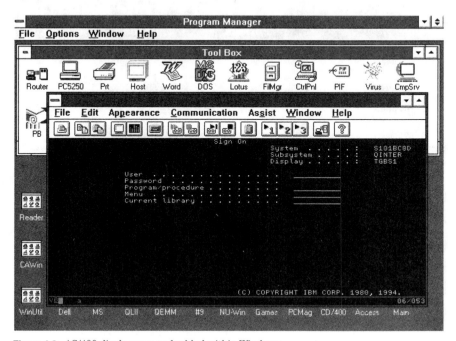

Figure 1.2 VISTA presents the results in a spreadsheet.

Figure 1.3 AS/400 displays are embedded within Windows.

designed for use in Windows and other GUI settings can accept data pasted into them from other sources. This feature is very valuable.

Visual Basic order entry system. Data entry personnel can use custom forms that make entry much easier, more appealing, and less prone to error (Figure 1.4). Pop-up lists offer valid choices for data entry, and edits can be extensive and field- or character-sensitive. Forms are much more easily and quickly designed on the PC than the AS/400, and much of the processing involved with accomplishing data entry can also be performed at the PC. The AS/400 CPU is then freed for tasks at which it is more suited, such as maintaining the database and its access paths and running batch jobs. The PC CPU can be used entirely for display and data capture purposes, as it probably has only one task to perform at a time.

1.5 Development Paradigm

We have already seen that client/server applications involve levels of complexity not inherent in single-platform development. Using two or more operating systems magnifies potential problems. It is important to choose your initial configuration carefully. Identify client/server projects consistent

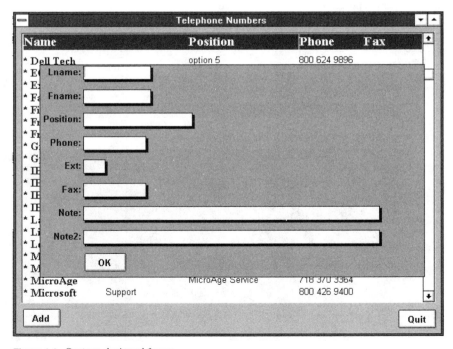

Figure 1.4 Custom-designed forms.

with your current level of expertise on all the platforms involved. Let the enterprise-wide solutions wait until basic or fundamental issues have been ironed out. Simplicity, to the extent possible, should determine the course of client/server applications development. The following suggestions can make implementation of a client/server system easier.

Educate top management and users as to the benefits obtained from client/server computing. Productivity enhancements and consequent changes in the work flow should be identified. Reasonable expectations on their part are important to development.

Begin a user training schedule to instill GUI skills. When client/server systems become available, users should be proficient in mouse techniques. The desktop environment should be comfortable to the employees, along with such techniques as point and click, cut and paste, window management, and other issues.

Decide which processes benefit from which platform. The client tends to perform well with CPU-intensive tasks, such as graphics, spreadsheets, and word processing. Anything that requires or benefits from the constant attention of the CPU should be considered for the client end. In addition, procedures that are single-user oriented, such as customized spreadsheet analyses connected to an AS/400 query, are obvious client applications. It is generally beneficial to place as much work as possible on the client to take advantage of the captive CPU at that end—no one else is using it. Save the AS/400 or the server for that which it does well—database management and security. Because the AS/400 is a more expensive environment, this approach is cost-effective and more efficient.

Be aware of resource usage and potential bottlenecks at the client, over the network, and at the server. This environment is dispersed, and each piece must work efficiently on its own as well as in concert with the others. Be especially wary of large data transfers, as they can place an inordinate load on the AS/400 and network traffic.

Analyze carefully security issues that result from PCs participating in AS/400 processing. Which files can the client access? Are they available for input, output, or both? The PC environment does not protect the AS/400 from security violations, so security must be controlled at the AS/400 side of the process. Designate personnel to be exclusively responsible for security measures and to whom all others will apply for access to objects.

Developers, and especially project leaders, should be aware of techniques and traps at all points of the distributed system. They must therefore be proficient in two or more platforms and in several languages or utilities on each, as well as in network connections. Potential problems can thus be spotted before they occur and ultimately avoided. It is essential to keep the big picture in mind to optimize the flow of data through the various components of the client/server configuration. An efficient program at the client end for data entry or query cannot be appreciated if the connectivity to the AS/400 is painfully slow.

Choose the elements of your client/server implementation very carefully. Many different combinations are possible, but not all of them are desirable. Be especially careful about the speed of the connecting link to the AS/400 database. ODBC is not as fast at data retrieval as the native methods of the servers, such as RPG.

Prototype the GUI interface so it can be tailored to user productivity requirements. The GUI interface is one of the main strengths of client/server applications, so it must flow smoothly and fulfill expectations. It is the face of the system and can be made quite attractive, then shown at an early stage to advantage.

1.6 Summary

The client/server environment is complex and productive. It requires developers who are familiar with multiple aspects of diverse platforms, operating systems, networks, and applications. Communications are important, as well as server batch processing and online client GUI interfaces and event-handling. If these issues are understood, elegant information systems can be constructed that repay the investment in technical knowledge. Executives can just click on an icon and receive an up-to-the-minute color chart of regional sales. Accountants can download database data into spreadsheets for further formatting and analysis. The less-friendly navigational aspects of the mainframe and midrange environments can effectively disappear in favor of the pictorial interface of the PC; the larger machines can still be used for their powerful database and security capabilities. Thus, each platform is used for what it does best.

Chapter

2

Graphical User Interface

The graphical user interface (GUI) is a very different way of working with computers compared to the traditional method of typing commands at the command line. Instead of remembering commands, with their often cryptic syntax and parameters, the user can simply point at various objects or options on the screen and click a button to execute them. The mouse is used to command instead of the keyboard. An arrow on the screen indicates mouse position (Figure 2.1). The arrow moves by moving the mouse or trackball. Buttons on the mouse are used to click and choose, with the left mouse button generally used to choose items. Icons or small pictures on the screen represent available choices or procedures. Other choices can be reached by clicking on options reached through pull-down menus. Necessary words or commands can still be entered, however, by using the keyboard. The traditional keyboard methods of navigation, such as arrow keys and PageUp or PageDown keys can still be effective and are sometimes faster or easier than the mouse. Usually, a combination of the two methods proves the most effective.

2.1 Common User Access

IBM has developed a standard for GUI environments. Common user access (CUA) is its concept of how a graphical environment should look and work. It has been adopted as the de-facto standard of the GUI world. CUA is the front-end of the client/server environment. It features a desktop, icons, menu bars, and windows that are movable and sizable. Various applications run next to or on top each other in adjustable windows. The user can switch between them at will without exiting one and starting up another. They are

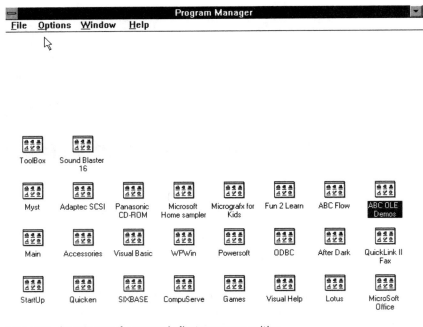

Figure 2.1 An arrow on the screen indicates mouse position.

all visible at the same time, and, while they might not be simultaneously active, it is easy to move between them and even cut and paste data between them.

The desktop

The whole idea of GUI is to provide an easier, intuitive way of working with computers for those who are not power users or programmers. This group includes the majority of computer users by far, executives as well as secretaries. Why require them to learn computer techniques when the computer should help them do their jobs faster and better? By replicating the physical desktop, with tasks visible and accessible, the GUI approach lets almost anyone use a computer effectively. Once one software package has been learned in the GUI environment, others work pretty similarly; a high degree of standardization exists between programs. For example, the same types of choices are available from a Microsoft Word menu bar as from a WordPerfect or even Excel menu bar. If you know how to open a file in one, you can open files in the others. This situation is a tremendous boost in terms of user productivity, especially when learning new software.

Title bar

Most windows feature a title bar at the top of the window that states the name of the window and possibly how it is being used (such as the name of the document you are editing). On the left of the title bar is a standard little box that produces a standard system menu (Figure 2.2) common to many windows. The middle of the title bar, in addition to having the name of the window, allows the window to be dragged. To drag a window, place the mouse pointer over the title bar, hold down the left button, and drag it to where you want it. The buttons at the right of the title bar are the minimize and maximize buttons. Clicking on them makes the window one of three sizes; full-screen, part of the screen, or minimized (hidden in an icon). As windows are opened, they can obscure other windows beneath them, much as manila folders on a desk can pile up.

Window sizing

Windows are sizable as well as movable. We have seen that a window can be snapped into three sizes using the buttons at the right of the title bar. The middle size, the one that takes up part of the screen, is adjustable. A win-

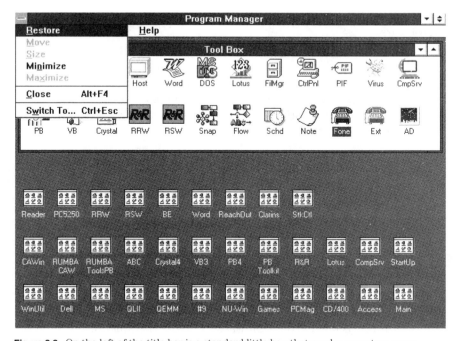

Figure 2.2 On the left of the title bar is a standard little box that produces system menu.

dow can be adjusted by placing the mouse pointer over the edge or border of the window. The pointer changes to a double-headed arrow to indicate that the border can be dragged larger or smaller. You can place it on a corner of the window to adjust both the height and width at the same time. Then, holding down the left mouse button, you can drag the window shape to the desired size. You can tailor the desktop just the way you want it.

Active window

When many windows are opened and placed on the desktop, it can get cluttered and confusing. Generally, you are only working with one window at a time. Any window visible on the desktop can be made the *active window* (the one you can work in) by clicking on it. The others become inactive. Even if you can only see a corner of a window, buried under other windows, clicking it will bring it to the top and make it active, or give it focus. Remember this phrase—*got focused*—because it will become very important in later discussions of client/server and GUI application design. If too many windows are open at one time to tell which is which, you can go to the task list or window list by pressing the Ctrl-Esc keys to list the open applications so you can pick one by name.

Scroll bars

Note the bars at the right and bottom edges of the window in Figure 2.3. These are scroll bars. They are used like the arrow keys to reach information that is off the screen. If more data exists than what you see on the screen, you can place the mouse pointer on one of the arrows on the scroll bar and use the mouse button to scroll the page. Of course, you can usually still use the arrow keys, as well as PageUp and PageDown.

Client area

The *client area* is the space on the inside of the window where the application runs. Any data processed by the application is contained here. Text for word processors, cells of spreadsheets, and database views all occur in the client area of the window. Various devices, such as pushbuttons and message boxes, are used within the client area to provide interaction with the user.

Menus

The *menu bar* is one of the main ways to access the functions of an application. All menus work alike (or should) in GUI environments. You click on a menu bar item, such as Help, and a pull-down or pop-up submenu appears (Figure 2.4). Sometimes, you must work your way down a branched struc-

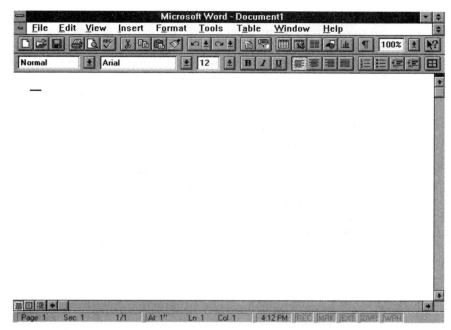

Figure 2.3   Scroll bars and a toolbar.

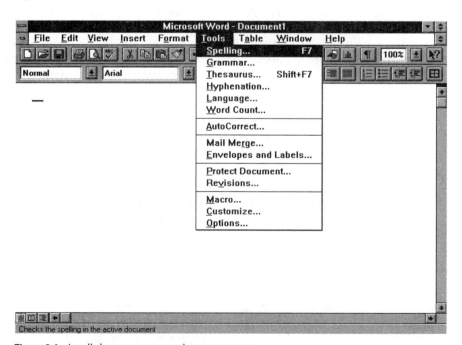

Figure 2.4   A pull-down or pop-up submenu appears.

ture of submenus to get to the function you want to perform. It is easy to look around the features of an application using menus. Everything is accessible by clicking through the menu options under the main menu bar. Menus are also familiar to users of non-GUI applications such as Lotus. At the top of the screen is a main menu with several options. Choosing one of them results in a pull-down submenu from which further choices are made. A menu choice can be selected either by pointing and clicking or by hitting a letter key if a letter in the menu choice is underlined (as Contents). The user works down through menu levels to the desired option and then chooses it. A dialog box opens to receive parameters. If several levels of menus must be navigated before the ultimate function is reached, it is probably faster to use a speed key combination (e.g., Ctrl-B for bold fonts). Familiarity with the application leads to a knowledge of these key combinations, thus bypassing the menus and increasing productivity. Many of these key combinations are also shown on the menus next to the functions they invoke. Icons on tool bars can be used to bypass menus as well.

Toolbars

Sometimes, it can become tedious to click through several levels of menus to get to a desired and often-used function, such as printing. To reduce the tedium, many windowed applications provide a *toolbar* (as was shown in Figure 2.3), which is a row of icons representing useful options. The printer is one of the icons. Just press this icon and the current document is sent to the printer with default settings. This method of working is familiar to Macintosh users, where many features are reached through icons. A toolbar is simply a row of icons representing common functions of the system.

2.2   The Mouse

Most features of a windowed system are accessed using the mouse. A *mouse* is any device used to move a pointer around the computer terminal screen. It can be the traditional mouse or a trackball. Mouse technique can be a little harder to acquire than one might at first imagine. It is necessary to develop a fair amount of dexterity with the mouse to use the full functionality of the GUI desktop. The following sections describe some of the main techniques to master.

Point and click

As you move the mouse across the desktop, or rotate the ball in the trackball, a mouse pointer on the screen moves correspondingly. If you move the mouse right, the pointer goes right. This pointer usually takes the form of an arrow, but sometimes changes shape, depending on the particular function or position on the screen. Sometimes, the pointer gets lost off the edge of the screen, but you can get it back by wiggling the mouse around to see where it is. When the mouse pointer is on something you want to do, click the left mouse button. A single-click usually chooses an option or opens a menu, while a double-click executes a program to open a window. No consistent rule exists about what single- and double-clicks do; you just have to experiment.

Drag and drop

This technique allows you to grab an object on the desktop and move it to another position. You place the mouse pointer over the desired object, press and hold the left mouse pointer, and move the mouse to the position on the screen where you want the object. You then release the mouse button to "drop" the item there. You can move icons, drop a document on the printer, drop a file in the shredder, etc., depending on the particular operating system and the functions.

Select or highlight text

This technique is important for word processors. It blocks or highlights a section of text or screen for further treatment. You might want to select a section of text to be put into a bold font, or copy a block of text from a mainframe emulation session into a document. To select text, move the mouse pointer to the beginning of the text to be selected. Press and hold the left mouse button. Then move the mouse pointer to the end of the desired text and release it. The selection is thus highlighted. You can now choose a function to apply to the selected text. To unselect text, move the pointer off the text and press the left mouse button.

Cursor placement

To position the cursor in a document, move the mouse pointer where you want to go and click the left button. Note that the mouse pointer is distinct from the cursor; which can be confusing at first. You see two movable pointers or place indicators on the screen. The mouse pointer allows you to place the cursor and select menu options. The cursor is where typing or data entry occurs.

Cut and paste

Cut and paste is one of the handiest features of the GUI environment. With it, you can mark out a section of one screen and paste it to another section of the same screen or into a completely different application window. You can cut out data from a server and paste it into a PC spreadsheet. You can mark out a section of a help document and copy it for sections of program code or share data or graphs between a spreadsheet and a document. Not only text, but any object that exists in a cut and paste enabled application, can be cut and pasted. *Cut* removes the selected object from the original location, while *Copy* does not. To cut and paste, you select the desired text or object as shown above. You then select the Edit option from the menu bar at the top of the screen. From the resulting pop-up menu, choose Cut to remove the object from the current location and place it into an intermediate holding area called the Clipboard. The Clipboard is a GUI device used to enable this feature and has its own viewer, accessible through the Main window. Once the object is in the Clipboard, it can be pasted into other applications. To paste, go to the other application or another location in the same application. Select Edit from the menu bar again and click on Paste to place the text or object at the desired location. A copy of the object is still in the Clipboard, available for further pasting, until another object is copied there.

2.3 Controls

Controls implement the GUI desktop. They are actually the pushbuttons, menus, icons, and other window devices used to interact with the user and display information or data. Designers of windowed environments place controls on the desktop in windows. They then associate code with each control to determine what happens when that control is activated or referenced. This relationship between controls and sections of code is how windows programs and applications are designed or implemented. Window controls are a standard group of objects defined by IBM in their CUA standard. Thus, most window type applications present the user with very similar interfaces. If you know how to use one, it is not difficult to figure out the next. Specific controls are described in the following sections.

Radio button

A radio button is a little round button, usually with a group of similar buttons. You can only choose one; they are exclusive. If you push one, it turns black in the center. If you push another, it turns off the previous one. These are used for choices where you can only make one selection, such as male or female.

Command button

A command button is a rectangular pushbutton with a label in it. It generally executes some underlying code function, such as Save or Quit.

Text

Text is the message in the window for the user. The information presented as text in the window cannot be changed. It is strictly for informational purposes, including descriptions or instructions.

Entry box

An entry box is a rectangular area where the user can enter data or where data is displayed. This area is the primary method of interacting with the keyboard in a window that takes the shape of a form and has an expected pattern of responses.

List box

A list box contains a scrollable list of items for selection. If more items exist than will fit into the allotted size of the list box, scroll bars appear to navigate the remaining information. The desired item is clicked on to be selected. List boxes are useful when it is necessary to limit the user to valid responses.

Combo box

A combo box is a combination of the entry box and the list box. The user can type something in the entry box or choose an item from the associated list in the list box using the mouse.

Message box

Message boxes provide a warning or informational message to the user. The message pops up and the user must respond by pressing one of the command buttons before continuing (OK, Cancel, Quit, etc.).

Spin button

The spin button is an entry box that has an up and down arrow next to it. Press one of these arrows with the mouse to cycle through increments and decrements of the response. An example of a spin button is when the system asks how many copies are to be printed. The default entry states one copy, but you can enter a number or spin through the numbers sequentially, using the arrows, if you do not want the default number of copies.

Dialog box

The dialog box is a window that contains messages and one or more controls for interacting with the user. Many functions and utilities that require a patterned set of responses from the user operate using dialog boxes.

2.4 Event-Handling

Events are actions that happen in the windowed environment. Generally, they refer to mouse actions. A double-click on an icon is an event. The GUI developer needs to place controls on the desktop and allow responses to events that occur in relation to the controls. This process is known as *event-handling* or *event-driven programming*. Application packages such as Visual Basic or PowerBuilder provide a mechanism for placing visual controls in windows. They also provide a menu-driven method for controlling the properties and event responses of these visual objects. Subroutines or code scripts are attached to each visual control for any action it recognizes. For example, a developer might place a command button on the desktop with the word *Quit* on it. She chooses the action or event for this button: "Click." The final step is to write the code that attaches through the chosen action to the button. This sequence is the standard drill for event handling—first the control, then the event, and finally the code.

Event-driven programming departs from the usual top-down approach of batch or mainframe programming. In top-down programming, a program starts at the beginning and progresses through a sequence of logical constructs and subroutines to the end. Then the program stops. It performs each line of code in turn, and goes on to the next when the current one is finished executing. In event-driven programming, however, the user is in more direct control and interaction with the program. The window opens and waits for the user to initiate an event. The window is placed into a message loop, waiting for a message or event it can transfer to the GUI application programming interfaces (API). The GUI system burns many computer cycles doing this, as well as in maintaining the graphics on the screen. It is forever asking its objects, "Are you clicked, are you clicked, are you clicked...?" which is one of the reasons a fast machine is required for GUI systems. Functions initiated in Windows programs are not necessarily sequential. For example, a line of code might spawn a process that runs for several minutes. While this process is running, the program might go on to the next line of code and execute it before the preceding line has finished.

When an event does occur, things become quite complex behind the scenes, usually in the "C" language. Fortunately, we do not have to worry much about what happens underneath the surface of event-handling. These things are handled by the new type of fourth-generation language (4GL) application package. These packages provide tools for visual programming, offering aids to streamline the development effort. All we need to do is associate events with controls and let the package take care of implementing the nasty details. Of course, it is always possible to code the whole thing from scratch, but it is often unnecessary and overly time-consuming, not to mention daunting. Only where extreme flexibility and performance are needed is original coding recommended. Many effective applications can be designed using the toolboxes of the 4GL packages, which provide standard visual objects written in "C" and available for easy use.

Some of the more common events handled in GUI programming are the following:

- *Click*: The user places the mouse pointer over an object and clicks the button.

- *Double-Click*: The user places the mouse pointer over an object and clicks the button twice in rapid succession.

- *Got Focus*: The given window or object has been activated. This event or property of the visual object can be used to change the appearance or functionality of the active window or object when it becomes active. For instance, if a particular window or form in a data entry sequence has been activated, you might want to populate it with default values. Otherwise, its controls could be blank or invisible.

- *Lost Focus*: A window or control has been deactivated. Lost focus is used to turn off properties of controls that should not be in effect unless they are active or have focus.

- *Change*: This event is used to monitor what is being input to an entry box by the user. If you want to know what the user is typing into an entry box and react to it, use the Change event of the entry box. Every time a change occurs (every time a key is pressed), the code executes.

2.5 Object-Oriented Programming

Object-oriented programming (OOP) is intimately related to GUI development. OOP is a fairly new concept in programming. The visual objects involved in GUI development have extremely complex inner mechanisms. That button so casually placed on the desktop might easily take longer to code than the rest of the user application. Luckily, we don't need to design an electronic fuel injection system to drive the car to work. Just access the incredibly complex object called a car and it performs for you, with a fairly simple user interface (steering wheel, brake pedal, etc.). Why reinvent the wheel, so to speak? Visual objects are much the same. Place them on the desktop and manipulate the handles provided for accessing their inner functions.

This approach represents a major departure from the traditional method of coding each system from the beginning. Most systems share typical functional requirements. You need to put data into a database through an input screen. You need edits on the data. You need to access the data in various relationships or views. Objects provide proven, universal components that can be combined to form systems and modified to individual needs. Developers, familiar with the available objects, can analyze the requirements in terms of these objects. Instead of thinking at the low level of code, it is possible to think in terms of objects. The problem can be defined in terms of entities or large-scale constructs which make up the whole. Instead of thinking about an address field, you think about a customer entity with all its defining properties, attributes, and attaching procedures. It is then possible to relate this concept to known objects in the application development environment or create one for it.

The following subsections define common OOP terminology.

Objects

A standalone collection of data and data structures with related methods or procedures. The data is defined, along with relevant operations on it. Grouping features and activities together into a higher construct is fundamental to our perception of the world and our work. For example, legs, eyes, lungs, cells, and many other features coalesce into the body. We are able to say *body* and have all the rest come along for free. Objects have several characteristics that enable rapid adaptation to various situations. They provide a simple exterior that masks a complex interior. The methods contained within the object determine its responses to the messages sent to it. For instance, an object might draw a circle. The actual mapping of pixels can get complicated, but all you need to do is tell the circle object where and how big.

Methods

Objects contain methods that define their behavior in various circumstances. These methods are like subroutines invoked in response to certain messages received by the object from its external interface, which might be the user or another program.

Classes

The highest form of an object is the *class*. A class is used as a generic template or blueprint from which specific objects are created as solutions for actual situations. The particular instance of the class is the object. Like a house developed from a blueprint, an object is created from a class. Classes are instantiated into specific, executable objects. The class might not be executable, as the blueprint is not livable. The higher class is called a *superclass* or a *virtual class*. The instantiated object of the class is known as a *subclass*. The subclass is tailored to a specific purpose.

It is much easier to design a human if you have concepts of both mammal and monkey. Animal is a superclass, mammal is a subclass, and monkey is an instance of the class or object. Human is another instance of the mammal subclass. As an object derived from the class, it inherits many characteristics of the parent and develops new ones of its own.

Inheritance

Objects share data structures and methods with their parent classes. Operations and definitions in the class are transmitted to the subclass or object, which can be altered with new operations added in the subclass. Only methods or definitions that need changing are touched. The rest retain inherited characteristics from the superclass. The more general a class is, the more adaptable it is to different circumstances. The more defined it is, the more useful in a given circumstance. Animals can live in more places than fish can, but they can't all read. Only one instantiation of the animal superclass can read. As you can see, there is an overlapping series of superclasses, subclasses, and objects that share characteristics through inheritance.

A rich body of classes available to the programmer enables the creation of objects by changing only the elements that are different, while leaving the bulk of inherited characteristics that are desirable. Once the technique becomes familiar, it is possible to develop very sophisticated objects quite easily. This process is a form of genetic engineering for computer systems.

Messages

Objects respond to messages. The user sends a message to an object, which responds by performing its interior methods on the relevant data. Often, it is not necessary to know the internals of an object; simply send it a valid message, and it will perform.

Encapsulation

The property of enclosing the inner workings of the object in a "black box" is known as *encapsulation*. The encapsulated object sits there, inscrutable, and you send it a message through a simple interface. It performs its function and returns the desired operation or value. This feature makes objects portable, combinable, and friendly.

Polymorphism

Polymorphism means "taking on many shapes." This feature of object-oriented programming means that a message should be able to produce desired results when sent to a derived class or its superclass. The result might not be the same, but the message is. If you say "Hi!" to different people, you might get very different responses, even though the request or message sent to the object is the same. Thus, objects related to the same class should respond to the same message, without changing the message. Derived classes should share a common message interface.

2.6 Types of Windows

The windowed GUI environment presents several standard types of windows, such as main windows, parent windows, child windows, multiple document interface (MDI) windows, pop-up, response, and message windows. These windows can operate in two ways, *modal* (requiring a response before continuing) and *modeless* (switchable at will). The window types are defined in the following subsections.

Main Window

The first window opened by an application is called the *main window*. It corresponds to the main menu in a character-based application. From the main window, all features of the application can be reached. Other windows, menus, and functions are activated from the main window. The title bar at the top of the main window contains the name of the application. Main windows can be moved, sized, and switched modelessly.

Parent and child windows

Parent and child windows are dependent windows in an application that can be opened from the main window by clicking on some object or icon on the desktop. The original window is the parent window, while the derived window is the child. Child windows belong to the parent in the sense that they do not possess the mobility or independence of the parent. You cannot move a child window outside the frame of the parent window; they move with the parent if the parent is moved. They close automatically with the parent and are modeless like the parent.

Multiple document interface

As seen above, the parent-to-child relationship between windows is based on dependency of the children on the parent. It is possible to open independent windows from the main window in an application. This technique or facility is called the *multiple document interface (MDI)* frame. It is a window used as a framework or platform for succeeding independent windows. An example is the initial window of a word processor such as Microsoft Word or WordPerfect. Independent switchable documents can be opened from the initial MDI frame. All windows opened this way are independent, even though they originate from the MDI.

Pop-up window

Pop-up windows are usually used for further choices in menus and for help or information to the user. Click on a menu bar selection and you often get a pop-up window, which contains further options that can provide their own pop-up windows when selected.

Modal window

If a dialog box or other window waits for the user to answer its prompts and questions, before switching to another window, it is called *modal*. The user is trapped in this mode until the required responses are provided. Message boxes are usually modal, requiring an answer or an acknowledgment before continuing.

Modeless window

If the user can switch at will between windows on the desktop, these windows are called *modeless*. This format is the desired norm for window application development. It is, however, much more difficult to manage than modal windows, because the programmer does not have the advantage of knowing where the user is at a given moment without resorting to various complex techniques. These techniques are discussed in the chapters on windowed application development.

2.7   GUI Platforms

Although Microsoft Windows is the most popular GUI platform, others exist that perform equally as well. Each have their own strengths and weaknesses. The following subsections describe the most popular platforms.

Microsoft Windows

Windows is the most popular GUI platform and offers the most software. It is easy to install and use. Windows 3.x, however, is not a preemptive multitasking operating system. It does not have a traffic cop to regulate or coordinate processing among the various contending windows or applications. It is possible for one ill-behaved program to seize up the whole environment, with resultant data loss. Windows also relies on DOS for basic input/output services (BIOS), such as disk access and terminal or printer output. Windows NT is Microsoft's answer to these problems. It is a true preemptive multitasking operating system like OS/2. It does not rely on DOS for basic input/output services but provides its own. NT's hardware requirements are consequently much higher than Windows 3.x.

OS/2

OS/2 from IBM is not nearly as prevalent as Microsoft Windows; yet it is in some ways a superior product. It has offered true preemptive multitasking for several years, something that Windows is only now attempting with NT. OS/2 is a robust operating system. System crashes, so common in the Windows environment (the infamous general protection fault), are less common in OS/2 because the preemptive multitasking environment monitors the performance of each application running on the desktop or in the background and arbitrates when necessary to resolve conflicts. OS/2 combines the easy-to-use icon approach of Apple Macintosh with true-blue IBM compatibility and communications. It is specifically designed to work with other IBM platforms like the AS/400 and 370 series. Communications Manager and Database Manager facilitate these connections. Unfortunately, there is nowhere near the proliferation of applications for OS/2 that exists for Windows. To address this shortcoming, OS/2 now has its own Windows environment, running under OS/2.

UNIX X-Windows

UNIX is a multiuser, multitasking operating system. Users usually dial in to a UNIX server or access it remotely or on a network. It is still primarily a command line operating system environment, but it does offer windowed features as well. UNIX has two primary windowed environments, OSF/Motif and Sun's Open Look. Like Windows and OS/2, UNIX X-Windows offers all the major GUI features but is not as prolific in application software as Windows. Communications programs such as Connection Program/400 provide cross-platform connectivity to the IBM AS/400.

Macintosh System 7

The Macintosh interface is the one that started the whole revolution with icons, point and click, and GUI. Mac users are loyal and claim that this environment is the easiest of all to use. This statement might well be true, not only in terms of actual software usage, but also with software and hardware installation. Plug-and-play is the norm in this setting. Much of the feature-rich software available for the Windows platform is also available for the Mac. Many institutions, such as schools and law firms, prefer the Mac for its ease of use and superior desktop publishing capabilities. Connectivity to IBM platforms is, however, more limited from the Mac. Projects in the works, like Pink, a hybrid operating system combining IBM and Apple software technology, will further integrate the Mac with the world of IBM.

2.8 Summary

GUIs are transforming the way people work with computers. Available on all major PC hardware platforms and operating systems, they are increasingly prevalent. Users who have point-and-click applications at home want them in the office, too. With the intuitive nature of the interface and advanced features like cut and paste, GUI applications are easier and more productive. It is unnecessary to memorize lists and strings of bizarre command syntax; just click on the picture of what you want. This change enables executive information systems (EIS), where high-level decision making can be supported by enhanced system access. GUI systems also increase input accuracy and efficiency. Integration of system functionality is a primary benefit of GUI. Everything is accessible and switchable on the desktop. Advanced object-oriented tools, contained in the 4GL development languages for the GUI environment, enable rapid and powerful application design. All these features, taken together, constitute an effective new platform to be used as the client in client/server systems.

Chapter

3

Client/Server Architecture

Client/server systems are made possible by a diverse array of technologies and software, including hardware architectures, operating systems, networks, communications protocols and devices, application development tools, and terminal emulation. As demands for interconnections associated with client/server development increase, more and more *middleware*, or software designed to translate between diverse environments, is developed. Obviously, standardization of elements and techniques is necessary to avoid complete chaos in connecting between different platforms.

3.1 Open Systems Interconnect Model

The International Standards Organization (ISO) has set standards for communications between computer platforms. These standards are known as the *Open Systems Interconnect (OSI) model*. OSI is at the heart of client/server systems. This model divides the communications tasks into seven layers, each of which is functionally independent of adjacent layers. The OSI model is modular; changes to one layer should not affect the operation of other layers. Thus, physical network schemes such as Ethernet or token ring at the lowest layer should work in the same manner with the upper layers. Vendors generally attempt to conform to the OSI standard. IBM's APPC, the PC LAN NetBIOS, and TCP/IP are compatible with the OSI model.

The seven layers of the OSI model are the following:

- *Physical layer*: the cable and cards that constitute the actual physical connection between network devices.

- *Data link layer*: This layer manages the flow of packets of information through the network with error control and synchronization.

- *Network layer*: This layer controls connections between network addresses.

- *Transport layer*: The transport layer monitors the accuracy of network traffic.

- *Session layer*: This layer coordinates between the session programs communicating on the network.

- *Presentation layer*: It acts as a data converter or translator between unlike symbol sets on the network.

- *Application layer*: This layer is where the real action is for client/server systems. Higher functions, such as file transfer or remote SQL requests, operate at the application layer.

3.2 Open Software Foundation and Distributed Computing Environment

The Open Software Foundation (OSF) is a nonprofit association of major vendors. IBM, Microsoft, Hewlett/Packard (HP), and Digital Equipment Corporation (DEC) are all represented, as well as many others. They select offerings from their members to provide open computing solutions, primarily with UNIX compliance.

The vendors call this overall selection of open systems technology the *distributed computing environment (DCE)*. OSF/DCE is the most widely accepted standard for developing open systems. IBM's SAA and the UNIX world are developing DCE-compliant software. DCE has been selected by the European Commission (EC) as the connection solution between multiple vendors. As such, DCE occupies the position of middleware, which means it operates between platforms, rather than being indigenous to a single platform. DCE contains the following components:

- *Network transport services* are responsible for the physical and logical transmission of packets around the network.

- *Threads services* control processing between contesting subtasks (threads) on the network, which is similar to the OS/2 scheme of processing. Thread services might provide increasing levels of parallel processing in the future, where threads are allocated to processors around the network.

- *Presentation services* handle the look and feel of the GUI.

- *Remote procedure call* enables a user on one system to execute a command on a remote system.

- *Name service* uses unique names to identify remote procedures by concatenating the time of day and network address of the remote computer.

- *Time service* synchronizes all clocks on the network to the network control node.

- *Distributed file system (DFS)* connects systems to provide cross-platform file access.

- *Directory service* maintains descriptions and network addresses of accessible objects or files.

- *Security* is implemented by the server calling back the requester or client to authenticate the command.

3.3 Bridges, Routers, and Gateways

Client/server systems operate almost by definition between unlike computer systems. A PC on one network might request a service from a server of a different type on a different network. This situation is like an American requesting the news of the day from a Japanese in Tokyo, when neither speaks the other's language. Several problems arise. A physical connection is necessary (network), along with translators (protocol converters). Neither person needs to know the other's language as long as the physical link and translators are reliable. Client/server systems work like this, too. They use bridges, routers, gateways, and all sorts of protocol converters to enable connections between diverse networks, hardware platforms, and operating systems.

A *network bridge* connects two networks, usually but not necessarily of the same type. The bridge sits between the two networks and operates at the data link layer of the OSI model. It interprets the flow of network packets and reads their destination addresses to determine when a destination address resides on the other network. When it does reside on the other network, the bridge switches the packet over there. The two networks are thus prevented from deluging each other with useless traffic. Local traffic is kept local, and the bridge is not allowed to cross over.

Routers are key to client/server implementations. They are programs that create a logical connection between different types of computers on networks, translating protocols back and forth. Routers operate at the network layer of the OSI model to connect separate devices of the same network protocol type (e.g., IBM SNA) but different operating systems (Windows to OS/400). Conversations can be conducted over this connection between unlike platforms and network addressing schemes. A pathway is thus provided for communications requests and services to be routed in the most efficient manner. The router, once started, is a pathway for the implementation of application program interfaces (API) between platforms. Terminal and printer emulation, remote procedure calls, and file transfer are some of the services that can be invoked once the router is started.

A *gateway* is used to connect unlike networks together. It is more complicated than the router because it must convert between incompatible network protocols, like IBM SNA to UNIX TCP/IP. Gateways operate at the top four layers of the OSI model. Often, a gateway takes the form of a dedicated PC with gateway cards in it. These cards provide communications functions to a server for a defined number of PCs or clients on the network. One gateway card might provide for up to seven emulation sessions on the PC network. These sessions can be allocated on a first-come-first-serve basis, or as dedicated sessions, each one assigned to a particular workstation address.

These devices, with their physical links between divergent platforms and their protocol converters, enable a wealth of client/server applications. Once a connection is established, as with a router, many different types of client/server activities become possible. These hardware and software devices are examples of middleware, which forms the connections between systems and applications.

3.4 System Application Architecture

System Application Architecture (SAA) is IBM's master plan for distributed processing. It provides a unified approach to software design and interplatform communications on the AS/400, System/370, and PS/2. The ultimate goal of SAA is an environment virtually transparent to the user, who might be accessing a 370, even if the user is signed on to the AS/400 or PS/2. These three machine architectures represent the components of the SAA triangle at the mainframe, midrange, and PC levels.

SAA provides intersystem connections and cooperative processing. It has several facets. One is to provide a standard and consistent interface for users across the various platforms. A user would not need much training to move productively from the AS/400 to the PC if the environments were similar. Common user access (CUA) implements this standardized approach, primarily in screens and keyboard usage. SAA also attempts to standardize the programming environments across the platforms, offering standard languages on all three. Common programming interface (CPI) is IBM's attempt to provide a consistent application development environment. Common communications support (CCS) is IBM's communications standardization scheme and perhaps the most successful of the three standards to date. The SNA-based ability for intelligent peers to communicate and share resources enables CCS. Obviously, IBM has a long way to go in providing a seamless integration of these different computer systems, but the APPC and APPN features of SNA and CCS lay a common basis for development.

3.5   Common Communications Support

CCS consists of a complex group of physical network connections, functions, and protocols which, taken together, provide a consistent way to
communicate between the PC, AS/400, and System/370. These functions
fall into the following groups.

Data link controls

Data link controls are the physical connections, hardware, communications
lines, modems, workstations, controllers, and protocols used to connect
network nodes. They include synchronous data link control (SDLC), token
ring, and X.25 networks.

Network node

Network nodes are the SNA node (type 2.1) devices being connected. These
types of nodes are capable of routing and handling directory services for APPN
to maintain the dynamic networking functions. These functions eliminate the
need for the mainframe to serve as both the host and router for attaching dependent devices. More organic and diverse networks thus become possible.

Objects

Objects are formatted data and tokens of discrete types, contained in data
streams and suitable for transmission and interpretation between SAA platforms. Objects include the following:

- PTOCA   Presentation text object content architecture
- IOCA   Image object content architecture
- GOCA   Graphics object content architecture
- FOCA   Font object content architecture
- FDOCA   Formatted data object content architecture

Data streams

Data streams are standardized formats for collections of objects used to
transfer data between SAA platforms for various purposes, such as print
serving or distributed databases:

- 3270   Data stream
- CDRA   Character data representation architecture

- IPDS   Intelligent printer data stream
- RFT:DCA   Revisable form text: document content architecture
- MO:DCA   Mixed object: document content architecture

Session services

LU 6.2 is a group of communications functions consisting of APPC protocols to provide data communications support.

Application services

Application services are features of APPC that provide distributed functions. Application services are the real benefits of SAA communications, the reason we go through all the rest. Application services are commonly applied as electronic mail, file transfer, remote data access, and the like. They include the following:

- DIA   Document interchange architecture
- SNADS   System network architecture/distribution services
- DDM   Distributed data management
- DRDA   Distributed relational database architecture
- SNAMS   System network architecture/management services

3.6 System Network Architecture

IBM's System Network Architecture (SNA) describes logical structures, protocols, formats, and procedures for implementing and controlling networks. Elements of SNA have been around for years in the form of the System/370 type connections to terminals such as the virtual telecommunications access method (VTAM). VTMA implements a type 5 SNA node, using a System Services Control Point (SSCP) to act as host, which is the traditional host relationship to the network. The host has the communications functions and the dumb devices that communicate with it. Dumb devices can activate functions on the host, but cannot do any processing on their own. This relationship is hierarchical in that the mainframe is the intelligent master and the peripheral terminal is the dumb slave. A 3270 terminal emulation allows remote systems such as PCs to communicate with the System/370 host, but only as dumb terminals.

These dumb terminal emulation sessions, however, can now be embedded in intelligent windowed environments. They can be integrated with the desktop metaphor and can share data with other windowed applications through cut and paste. They are also switchable with the other windows in that you can point at a window with the mouse and make it active. It is a question as to how dumb these emulation sessions really are when operating in a GUI setting with cut and paste, file transfer, printer emulation, push button remote procedure calls, and the like. It is clear that SNA enables a constantly evolving set of standards and features for IBM connectivity and client/server design.

SNA is a protocol stack comprising seven layers. Note the similarity to the OSI model discussed above:

- Physical control

- Data link control

- Path control

- Transmission control

- Data flow control

- Presentation services

- Transaction services

The first three layers of SNA are the lower layers and are concerned with the physical connection on the network. These layers are called the node type. The top four layers of the SNA protocol stack are called the *logical unit (LU)*. They handle the software services of communications.

Mainframes (type 5 nodes) represent the most powerful node types with their communications controllers (type 4 node). Known as the *subarea node*, they provide a powerful and extensive set of networking facilities. They route network traffic and support a multitude of connections. This type of node supports the traditional host/workstation network scheme. Peer-to-peer capability, however, is not supported.

3.7 Advanced Peer-to-Peer Networking

SNA node type 2.1 was introduced to enable peer-to-peer connectivity as an advanced alternative to 3270 type terminal emulation. These nodes are called low-entry networking (LEN) nodes, network nodes, or end nodes. They do not require the mainframe. Although the mainframe is a type 4 and 5 network node, it can look like a type 2.1 node to the network when running VTAM and NCP together. In this way, the mainframe can participate in node type 2.1 peer-to-peer networking, but only as an end node. Advanced peer-to-peer networking (APPN) is a recent enhancement to node type 2.1 networking that implements dynamic networking capabilities between network nodes. APPN allows network nodes to reconfigure themselves automatically in response to changes in the APPN network. This "autoconfig" capability is a dramatic improvement compared to the need to manually configure every attached device. In many cases, an APPN device can simply be plugged in to a configured line, and the target machine on the network can recognize it, configure it, and bring it to active status automatically. A mainframe node is not required to direct traffic between 2.1 type nodes. APPN services include connectivity, directory, route selection, session, and data transport services.

Independent, or peer-to-peer, type connections involve establishing and maintaining links between network nodes that function as equals and do not require the services of an SSCP or mainframe host to mediate between them. APPN is the AS/400 implementation of this strategy. Mainframes do not use APPN; it is a cutting-edge feature of the AS/400, making it much easier to configure than mainframes. APPN, coupled with ever-increasing horsepower and storage on the AS/400, positions the AS/400 as the server of choice in client/server systems.

Network topologies such as token ring are supported at the physical or data link layer to support peer-to-peer connections. These topologies can be used to connect three families of IBM computers:

- System/370
- AS/400 (System/36 and System/38)
- PC (PS/2)

In turn, these three families of computers can be connected together in varying relationships as node types. End nodes are those that can function as a host, receiving requests from the network and furnishing a response in the form of an object or data stream. Network nodes can originate, serve, or simply route a request through to the appropriate node for a response. SNA node type 2.1 is essential for SAA type communications because it supports peer-to-peer connections, where each node can initiate, respond, pass through, or terminate. Very flexible and responsive networks can be designed this way. Nodes of type 2.1 can function as peers, integrating PCs with the AS/400 and mainframe on a network. The AS/400 can function either as an end node (host) or as a network node. Generally, PCs are used as network clients, requesting data services from larger machines because of the superior CPU power and DASD capabilities of the 370 and AS/400. PCs (especially those running OS/2), however, are also being used as servers, as they become more powerful.

Three types of nodes can be used in the APPN network:

- *LEN end node*: no APPN dynamic networking functions but it still can connect as node type 2.1 to APPN network.
- *APPN end node*: APPN auto-configuration but only as end of network. No routing or directory services.

- *APPN network node*: full APPN functionality, including routing, directory services, dynamic reconfiguration. No System/370 support, only AS/400 and PC.

APPN is an important feature of SAA/SNA connectivity and node type 2.1. Dynamic networking capabilities allow network nodes to configure themselves automatically and to recognize the addition or removal of remote nodes. It is what provides the ability to connect as peers without using the services of the System/370 as interpreter or host. It runs on the AS/400, System/36, and PC, providing dynamic networking capabilities between the machines. APPN also allows display station pass-through, in which a user can sign on one system and pass through it to another peer system on the network, accessing the remote system's data and programs.

For example, the user can be on a PC, sign on to one AS/400, and access data on another AS/400 without the PC and the second AS/400 being directly connected. This connectibility is a very important feature of APPN and SNA because it allows network connections to configure themselves dynamically in an any-to-any relationship. True distributed processing is a result of this type of peer relationship between network nodes. Only these peer-to-peer features of SNA are included in the SAA network definition, although the hierarchical host-to-workstation relationship is still supported.

3.8 Advanced Program-to-Program Communication

LU 6.2 was designed to work with SNA node type 2.1, providing advanced program-to-program communications (APPC) facilities to interconnect the PC, AS/400 (also System/36 and System/38), and System/370. LU 6.2, or APPC as it is more often called (these terms are virtually interchangeable), allows remote systems to communicate and synchronize distributed processing between themselves. LU 6.2 has features to control transaction and commitment if an error occurs on the network. LU 6.2 controls conversations between programs and platforms involved in distributed processing, supporting multiple sessions at the same time between 2.1 type nodes. Application services, such as DIA, DDM, SNADS, SNAMS, and DRDA are implemented through LU 6.2 by transaction programs. The LU handles the SNA protocols for transfer of requests and answers between local and remote transaction programs. LU 6.2 support is provided by VTAM/NCP on the mainframe, OS/400 APPC on the AS/400, and OS/2 EE Communications Manager on the PC.

3.9 Application Program Interface

APIs were designed to allow communications between systems and platforms to provide true distributed processing. This scheme takes advantage of the fact that all three platforms in the SAA world are intelligent, and each can offer its own advantages. Systems can be developed that run across the boundaries of platforms, using the strengths of each. APIs are the handles on each system accessible from remote points.

LU 6.2 (APPC) contains verbs that can be used in programs to invoke networking functions. These function calls from an application program to the LU are known as APIs. They enable high-level languages to communicate directly with the operating system and networking features of the LU. Programmers can access APIs from within an application program to interact with remote services. It is the use of these APIs that enable the development of software and application services such as electronic mail.

IBM has provided SAA common programming interface for communications (CPIC) to standardize programming access to LU 6.2. A standard set of LU 6.2 protocol boundary verbs can be used to communicate with remote LU 6.2 applications. A conversation is set up between partner programs running on different platforms.

These API and APPC conversations are not easily accomplished. It takes a very advanced knowledge of "C" and the intricacies of the APIs and APPC conversation verbs to develop these systems. Mostly, it is the province of software development houses, with teams of API wizards. The rest of us usually opt to use tools they develop for interplatform connection capabilities.

3.10   Application Services

Part of the LU (upper) section of the SNA protocol stack is the applications services. This group of functions serves the needs of network users. They can be requested by any LU 6.2 of any other node on the SAA network. Each is described in the following subsections.

DIA

Document interchange architecture (DIA) enables electronic mail and the exchange of information and documents between OfficeVision/400 users and applications. Users can send and receive documents and messages both locally and remotely. Document library services offer a filing system for documents that allow their storage, retrieval, and distribution across the full range of SAA platforms. This service is implemented as a client/server relationship between a source-recipient node (SRN) and an office system node (OSN). DIA is supported in OfficeVision/MVS and DISOSS on the mainframe, OfficeVision/400 on the AS/400, and in OfficeVision/2 on the PS/2.

SNADS

System network architecture/distribution services (SNADS) is an asynchronous distribution service capable of storing data or information for later delivery. Sometimes called *store and forward*, this ability is central to the electronic mail function. It is also useful in other respects, however, such as distributing files, programs, messages, or other types of objects to multiple remote users. For this function to work, SNADS must be supported on all platforms involved in the exchange. Distribution queues such as document library service queues and VM/MVS bridge queues are used to route objects to other systems. A system distribution directory contains system addresses and names of authorized SNADS users. OS/400 can use SNADS to exchange objects between systems using APPC and APPN. DSUs use routing tables that contain unique system and user names to coordinate the network distribution of objects.

VM/MVS bridge

The VM/MVS bridge enables the transfer of DIA documents, OfficeVision documents, notes, messages, and other objects such as print files and data files between the AS/400 and VM/370. AS/400 SNA communicates with System/370 VTAM/NCP and VM/RSCS. This facility was once called PROFS bridge and is contained in the AS/400 communications utility.

DDM

Distributed data management (DDM) allows AS/400 users and applications to access data on remote systems and vice versa. The AS/400 is the source system, and the remote system is called the target system. APPC and APPN support enable DDM to access files and records remotely. You can find, update, delete, and add records to the target database just as if it were right on the local PC disk drive. Also supported are file operations such as copy, delete, and rename. For example, a file can be copied from target to source computer. The user, programmer, and application do not need to know where the file resides; DDM handles that transparently. DDM, part of the database manager (or DB2/400), performs client/server requests between the source and target systems. Of course, both ends of the source/target connections must be running SAA-compliant DDM. Security considerations come into play when updating between platforms, especially when updating an AS/400 file from the PC. DDM/CICS on the mainframe supports target functions, while AS/400 DDM can be both source and target.

DRDA

Distributed relational database architecture (DRDA) is an SAA enhancement to remote database access using DDM Level 3. An SQL interface allows applications to access a relational database which is spread out on the SNA peer network. DRDA manages the remote portions of SQL data requests using the FDOCA and CDRA standard formats for data interchange between systems. A system of two-stage commitment control is implemented by DRDA to ensure database integrity across the network.

SNAMS

System network architecture/management services (SNAMS) provides a way to maintain the entire network from a central point. Issues such as configuration and problem management, as well as performance tuning, can be monitored from one machine. Alerts originating anywhere on the SNA network are forwarded to the focal point for centralized control. Network nodes fall into three SNAMS categories:

- *Entry point*: An entry point is a network node that has its own management support.
- *Focal point*: The focal point is a central control location that monitors information and alerts from other points in the network.
- *Service point*: The service point is a non-SNA device that uses a protocol converter to communicate and relay information to the focal point for network management.

NetView running on the mainframe is an example of an SNAMS control point. It offers several useful facilities to monitor and control the network. NetView can monitor response time, performance, and hardware faults and distribute network management commands around the network.

3.11 Remote SQL

Remote Structured Query Language (SQL) is an important component of client/server systems. Developed by IBM as a powerful and easy data access language, SQL has become a mainstay of IBM client/server connections. It represents a very convenient way to access remote data, using the built-in functionality of database managers like DB2 (formerly known as database manager). The client simply issues an SQL call, which is routed through the network to the server. Communications configurations provide the link to the server. The server intercepts this remote SQL request and initiates a query using its own native SQL-based database handler. The requisite processing occurs on the server, which is designed to handle this type of database management. It maximizes the use of existing access paths and determines the optimal way to service the request. The resulting data extract is then returned to the requesting client. All this activity happens without the developer needing to manage complex conversations between different platforms. SQL provides both the universal data access language and the means of furnishing the results. The SQL API is accessed to submit the request to the server.

3.12   Open Database Connectivity

Microsoft has developed a technique for accessing data on remote platforms. This remote platform might be an AS/400 on the network or even a database on the same PC but in a different format. Open database connectivity (ODBC) is implemented as a dynamic link library (DLL) that translates between the requester database and the server database. ODBC forms a connection between the requesting program, running in Windows, and the server. The request takes the form of a standard remote SQL call. This proprietary feature of Windows development can connect to diverse platforms such as Macintosh data access language (DAL) and AS/400 SQL. ODBC is an important feature of Windows client/server development because it provides a virtually plug-and-play access to remote data. Once the connection is defined using ODBC, remote data can be accessed as easily as if it were local (but not as quickly, unfortunately).

3.13   Remote Procedure Call

The remote procedure call (RPC) is a function executed on a remote platform. The client program issues an RPC and then waits for it to complete. The RPC is routed to the appropriate location, which receives it using an activated server process, and executes it. The results are returned to the calling program on the client, which then resumes processing. It is like a program running synchronously in two places. Basically, it is very similar to a subroutine call or a call to another program. The difference is that this other program is on a different computer. This consideration raises a number of problems that need attention, such as security, error checking, and multiuser record locking. Performance is always a primary concern in remote operations. If multiple RPCs are to be submitted to a server, they can be bundled into a session to save network traffic and processor overhead. Single RPC service is called *connectionless*, while RPC sessions are *connection-oriented*. Connection-oriented RPC sessions offer a diminishing cost in terms of processor overhead, based on the number of bundled requests. The more requests, the more efficient it is to send them in a session connection. Parameters can be passed, generally by value, along with the RPC.

3.14   Summary

Client/server architecture is supported by a growing body of standards and devices. OSI, OSF, and DCE offer cross-platform techniques and scenarios. IBM can connect between all its own platforms, as well as with UNIX, Apple Macintosh, and others. A rich array of connections is available, with products entering the market constantly. Bridges, routers, and gateways are devices that create physical links between networks. SNA is a collection of IBM networking protocols and procedures to implement connectivity derived from the OSI standard. SAA is IBM's grand plan for connecting diverse platforms and architectures. It is based upon three platforms, the System/370, the AS/400, and the PC or PS/2. Distributed functions and cooperative processing depend on intelligent peer-to-peer communications between these three platforms. APPN provides dynamic network configuration and intelligent routing of network sessions. Applications services such as DIA, SNADS, DDM, DRDA, and SNAMS provide the real benefit of connectivity. Remote SQL is a high level, nonprocedural language that allows queries submitted on one system to access data on another system and return the results. ODBC is a special middleware driver that allows Windows programs to connect to a variety of local and remote databases. RPCs run programs on remote systems and wait for the results, like a remotely executed subroutine. Client/server systems are derived from these facilities.

The AS/400 Server

*The AS/400 is a machine well aware of the needs of
client/server development. It provides several useful and
efficient functions to enable these distributed projects. Its
database is redesigned and enhanced. It can function on its
own as a database and interactive machine, using its own
native data and languages. It can function as an optimized
server for remote data access. It can also provide a
simultaneous combination of these two services. The AS/400
has several programs, such as Client Access and SQL, which
help in designing client/server applications.*

*Client Access/400 is IBM's own software for accessing
the AS/400 from PCs. It was called PC Support, but now the
Windows clients are rewritten in C for speed, while the
extended DOS version remains pretty much the same.
Installing Client Access/400 is not the most simple operation;
it requires planning and reading. Once in place, however, it
gives you a good start on developing client/server systems.
Terminal emulation provides the AS/400 screens within the
Windows desktop. Printers can be emulated so that your
desktop printer can be used to print AS/400 jobs, just as if it
were a printer attached to the AS/400 itself.*

*Submit Remote Command allows the user or a PC program
to run a command on the AS/400 from the PC end, just as if
signed on to the AS/400. This ability has obvious value in
designing client/server systems. File Transfer can be used
from a menu or from program code to transfer files or parts of*

files from the AS/400 to the PC. Entire files can also be uploaded from the PC to the AS/400. Data queues are AS/400 memory areas that can be read from the PC. These are useful in setting flags in cooperative processing. A batch job might, for instance, send a message to a data queue when it is finished processing. Thus, the PC can know when to proceed to the next step. Integrated file system offers enhanced file types and processing speed for AS/400 disk drives, which appear to the PC as local drives. Application programming interfaces can be used by programs to access various features of Client Access from within the program. For example, Visual Basic could start a file transfer. Client Access can form the basis for extended client/server development.

DB2/400 is the AS/400's new database. It offers many new features that enable or implement distributed processing. In addition to the machine's previously existing database functions, such as maintaining indexes or access paths, features now exist that round out the database functionality of the AS/400 and make it competitive with other industry server databases like Sybase. Referential integrity ensures that dependencies between records in relational databases are preserved.

Stored Procedures are programs stored in compiled format on the AS/400. They can be executed from the PC side, saving interpreter time and communications overhead. Triggers are often used to set off automatic edits whenever a record in the database is added, updated, or deleted, no matter what program performs the change. Triggers operate at the database level, eliminating the need to code these edits into every program which accesses the data, and even operating on programs like DFU, over which the programmer has little control. The EXPLAIN *function is useful in determining how SQL actually does its work, enabling analysis and optimization. The predictive query governor estimates how long a query will take to run and notifies the user if it is over a system limit. The user can choose to end the query if it takes too long—a common situation. Two-phase transaction management ensures the validity of an entire transaction across the distributed platforms, so that the client does not get updated unless the AS/400 does. A system-wide database catalog allows local and remote applications to find out about AS/400 databases and fields. Distributed data management (DDM) and distributed relational database architecture (DRDA) offer SQL-based methods for remote data access. System-managed access path protection (SMAPP) ensures* that system access paths are maintained in such a way as to ensure a timely re-IPL if a failure occurs. The system can now automatically maintain its journals through system change journal management. These much needed additions make the AS/400 a flexible server for client/server.

Remote SQL is one of the mainstays of client/server systems using the AS/400. Its English-like syntax allows programmers from diverse backgrounds and platforms to communicate with remote systems about which they know little. Actually, it is possible for a PC programmer who does not know much about the AS/400 and DB/2 to access its data through the universal language of SQL. SQL is IBM's SAA standard for nonprocedural data access. The open database connectivity (ODBC) drivers that form the important link between Windows and the AS/400 are based in SQL. Thus, you can write a Visual Basic SQL statement that is transmitted to the AS/400 through the Client Access router and that returns data from the AS/400's databases. SQL can be interactive, which means, of course, that it is interpreted every time it runs and is relatively slow. Or it can be compiled, which makes it more efficient. SQL can also be embedded in other host languages, such as RPG or PowerBuilder. SQL uses table views and indexes to manage its data. It is one of the easiest languages on the AS/400 or any machine to learn, and is extremely useful in client/server development. It is such a relief to find a language that works in virtually the same form on different platforms.

IBM has created the Advanced Server Series of AS/400s to accommodate remote data requests. These new models provide enhanced, efficient data server features. They come somewhat at the cost of ordinary AS/400 interactive processes, so they are not for everyone. Actually, the standard AS/400 has been revamped in the current models and V3R1 of the operating system provides much snappier remote response to communications and data requests, especially through SQL. Client Series Software is available for immediate client/server functionality, such as Rumba and VISTA. The file server IOP (FSIOP) is a 486-powered disk processor right inside the AS/400. It behaves as a PC network drive, offering greatly boosted performance over Shared Folders. LAN Server/400 is a network operating system that can run on the FSIOP, bringing the PC file server completely within the AS/400 box. PC types of data access such as stream I/O are supported by the IFS to allow PC programs to read AS/400 data in the manner to which they are accustomed.

Chapter

4

Client Access/400

Client Access/400 software attaches a PC to the AS/400, bringing AS/400 functionality to a desktop window or the DOS environment. It replaces PC Support, the product formerly used for this purpose. Client Access/400 has most of the same features as PC Support, including terminal emulation, shared and virtual printers, remote commands, file transfer, data queues, messages, and shared folders. Client Access/400 is PC Support but with the Windows and OS/2 clients rewritten in C++ to improve efficiency. It can run in DOS, Windows, and OS/2. The DOS version is basically the same as the old PC Support for DOS. Client Access/400 is compatible with PC Support version 2 (V2) running on the AS/400, and the original PC Support can be used with version 3, revision 1 (V3R1). Client Access/400 will not run in the OS/2 Windows environment.

One of the big problems with PC Support was its use of terminate and stay resident (TSRs) programs that implemented the program. These programs had to be loaded into memory at start-up time before Windows initialized. The TSRs stay resident in memory, eating up scarce DOS resources and causing a number of problems. The two major TSRs necessary to load before Windows were router and shared folders. Client Access/400 provides native Windows drivers implemented as data link libraries (DLLs). They are only called when needed and do not cause the incompatibility problems of DOS TSRs. With Client Access/400, you still need a small TSR before Windows is initialized, but it is a major improvement over PC Support.

Rumba can connect to both Client Access/400 and PC Support through Windows. In fact, it is a recommended front-end for Client Access/400. The Rumba chapter provides details of Rumba access to Client Access/400.

4.1   Installing Client Access/400

Client Access/400 consists of two parts, the part that runs on the AS/400 and the part that runs on the PC. Once it is installed on the AS/400 (for Windows it is in QPWXCWN), it is a simple matter to install it on the PC. Client Access/400 is user-licensed. It is necessary to enroll users on the AS/400 and to configure their PC connections. Client Access/400 can be installed into various environments, and PC Support installations can be migrated into Client Access/400 to preserve existing configurations. The system administrator, however, must perform a few tasks first. (Refer to the IBM manual *Client Access/400 for Windows Getting Started* to migrate configurations.)

Following is the procedure for installing Client Access/400 into Windows 3.1:

1. Place installation disk in drive A:.
2. Select Run from the Windows File menu.
3. Type A:install in the Command Line text box and press Enter.
4. Follow the instructions (see Appendix B for more details).
5. Exit Windows.

To configure Client Access/400 for AS/400 systems, shared folders, virtual printers, start-up options, and automatic application program updates from the AS/400 to the PC, follow this procedure:

1. Restart Windows, and the setup program automatically starts.
2. Run the configuration program from the configuration icon in the Client Access/400 program group.
3. Double-click an option or icon to be configured.
4. Enter your connection information into the Common Options dialog box.
5. When connection information is complete, you are connected to the AS/400.
6. Enter user ID and password.
7. Client Access/400 Setup window appears, and you can configure PC5250 or Rumba.
8. Follow the instructions.

Double-click on the Help icon in the Client Access/400 group to display error recovery information on particular messages for the installation process or for any other errors. An online introduction to Client Access/400 is also available from the Help icon.

To begin the Client Access/400 session in Windows, you must double-click on the Startup icon in the Client Access/400 program group. Until you perform this step, no connection exists with the AS/400.

4.2   Terminal Emulation

The main function of Client Access/400 is most likely the ability to run an AS/400 display session in a window (or DOS), emulating the AS/400 5250 terminal on the PC. It is not necessary to use a special display device to run an AS/400 session. The PC on the user's desk can function both as a personal computer and an AS/400 terminal. You can even switch back and forth between the two functions at the touch of a key (actually, two keys: Alt and Esc). If using Windows, you can even cut data out of the AS/400 session and paste it into a PC application.

Terminal emulation offers the following features:

- 5250 display emulation
- Workstation printer emulation
- Keyboard mapping
- Cut and paste
- Hot link to spreadsheet or other PC application
- Mouse actions on the AS/400 screen
- Macros to automate frequently repeated sequences of commands
- Window sizing, moving, and font adjustment
- File transfer

Client Access/400 comes with two different front ends from which to choose. You can use the Client Access/400 PC5250 emulator, or you can use Rumba. Both offer Quick Step pushbuttons for macro execution and Hot Spots on the display that respond to mouse actions.

4.3   Printers

One of the benefits of connecting your PC to the AS/400 through Client Access/400 is the ability to use PC printers as AS/400 printers. This feature is called *shared printers*. It is a part of the workstation emulation. The printer session automatically creates a printer definition on the AS/400 as a result of the AS/400 auto-configuration capability. You can name the printer session as you wish, such as PRT08 or PRT_FRED. When print jobs are sent to that AS/400 printer by an AS/400 program, your active Client Access/400 session intercepts the data and routes it to a locally attached printer, such as a laser jet or other PC printer attached to the workstation.

You can even direct an AS/400 print job out over the PC network to a network printer through a combination of Client Access/400 and network services such as Novell's Capture command. To set up a workstation printer, use the workstation configuration. It is necessary to open the printer session, configure it, and save it.

1. Select New from the File menu.

2. Click the radio button for 3812 printer and click OK.

3. Select Print Options, Application Print Setup, or Change Printer to configure the workstation printer emulation.

4. Click Save to save the configuration for future use.

Now, whenever you want a local printer hooked up to the AS/400, just open the session you created. Once started, the printer emulation session appears in a window. You can control the printer emulation from this window, using the commands Start, Stop, Cancel, and Test as well as Online and Ready. You have a printer control panel right in Windows.

It is also possible to use printers attached to the AS/400 as if they were local PC printers. The print job, initiated on the PC, is routed through the services of Client Access/400 to an AS/400 printer. This feature is called *virtual printer*. It is not used as much as the shared printer function because the usual idea of client/server functionality is to offload work from the AS/400 to the PC. But this feature might be needed if you use printer features not available at the PC end of things, such as speed or quality. Or you might want to print from the local PC to an AS/400 printer at a remote site. To set up virtual printing, double-click on the Configure icon in the Client Access/400 program group to set up an AS/400 printer as a local workstation printer. Then double-click on the type of printer you want to set up. Virtual printer configures an AS/400 printer as a PC printer. The resulting dialog box allows you to add, delete, or change a printer definition.

4.4 Submitting Remote Commands

Client Access/400 provides a method for running an AS/400 command from the PC platform. A PC program can run an AS/400 program, wait for a response, and continue processing. The client/server implications of this function are extensive and powerful. Merely by clicking on a desktop icon or pushbutton in Windows, the user can transparently initiate remote AS/400 processing and receive the results on the PC.

4.5   File Transfer

File transfer is a function that allows the user to copy files or parts of files from the AS/400 to the PC and from the PC to the AS/400. Although two-way transfers are possible, the more frequent direction is to transfer data from the AS/400 to the PC to get the results of a query, for example, into a PC spreadsheet for further analysis. File transfer enables a data link between the AS/400 and the PC, eliminating the common problem of keying information from AS/400 reports into a PC spreadsheet, which comes with all the accompanying extra work and input errors. Data that originates on the PC might also need to be mirrored on the AS/400 for universal access. File transfer enables these types of replications of data between platforms.

The SQL-based interface of the file transfer enables a query-like request to be submitted to the AS/400's Database Manager, which is part of DB2/400. It is possible to request that only certain records (rows) that meet a specified condition be returned from the AS/400, selecting only certain fields (columns).

Simply double-click on the transfer icon to start a file transfer.

4.6   Data Queues

Data queues are named areas on the AS/400 that can be accessed from the PC in programs. An AS/400 program can be run that loads data into the data queue. The PC can then read lines off the data queue, providing a fairly simple method of passing information between the AS/400 and the PC. If only a simple message needs to be passed to the AS/400, data queues can suffice. More complex cross-platform access can be accomplished in a number of ways, including file transfer, ODBC, remote SQL, and APPC connections.

4.7   Integrated File System

The integrated file system (IFS) replaces PC Support's shared folders. Shared folders was a PC Support feature that turns part of the AS/400 disk drives into a local network drive for the PCs attached to it. It is usually accessed as drive I: on the network. Shared folders has always been rather slow and cumbersome to use, however, compared to an actual network drive.

Now, with Client Access/400, this function is optimized and works much faster because of the AS/400's IFS and new file server input/output processor (FSIOP). These features use an allocated portion of the AS/400 DASD for holding PC files like databases, spreadsheets, and word processing documents. The IFS supports PC-style stream I/O as well as the traditional AS/400 file systems such as QSYS libraries for AS/400 files and QDLS for shared folder documents. This method is efficient for client/server processes. The new file system supports QLANSrv files for the LAN Server/400 and QOpenSys files for portable open system interface for computing environments (POSIX). Thus, AS/400 is opened as a file server to a variety of clients. Data and files can be organized similarly to PC directories and subdirectory trees. A common interface lets the user access files and databases on the AS/400 much more flexibly than that previously available with PC Support's shared folders.

The FSIOP is actually a 486 chip on board the AS/400. This chip is used to process file requests from the client, providing rapid access comparable to native PC LAN access times and reducing demands on the AS/400 IOPs to virtually nothing. It is thus possible to run an entire network file server function from within the AS/400 disk drives.

Simply double-click on the configuration icon in the Client Access/400 program group to configure AS/400 DASD as a network drive. Then double-click on the folders icon. In the resulting dialog box, you can add or remove a drive and adjust the memory cache.

4.8 National Language Support

The AS/400 speaks many different languages. As the interface between the AS/400 and the PC, Client Access/400 is no exception. Any language supported by the AS/400 is available as the interface to Client Access/400. These language features are installed by the system administrator. The EHNL parameter in WIN.INI specifies which language to use. The MRInnnn library in QPWXCWN contains the relevant language support.

4.9 Application Programming Interfaces

Client Access/400 supports the APIs from PC Support. Client Access/400 Tools is an additional product that has new features and functions for API developers. The emulators that constitute Client Access/400 support the emulator high-level language program interface (EHLLAPI) to form a link between external programs and the emulator functions. The following APIs are supported:

- Windows Open Services Architecture (WOSA).

- *License service application program interface (LSAPI)*: Windows license management for developers.

- *Messaging application program interface (MAPI)*: Windows message access.

- *Open Database Connectivity (ODBC)*: the Windows standard SQL-based database access method for AS/400 and other external platforms.

- *APPC communications router*: a high-level method for accessing the low-level functions of the communications link to the AS/400.

- *Data queues*: holding areas for data on the AS/400 that can be accessed from the PC through the API.

- *Data transform*: data conversion routines for PC-to-AS/400 communications.

- *Network driver interface specification (NDIS)*: to access adapter drivers and cards for networks.

- *Network drives (shared folders)*: to assign and release AS/400 disk drive space as local PC disk drives.

- *Network redirector*: network access to drives and printers, local and remote.

- *Node operator facility (NOF)*: to control the functions of the logical unit (LU).

- *Remote SQL*: AS/400 database access from the PC platform.

- *Transfer*: query function to AS/400 for entire files.

- *Submit remote command*: run an AS/400 command from the PC and wait for completion.

- *Virtual printer*: assign and release AS/400 printers from the PC side.

The above APIs enable a wide variety of client/server functionality from the PC end. They do, however, require some programming expertise to implement.

4.10 Requirements

A minimum level of hardware and software is necessary to connect your Client Access/400 PC to the AS/400 through the network. IBM's suggested minimum configuration for running Client Access/400 is as follows:

- 386 or better computer
- 4Mb RAM
- 10Mb available disk space
- DOS 5.0 or later
- Microsoft Windows 3.1
- Adapter card for the network
- IBM local area network support program

Although Client Access/400 can work in that configuration, it will be happier with at least 8Mb of RAM. In fact, any Windows installation runs better with this much memory, especially if any degree of task swapping occurs (switching between active windows).

4.11 Summary

Client Access/400 connects the desktop PC, which is running Windows or DOS, to the AS/400. It replaces PC Support and is an improvement over that product. Written in C++, Client Access/400 is much more efficient than PC Support, especially for client/server tasks. Shared folders is replaced by the IFS. The FSIOP dramatically speeds up file access from the PC client to the AS/400 server. Now, the AS/400 supports stream access as well as its own native file types. Two GUI front-ends for Client Access/400 are provided. PC5250 is the IBM emulation offering, while Rumba is also bundled with the software. Both offer extensive connectivity features. You can set up a local PC printer as an AS/400 printer emulation, or an AS/400 printer as a local PC printer. APIs are supported that provide access through high-level language routines to low-level functions of the communications environment and protocols. AS/400 commands can be run from the PC with the submit remote command utility, which is very useful for client/server systems. Client Access/400 also supports data queues that enable PC programs to access data areas on the AS/400 for cross-platform messaging.

5

DB2/400

5.1 The Database

The AS/400 has been around since 1988, but its database never had a name. It has been called the AS/400 database or the Database Manager. Now, it has been brought up to DB2 standards by IBM, with version 3, release 1 (V3R1) of the OS/400 operating system. It is now comparable to DB2 on the mainframe and OS/2 on the PC. The new AS/400 database is called *DB2/400*. It has several new features that make it more suitable as a server in a heterogeneous client/server environment.

The AS/400 has always been an object-oriented system, at least in terms of storage if not procedures. Everything on the system is an object accessible by name, including programs, databases, printer descriptions, and whatever else found on the system. Every object has a header associated with it that defines it in terms of type and usage. The headers ensure that a particular object is used correctly and consistently, and only by authorized users.

The database of the AS/400 is said to be an *integrated relational database*. *Relational* means there are interconnections between the files in the system, related through key fields. One file might contain a number of transactions for a particular customer, and another the name and address of the customer. A customer number field could relate the two files so that it is possible to construct a link, or relation, between the name of the customer (one record) and the transactions for the customer in the other file (multiple records). Each file has the customer number field, which functions as the link. Once the files are linked by key field, every customer in the master file is connected to the relevant records in the transaction file. In turn, the transaction records for the customer might have a code that relates to product descriptions in a third file. The relationships between files can become complex and are based on key field links (Figure 5.1). This type of relational database is uniquely suited to structured query language (SQL) access. Once an SQL relationship is set up between files, it is a simple matter to select records and fields from each file. SQL has become an industry standard for accessing data in relational databases and is central to client/server system development.

The fact that the AS/400 database is integrated refers to the tight bundling of database functionality into the operating system architecture, making the database very efficient and reliable. This machine was designed as a database handler, which probably accounts for much of its popularity worldwide. You do not need to buy a machine and then shop around for a good database to run on it; it all comes as a tightly integrated package with advanced and fairly easy-to-use functionality. Database management, security, and other features of the OS/400 operating system are a well-integrated whole. They are efficient because they all work at the operating system level, in machine instructions, eliminating an entire level of functionality and speeding things up considerably. In the arena of client/server development, such a database is desirable. Remote calls to the AS/400 as a data server can be serviced right at the operating-system level, without complex calls to additional database programs.

SQL is the industry standard interface for the AS/400 database. DB2/400 has another interface, however, that can be used to access its data. This native interface is not an SQL approach, but is quite familiar to AS/400 programmers—more so than the SQL interface. It consists of the data description specifications (DDS) for defining databases and programming languages like CL, RPG, and COBOL for accessing the databases through special commands integrated with the operating system. In fact, these languages access the data-

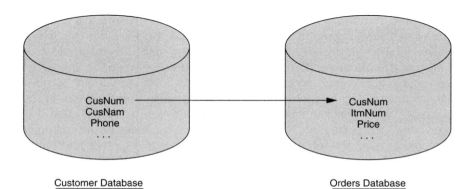

CusNum
CusNam
Phone
. . .

CusNum
ItmNum
Price
. . .

Customer Database   Orders Database

Figure 5.1 Relationships between files are based on key field links.

base using the machine instruction set (MI), which is at an even lower and consequently more efficient level than the operating system. DB2/400 can be accessed by the SQL interface or by the native RPG/COBOL interface. In addition, SQL statements can be included in RPG and COBOL programs to create a hybrid form of data access.

Both the native and the SQL interface can access databases created by the other. The native interface is good at keyed single-record processing or transactions. SQL excels at returning subsets of data, using existing access paths or creating its own. SQL has its own terminology and methods for accessing the database.

5.2 Access Paths

The AS/400 builds and maintains access paths to its data. Once defined, keys and views, or subsets, are handled by DB2. There is no need to ensure that an index is current or a change to one is reflected in all other relevant indexes. The traditional or native AS/400 programming interface uses DDS to describe databases and views of them. The database itself is called a *physical file*. It might or might not contain a key to sequence the records. Logical files are also defined in DDS to create logical views of the data in a physical file. These logical files do not contain the actual data, just a sequence of pointers to the data in the physical file. They redefine the view of the data in the physical file. Here is where you might define an alternate keyed access path to the data by customer number, name, or region of the country, etc. Connections between physical files can also be accomplished through *logical files*. Multiple logical files can be defined for a given physical file. Once defined, the AS/400 manages these access paths. Even if the machine suffers a power outage, the operating system can attempt to rebuild the access paths, and is usually successful.

When record retrieval is performed by the native keyed access path, response time is excellent. This method is probably the fastest way to access a record on the AS/400. When a query or SQL statement is run, DB2 (and the previous Database Manager) is smart enough to look for an existing data path to use in constructing the result set. If you submit an SQL statement to return the records for a particular customer, DB2 looks for an index keyed on customer. If it finds one, it can return the results immediately, without constructing an access path first. The performance savings can be impressive, especially as the target database grows in size.

5.3 Referential Integrity

DB2/400 provides a way to ensure that relational databases are used in accordance with primary business rules. For example, you would not want to delete a customer from a customer master database when transaction records exist in another database for that customer. Otherwise, the transaction records would be left without a master or header record. *Referential integrity* is a function of DB2 that ensures that files have correct relations between them. These correct relations are definable by the user. It is possible to set up rules that only allow records to be added, updated, or deleted when they do not violate the referential integrity rules as defined. A violation results in an error message from DB2/400, removing the burden from the programmer and placing it at the data definition level, where it belongs. It is unnecessary for the programmer to worry about whether the record being deleted is required by another file; referential integrity automatically checks once the rule is defined. Any time the file is accessed by any program or procedure that changes records, DB2's referential integrity procedure is invoked. RPG, COBOL, SQL, and even CL updates to databases are monitored by referential integrity to maintain database dependencies.

Referential integrity basically ensures that one file has matching records in another file, related by a key field. If you did delete a customer that had a transaction in an invoice file, you would have an invoice for a customer who no longer exists, and the transaction might have a product code in it that identifies what the customer bought. This product code would be linked to a product file, containing full descriptions of the product with name, price, vendor name, address, etc. It would therefore be unwise to allow a product master record to be deleted when referenced by records in the transaction database. Each transaction record references records in at least two other databases—records that should not be deleted if they have active external references.

Most relational databases have this type of interdependency between files. It is common to have some sort of header or master file associated with multiple transactional records for that particular header file record (Figure 5.2). It is also common to have lookup tables associated with codes in other files, such as vendor codes, state codes, or company codes. In general, database records can reference a full description of an entity by a simple, short code. When the full attributes of the entity are required, the relational database program can access it by the code key. These types of lookup table and master/detail relationships must be preserved. Some file records can be added without constraint, but cannot be deleted. You can add any new vendor to the list, but you cannot delete one referenced in other files without making those records meaningless. Some files can only be added to when the new record contains a reference to an already existing record in another file. For example, you can only add an invoice for an existing customer. Some files can have records added, updated, or deleted without constraint.

Referential constraints define these dependencies between files for all subsequent usage. These relational constraints exist between a parent file and a dependent file. The rule states that every record in the dependent file must have a matching record in the parent file. The files are matched on identical field types, such as a five-digit alphanumeric code in both files. If

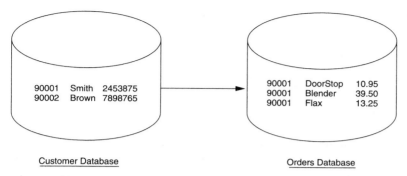

Figure 5.2 Header or master file associated with multiple transactional records.

you try to add BC901 to a constrained field in the dependent file, referential integrity checks for that value in the key field of the parent file. The field in the dependent file is called the *foreign key*, while the field in the parent file is the *parent key*. Referential integrity ensures that the foreign key matches a parent key.

Referential integrity constraint rules offer various actions to be invoked when records in the dependent file are inserted, updated, or deleted:

- Records can only be inserted in the dependent file when a matching parent key is found.

- Parent keys cannot be changed if they match existing dependent or foreign keys. Foreign keys cannot be changed unless the new value matches an existing parent key.

- Parent key records cannot be deleted if they match existing foreign keys in dependent files. Alternatively, the delete constraint rule can be set to Cascade, which causes all foreign keys to be deleted along with the parent record. It can also be set to Set Null, which sets all foreign keys to null (not the same as blank or zero) when a parent key is deleted.

Referential constraints can be added to files with the ADDPFCST command. It is necessary to add both the definition of the parent key to the primary file and the foreign key in the dependent file. To add a referential constraint such that the CUSTTRAN transaction file must have records that match the CUST MAST file, on the CSTCOD key, use one of the following programs:

Using native interface (CL):

```
ADDPFCST FILE(CUSTMAST) TYPE(*PRIKEY) KEY(CSTCOD)
    CST(CUSTKEY)

ADDPFCST FILE(CUSTTRAN) TYPE(*REFCST) KEY(CSTCOD)
    CST(TRANKEY) PRNFILE(CUSTMAST) PRNKEY(CSTCOD)
    UPDRULE(*NOACTION) DLTRULE(*NOACTION)
```

Using SQL interface:

```
ALTER TABLE CUSTMAST ADD CONSTRAINT CUSTKEY
    PRIMARY KEY (CSTCOD)

ALTER TABLE CUSTTRAN ADD CONSTRAINT TRANKEY
    FOREIGN KEY (CSTCOD)
    REFERENCES CUSTMAST (CSTCOD)
    ON UPDATE NO ACTION
    ON DELETE NO ACTION
```

The above commands set up a relationship for referential constraints between the CUSTMAST file and the CUSTTRAN file. Once these constraints are defined, DB2/400 checks to verify that all existing records in the two files meet the constraint rules. It monitors commands on an ongoing basis to ensure that all procedures affecting the records in the dependent file are subject to the referential constraint, including high-level language programs as well as CL commands, system utilities, and SQL statements.

5.4 Stored Procedures

Stored procedures optimize the execution of remote SQL. Without stored procedures, each remote SQL statement is sent over the communications connection from the client to the server, processed on the server, and sent back again (Figure 5.3). The whole process is then repeated until the remote SQL statements are finished. Why do it this way? Why not put the remote SQL requests on the server and just ask it to run them? Using this method, only two communications occur: one from the client to the server to initiate the procedure, and one more when the procedure is finished. Stored procedures can minimize remote procedures because they reduce what is least efficient in client/server systems—remote conversations.

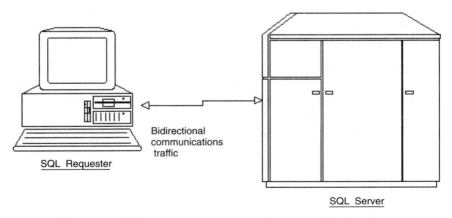

Figure 5.3 Each remote SQL statement is sent over to the server and back again.

The DECLARE PROCEDURE and CALL statements in SQL are used to in-voke a procedure which is stored on a remote system. This procedure can be written in any language native to the AS/400, including RPG, COBOL, CL, REXX, or SQL (not S/36 programs). The program on the remote system is treated like a subroutine that is invoked locally but run remotely. When the subroutine is finished executing, control returns to the calling program on the local system. In general, it is best to design client/server systems to min-imize communications flow between platforms. Stored procedures can help.

5.5 Triggers

Like referential integrity constraints, triggers determine what happens if the user tries to add, change, or delete a record from a database. Triggers are a way to attach a user-defined procedure to these database actions. If the user adds a record to the database, the trigger can automatically exe-cute a specific routine. Triggers can be set to go off either before or after the file is altered. If it is necessary to notify a particular member of the company every time a record is deleted from a database, you can attach a delete trigger. Then, whenever a delete occurs, no matter how it is accom-plished (SQL, RPG, CL, etc.), the notification program is executed. Once defined, the trigger fires automatically for its defined event, so it is unnec-essary to write it into every program or event that affects that database.

Triggers are also useful for edits. You can set one up so that, any time a database record is changed or added, a set of edits is run on the data fields. A trigger automatically ensures that the edits are performed, regardless of how the record is changed. Anything that needs to happen, local or remote, when a record is added, changed, or deleted, can be accomplished through triggers.

To define a trigger, you need to specify the following:

- *Base File*: the file that has the trigger attached.

- *Trigger Event*: which type of event fires the trigger: add, update, or delete.

- *Trigger Time*: when the trigger executes; before or after the actual data-base change.

- *Trigger Program*: the name of the program that executes when the trig-ger executes.

Set up a trigger with the ADDPFTRG command as follows:

```
ADDPFTRG FILE(CUSTMAST) TRGTIME(*BEFORE)
    TRGEVENT(*DELETE) PGM(MYPROG)
```

This command defines a trigger, attached to the CUSTMAST database, that executes the program named MYPROG before any actual delete func-tion is allowed to alter the database.

5.6 EXPLAIN Function

SQL can use a lot of system resources. The EXPLAIN function lets the user find out just exactly how SQL is going about its business. Perhaps a logical file could cut way back on the time required to process a recurring query. EXPLAIN provides information that can be used to tune the query. The CL command PRTSQLINF is used to print the SQL information:

```
PRTSQLINF OBJ(MYPROG) OBJTYPE(*PGM)
```

5.7 Predictive Query Governor

SQL and Query/400 are very useful tools for both local and remote procedures. They can, however, use an inordinate amount of system resources, especially in building access paths to the data. It is desirable to limit these tools using reasonable parameters to avoid slowing down the system too much during peak usage. The predictive query governor determines whether a query will take too long to run based on how the query is defined and which access paths already exist for optimizing the run time. The user can specify a time limit for a given procedure involving the query function. If the predictive query governor determines that the query will exceed this limit, the query is either aborted automatically or the user is prompted to indicate if the query should continue. The query is not started without user intervention if the predictive query governor sees that it will exceed the time limit. This process is different from other query governors, which terminate the query only after it actually reaches its limit, thus wasting system resources.

You can use the CHGQRYA command to change query attributes for a user or job. The time limit for queries remains in effect for the duration of the job or interactive session. The query limit can be set at the command line, or within CL programs:

```
CHGQRYA QRYTIMLMT(120)
```

Predictive query governor works with Query/400, SQL, OPNQRYF, Query Manager, and S/38 Query.

5.8 Two-Phase Transaction Management

When dealing with distributed environments on remote platforms, it is important to ensure that a transaction has been completed successfully on all databases. If it has not, it must be backed out automatically. Anything can happen, especially when dealing with diverse platforms and communications links. The remote system could be down, or the phone lines could go out. Database integrity must be ensured. Distributed relational database architecture (DRDA) Level 2 provides a facility for this. DRDA provides a distributed unit of work (DUW), consisting of all relevant transactions on the distributed network, including the local and remote unit of work. SQL statements can be served on a variety of local and remote platforms. When the platforms involved report that all the requisite processing is complete, DRDA can respond with a two-phase commitment control, verifying that the databases have all been updated correctly. All communications connections are kept open until the entire distributed transaction is complete and the COMMIT has been invoked.

DRDA DUW and two-phase COMMIT protect networked database integrity for client/server systems. The application requester requests data from the application server, which correspond respectively to the client and the server. The connection is made, then the remote database updates are performed. Finally, the commitment control ensures that all has gone well. It asks all the server databases if their updates are complete. It they are, the data is committed on all databases. If not, all updates in the current transaction on all participating platforms are rolled back to their state before the transaction.

When you create the SQL programs involved in these distributed transactions, you can specify the RDBCNNMTH parameter to set up the remote database connection method:

```
CRTSQL... RDBCNNMTH(*DUW)
```

DUW performs better than its predecessor RUW because it does not terminate each communications link to a remote database when a new link is established. It simply inactivates them. Therefore, the links do not need to be reestablished for further processing or commitment control. In addition, DUW and two-phase commitment control ensure successful database updates for a transaction across multiple local and remote databases.

5.9 System-Wide Database Catalog

DB2 maintains a system-wide catalog to describe the data in files and fields. Whether the data is described using the native or SQL interface, DB2 creates system-wide catalog entries. This catalog can then be used by software packages to determine which fields are contained in which files. The catalog is a centralized and known source of data definitions that can be used locally or remotely when building applications.

5.10 DDM and DRDA

IBM has two methods that can be used to access data on remote platforms. Distributed data management (DDM) allows a connection to be made through a DDM file. The CRTDDMF command in the command language identifies a file on a remote system and creates a DDM file to access it. The OVRDBF (override database file) command redefines or connects the file named in the high-level program to the DDM file. The operating system connects the DDM file to the remote system and file (assuming all intervening configurations are in place). The data is accessible to a native programming language such as RPG or COBOL, just as if local data were being referenced. The difference, of course, is in response time. The local program must wait for the data request to be funneled through intervening files and communications lines, satisfied by the remote server, and then returned by the same route. This process is obviously not as fast as performing a record retrieval on the local machine.

DRDA Level 2 is an SQL-based method for remote data access. The relational database directory is used to define system and data locations in the distributed environment. System names and file names are entries in the directory that point to files or access paths. The SQL CONNECT statement is used in program code (remember that SQL can be embedded in RPG and COBOL programs) to connect to a remote database. It works through the specifications in the relational database directory. The remote SQL request is sent to the server system, which responds by returning a data excerpt to the requesting system. DRDA is thus able to request the results of a remote SQL statement.

5.11   System-Managed Access Path Protection

System-managed access path protection (SMAPP) allows the system to protect the all-important access paths on the AS/400 from power outages and other disasters. Access paths chosen for SMAPP are automatically logged to minimize IPL time required to rebuild these access paths. The system determines whether the time estimated for rebuilding all access paths will exceed a maximum allowable IPL time. If so, it begins the logging process on selected database access paths. This maximum allowable recovery time can be set by the user, but the shorter the time, the more system resources it consumes in ensuring the shorter recovery time. SMAPP takes much of the manual time and effort out of maintaining the journal receivers. It is an automatic feature of OS/400 V3R1.

5.12   System Change Journal Management

System change journal management (SCJM) automates journaling. It attaches new journal receivers to databases when the existing one fills up to a specified level. SCJM can then delete the old receivers if desired. Other features of DB2/400, such as referential integrity and two-phase commitment control, depend on journal receivers. SCJM eases this process by automatically managing the journal receivers needed for these functions and their related databases. Use the `MNGRCV(*SYSTEM)` parameter of the `CRTJRN` command to implement SCJM.

5.13 Summary

DB2/400 brings the AS/400 database up to DB2 functionality and standards. Referential integrity ensures that files maintain correct relations between themselves according to user-defined constraint rules. Stored procedures optimize remote SQL by permitting the client to ask the server to run its own SQL routine, rather than sending each SQL statement to the server, one at a time. Triggers can be attached to a database as extended attributes that cause a user program to be executed automatically upon add, update, or delete of a record in the database. The `EXPLAIN` function and the predictive query governor help the user determine performance characteristics of queries running on the AS/400 and tune or limit them. Two-phase commitment control is a DRDA feature that ensures that all remote updates in a distributed unit of work are successful. DDM allows the user to establish a communications file that can be accessed from within a local RPG or other program to access a remote database. DRDA uses a relational database directory to establish SQL requests between remote systems. Taken together, these features greatly increase the client/server capability of the AS/400.

Chapter

6

SQL

Structured query language (SQL) is a universal language used to access data in relational databases. It is one of the most convenient and yet powerful ways to access data on the AS/400. SQL lets you create, manage, query, and report on DB2/400 databases. It is the easiest language to learn for AS/400 database access, as well as the most widely supported for remote access to DB2/400. SQL is smarter than many other languages because its tight interface with DB2/400 enables it to determine how to access the data using existing access paths. You do not have to specify explicit data access commands in SQL routines. A single, simple SELECT statement naming a DB2/400 database is enough to notify the AS/400's operating system to serve the request. The database manager (DB2/400) takes care of data access paths automatically, maintaining them and making them available to both SQL and native access methods, such as RPG and COBOL. This partnership of the simple and powerful SQL language accessing the advanced server features of DB2/400 is one of the best ways to access AS/400 data.

SQL's learning curve is not very long, but it does present some complexities. SQL is essentially a tool for querying the database and returning a subset or selection of the data. It does not have the full power of a third generation (3GL) programming language like RPG; interactive displays, data edits, and complex or recursive data access methods are outside its jurisdiction.

6.1 SQL and SAA

SQL is an important element in IBM's plan for making its systems applications architecture (SAA) an open architecture. It allows application programs to access data on remote platforms, regardless of architecture or access methods. As long as the remote platform is SQL compliant, adhering to a recognized set of standards (which are currently evolving), the requester or client can submit an SQL request to the platform. It does not matter to the client how the server processes that request. The client sends an SQL request to the server and waits for a data excerpt to come back. The client then continues processing, using the server data returned from its remote SQL request. This process is a very convenient method of receiving remote data. The client programmer does not need to know much about the server's architecture or languages; as long as the communication link is in place and configured correctly, the client can send a remote SQL request.

6.2   Open Database Connectivity

Open database connectivity (ODBC) is a Microsoft Windows method for accessing data on remote platforms based on SQL. The remote platform might be an AS/400 or mainframe on the network, or even a database from another application language on the same PC. ODBC is implemented by a Windows dynamic link library (DLL), which converts the request from the server database format to the client database. ODBC forms a connection between the requesting program, which is running in Windows, and the server. The request takes the form of a remote SQL call. This Windows feature can connect to diverse platforms, such as Macintosh Data Access Language (DAL) and AS/400 SQL. ODBC is an important feature of Windows client/server development because it provides a virtually plug-and-play access to remote data. Once the connection is defined using ODBC, remote data can be accessed as easily as if it were local (but not as quickly, unfortunately). ODBC is the most convenient and painless method for accessing AS/400 data from Windows programs like PowerBuilder and Visual Basic. As the AS/400 and DB2/400 become more optimized for client/server applications, the response time will certainly improve.

6.3   Interactive SQL

Interactive, or dynamic, SQL enables the user to submit immediate queries against a database. No programming or compiling is required. Ad-hoc SQL statements are the fastest and easiest way to access AS/400 data. To start an interactive SQL session, type the following at the command line:

```
STRSQL
```

to initiate an interactive SQL session allowing you to enter interactive SQL statements and receive immediate responses (as quickly as the system can)

(Figure 6.1). Interactive SQL is resource-hungry, however, and should be used sparingly, like interactive query, which is essentially the same thing. Interactive SQL is the fastest way to look at a subset of data or delete or update certain records in a database.

6.4 Embedded SQL

A more useful application of SQL for client/server systems is to embed SQL statements inside another language or application program. This other language could be RPG or COBOL on the AS/400, or PowerBuilder or Visual Basic on the PC. Any platform capable of establishing a connection with the server's SQL manager can handle embedded SQL, also called *static SQL*. The SQL statements are precompiled by the system before the other program is compiled. The embedded SQL returns a data subset to the program in which it resides. Embedded SQL is a handy way to access data from other sources, as long as an ODBC or similar connection is in place. The program containing the embedded SQL, like RPG or COBOL, is called the *host structure*. Not all languages are enabled as SQL host structures, but the main players in the client/server arena are. Some static or embedded SQL statements cannot be implemented interactively.

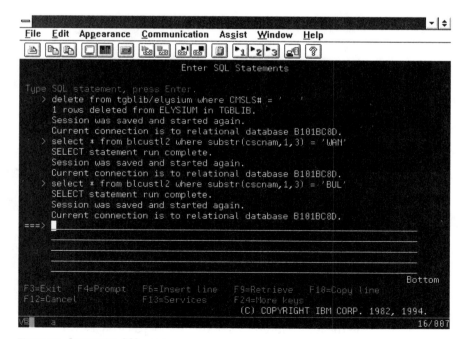

Figure 6.1 Interactive SQL session.

6.5 Remote SQL

For ODBC drivers to establish a connection between the different platforms, they need to be configured. Once configured, an open data path is available with SQL running at both ends. Like embedded SQL, remote SQL establishes a data connection between the client and the server. With embedded SQL, the client is actually an RPG or another program running on the AS/400. The embedded SQL connects to the database manager and returns a data excerpt to the RPG program. With remote SQL, the process is similar, except the client program runs on a different system, which is accomplished through the CONNECT statement in the client program and the RDB definition for a remote database on the AS/400.

6.6 Tables, Views, and Indexes

SQL has its own names for the components of the database. In fact, it does not use the word *database*. Table 6.1 shows corresponding SQL names for database terminology from languages like RPG:

TABLE 6.1 Corresponding SQL Names

3GL	SQL
Library	Collection
Database	Table
Record	Row
Field	Column
Logical File	View or Index

Whatever you call these items, they refer to the same objects within DB2/400. There are two access methods, but only one database. An SQL table is created with the CREATE TABLE statement:

```
CREATE TABLE EMPLIB/EMPTABLE
    (NAME      CHAR(15),
     SALARY    DECIMAL(9,2),
     DEPT      CHAR(3) )
```

These commands create an SQL table named EMPTABLE in the EMPLIB library with three fields: NAME with 15 characters, SALARY with a 9-digit number containing two decimals, and DEPT with three characters. This table, even though created through SQL, is a DB2/400 database and is accessible through the native interfaces of the AS/400, as well as SQL.

Views provide alternate selections or data ordering. They correspond to logical files or indexes. No actual data is contained in a view. It is merely a set of pointers to the data contained in the table. We might want a user to access the above defined table called EMPTABLE, but not be able to see the salaries. We only show people with salaries over $30,000, but we do not show the actual salaries. The following view definition accomplishes this objective:

```
CREATE VIEW EMPVIEW
    AS SELECT ALL
    DEPT, NAME
    FROM EMPTABLE
    WHERE SALARY > 30000
```

Indexes can greatly improve the response time of table access. An *index* is an ordered reference list for a table or database. It does not contain the actual data, but rather how to access it in a particular order. It might, for example, contain a set of pointers to the records or rows of data in alphabetical order for the name field. The index is external to the data. Whether the index is created through SQL, DDS, or another method, DB2/400 maintains it. Once defined, it becomes part of the access path for the database. SQL automatically looks for an existing index when requested to return a data subset from a database. If it finds an appropriate index, it does not need to build a new access path to access the data. In a database with hundreds of thousands or even millions of records, this fact can save significant time when SQL responds to a data request. An SQL index can be built with the CREATE INDEX statement. SQL will also use a logical file defined through DDS as the keyed access path for a query if a relevant one exists.

6.7 Language Elements

The English-like syntax of SQL facilitates data access. It is essentially a very simple language. The following statements are the basis of SQL/400:

SELECT   select rows from table, based on search criteria
UPDATE   update columns in rows
FETCH   return row of table into host variables in calling program
INSERT   insert row into table
DELETE   delete row from table

SQL statements can contain clauses. Common SQL clauses are the following:

FROM   specifies the table for data access
WHERE   which rows to return
GROUP BY   group the rows
HAVING   select groups based on their subtotals
ORDER BY   index the rows returned, based on column values

Many operations are possible just using these few keywords. It is not necessary to know how a file should be opened, as it is in many other 3GL languages. It is not necessary to know verbs for moving around within the file or table. SQL handles all this for you.

SQL uses *predicates* to define many of its clauses. An SQL predicate is an expression containing an operator that compares two values or variables. The predicate returns a value of true or false. A typical example of a predicate is `x = 1`, which is combined with a clause to form a condition: `WHERE x = 1`.

SQL uses these comparison operators in its clauses:

```
x = y     x is equal to y
x ¬= y    x is not equal to y
x <> y    x is not equal to y
x < y     x is less than y
x > y     x is greater than y
x <= y    x is less than or equal to y
x >= y    x is greater than or equal to y
x ¬< y    x is not less than y
x ¬> y    x is not greater than y
```

Other predicates are the following:

```
BETWEEN: x BETWEEN y AND z
IN: x IN ('A', 'B')
```

SQL has functions for use with SELECT and other statements. They include the following:

```
SUM    add the column
AVG    average the column
MAX    return the maximum value in the column
MIN    return the minimum value in the column
```

The SELECT statement returns a subset of the table. This SELECT statement returns only fields NAME and DEPT from EMPTABLE:

```
SELECT DEPT, NAME FROM EMPTABLE
```

The WHERE clause limits the rows returned to those that satisfy the condition:

```
SELECT DEPT, NAME FROM EMPTABLE
    WHERE SALARY > 30000
```

The GROUP BY clause causes the resulting set to contain only one row for each unique value in a particular column. In other words, if EMPTABLE contains 100 records, but only three distinct DEPT values, the following returns only three rows, containing just the names of the departments:

```
SELECT DEPT FROM EMPTABLE
    GROUP BY DEPT
```

GROUP BY is often used in conjunction with the SUM function to show subtotals for groups. The following shows the subtotals of SALARY for the various departments:

```
SELECT DEPT, SUM(SALARY) FROM EMPTABLE
    GROUP BY DEPT
```

The HAVING clause is used to select only those group records that meet a given condition, such as the WHERE clause in the SELECT, which shows department subtotals when someone's salary in the department is over $50,000:

```
SELECT DEPT, SUM(SALARY) FROM EMPTABLE
    GROUP BY DEPT
    HAVING MAX(SALARY) > 50000
```

The ORDER BY clause indexes the results set by the values in a column. The following indexes the data on DEPT and then NAME:

```
SELECT DEPT, NAME,SALARY FROM EMPTABLE
    ORDER BY DEPT, NAME
```

The UPDATE statement is used for changing the values in a table column, selectively or as a whole. You could give the MIS department a 20 percent raise by the following:

```
UPDATE EMPTABLE SET SALARY = SALARY * 1.2
    WHERE DEPT = 'MIS'
```

Remote SQL can be implemented using stored procedures available through DB2/400. These are SQL procedures stored on the server and executed from the client using the DECLARE PROCEDURE and the CALL statements. DECLARE PROCEDURE defines the server system and the procedure to be invoked. CALL actually executes the remote procedure. Refer to the technical documentation of each client package for the exact syntax of remote SQL connections.

6.8 Summary

SQL provides a very powerful and convenient data access method for local and remote platforms. It has become an industry standard for remote connections. SQL can create tables and views that can be used by SQL as well as other languages. Its syntax is much simpler than other computer languages, allowing users to access databases easily. In a short time, users can learn to query, update, and delete data in a database.

SQL is at the heart of many database engines, including DB2/400 on the AS/400. Remote requests to DB2/400 can be served and subsets of data returned to the requesting client. This distributed data scenario is available on the PC, the AS/400, and mainframes, as well as on systems from a multitude of vendors. It is likely that an SQL standard will become the norm for distributed processing. SQL is not bundled with OS/400 but must be ordered separately.

7

Integrated Language
Environment RPG IV

7.1 Overview of RPG IV

Although client/server systems depend heavily on PC interfaces, RPG can still be the core of the system. A PC program can call an RPG program as a remote procedure, keeping some of the processing on the AS/400, where the data is native and the processing and data handling is powerful. By using a remote procedure call, and allowing RPG to process on the AS/400, communications overhead can be kept to a minimum. RPG is enhanced as of version 3, release 1 (V3R1), with many new features that make it more productive as an element in the client/server mosaic. Many times in a client/server application, data must be gathered from many different databases on the AS/400 for presentation in a simplified format on the PC. RPG is a good method. You simply call an RPG program remotely from the PC, wait for it to finish processing, and then access the resulting data set from the PC or download it for further manipulation and reporting. This approach really uses the strengths of both platforms—the data crunching power of the AS/400 and the presentation and manipulation tools of the PC.

Integrated language environment

The AS/400 languages and compilers have been revamped for performance and syntax. Programs are now compiled with more efficient binding, which means that calls to external programs are executed much more quickly. Iterative external program calls are now feasible in situations where they used to be too slow. To notify the AS/400 that you want to write in the new style of RPG IV, you specify the source type as RPGLE and create a source physical file called QRPGLESRC to hold the source files.

RPG IV now has expanded names of up to 10 characters. Mixed case typing is allowed. Free-form expressions in the EVAL opcode finally bring algebraic formulas in to RPG, making the code much more readable. There are built-in functions and date and time support. Many new keywords at the F-spec level allow the programmer to define file usages more precisely and conveniently. Factors and result fields are 14 characters. Finally, a source migration tool can aid in converting the old RPG programs to the new format.

Columns

RPG has loosened up its column-oriented nature. It is finally not true that everything in an RPG program must be in the correct column. Now, only *most* things must be in the correct column. RPG is still not a free-form language, but the improved freedoms are welcome and very helpful in terms of readability. The program source entry utility (SEU) still helps in placing those elements that require strict positions. Consider the following, which figures out how many months ago (up to 15) a date is:

```
C           Eval     n = 15 - (NowYYMM - ((ThenYY * 12) + ThenMM))
```

This is not the RPG we have struggled with to create algebraic expressions in the past. Now, you can write any kind of expression with the Eval statement, much more easily than before. Also, note the longer (10 character) variable names and mixed case. All of these things, taken together, make the new RPG a delight compared to the old version, which looks positively archaic in comparison:

```
C      YY1    MULT  12          N
C             ADD   MM2         N
C      YYMM2  SUB   N           N
C      15     SUB   N           N
```

I think this difference alone is worth the price of the new RPG IV.

7.2 Sections and Specifications

RPG programs are still written in sections, called *specifications*, that must occur in order and are identified by a letter in column 6. Now, however, instead of having E and I specs for data definitions, we have the D spec (for data). The sections are shown in Table 7.1.

7.3 Specifications

RPG is coded in different sections, each with its own type of specification. Figure 7.1 is a sample RPG program, which gathers sales information for a given group of products and items. It is written in the new RPG IV style.

TABLE 7.1 RPG Specifications

H	HEADER SPECS	program identification
F	FILE SPECS	file definitions
D	DATA SPECS	array and data structure declaration
C	CALC SPECS	commands and main program
O	OUTPUT SPECS	report writing

Figure 7.1 Sample RPG program.

```
H*   SALES rpg
H*   Tony Baritz
H*   06/26/95
**-------------------------------------------------------------------
FProdFil    IF    E              Disk
FItemFil    IF    E         K Disk       Rename(ItemFil1:itm)
FSaleFil    IF    E         K Disk
FOutFil     UF A E         K Disk
**-------------------------------------------------------------------
D                   DS
D     YYMM                     4  0
D     YYx                      2        OverLay(YYMM:1)
D     MMx                      2        OverLay(YYMM:3)
D     YY#                      2  0     OverLay(YYMM:1)
D     MM#                      2  0     OverLay(YYMM:3)
**
D                   DS
D     ThenYYMM#                4  0
D     ThenYY#                  2  0     OverLay(ThenYYMM#:1)
D     ThenMM#                  2  0     OverLay(ThenYYMM#:3)
**
D     Sales         S          6  0     Dim(15)
**-------------------------------------------------------------------
C         *Entry      Plist
C                     Parm                   MM              2
C                     Parm                   YY              2
**-------------------------------------------------------------------
**    Cycle through the list of relevant products
**-------------------------------------------------------------------
C                     Read    ProdFil                              99
C                     DoW     *in99 = *OFF
**-------------------------------------------------------------------
**    Cycle through the Items for each product
**-------------------------------------------------------------------
C         ItmKey      Chain   ItemFil                              98
C                     DoW     *In98 = *Off
**-------------------------------------------------------------------
**    Get Item Sales
**-------------------------------------------------------------------
C                     If      Status = ' ' or (Special = 'N' and MM <> 9)
C         IvtKey      SetLL   SaleFil                              97
C                     Read    SaleFil                                  97
C                     DoW     *In97 = *OFF    and PrItem = IvItem
C                                             and IvYMpd <= YYMM
**
C                     Move    IvYMpd    ThenYYMM#
C                     Z-add   0         n                   2 0
C                     Eval    n = 15-(NowYYMM#-((ThenYY#*12)+ThenMM#))
```

Figure 7.1 Continued

```
C                      Z-add     IvChS1    Sales(n)
**
C                      Read      SaleFil                              97
C                      Enddo
**----------------------------------------------------------------
**     Write the record
**----------------------------------------------------------------
C                      MoveL     F1PdCl    IrProd
C                      MoveL     ItDesc    IrDesc
C                      Move      YY        AsofYY
C                      Move      MM        AsofMM
**
C                      Z-add     Sales(1)  Sale01
C                      Z-add     Sales(2)  Sale02
C                      Z-add     Sales(3)  Sale03
**
C                      Write     OutFil
**
**----------------------------------------------------------------
** Next Item
**----------------------------------------------------------------
C                      Endif
C                      ReadE     ItemFil                              98
C                      Enddo
**----------------------------------------------------------------
** Next Product
**----------------------------------------------------------------
C                      Read      ProdFil                              99
C                      Enddo
**----------------------------------------------------------------
C                      Seton                                         LR
**----------------------------------------------------------------
```

We still have the different types of specs, and most of the specifications are familiar, but the readability is greatly improved.

Header specs

The first type of spec coded in an RPG program is the *header spec*. While the header is optional, it provides identifying information about the program and should be included. You can specify your name, the program name, and a description of the program's function. The * in the seventh position indicates a comment line.

```
H* SALES rpg
```

File specs

File specs are critical to an RPG program. They identify each externally defined file to be referenced by the program, and indicate what their functions will be. Remember that screens are considered to be files, in addition to the physical and logical files. The following spec identifies a data file to the RPG program:

```
F   ItemFil   IF   E    K Disk    Rename(ItemFil1:itm)
```

Note the `Rename` keyword on the same line as the file spec. This command used to take two lines. Many items must be defined about the files in the file specs. Here is a breakdown of the first file spec listed above:

- `F`: indicates that it is a file spec
- `ItemFil`: the filename
- `I`: file is used for Input
- `F`: file is full procedural, can be used for chaining, reading, etc.
- `E`: file is defined externally to RPG (in DDS)
- `K`: file is keyed, will automatically use the index
- `Disk`: file resides on disk

It is important to accurately define the type and program function of the files you need to use, or the program will not work. In fact, it probably will not even compile if it has bad file specs. File usages are the following:

- `I` = input
- `O` = output
- `IP` = input primary
- `UF` = update full procedural (for chaining or finds)
- `CF` = combined full procedural (for screens)

SEU, the program source entry utility, provides you with a fill-in-the-blank prompt screen after you type the `F` in column 6, so that the SEU knows for which type of RPG spec to prompt.

Data specs

Extension and input specs have been replaced by the data spec.

```
D    ThenYYMM#    4   0
D    ThenYY#      2   0   OverLay(ThenYYMM#:1)
D    ThenMM#      2   0   OverLay(ThenYYMM#:3)
```

The above defines a data structure called `ThenYYMM#`. It has two subfields. `ThenYY#` is numeric (2 digits, no decimal places) and overlays two places of `ThenYYMM#`, starting at position 1. `ThenMM#` similarly overlays two places of `ThenYYMM#` starting at position 3. Note the indentation, which makes the data structure components easier to read.

```
D  Sales        S                6   0  Dim(15)
```

Next, we define an array called `Sales`. This array has 15 elements, each consisting of a six-digit number with no decimal places. These array elements can be referenced in the program by array name and element number, such as Sales(3).

Calculation specs

Calc specs are generally the heart of an RPG program. It is here that the specific file and data processing takes place, commands occur, and logic flow is implemented. The following is a calc spec that places a numeric field into our data structure:

```
C              Move   IvYMpd        ThenYYMM#
```

The main components of a calc spec are the C, which identifies the line as a calc spec, Factor1, which is related somehow to Factor2 through the action of the opcode, and Result, which is where the outcome is placed.

Additional parameters include the N01 on the left of the syntax line above for indicator use, and the HiLoEq on the right of the syntax line, which is also for indicators.

Assignment operators and variable initialization

RPG variable names can now be up to 10 characters long. This rule also applies to arrays with their indexes, as in Sales(12).

If a data file is correctly identified in the F spec in an RPG program, all its field names become automatically available to the program. RPG creates variables with the same names as the DDS field names for RPG's internal use. These field names are automatically passed to and returned from any screen called from the RPG program. This action can lead to some confusion if duplicate field names exist in two or more files. The solution for this problem is the Prefix option of the file spec:

```
F   ItemFil   IF  E            K Disk    Prefix(xx)
```

This command attaches the prefix xx to all fields in the ItemFil, so they cannot be confused with fields from another file. Field names produced by this method look like xxSalary and xxName. With the prefix, the field names must still be 10 characters or less.

Table 7.2 shows some of the more useful opcodes that handle data.

Variables can be initialized simply by adding the defining parameters—length and decimal positions—to the opcodes. For example, to define and initialize the variable n, use the following:

```
C    Z-add  0  n  2  0
```

This statement tells RPG to set up a variable called n with two digits and no decimals, and to initialize it to zero (Z-add 0). It is simply the two numbers, 2 and 0, in the appropriate columns that tell RPG to declare this variable. If you forget this step, you will get an undefined variable error at compile time.

TABLE 7.2 PPG Opcodes

Command	Definition	Example
Z-Add	initialize to zero and add a number to a numeric variable	C Z-Add 0 ThenYYMM#
Move	move a variable to another variable (left-truncated if necessary)	C Move IvYMpd ThenYYMM#
MoveL	move a string to a character variable (right-truncated if necessary)	C MoveL 'Hello' Greeting
MoveA	move a string to an array or vice versa	C MoveA 'Hello' Array1

A variable needs to be defined only once. After definition, you can refer to it without the defining numerals. To define a character variable, put in the variable length only, leaving out the decimal portion.

```
C Move 'ABC' var1 3
```

The missing decimal of this initialization is an example of how, in RPG, when nothing is in a certain column, it means something, such as that this variable is declared as a character.

Mathematical operators

RPG used to be unwieldy for complex mathematical calculations because only one operator could be used on any line of code. This limitation has been changed with the Eval opcode. Therefore, algebraic expressions like the following are now available in RPG:

```
C Eval n = x - ((a/b) * c)
```

Logical constructs are also simplified in the new RPG. We can now represent the statement, "If A is greater than B or C is equal to 1" as the following:

```
C If a > b or c = 1
```

And "Add 1 to x while y is less than 25" can be written as:

```
C     DoW x < 25
C     Add 1 x
C     Endif
```

I/O: Record, find, read, update, and write

RPG opcodes for database I/O are shown in Table 7.3.

SEU provides a prompting screen to help with the construction of RPG I/O statements in the calc specs.

TABLE 7.3 RPG Opcodes for Databases

Command	Definition	Example
EXFMT	executes a screen which has been designed and compiled externally to RPG, passing RPG fields to it.	`C ExFmt Order`
CHAIN	finds the named value in the index, reads the record, and sets on an RPG special indicator (98 in this example) if not found.	`C ItmKey Chain ItemFil 98`
READ	reads the next record, sets on indicator 77 if end-of-file.	`C Read ItemFil 77`
READE	sets the pointer to next record with same index value, and sets on special indicator 77 if not found.	`C ItmKey ReadE ItemFil 77`
SETGT	sets the pointer to the next record with a value greater than the named value, and sets on indicator 77 if not found. It does not read the record, so you must issue a READ as well.	`C ItmKey SetGt ItemFil 77`
UPDAT	updates the current record (requires record format name rather than the database name).	`C Updat ItemFil 77`
WRITE	adds a new record to the database (requires record format name, not database name).	`C Write ItemF1 98`

7.4 Indicators

RPG maintains special indicators to help with program logic flow and control. These indicators can be referenced by the program to influence logic and branching. RPG allows the setting of indicators 01 through 99 to be used by the programmer as program flags. These indicators can be used to recognize when a file is at end-of-file, when a certain condition is true, what key a user has pressed in a screen, etc. They can be accessed with the *INnn syntax:

```
C If *In99 = *OFF
```

The programmer can set on indicator 12 with this statement:

```
C SetOn 12
```

and set it back off with this one:

```
C SetOf 12
```

RPG maintains a set of special indicators to determine program flow and branching. The only one we need concern ourselves with is LR, which tells

RPG whether the last record has been read in an input file. RPG can then exit the program because LR is set on, either by the RPG cycle or programmer intervention.

```
C Seton LR
```

7.5 The RPG Cycle

RPG has an automatic cycle that it follows. The programmer can define one of the data files as an input primary (IP) file in the F spec. RPG then reads one record at a time from this file, performing all the logic in the calc specs for each record in the input primary file, and set on LR (last record) when the input primary file is at end-of-file.

Input primary files

A file is defined as input primary with this syntax:

```
F   ProdFil IP E    Disk
```

This file definition reads one record at a time from the file defined as IP (input primary) and performs all calc spec logic for each record.

Circumventing the RPG cycle

Input primary works only if you can read one record at a time from the file until it is finished, and then quit. If you need to jump around in the file, you must maintain your own program I/O logic with CHAINs and GOTOs, and SETON LRs as in our sample program. Some programmers ignore the RPG cycle or do not learn it, preferring to explicitly manage the logic and flow of RPG I/O themselves.

7.6 Summary

RPG is a powerful language. It has been greatly enhanced in its latest version, which is called RPG IV. It retains its concise nature while gaining some free-form aspects, making it much easier to code and read. It binds much more efficiently to external programs. Many new features and functions make it more convenient. In conjunction with programs running on the PC platform in client/server applications, RPG IV can be the main data crunching engine, collecting and processing data from the AS/400 and making it available to the client.

Advanced Server Series

The AS/400 has optimized its hardware and software to support client/ server features such as remote SQL access and network connections. These AS/400 machines are called the *Advanced Server Series*. The AS/400 operating system (OS/400) provides many new and enhanced client/server type of features as of version 3, release 1. IBM also recommends PC software that works well with the AS/400 in client/server environments called the *Client Series*. The integrated package of client and server hardware and software eases system configuration and represents a major advantage over other environments where the user is responsible for choosing system and application tools on both the server and the clients, who must then get everything to work together. The AS/400 components and features are all designed to work together out of the box. They support clients such as Microsoft Windows, OS/2, Macintosh, AIX, and others. Remote data access and terminal emulation, as well as mail and messages, are provided to these clients. Protocols supported include APPC, TCP/IP, ODBC, IDAPI, and DAL. In short, the AS/400 is accessible from a wide variety of platforms and clients with minimal configuration.

The main features of the AS/400 as a distributed network server include the following:

- Transparent access for a wide variety of clients and protocols
- Versatile and efficient application development platform
- Centralized node for network services and management
- Powerful, reliable database management (DB2/400)

- Open communications

- Ease of installation, maintenance, and programming environment

It is now feasible to use the AS/400 as a server in a diverse network. It can actually function both as a server and client, but it is much more adept at being a server. DB2/400, along with the Client Series software, forms an efficient and dependable distributed platform for client/server development.

8.1 New Models

The AS/400 offers models optimized from the hardware through the operating system to the utilities for client/server procedures. They still have all the features for which the AS/400 is known, including ease of use, integrated software and hardware products, and superior security. In addition, they serve remote data requests much better and faster than the older models. A Server Series AS/400 is designed to divert resources away from interactive user jobs and toward the noninteractive jobs that typically constitute server functions. The resources are diverted even if the run priorities of the jobs are set to maximize interactive resources. Systems that depend on interactive processes, as opposed to server processes, should not use a Server Series AS/400; they are better off with traditional models. On a traditional model, the interactive function is usually optimized to provide quick display response for the users. IBM recommends that a Server Series AS/400 should be used if 70 percent or more of the applications are in the client/server area. Client/server type applications include the following:

- APPC
- Shared folders
- Compiling
- Background jobs
- Distributed processes
- Remote data requests

Interactive applications are the following:

- PC Support or Client Access
- 5250 terminals
- RUMBA/400
- Applications that use the keyboard and/or display extensively

The Server Series models, compared to their traditional model equivalents, are shown in Table 8.1.

**TABLE 8.1 Server Series Compared to
Traditional Model Equivalents**

Server series	Traditional model equivalents	
	Interactive equivalent	Server equivalent
9402 Model 100	9402 F02	9406 F45
9404 Model 135	9406 F10	9406 F50+
9404 Model 140	9406 F20	9406 F70+
9402 Model 20S	9402 F02	9406 F45
9404 Model 30S #2411	9406 F10	9406 F50+
9404 Model 30S #2412	9406 F20	9406 F70+

As you can see, the Server Series models support both interactive and server applications, but they excel at client/server tasks at the expense of interactive processes. Use them only in environments that demand optimization for communications to remote platforms. Avoid them for online native program data entry and transactions.

8.2 Client Series Software

IBM offers the Client Series to complement the Server Series. The Client Series consists of software specifically designed for easy installation on the PC client and for interoperability with the AS/400 as a server. The software consists chiefly of end-user tools, application development packages, and 5250 emulators. Some of them are the following:

- RUMBA/400 GUI front-end for AS/400, replaces PC Support
- Macintosh Connections GUI front-end for AS/400 on the Macintosh
- ShowCase VISTA Query AS/400 data from PC GUI interface
- SQL Windows SQL interface to AS/400 data from Windows
- VisualAge object-oriented development
- SYNON CSG CASE tool for client/server development
- LANRES/400 Novell network interface
- DAL Macintosh Data Access Language
- OMNIS 7 Macintosh SQL interface
- TRACK Executive Information Support

These software packages are easy to install and are recommended by IBM as client/server solutions. See the specific chapters on RUMBA, VISTA, and Apple for more details about the software.

8.3   Performance Enhancements for Client/Server

The AS/400 has always been able to handle a wide variety of job types. Interactive, batch, communications, transaction processing, and database management all coexist efficiently. Now, the AS/400 has been optimized for the types of jobs involved in client/server applications. Jobs that access the AS/400 from other platforms, such as shared folders or remote SQL requests, run much faster than before. Many of the features available through DB2/400, such as referential integrity, triggers, and stored procedures, combine with the enhanced hardware speed of the server to make the AS/400 an efficient server platform in distributed environments.

In addition, the AS/400 is being redesigned to adhere to object-oriented standards so it can participate in enterprise client/server application development, representing a major increase in programmer and developer productivity. Tested and reliable object modules are available for use in the distributed environment, eliminating the need to write the client/server application from scratch. The programmer or developer works, according to the object-oriented paradigm, with objects that represent business modules at a high level. Objects, once designed, are adaptable to various situations. They enable the developer, for example, to place an icon on the GUI desktop that seamlessly accesses an AS/400 database query and returns a color graph showing regional sales to a sales manager at a remote site. The whole bundle of functions and processes that lead to the graph can be thought of as a regional sales object. It can then be adapted fairly easily into a quarterly sales object. This type of network integration, using object-oriented tools and utilities, represents the future of business application development, according to many industry analysts, and the AS/400 is committed to supplying the tools and platforms that support it.

8.4   File Server Input/Output Processor

The AS/400 now offers a feature that allows you to use AS/400 disk drives as if they were local PC network disk drives. Actually, it has had this function for quite some time under the name of Shared Folders, where PC files are stored and accessed on the AS/400 disks. Shared Folders, however, has always been slow. Now, the AS/400 serves PC file requests by having its own PC-type file server. It uses a dedicated 486 microprocessor on an AS/400 I/O card called the *file server input output processor (FSIOP)*. This feature uses an AS/400 disk drive or an allocated portion of a drive as a PC file server. The FSIOP handles the processing of PC file disk requests, minimizing impact on the AS/400 itself. FSIOP can replace Shared Folders or be used in addition to Shared Folders. The performance of FSIOP, however, is far superior to the disk access of Shared Folders. Security and system management for these drives can be controlled from the AS/400. It is possible to eliminate a separate PC network server; you can run the entire AS/400 to PC network from AS/400 disk drives.

The FSIOP looks like any other I/O processor to the AS/400 in terms of system management. System Service Tools can be used to inspect error logs, trace points, and debug. Performance Monitor works with FSIOP as well as with other AS/400 disk drives. To the PC, the FSIOP looks just like any other PC network disk drive; it leads a double life. The FSIOP is configured as a network server description (CRTNWSD) on the AS/400.

8.5 LAN Server/400

To implement the FSIOP as a PC network file server, IBM provides LAN Server/400. This network operating system software is designed to work with the FSIOP on the AS/400. It fully integrates the PC network into the AS/400 box, eliminating the need for an external file server and operating system, such as Novell. Whether you choose this route or another is a matter for careful comparison and consideration; there are advantages on either side.

LAN Server/400 is a licensed program on the AS/400 that manages the FSIOP, creating a file server network for PCs entirely contained within the AS/400. The AS/400 thus becomes not only the server for AS/400 files, but also the server for PC type files—spreadsheets and word processor documents, for example. Problems such as decentralized database administration, operating system incompatibilities, and configurations for coexistence disappear with this solution. AS/400 backups can now capture AS/400 files and PC files because they all reside on the AS/400's disk drives. The whole system can thus be managed from the AS/400. Performance monitoring and tuning can be accomplished from a central location for all AS/400 and FSIOP processes. User profiles known to the AS/400 are automatically reflected in a database of FSIOP user information, simplifying network security.

This technology supports OS/2 LAN server clients. DOS, Windows, and Netware clients will be supported at a later date. Token Ring and Ethernet LANs will also be supported. Access time is greatly improved over Shared Folders access time. In fact, this approach can eliminate the use of Shared Folders altogether. The reported response time of FSIOP is almost equal to high-end PC file servers. IBM reports that FSIOP offers 80 to 90 percent of the performance of a 486/66 file server. LAN Server/400 uses a file system similar to OS/2's high-performance file system (HPFS), which is mounted on the AS/400 as QLANSRV. AS/400 DASD must be allocated for this purpose before use, unlike the dynamic allocation of AS/400 native file space.

LAN Server/400 allows system administrators (QSECOFR) to set up domains of servers. A *domain* is a group of servers that treat distributed network disk drives as a single logical drive, visible to the network users. The domain controller is a server that controls the distributed logical file domain. It performs routing and coordinating tasks for the FSIOP and OS/2 LAN Server on the network. The administrator can manage server resources, view system utilization, and monitor domain security.

Clients have the choice of running Client Access/400 or LAN Server/400 or both. Both can access the FSIOP files. Client Access/400 running alone can access the files, but cannot take advantage of the performance edge of the FSIOP. Instead, QCMN services Client Access/400 requests routed to the FSIOP without LAN Server. Using LAN Server with Client Access is the most versatile and powerful solution. It makes a wide range of services available through Client Access, along with the marked performance boost for PC file sharing of FSIOP. OfficeVision/400 cannot yet access these files through the FSIOP and must still be used with Shared Folders.

To implement FSIOP, DOS and OS/2 must run LAN Requester client code. This software provides the protocol conversions necessary to allow DOS and OS/2 to access the FSIOP and the files on the AS/400. This code can be downloaded to the workstation through Client Access/400 or some other file transfer product or installed on the PC from a floppy disk. LAN Server is user licensed and additional licenses must be purchased for additional users.

8.6 Integrated File System

Integrated file system (IFS) allows file access methods that are alien to the AS/400 to operate on its files. For instance, a BASIC program on a PC might access the AS/400 database using a byte stream method. The AS/400 does not know what a byte stream is. This database access, once completed through IFS, however, would be subject to all the DB2/400 database management utilities, such as referential integrity and triggers. It therefore combines remote file access technology with the native features of the database manager.

8.7 Summary

The AS/400 makes it easier to implement client/server environments. The Server Series consists of new models of the AS/400 optimized for client/server processes, including remote data requests, batch processes, and network services. The Server Series can deliver performance increases of three to five times the comparable traditional models for these jobs. The interactive environment is not primary on these machines, and what is gained in client/server performance is taken from the interactive environment.

The FSIOP is a 486 card located inside the AS/400 that operates like a PC network disk drive. This means you can thus run a PC network from inside the AS/400 box, complete with AS/400 performance, management, and security features. This option eliminates the requirement to purchase and support a separate PC file server. LAN Server/400 is the software that enables this functionality between the PC and the AS/400 FSIOP.

In conjunction with these new models, IBM offers the Client Series of software, which is designed for easy installation and use on the PC side of things. Many of the headaches intrinsic to implementing distributed processing are eliminated by this integrated approach to the entire client/server concept. Client Series software includes RUMBA, ShowCase VISTA, SQL Windows, Macintosh Connections, and many others.

PC Clients and Operating Systems

A significant part of client/server actions occur on the client, so it is essential to understand the various clients' operating systems. We generally mean PCs when we say clients, although the AS/400 could function as a client to the mainframe server or even to a PC server. We will stick to the norm for our purposes—an AS/400 server and PC clients. The operating systems that primarily constitute this view of client/server systems are Windows, DOS, OS/2, UNIX, and System 7 from Apple. The AS/400 has varying degrees of services designed for use with each of the preceding operating systems. Simple terminal emulation is available, for example, to all of them, while data queue access is available only to some.

DOS is the old mainstay of the PC world. Everyone said it would be gone by now, but it refuses to leave. It actually gets better all the time. Most people would not think of DOS in terms of client/server development, but actually it offers a lot of potential. Its implications in terms of Windows bear some investigation, too. DOS is a character-based interface, unlike the pictorial nature of GUIs. You must be careful about memory management with it because it is all too easy to max out its limited memory space. Utilities such as Memmaker and QEMM can help. DOS can provide terminal emulation through Client Access and can provide client/server programs and systems through extended DOS Client Access features, including file transfer and remote command. With these, you can write a DOS program that runs an AS/400 program and brings the data down to the PC, allowing massaging of the data and printing at the PC. This function is client/server. It might not be as attractive or powerful as Windows-based client/server applications, but it is client/server nonetheless. More on this topic is described in the DOS client/server sample section.

Windows is probably the image that comes to mind when we hear the phrase client/server. *This platform offers itself admirably to the development of easy programs for the user to gain access to remote AS/400 data. Except for certain system instabilities (including the general protection fault, or GPF), Windows provides an attractive and productive platform for use as a front-end to various back-end database systems, like the AS/400. Windows 3.1 and DOS are related in that it is necessary to start DOS before Windows. Windows 95 eliminates this, along with the resulting system crashes. Windows NT is a full-blown networking operating system, which can run at the PC network file server as well as the workstations. The Program Manager is the desktop of Windows. It contains the familiar icons and menus of the Windows system and GUI. From here, you can access terminal emulation, Lotus, Word, and other Windows applications. Cut and paste, DDE, and OLE are also features available to applications running under Windows. Programs that run in Windows use concepts such as event-handling and object-oriented programming to implement their features. Open database connectivity (ODBC) is the SQL-based Windows interface to external data sources, whether they reside in another Windows application or on a remote AS/400. Because Windows 3.1 depends on DOS, memory management becomes an important issue. Windows 95 is a 32-bit preemptive multitasking environment similar to Windows NT or OS/2. It offers a more intuitive interface than the other Windows operating systems. It also features plug and play for much easier device configuration. Its memory requirements are much less than those for Windows NT, which could be an attractive compromise between the full blown network power of NT, the lower memory requirements of Windows 3.1, and the more intuitive interface of OS/2. In later sections on sample applications, we develop several client/server systems in the Windows environment.*

OS/2 is IBM's operating system intended to provide a GUI with true preemptive multitasking. Windows 3.1 was unable to provide this feature, despite its popularity. OS/2 has a slightly different shell than Windows. The Presentation Manager and Workplace Shell are its paradigm. Folders instead of icons populate the desktop, and inside the folders are pages containing needed functions. Preemptive multitasking is the ability of the operating system to manage different threads or pieces of processes in an orderly manner. OS/2 does not depend on DOS in any way, so the memory constraints and conflicts inherent in the Windows 3.1/DOS partnership are eliminated. OS/2 can emulate DOS and Windows from within the Workplace Shell. Communications Manager offers terminal emulation and other connection services to the AS/400. A Database Manager and two different file systems can be used. OS/2 is a fully featured if not very widely used operating system for client/server development. Because it is IBM software, in some ways it fits very neatly into the remote data access capabilities of the AS/400, as in the case of VRPG, an AS/400 language that now has a GUI front-end.

UNIX comes from a different perspective altogether. It is not from the IBM world, as are OS/400, OS/2, DOS, and Windows. UNIX was designed to provide an open-ended nonproprietary operating system to run "C" programs at Bell Labs. It features open connections and is not as easy to use as operating systems in the IBM world. Its GUI is known as X-Windows. The AS/400 offers Connection Program/400 to connect to the UNIX world and has 5250 terminal emulation, remote printers, data access APIs, file transfer, and remote commands. This group of services provides a good basis for developing client/server functionality across the IBM/UNIX boundary. No longer can it be said that UNIX is open and IBM closed; they are converging. SNA and TCP/IP are the two networking protocols that constitute a very large part of the applications in production today. As they mature, they become more interoperable, enabling more and more cross-platform ideas to be implemented.

Apple is known as the home computer. Increasingly, though, it is finding its way into businesses, especially in the domain of desktop publishing, where its ease of installation and use is appropriate to the nontechnical user interested in productive graphical output. Now IBM offers several connection methods to bring the Apple Macintosh into the data-crunching world of IBM. The SNA Gateway Connection, TCP/IP Connection, and AppleTalk Connection all provide links to the AS/400. Terminal emulation and printer *emulation are available so that the Mac can operate like an AS/400 terminal or printer. Data access language (DAL) and SQL provide methods for gaining access to the data stored in the AS/400's files from the Macintosh. File Services enables transfers of files between the platforms. While these are not the most powerful group of tools on the market for connecting the AS/400 to other clients, they are sufficient for developing some client/server functions.*

Now that we have all these operating systems, how do we tie them together? Networks. Various types of interface cards connect computers and other devices through cabling (or microwave, satellites, etc.). Protocols are the sets of rules and communications standards that control the transmissions across the networks. Local area networks (LANs) connect devices in a single location, like an office. WANs connect across distance, using phone lines or other types of links. Two types of network topology are predominantly used with the AS/400. IBM's token ring uses a token ring card in each computer and in the AS/400 to provide connectivity, which was used for years to connect IBM computers. Ethernet has lately made inroads as the other type of card generally used with the AS/400 and PCs in LANs. More and more, Ethernet is becoming the standard. Now that the computers are connected physically to the AS/400, we need to think about what type of PC file server we want to run for the shared PC applications. The AS/400 functions as a major database server, while the PC file server offers spreadsheets and word processors as well as shared peripherals and backups. In addition, our client/server PC applications might well reside on the PC server, eliminating the need to install them on each user's PC. Novell Netware is the predominant operating system for PC networks, with Windows NT coming up fast in second place. Making careful and appropriate selections from the above components, an efficient network can be constructed. For example, we might run Ethernet cards over unshielded twisted pair (UTP) cable, connecting the PCs with the AS/400 and a Novell file server. Now we have all the pieces in place to create distributed functionality.

Chapter

9

DOS

9.1 Character-Based Interface

DOS is an acronym for disk operating system. Originally developed as a rather simple operating system for the IBM PC, it rode the rapidly expanding PC marketplace to a position of dominance. Other, more sophisticated operating systems such as Windows and OS/2 have been introduced to the PC since DOS was introduced, but DOS continues to hold a significant section of the market. DOS is sufficient for many of the standalone applications that users are running on PCs. Even systems that now run in Windows 3.x depend on DOS for services. It is necessary to start DOS first, and then run Windows on top of it (which is not true of Windows NT).

DOS knows how to store and retrieve files on the disk drives, send output to the printer or terminal, manage directories, and execute programs. Application programs are run on top of DOS and generally handle any advanced system requirements such as indexing and security. DOS is not a full-fledged operating system that presents the user with a myriad of system functions and features. The IBM PC and DOS were not really conceived of in terms of enterprise-scale corporate systems. Problems of connectivity and security, for example, which come with full-scale solutions, are beyond the scope of DOS. Simplicity is both its strength and weakness.

Many features of more sophisticated operating systems like UNIX or OS/400 are not part of DOS. Because DOS is a single-user environment, no security exists. You can erase any local files (on the disk drives in the PC) you want, as they are all yours. File locking and sharing are topics that are outside the scope of DOS because DOS is designed as a single-user system.

Once the user logs into a network, the network operating system takes over for any tasks related to security. A PC running DOS has unlimited access to its own internal disk files, but submits requests to files on the network drives using the security of the network operating system. Physical files residing on the AS/400 are managed by the security features of OS/400. Requests to these files, which originate on the PC, are passed through the security functions of the AS/400 user profile, used to connect the PC into the AS/400 as a client. Another type of file is the file stored on the AS/400 through shared folders. It looks like a local disk file to the PC but actually resides on an AS/400 disk drive. DOS handles none of these security issues.

One of the more stringent constraints of DOS is the 640K barrier for random access memory (RAM), which is where the computer does most of its work, or thinking, if you will. When DOS was designed, it seemed that 640K was all the memory anyone would need on a PC. In fact, PCs generally had 256K or less in the early 1980s, and plenty of software ran in this. As PCs gained in popularity and functionality, applications rapidly became more powerful, feature-laden, and memory intensive. 640K quickly became insufficient for the needs of advancing software. Most PCs running Lotus now require a minimum of 1 to 2 megabytes of RAM. Windows running on top of DOS needs 4 to 8 megabytes of RAM. This memory squeeze is one of the ongoing problems with DOS as a primary operating system.

Because DOS is a single-user operating system, it cannot perform multitasking or swap jobs in and out of memory the way the AS/400 does. *Preemptive multitasking* is an orderly arrangement whereby a task manager coordinates or juggles various jobs. As these jobs contend for the same system resources, the operating system decides which ones to activate and which to put on temporary hold, according to preset priorities. DOS cannot perform this function. Any job running in DOS has the system's full attention, until it releases the CPU, which is sufficient for many procedures on the PC and even desirable at times. When you are running a spreadsheet or database update, you are not sharing system resources with anything else. All the CPU power is available for recalculations or WYSIWIG (what you see is what you get) or whatever you are doing. If a PC is to be used for a single purpose, by a single user, it is hard to beat DOS for performance. It is still a viable option as a single-user application platform, even in some client/server settings.

DOS is a character-based operating system, as opposed to a graphical interface, which means there are no pictures in DOS. The screen can only show ASCII characters or images made from the characters. This fact is not true of all software invoked and run from DOS; some use the mouse and graphics. When you are in the operating system itself, in DOS at the c:> prompt, however, you must know commands and program names. There is no point and click with the mouse to navigate the various features of the operating system, no pictures of available programs to run, and no hunting around in visible tree images of the directory structure for files.

Several add-ons are available for the DOS environment that provide the user with menus or shells. These can insulate the user from the barren c:> prompt. It is possible to place users into a menu system at startup so that all they need to do is select options to navigate the system and execute programs. Users type a number representing a menu option or use the arrow keys to get to the desired option. When the program is finished running, they are returned to the menu. Although this menu is not a GUI environment where you just point at pictures and click, it does provide a level of user comfort and intuitive interaction.

Many of the more state-of-the-art tools for remote database access are not available to DOS. The Microsoft open database connectivity (ODBC) standard is implemented in Windows. OS/2 has its own DB2 implementation, which enables remote SQL calls to the AS/400. These online links to the AS/400 DB2/400 database are implemented in platforms other than DOS. It remains to be seen, as the world of client/server develops new tools, if this functionality can be brought into the DOS world.

For the above reasons, DOS is usually dismissed as a suitable platform for client/server applications. There are exceptions, however. Many client/server applications can be used quite advantageously from the DOS platform. These include the following:

- *Terminal emulation*: The PC behaves like a 5250 AS/400 display terminal.

- *File transfer*: Files are moved from the AS/400 to PC or the reverse.

- *Shared or virtual printers*: A PC printer is used as an AS/400 printer or the reverse.

- *Shared folders*: AS/400 disk space is accessed as local PC disk space.

- *Remote commands*: AS/400 commands are submitted from the DOS command line.

Many of the bells and whistles available through GUI client/server functions, such as cut and paste, are not possible in DOS terminal emulation. If you need to cut out a piece of an AS/400 screen and pop it into a PC application, DOS is not the answer. DOS does, however, offer the advantage of a simple environment and much lower system hardware requirements (i.e., cost) than any other platform. Simple client/server systems can be implemented at the PC end through DOS.

9.2 Memory Management

As mentioned above, the 640K memory ceiling on conventional memory in DOS is one of its primary limitations. Several ways around this limitation have been developed in recent years. It is now possible to add memory chips or boards to increase the capacity of DOS RAM to several megabytes. Memory management software run at startup prepares or formats this extra memory for later use by applications. This solution is a bit of a workaround, but it is effective in many cases. Lotus now knows to look for this expanded or extended memory to increase the size and speed of its spreadsheets. Many other software packages for DOS also take advantage of expanded memory. While memory cramping in the lower 640K has not been eliminated, it has been eased by these techniques.

There are basically five types of memory available to DOS (Figure 9.1):

- *Conventional*: the lower 640K, which is where the RAM cram occurs. DOS applications contend for space in conventional memory. It is desirable to load as many programs and drivers as possible outside conventional memory. Loading programs into other types of memory conserves conventional memory for application program needs.

- *Upper*: the space between 640K and one megabyte, which is usually used to load device drivers. The system uses this area to manage hardware devices, but does not generally use all of it. Free areas here are called *upper memory blocks (UMBs)*. They can be used by memory management programs to load device drivers out of conventional memory.

- *Expanded*: memory accessed above one megabyte by applications such as Lotus. Expanded memory is an interim solution that has been largely replaced by extended memory, described next. Expanded memory can be emulated by extended memory management programs for applications that require it.

- *Extended*: memory accessed above one megabyte for applications such as Windows. It is necessary to run a memory manager to configure extended memory at boot time.

- *High*: the first 64K of extended memory. This area is often used to load DOS itself, removing it from conventional memory.

The last three types of DOS memory were added to PC architecture to alleviate the problem of insufficient conventional memory for growing application needs. Programs called *memory managers* are run at boot time (startup) to allocate these extra memory blocks and make them available to subsequent applications.

Memory managers include the following:

- HIMEM.SYS: comes with DOS and is used to load DOS high. Third-party memory managers that have their own scheme can replace this file on installation.

- EMM386.SYS: comes with DOS and Windows, configures extended memory for use with Windows.

- QEMM386.SYS: a third-party memory manager that is highly recommended. It configures extended memory, emulates expanded memory, and loads devices high. On installation, it reads the PC system configuration. It makes necessary changes to system files CONFIG.SYS and AUTOEXEC.BAT to automate optimized memory usage.

9.3 Batch Files

DOS uses files containing plain text (ASCII) instructions as batch files to execute streams of DOS commands. They can be edited with a plain text editor. Two of these types of files are sought by DOS at boot time to configure the system. If you edit these files, do not use a word processor with a proprietary format on them because they will become unreadable by the operating system, and the PC might then become unbootable. Make sure you have a boot disk handy before attempting changes to these files.

CONFIG.SYS

This file contains information such as which device drivers to load and how many files can be open at any one time. DOS automatically looks for it and

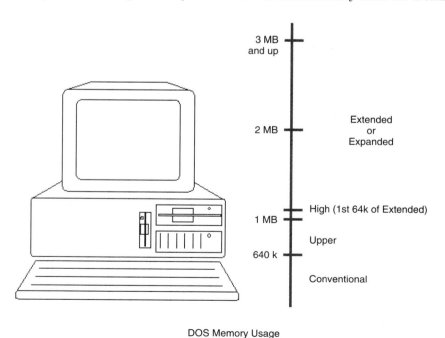

DOS Memory Usage

Figure 9.1 Five types of memory available to DOS.

executes its instructions. When configuring a DOS environment, this file is of critical importance. A typical CONFIG.SYS might look like this:

```
DEVICE=C:\DOS\HIMEM.SYS
DEVICE=C:\DOS\SETVER.EXE
SHELL=C:\DOS\COMMAND.COM C:\DOS\/P
DOS=HIGH

BREAK=ON

FILES=50
BUFFERS=30

DEVICE=OC01IA.SYS 000
DEVICE=OC02DLC.SYS
```

HIMEM.SYS enables high memory.

SETVER.EXE allows older programs, which expect to run in older DOS versions, to coexist with newer versions.

SHELL defines the location and behavior of the command processor.

DOS=HIGH actually loads DOS into high memory, saving conventional space.

BREAK=ON activates the Ctrl-Break key combination to terminate running programs.

FILES=50 sets the number of files that can be open at one time to 50. This line is critical in DOS to avoid the "Insufficient file handles" error.

BUFFERS=30 sets up buffers to be used to manage data transfers to and from the disks.

DEVICE= these lines load device drivers. The last two lines load two network device drivers.

After QEMM386 has been run to configure extended memory, CONFIG.SYS might look like this:

```
DEVICE=C:\QEMM\QEMM386.SYS R:2 RAM ST:M
DEVICE=C:\DOS\SETVER.EXE
SHELL=C:\DOS\COMMAND.COM C:\DOS\ /P
DOS=HIGH
BREAK=ON

FILES=50
BUFFERS=30
LASTDRIVE=K

DEVICE=C:\QEMM\LOADHI.SYS /R:1 OC01IA.SYS 000
DEVICE=C:\QEMM\LOADHI.SYS /R:2 OC02DLC.SYS
```

Note the extra parameters added by the automatic configuration facility of QEMM. These instruct the operating system how and where to load particular drivers for maximum memory usage.

AUTOEXEC.BAT

DOS automatically looks for this file at startup. Any commands contained in it are executed, tailoring the system to user requirements. Commands here set up the search path for files, connect to the network, load an initial program or menu, etc. AUTOEXEC.BAT might look something like this:

```
PROMPT $P$G
SET COMSPEC=C:\DOS\COMMAND.COM
PATH C:\;C:\DOS;C:\UTIL;C:\WINDOWS
DOSKEY
C:\DOS\MODE CON RATE= 32 DELAY= 1
SET TEMP=C:\DOS
C:
CD\
IPX
NETX
L:
LOGIN
```

PROMPT PG sets the command line prompt to indicate the current directory. For example, C:\LOTUS>.

SET COMSPEC=C:\DOS\COMMAND.COM sets an environment variable containing the location of the command processor (COMMAND.COM).

PATH C:\;C:\DOS;C:\UTIL;C:\WINDOWS sets up a search path for programs. This path will be used automatically when the user tries to run a program from the command line. If the command does not contain an explicit path to the program, the system searches through the directories from the PATH statement, in order.

DOSKEY starts up a program that enables the user to recall previous DOS commands at the command line and edit them, avoiding retyping repetitive or complex sequences.

C:\DOS\MODE CON RATE= 32 DELAY= 1 sets the cursor speed to the fastest possible setting.

SET TEMP=C:\DOS sets up an environment variable specifying C:\DOS as a working directory for temporary files.

C: makes sure the system has the C: drive as the current drive.

CD\ sends the command line to the root directory.

IPX loads the protocol for physical-layer connection to the network.

NETX attaches to the file server on the network.

L: makes a network drive the current drive.

LOGIN logs the user into the network.

After QEMM386 has been run to configure extended memory, AUTOEXEC.BAT might look like this:

```
PROMPT $P$G
SET COMSPEC=C:\DOS\COMMAND.COM
PATH C:\;C:\DOS;C:\UTIL;C:\WINDOWS
C:\QEMM\LOADHI /R:2 DOSKEY
C:\DOS\MODE CON RATE= 32 DELAY= 1
SET TEMP=C:\DOS
C:
CD\
C:\QEMM\LOADHI /R:1 IPX
C:\QEMM\LOADHI /R:2 NETX
L:
LOGIN
```

By using these two files and possibly calling other .BAT files, it is possible to set up a custom environment in which the user is virtually unaware of the operating system. In this way, simple client/server systems can be accomplished in DOS.

9.4 Terminal Emulation

Terminal emulation makes the PC behave as if it were a 5250 terminal attached to the AS/400. The AS/400 sees a 5250 connection, while the PC can toggle between DOS functions and 5250 functions. By using PC Support or Client/Access, two environments can be available on the computer. These environments are not available simultaneously, but rather sequentially. The user can have both the AS/400 and the PC network loaded at the same time, but can only access one at a time. It is possible to switch back and forth between them.

9.5 File Transfer

File transfer is the ability to move files or extracts of files from the AS/400 to the PC or vice versa. File transfer is often used to place AS/400 data into PC spreadsheets like Lotus 123 or Excel. Once imported, the data can be formatted into analyses required by the accounting department, for instance, with much more flexibility than possible on the AS/400. File transfer is a very productive yet simple client/server application. In the Client/Access scheme, file transfer uses remote SQL to access the AS/400 database. Selected fields and records of files can be transferred if so desired. Downloaded files can be sorted on the way down to the PC. Uploading is also possible, although obviously a high degree of security should be invoked when allowing the PC to update AS/400 files. It is possible to set up an automatic or batch file transfer, which executes at a given time or from a menu prompt on the PC. In this way, a mirror image of an AS/400 database can be maintained on the PC.

9.6 Remote Command

Remote command is a very powerful feature of client/server available to DOS environments. The RMTCMD command at the DOS command line invokes an AS/400 procedure through the router, which means that DOS programs can initiate AS/400 processing. Used in concert with file transfer, it is possible to write a PC program that runs an AS/400 program and then downloads the resulting data to the PC for further processing. All this processing can be invisible to the user, which is true client/server functionality. The PC submits a request for data to the server and then receives the data back into its own environment.

9.7 Summary

DOS is a basic but very efficient operating system for the PC. It is lean and mean. The whole system is available to the single user and the single program running. System hardware requirements are low so that it is more affordable than GUI systems. It has been successfully running thousands of software programs for years and has a loyal user base. If user client/server requirements are simple, such as terminal emulation or file transfers to spreadsheets, DOS is sufficient. It is possible to download data to various DOS applications on an ad-hoc or periodic basis for further processing. Powerful client/server features, such as remote commands and data queues, are also available to DOS. When requirements progress to the point where a live connection is needed between application platforms or task switching becomes necessary between applications, a more sophisticated, multitasking operating system should be implemented.

Windows

10.1 Windows and DOS

Windows is a very popular operating system. Many corporate users are accustomed to Windows, or another similar interface, from their home computers. They want the same functionality and user friendliness at work. Windows is capturing more and more of the PC DOS market as the operating system of choice. Windows 3.x is not, however, a replacement for DOS (Windows NT is). Rather, Windows 3.x rides on top of DOS, requesting and receiving disk and other services from DOS. Marketed as a multitasking operating system by Microsoft, Windows 3.x provides some multitasking features but does not offer true preemptive multitasking. It can run different applications simultaneously, each in its own window. Each active program, however, has the option of seizing all the resources of the computer and holding them until ready to release them. The individual application decides when to release system resources to other tasks, not a preemptive multitasking manager. Most applications designed for Windows, however, do not generate conflicts. Custom client/server software should behave accordingly.

The ability to toggle back and forth between open applications is a very productive and appealing feature of Windows. It is possible to have an AS/400 session open in one window, Microsoft Word open in another, and Lotus 123 open in yet another (Figure 10.1). You can move smoothly and instantly between these applications simply by pointing at them with the mouse and clicking the button (or by using the Alt-Esc key combination). You can cut out data from an AS/400 query result, paste it into Lotus or Excel for reformatting and further calculations, and maybe create a graph. You can then

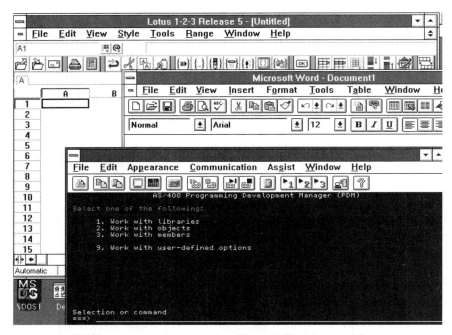

Figure 10.1 AS/400 session open in one window, Microsoft Word, Lotus 1-2-3.

paste it into Word as a financial illustration. All these steps are accomplished easily and quickly. No DOS or character-based interface can provide this type of seamless integration between unlike platforms and applications. Users who become accustomed to working in Windows are generally unwilling to go back to separate programs, data, and command-line interfaces.

Windows handles printing in a manner far superior to DOS or OS/400. It is easy to choose font types in a document. Bold, italics, font sizes, footnotes, bullets—the features readily available for documents through Windows are much too extensive to list here. Many fonts are native to Windows and many more available as add-ons. Just point at one in a pop-up menu and click—and it's active. You can mix fonts and styles in a Windows document. The printer need not have these fonts resident or on a cartridge. True Type fonts are scalable from tiny to huge and show on the screen exactly the way they print. Creating professional looking desktop publishing documents is greatly eased by the Windows environment.

10.2 Windows NT

Windows NT (new technology) is a true preemptive multitasking operating system. It began life as the OS/2 version 3.0 project at IBM, so it has many of the same features as OS/2, but Microsoft and IBM parted ways, and Windows NT was born. It solves many of the problems of Windows 3.x and eliminates its dependence on DOS services. Windows NT eliminates the need for DOS entirely, although it can run DOS programs.

DOS gives complete and unlimited access to the process running; only one process can run at a time. Windows NT divides the work of simultaneous applications into multiple threads and then allocates system resources to each of these threads. These threads are then submitted by the operating system to the processor, which executes them sequentially. Preemptive multitasking continually monitors the executing and waiting threads, swapping system resources between them. This technique allows several unrelated tasks to run simultaneously in segments. It also eliminates the problem of a process seizing too much of the system's resources, or of even locking up the system in the event of failure. The multitasking operating system can be printing a large word processing document in the background while the user is in a spreadsheet, graphing results.

Windows NT is self-sufficient and robust and looks very much like the old Windows while incorporating some user-friendly features similar to the Apple Macintosh interface. The hardware requirements of Windows NT are much more extensive than those of Windows 3.x. It is an extensive, 32-bit operating system and is happiest on a PC with a fast processor of at least the 486/33 class. 16 megabytes of internal memory (RAM) is also desirable for the full-fledged version of NT.

Windows NT is designed with network functionality built in. It can run on many different platforms. It is intended by Microsoft to be implemented as an enterprise-wide operating system. The server and the workstation can both run Windows NT.

10.3 Program Manager

The Program Manager is the desktop of Windows. When you start Windows, the first screen that comes up is the Program Manager (Figure 10.2). The features seen on the Program Manager screen are common to all Windows programs; they all look and feel the same. Program Manager is like the top of a desk: various projects sit in the desktop; you can pick them up and work with them at will. Just as you would open a folder on your desk to work with the project or materials inside, you can open a window. Program Manager contains different icons that represent program groups—for instance, the Microsoft Word group. These icons can be expanded by clicking on them into groups of related programs, themselves shown as icons. Click on these icons to execute the programs. To run Word, for example, click on the group and it opens up. Then click on the Word icon in the group, which opens the Word application. All applications are run in the same way in Windows: just point at them with the mouse and double-click the left button.

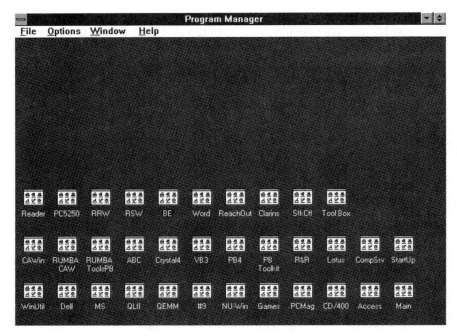

Figure 10.2 Program Manager.

The program groups and their icons and windows are in the middle of the screen. Around the edges are various tools for navigating the desktop. Note the menu bar at the top of the screen. Most Windows applications have a menu bar at the top. The user can point at these menu items and click the mouse to open them up into several options. Some of these lead to other options or menus, and others directly to the desired operation. The scroll bars at the right and bottom of some screens indicate that more data exists than will fit in the single window. This data can be viewed by pointing at the scroll bar and holding down the left mouse button. Many of these scrollable screens respond to the arrow keys and the PageUp/PageDown keys as well as the mouse.

The arrowhead pushbuttons at the upper right of Windows screens are used to expand or shrink the windows. A window can be made to occupy the full screen or can be shrunk down to various smaller sizes within the screen. It can even be minimized to an icon by clicking the minimize button at the upper right of the screen. Minimized, the window is still running and can be activated by double-clicking it. Minimizing active applications to icons reduces screen clutter. Windows are sizable by placing the cursor on the edge of the window and holding down the left mouse key while dragging the mouse. If you place the cursor on the window corner, you can change height and width at the same time. If you place the mouse on the title bar at the top of a window, you can move the whole window around the screen. In this way, you can tailor the desktop to your liking. Make a window active for work by pointing at it and clicking, or by using the Alt-Esc key combination to cycle through active windows. The Ctrl-Esc key combination brings up the task list, from which you can select an active window.

The Main group contains the essential Windows utilities (Figure 10.3) used to control and configure Windows. The primary utilities found in Main are described in the following subsections.

File Manager. *File Manager* provides a visual approach to file handling (Figure 10.4). It is easy to choose directories and subdirectories shown in the directory tree at the left of the screen. Double-click on a directory to show the files contained in it on the right of the screen. If more files are in the directory than you can see in the right of the window, use the scroll bars to pan through the rest of them. These files can be renamed, copied, moved, deleted, and executed right from the File Manager screen. The different disk drives available in your system are shown as icons at the top of the File Manager. If you are logged in to a network, its drives are shown here as well. Click on one of these icons to change to that drive, and you will see the directories and files appear on the screen.

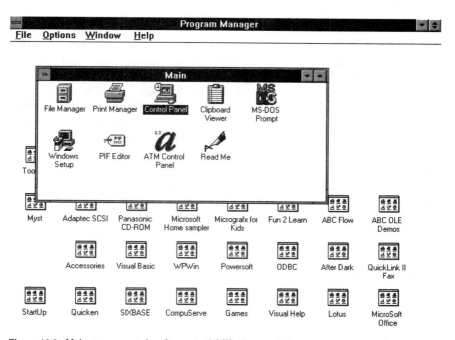

Figure 10.3 Main group contains the essential Windows utilities.

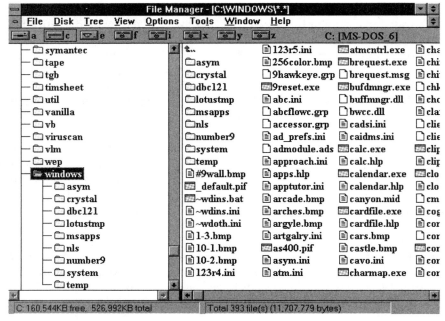

Figure 10.4   File Manager provides a visual approach to file handling.

Control Panel. *Control Panel* allows the user to configure the system, tailoring it to individual preferences (Figure 10.5). Within it are Fonts, Mouse, Desktop, Keyboard, Printers, Network, 386 Enhanced, and other settings. Use these icons to set cursor speed, screen savers, colors of windows, network settings, fonts used by printers, etc. Dialog boxes open to ask further questions about what you want to do (Figure 10.6). You simply fill in the values you want and click on the OK button to save the changes.

Print Manager. *Print Manager* controls documents sent to the printer (Figure 10.7). From here, you can pause or cancel the printing of a document. You can check on the status of a printing document and change the order of print jobs queued up. Printer setups can also be changed. Simply select the print job by clicking on it and choose an action to be performed on it from the menu bar at the top of the screen.

MS-DOS Prompt. *MS-DOS Prompt* starts an emulated DOS session in a window (Figure 10.8). Within this DOS session, it is possible to run DOS applications and utilities, but some configurations and limitations apply. When the DOS session is started, it does not have the same characteristics or settings of the original DOS session that started Windows. This fact requires an explanation: in Windows 3.x, Windows runs on top of DOS, which means that the com-

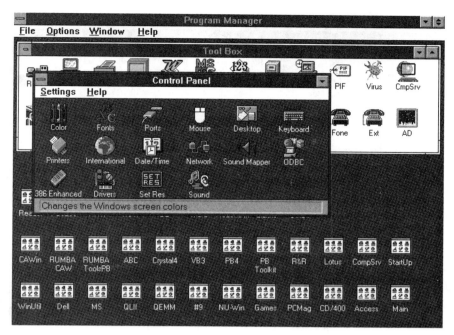

Figure 10.5   Control Panel.

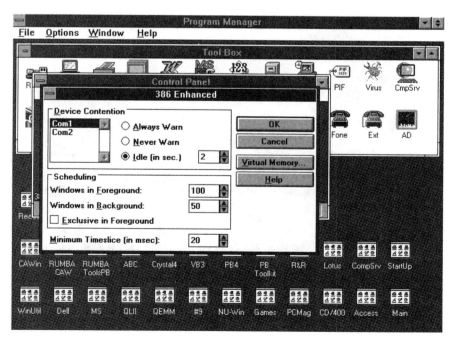

Figure 10.6   Dialog boxes open up.

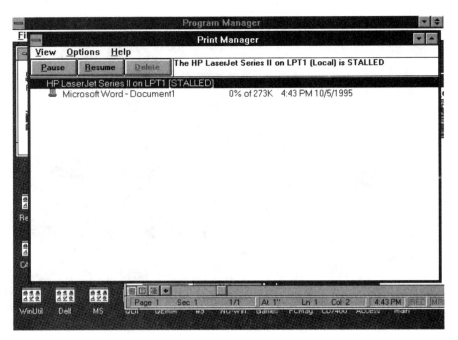

Figure 10.7 Print Manager.

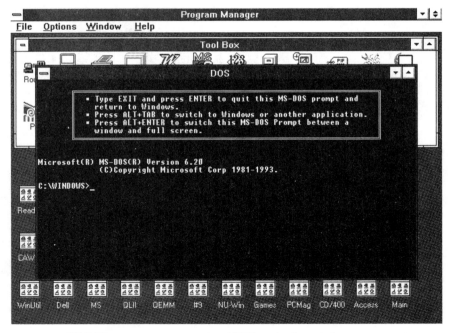

Figure 10.8 MS-DOS prompt starts an emulated DOS session in a window.

puter first starts DOS, then Windows. We then run yet another DOS session, inside Windows. We are running DOS within Windows on top of DOS (who's on first?). The DOS session within Windows is not actually a true DOS session but a Windows emulation of one. Some problems thus arise. Primarily, the problem of the 640K conventional memory limit becomes more severe in Windows DOS than in native DOS. Also, the path and other settings of the original DOS session are not inherited by the Windows DOS session, so it is necessary to use a .PIF file to restore or set these. But problems can still beset this environment. Even if configured correctly, MS-DOS within Windows can provide DOS functionality concurrently with Windows, depending on how much RAM is available to the DOS session after resident programs and drivers.

Other groups. In addition to the Main group, other groups are contained within the Program Manager desktop (Figure 10.9). *Client/server applications* can be designed and placed on the Program Manager desktop using icons. The user can simply click on them to execute or activate them. If they open up their own windows, data displayed by them can be copied and shared with other applications. Communication links with other hardware platforms can be automatically connected by routines attached to these icons. It is unnecessary for the user to know anything about communications or even that communications are occurring to access remote data and client/server applications.

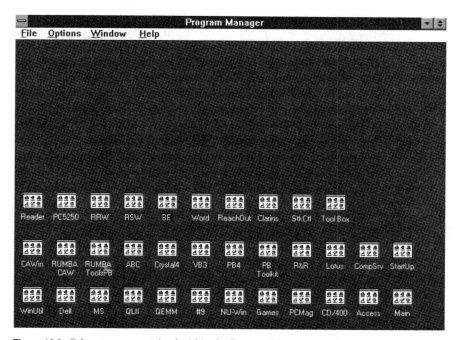

Figure 10.9 Other groups contained within the Program Manager desktop.

10.4   Graphical User Interface

Windows provides point-and-click functionality via the mouse. It is thus possible to navigate all the features, programs, and configurations available in the Windows environment without knowing a single command. You just point at pictures (or icons, as they are called) and click the mouse button. Menu bars and extensive online help make Windows even easier to use.

In addition, all Windows applications look and work alike. Once the user becomes familiar with the environment, the learning curve associated with entering a new application is minimized. All applications work almost the same. The menu options listed at the top of the screen are virtually identical in all Windows software (Figure 10.10). The point-and-click function and the cut-and-paste feature are identical in all packages. Windows word processors are much easier to use while, at the same time, being more fully featured than DOS word processors.

10.5   Terminal Emulation

One of the windows on the desktop can be an emulation session for a server platform. The AS/400 can be used in the Windows environment along with

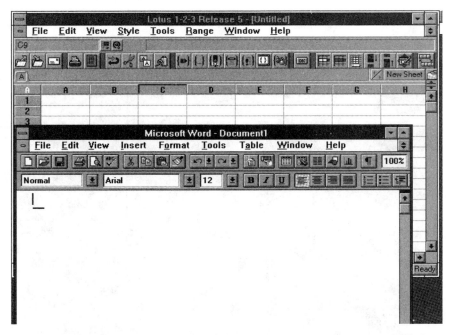

Figure 10.10 The menu options at the top of the screen are virtually the same in all Windows software.

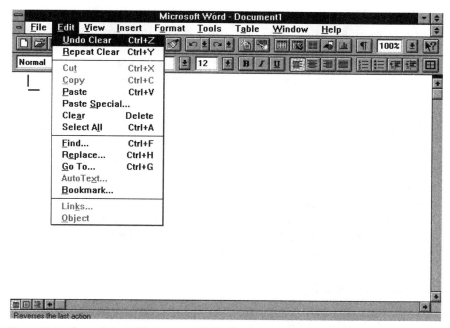

Figure 10.11 Copy, Cut, and Paste are available through the Edit menu.

other Windows applications such as Word or Excel. The same facilities that enable other Windows applications, such as cut and paste, can also be used in an AS/400 window. PC Support and Client Access are two IBM terminal emulators. Rumba is one of the most common and feature-full AS/400 terminal emulation facilities. Using Rumba, the user can set up pushbuttons that execute AS/400 programs. You can also mouse around the AS/400 screen, cut sections of data, and paste them into Windows applications. This feature is very useful for small excerpts of data that are to be inserted in spreadsheets and word processors. It is also handy for documentation of AS/400 systems or applications. AS/400 displays can be inserted right into Windows documents.

10.6 Cut and Paste

Cut and paste is a very useful feature of Windows. You can highlight a section of a screen in a window by using the mouse (hold down the left mouse button while dragging the mouse) and copy it to a Windows holding area called the *Clipboard*. Copy, cut, and paste are available through the Edit menu at the top of most Windows screens (Figure 10.11). Once the data is in the clipboard, it can be pasted into other Windows applications. Even though it is called *cut and paste*, the function also includes copy and paste, which means that you can share data between applications. It is a simple matter to mark a section of a Lotus spreadsheet and copy it into a Word-Perfect document or Microsoft Excel, for example. This facility enhances presentations and enables illustrations in company correspondence. Cut and paste is one of the most productive features of the Windows environment. It provides integration between various software packages running in different windows.

The cut-and-paste facility is very useful for documentation. It is possible, for instance, to open an AS/400 session in a window and a WordPerfect session in another window, as we have seen. It is then a simple matter to highlight pieces of the AS/400 application displays and paste them into the PC documentation. In this way, you can easily show AS/400 screens, as well as screens from other windows, in the document. Just put a frame around it and you have a sample application screen in the documentation. Point the mouse at the application being described to make it active, then point at the document being written to switch to that application.

10.7   DDE and OLE

Dynamic data exchange (DDE) is just what it sounds like: an online hot link between application packages. Changes made to data in Lotus, for instance, can be automatically reflected in a Microsoft Word document when that document is called up, ensuring that external data references are refreshed without further user interaction. It is even possible to have DDE refresh a PC document from an AS/400 query result. Whatever the current state of the AS/400 data, it is reflected in the document. This sort of link obviously does not execute instantaneously. It takes time to connect to the AS/400, run the query, and download the results. The link does, however, ensure timeliness and accuracy of data references. For example, a periodic report can have automatically refreshed data from the server. DDE links are customizable through macros in the different applications. They can be set up to execute at specific times or upon initial application loading. It is possible to set up a spreadsheet to execute automatically and produce reports at prearranged times, drawing data from various external sources. Color Excel graphs can run automatically at night from AS/400 data, and be waiting at your desk in the morning, or at a remote location.

Object linking and embedding (OLE) is an enhancement to DDE. An object can be in the form of data, a spreadsheet, a graph, or virtually any excerpt from another OLE-enabled software package. This object, once created, can be embedded or implanted into a second OLE-enabled application. In other words, you can embed an Excel graph into a WordPerfect document or a Word document into a Lotus spreadsheet. The link between the embedded object and its native source application is live, or dynamic. Any changes made to the original object are automatically reflected in its linked object embedded in the other application. It is unnecessary to run the package from which the object originated if you want to change it. You can just click on the embedded object, and Windows can run the application from which it came, automatically, allowing editing.

The representation of the embedded object can take different forms. It is possible to embed the object as itself or as an icon. When embedded as an icon, the object looks and behaves like any other icon in Windows. This type of OLE is called a *package*. Any process that can be executed from an icon can be embedded as a package into an application. It is thus possible to put a pushbutton into a document to execute a spreadsheet or various multimedia effects. The user can then click on the icon to execute it. This technique saves space for embedded objects that do not always need to be expanded. Embedding a package object allows the user to choose whether or not to activate the underlying process. Backup detail or notes that might be of interest can be included as a package object. It is even possible to package Windows utilities such as the calculator, if the user should need it.

OLE is a form of client/server computing. It does not necessarily involve different hardware platforms or operating systems, although it very well might. It does represent one software platform acting as a server to a client platform and providing data in response to a request. You can link graphs to documents, mailing lists to form letters, and databases from various platforms through SQL to spreadsheets, to name a few options. This facility is very powerful in terms of user productivity.

10.8   Event-Handling

Event-handling is the core concern of Windows programmers. It is necessary for the system to know at all times where the mouse pointer is and what buttons have been clicked. These actions are called *events*. Event-handling is how Windows removes navigational headaches from users. They just mouse around the screen, looking at different options and activating some of them. They open submenus and click on icons. Different levels of screen awareness, from the individual pixel level to windows and icons, enable the programmer to track what the user is pointing at and what action to take as a result. Many development packages, such as Visual Basic or PowerBuilder, include possible choices for events in pop-up windows. The developer can place a button or icon on the screen, choose an event (such as double-click) and attach a section of program code to it.

10.9   Open Database Connectivity

Microsoft developed a standard for connectivity between client Windows applications and external databases called open database connectivity (ODBC). ODBC takes the form of drivers invoked by the software package to connect it to a server's remote database. The database can be as near as a dBASE file in the same directory or as far away as an AS/400 in another country. The ODBC configurations and parameters handle the connection requirements and data conversions transparently, allowing the application program simply to submit data requests and await their return. ODBC allows Windows programs to connect to a multitude of back-end databases without knowing anything about their native formats or access methods. ODBC takes care of the details for you. Version 3, release 1 of the AS/400 operating system provides a much-enhanced and optimized ODBC driver for use in Windows programs.

10.10   Memory Management

Windows 3.x runs on top of DOS, requesting files and other services from it. Therefore, when configuring Windows, it is necessary to consider the underlying DOS configuration as well. Windows does not suffer from the 640K barrier that is so problematic in DOS. It can access extended memory that has been installed in the form of a board or a chip and invoked by loading a memory management program like EMM386 or HIMEM.SYS.

Windows can swap or page RAM to disk to create virtual memory. This technique allows Windows to run more programs at one time. It saves inactive programs to the disk if not enough RAM is available to run them. This use of memory is much slower, however, than using RAM. SMARTDrive is a Windows utility that enables disk caching, which speeds up the process of accessing disk information. Regardless, RAM is much faster than virtual memory, so it is advisable to have plenty when running Windows. At least 8Mb of RAM should ensure good performance for Windows users, but more is even better. Microsoft says the minimum is 4Mb, but this is pretty slow and causes a lot of swapping. Use the DOS MEM command to show how much memory of what type is installed on the PC.

Refer to the DOS chapter for tips on how to configure DOS memory for optimal performance. Remember to make copies of CONFIG.SYS and AUTOEXEC.BAT before changing them, because invalid entries can make the computer unbootable. Be sure to have a spare boot disk around for this contingency.

The Windows setup program modifies CONFIG.SYS and AUTOEXEC.BAT when it is run. HIMEM.SYS is added to CONFIG.SYS. When using Windows, check to see that the BUFFERS command in CONFIG.SYS is set to 30 (BUFFERS=30) to optimize disk access. Remove any terminate-and-stay-resident programs (TSRs) or menu systems from AUTOEXEC.BAT. Many TSRs can be invoked from within Windows. Menus are superfluous because Windows will take the place of them.

Windows uses two files called WIN.INI and SYSTEM.INI to specify settings for the Windows environment and the programs that run in Windows. These files work much the same as the DOS use of CONFIG.SYS and AUTOEXEC.BAT. WIN.INI sets up the Windows environment for individual user options (Figure 10.12). SYSTEM.INI contains instructions to configure Windows to the PC's system hardware (Figure 10.13). Refer to the Windows manual for details about specific settings in these files. Many Windows software packages automatically make entries to these files at installation time.

10.11 Windows 95

Windows 3.1, despite its pervasive popularity and market share, has drawbacks. The 3.1 version relies on outmoded DOS services, and is prone to the frustrating general protection fault, or *GPF*, where one application crashes the whole system. These problems can happen because Windows 3.1 is not

```
[windows]
spooler=yes
load=c:\afterdrk\ad.exe c:\afterdrk\adinit.exe c:\quickenw\BILLMNDW.EXE printman.exe
run=
Beep=yes
NullPort=None
BorderWidth=3
CursorBlinkRate=530
DourbleClickSpeed=452
Programs=com exe bat pif
Documents=
DeviceNotSelectedTimeout=15
TransmissionRetryTimeout=45
KeyboardDelay=2
KeyboardSpeed=31
ScreenSaveActive=0
screensaveTimeOut=60
CoolSwitch=1
MouseThreshold1=4
MouseThreshold2=9
MouseSpeed=2
MouseTrails=7
DosPrint=no
device=HPLaserJetIII,hppc15a,LPT1:

[Desktop]
Pattern=(None)
GridGranularity=0
IconSpacing=75
TileWallPaper=1
wallpaper=(None)
```

Figure 10.12 WIN.INI sets up the Windows environment for individual user options.

```
[boot]
shell=progman.exe
mouse.drv=mouse.drv
network.drv=
language.dll=
sournd.drv=mmsound.drv
comm.drv=rhsicomm.drv
atm.system.drv=system.drv
386grabber=vga.3gr
oemfonts.fon=vgaoem.fon
286grabber=vgacolor.2gr
fixedfon.fon=vgasys.fon
display.drv=vga.drv
keyboard.drv=keyboard.drv
system.drv=atmsys.drv
SCRNSAVE.EXE=C:\WEP\IDLEWILD.EXE
drivers=mmsystem.dll
oldcomm.drv=comm.drv
COMM_DRV_OLD=bicomm.drv

[keyboard]
keyboard.dll=
oemansi.bin=
subtype=
type=4

[boot.description]
mouse.drv=Microsoft, or IBM PS/2
netowrk.drv=NoNetwork Installed
language.dll=English(American)
system.drv=MS-DOS System
codepage=437
woafont.fon=English (437)
aspect=100,96,96
display.drv=VGA
keyboard.typ=Enhanced 101 or 102 key US and Non US keyboards
```

Figure 10.13 SYSTEM.INI contains instructions to configure Windows to the PC's system hardware.

a true preemptive multitasker. Every program is capable of seizing the operating environment, and even of invading the memory space of another application. When this happens, everything grinds to a halt, and the Windows
environment itself becomes unstable. Windows NT solves this problem, but
has drastically higher hardware requirements.

Now Microsoft is offering Windows 95. It is a true 32-bit operating system
that features preemptive multitasking and multithreading. Applications can
run simultaneously and gracefully. Windows 95 (originally code-named
Chicago) takes much of the fear out of your desktop. Its nonsegmented memory model is much more robust than the juggling act going on in Windows 3.1.
It offers long filenames to free us from the constraints of the 8-character DOS,
and consequently Windows 3.1, naming conventions. In these respects, it is
very similar to Windows NT, although it has no server component.

Unlike Windows 3.1 and Windows NT, Windows 95 does not share the
Windows desktop metaphor so familiar to us by now. It has a more intuitive,
advanced interface. It uses folders instead of icons (a concept akin to the
OS/2 or Apple interface). A Taskbar at the bottom of the screen allows easy

tracking and switching between open applications. No more hunting for that other application; they are all accessible through the Taskbar. The Taskbar features a start button that has seven choices attached to it. This approach is much more integrated than Windows 3.1, where you had to look in several different places for system management tools such as File Manager, Program Manager, or Control Panel—they are combined into a single interface. The start menu remembers 15 of the last documents you worked on and knows which applications you used to work on them. Shortcut creates automatic links to system and network objects so that you just need to open one object to use, for example, a particular word processor on a specific document on a network drive. When you select the Shortcut object, you are automatically placed in the correct package with the document open.

Windows 95 is much more network aware and sophisticated than Windows 3.1. It has easy Internet connectivity, as well as being able to run multiple network protocols at the same time. This capability is good news to those of us who have been trying to wrangle coexistence between DOS, Novell Netware, Windows 3.1 and the AS/400 PC Support or Client Access drivers. Client/server applications should become easier and more powerful in this environment.

Windows 95 is fully downwardly compatible with DOS and Windows 3.1 applications. You can thus run your existing DOS and Windows 3.1 applications from Windows 95. It uses the concept of a virtual DOS device driver to create a run environment for DOS applications. Windows 95 native applications do not run under OS/2, however, so the dichotomy is widening between Microsoft and IBM.

Plug and Play is another improvement in the Windows 95 environment. You no longer have to read manuals and fool around with dip switches and IRQ settings for new devices. You can just plug your device in and let the operating system search its databases of devices for the correct settings to set up the environment.

Windows 95 needs a minimum of 4Mb of RAM to run, and 8Mb to run happily. A 486/33-MHz machine is the minimum realistic platform for this operating system. Here, too, more is better. 12Mb on a Pentium 90 is very nice. Windows 95 requires about 25Mb of disk space. Microsoft expects to supplant its existing Windows 3.1 base with Windows 95 (as Windows NT does not seem to be doing this). Microsoft thinks it can sell 50 million copies of it in a year. In fact, it will probably come already installed on new machines, just like Windows 3.1.

10.12 Summary

It is clear why Windows has been so successful in the PC marketplace. It offers an easy-to-use, appealing environment that is also extremely productive. Point-and-click procedures using the mouse permit the user to navigate easily through the various features of the operating system and applications. Once a Windows application has been learned, it is easy to use others, because they all look and work alike. Windows 3.x runs on top of DOS, while Windows NT is a true preemptive multitasking 32-bit operating system and can be used as a complete enterprise network solution.

Windows allows the user to have several applications active at one time. An AS/400 emulation session and virtual printer can coexist with Microsoft Excel and WordPerfect, for example. They are all open in their own windows, visible and available. The ability to look something up instantly in one package for use in another package is very productive. Data in any one of these windows can be cut and pasted or copied to the others (if the destination window has that ability). The integration between software and even hardware platforms available in Windows is a major advantage in developing client/server systems. Many client/server tools, such as ODBC and remote SQL, are available for use in this environment. Several vendors offer development software for writing or creating Windows GUI applications that access behind-the-scenes connections to remote servers. Windows must be considered carefully as a platform for client/server development.

Chapter

11

OS/2

OS/2 is a full-featured multitasking operating system for the PC. It can run multiple programs simultaneously, each in its own window on the graphical desktop. In addition, it has a command-line environment, similar to DOS, and uses many of the same commands as DOS. The user then can choose either graphical or character-based operations. IBM claims OS/2 is a better DOS than DOS and a better Windows than Windows. It provides a very productive environment and an excellent platform for client/server development. In fact, OS/2 was designed by IBM with client/server type communications in mind. It does not suffer from the memory limitations of DOS nor the DOS-dependency of Windows 3.x. Its multitasking competition is from neither of those platforms but from Windows NT, another true multitasker. There are those who say that OS/2 has the advantages of UNIX without many of the limitations of that platform. OS/2 uses PCs that are 386 or 486, with plenty of RAM. OS/2's main limitation is that many industry-leading vendors have not yet provided software written for it. Many of them preferred to go with Windows. OS/2 counters this lack of support by providing its own Windows environment for running Windows software.

11.1 Presentation Manager and Workplace Shell

OS/2's Workplace Shell, a feature of Presentation Manager, looks very much like Apple's Macintosh interface. It also has much in common with the Windows interface because Windows and OS/2 have a common background—IBM. Before Microsoft split off and began developing Windows on its own, Microsoft and IBM were in a joint venture to develop OS/2. Even today, they share trade secrets and licensed code. Like Windows, OS/2 offers an array of pushbuttons, icons, menu bars, and other GUI gadgets to make navigating the operating system as easy as possible. It is a desktop format that holds folders and icons on its surface. The user chooses to work with these by pointing and clicking the mouse. The OS/2 graphical user interface (GUI) is even simpler and more intuitive in nature than Windows. Online help is extensive and context-sensitive.

OS/2 uses folders to contain objects. These folders are what you see on the OS/2 desktop when it starts up. The desktop itself is a type of folder in Workplace Shell, called the *desktop folder*, and it is always open. Some folders on the desktop contain the documents and projects or objects composing your daily tasks. You just click on them to open them and begin working. A convenient feature allows you to click on a document in a folder, and OS/2 will start the software package used to create that document. It is unnecessary to start the word processor and then search around for the document to edit. Another nice feature is the ability to drop a document onto the printer. Point at the document with the mouse, press the left button and drag it over to the printer icon, and drop it (release the button). The folders and the objects they contain can be copied, moved, deleted, printed, or opened. Opening folders is one of the main methods of looking around the environment to find what is available.

Other folders are represented as icons within the Workplace Shell desktop folder. They can be opened by pointing at them with the mouse and clicking. These icons tend to look like what they represent. For instance, a printer interface is represented on the desktop as a miniature picture of a printer. There is a shredder, which does what you would think. You can drop either files or documents into the shredder. A Master Help Index is represented as a book with a large question mark on the cover.

Clicking on icons generally opens a window. Programs run in foreground mode in OS/2 execute in their own windows. These windows can be moved, sized, and closed. Most windows have the same format. Multiple programs or applications can be run in separate windows at the same time. You can make one interactive by clicking on it. Often, when a menu bar option is chosen, it creates a pop-up menu.

Some of the more important icons available in the Workplace Shell are the following:

- *OS/2 System*: This folder contains the most useful OS/2 utilities.

- *Drives*: Located in the OS/2 System folder, this icon shows disk drives available on the system, including network drives, as icons. Just click on one to open up a pictorial directory tree structure of that drive. You can follow the branches of the tree to find and manage individual files.

- *System Setup*: You can configure features of the system using this icon. Keyboard, Mouse, Windows, Fonts, and Colors are some of the configurable objects available here.

- *Printer*: Active print jobs and jobs in the print queue can be managed from this icon.

- *Master Help Index*: This icon is in the Workplace Shell. The Information icon also has extensive help. These icons offer help screens that contain explanations of various topics and pointers to related topics. Important phrases within these explanations are highlighted as hot links. You can click on the hot link to pop you into another screen, expanding on that topic.

- *Command Prompts*: These prompts access the command line to enter DOS-like OS/2 commands. It is usually not necessary to work here to take advantage of the Workplace Shell. Some procedures, however, can only be initiated from the command line.

11.2   Preemptive Multitasking

OS/2 has, for several years, been the true multitasking operating system for the PC, as has Windows NT recently. OS/2 can run multiple jobs at the same time. It is an operating system that divides contending, simultaneous sessions into processes and threads and then executes the threads sequentially. Threads from different jobs or sessions run through the processor in an order determined by the operating system. The preemptive priority-based scheduler handles this arrangement, giving each thread an appropriate time slice. Programs do not grab system resources directly, as they do in DOS. They request virtual resources from the OS/2 kernel, which maps these requests in an orderly fashion to real system resources, avoiding simultaneous contention. In this way, several jobs can have the appearance of running at the same time, although they really are swapping threads in and out of the processor very quickly. OS/2 can run Windows as well as DOS programs, as well as different types of sessions concurrently. Interactive foreground sessions let the user participate in the program, using the mouse and keyboard. Background sessions run on their own at the same time as the foreground sessions, performing lengthy batch database updates or printing large reports or performing any other time-consuming processing. Background sessions are not connected to a screen session, which means that the user does not have to stop working on the PC when running a lengthy process. To run a job in the background, you just start the job with the DETACH command and switch to another window to perform a foreground task.

Programs running in OS/2 can communicate with each other and with programs running on remote systems. This ability is fundamental to developing client/server systems. It is implemented through the use of inter-process communication protocols (IPC) and interprocess synchronization. Interprocess communication protocols connect client/server programs through a variety of virtual devices:

Named pipes. This method is the preferred way of communication between separate local or remote programs on the network. The named pipe is created by a server process and read by a client process as though it were an ordinary disk file. Two-way, or full-duplex, communication between these processes co-ordinates the sequence of writing and reading, providing a simple way to handle remote calls to file servers. This communication is one of the main reasons for considering OS/2 as a contender in the client/server arena.

Shared memory. Shared memory processes can access objects stored in shared memory areas by name. Shared memory is accomplished through the use of semaphores.

Data queues. These data queues are similar to the data queue on the AS/400. It is a byte stream that can be accessed by name from a remote platform. A local program can write to the queue, and a remote program can then read from it, or vice versa.

Semaphores. Like the semaphores used on train tracks, OS/2 semaphores are a type of flag used to regulate traffic—in this case, between requesting clients rather than locomotives. In both cases they help avoid collisions. Semaphores are accessed through API calls.

11.3 Memory Management

As with DOS and Windows, memory management is a prime concern of the OS/2 environment. Unlike DOS, OS/2 manages its requisite memory spaces, known as virtual address spaces, automatically. OS/2 creates one for each application process running. It also protects these assigned address spaces against encroachment by other applications. This invasion of memory by another program is called a *general protection fault*. OS/2 politely shuts down any application that generates this fault, unless the application tells OS/2 it is prepared to do this itself. There is no maximum on these memory spaces allocated to programs as there is in DOS. In fact, OS/2 can allocate up to 512Mb of available RAM for each application. It is unlikely, however, that your PC has anything like 512Mb of memory available. OS/2 is ready to accommodate less RAM by paging the programs in and out to disk, using de-mand-paged virtual memory. This technique uses a combination of RAM and disk space to create a virtual memory environment capable of support-ing multiple OS/2, Windows, and DOS sessions simultaneously.

These memory management features are built into OS/2. It is not necessary to run additional memory management software to implement them. It is advisable, however, to run OS/2 with as much available RAM as possible. Swapping programs to disk to accommodate other program needs is a much slower multitasking expedient than swapping within electronic memory. A good base for OS/2 is 16Mb of installed RAM. This amount is not the minimum suggested by IBM, but you will be happier if you are not waiting an inordinate amount of time for the system to search the disk to swap files.

11.4   Extended Services

OS/2 has optional add-ons for services beyond the standalone PC. Communications Manager and Database Manager offer emulation and data access to remote platforms, packaged as Extended Services. Extended Services comes in two versions, Extended Services with Database Server for OS/2 and Extended Services for OS/2. The first has more database connectivity features, as you would expect. We are primarily interested in the AS/400 connections, but these products also connect to the System 370 family of mainframes and DEC minicomputers. These are industrial-strength tools for connecting the PC workstation to midrange and mainframe platforms. As such, they are difficult to install, yet provide a more powerful and accessible link to the servers. These packages make the OS/2 PC a full participant in remote connectivity. They can even function as network nodes, passing a remote session through to a third location with routing functions.

11.5   Communications Manager

Communications Manager is a feature of OS/2 that enables a number of communications services and client/server applications. It is an additional platform, available from IBM at extra cost, to supplement the OS/2 base operating system package. Once installed, Communications Manager appears, of course, as an icon on the desktop. Click on it to reveal its contents. Communications Manager can act as both a client and a server. It can request data from a server, and it can furnish services to a requester or client. In our context, the PC OS/2 environment acts as the client, requesting services from a network server. OS/2 is IBM software and, as such, specifically designed to coexist and cooperate with other IBM platforms. The IBM servers in the midrange and mainframe arenas, the AS/400 and ES/9000 or 3090, are platforms that are easy targets for the Communications Manager and its facilities, being designed to work with it. UNIX connectivity is also possible. The server accessed can be local or remote, with a number of connections supported, including SNA, LAN, SDLC, X.25, Twinaxial, ISDN, and others. System application architecture (SAA) features from the IBM world are available to OS/2. Distributed Computing Environment (DCE) features from the UNIX world are also available for connections to OS/2. These features enable an open-architecture approach to client/server development in OS/2.

Client workstations can access communications functions of other OS/2 Communications Manager Client Server/2 stations on the network. This connectibility is a form of passthrough, common on larger platforms. OS/2 incorporates many of the SNA features of midrange and mainframe connectivity. APPN and APPC are supported by OS/2.

Advanced peer-to-peer networking (APPN) is a mainstay of IBM's SNA communications. In this scheme, SNA workstations can function as end nodes or network nodes, providing network directory and routing services. Automatic connection between nodes without explicit configuration of network addresses is one of the primary advantages of APPN, along with automatic configuration of communications services.

Advanced program-to-program communications (APPC) is an SNA feature that allows networked computers to share data and services. Also known as LU6.2, a set of APPC application program interfaces (APIs) permits programmers to access information on other platforms. This method is one of the fastest and most efficient ways of requesting data from the server, although it is not the easiest. As a technique for getting records from the server to the client, it can beat remote SQL in most cases. A much higher level of technical expertise is required to implement APPC conversations, however, than the remote SQL interface.

Terminal emulation is one of the primary facilities of Communications Manager. It places a server terminal session into an OS/2 window with all the typical characteristics of the Workplace Shell available. Cut and paste is active as is window sizing. Both 5250 and 3270 type sessions are supported. You can run both at once in separate windows, if so desired, giving access to the AS/400 and S/370 simultaneously.

Remote printer allows server data to be printed locally on the PC or network printer.

File transfer allows users to move files or parts of files from a server to a client.

Remote command permits the user to run a command on a remote server from a client workstation.

11.6 Database Manager

IBM developed SQL as an easy, English-like relational database access tool. Remote SQL is the core of Database Manager, so you can submit SQL requests, which are particularly serviceable by the AS/400's Database Manager, or DB2/400, as it is now called. The PC sends an SQL request to the AS/400, which responds with a data excerpt from its relational databases. This process is the essence of client/server functionality, much of which functions through remote SQL. The database server can be another OS/2 machine that has been set up for this purpose on the network or a networked midrange or mainframe. The database server provides the search or update functionality.

Security is, of course, an important consideration when connecting to remote databases. Not all users should be allowed to change or even see information in some of these files. User profile management (UPM) provides utilities for controlling user logon. A user ID and password can be set up for remote OS/2 connections. Once the user has connected to the server, the usual authorities are invoked for that user, just as if the user had signed on at a 5250 terminal. Rights attach to the user's name or group.

Database Services is the core of Database Manager, and serves submitted SQL statements and transaction management. When an SQL statement is received by Database Services, it is translated (prepared and bound) into machine-executable instructions. Database Services handles both interactive (dynamic) SQL statements and precompiled (static) requests. Dynamic SQL is slower than static SQL, which is why static SQL is embedded in programs for faster execution. Database Services is not called upon to translate the static SQL request at run-time. Record locking and transaction management are also handled by Database Services. When SQL requests an update to a relational database, Database Services locks the records that need to be updated. It then attempts to complete the unit of work requested by the SQL statement. If successful, Database Services sends a COMMIT statement, indicating that the transaction is good. If, for some reason, the transaction cannot be completed, Database Services sends a ROLLBACK statement, restoring the database to the state it was in before the operation started, maintaining database integrity.

Database Tools offers three utilities to configure Database Manager for your particular needs. Configuration Tool lets you manage transaction logs, the number of active applications, and the memory usage for database operations. Recovery Tool manages backup and recovery of databases. Backups can be incremental or complete. Directory Tool creates databases and sets user access rights. Local and remote databases can be seen with Directory Tool, complete with catalogs or full descriptions. Database Tools can be a system-wide database access tool, if set up properly.

Query Manager assists in the construction of SQL syntax and statements. If you do not want to write the SQL yourself at the command line, you can use this utility as an aid in submitting SQL requests to Database Services. Query Manager allows you to create user profiles for each user, automatically setting up the access rights, available databases, and printing options for that user. Menus help you construct the desired SQL statement and submit it to Database Services for execution. Query Manager can also create databases and query them. It can create specialized relational views of databases, along with forms and reports. Queries can be saved for future recall and use by selecting items from menus and lists of databases, fields, and operations. Query Manager is very configurable, providing custom environments to users, depending on their needs. It can even be used to provide a front-end data entry system for database access.

Remote Data Services enables connections to remote platforms, such as the AS/400. Using Token Ring, Ethernet, SDLC, PC LANs, or X.25 topologies, connections can be made to remote database servers. Database Manager connects to the remote server through the functions of Communications Manager and NetBIOS or APPN protocols. Remote Data Services can find files on remote locations through the catalog files of Directory Services and Communication Manager parameters. A system administrator controls these settings. Remote databases accessed in this way appear to be local and are transparent to the user.

DOS and Windows Database Client Support is a feature that allows DOS or Windows clients to access an OS/2 workstation or database server on the network. Using NetBIOS and a special database enabler, the DOS workstation can access OS/2 on the network through programs specially developed for this function. These programs access the OS/2 API, usually through the "C" language on the DOS client. A limited access to remote data is provided in this way, although the standard services of OS/2 are not available.

11.7   DOS and Windows in OS/2

It is possible to run the DOS operating system and programs within the OS/2 Workplace Shell. The DOS environment can run in a window, or it can take up the full screen. If given the full screen, it runs faster. It is also possible to run multiple DOS sessions. Each session can be configured through the use of DOS Settings to provide a custom environment. OS/2 sets up a virtual DOS machine (VDM) for each DOS session started in a window. This VDM has several advantages over a traditional DOS session. Each of these sessions is given 620K of memory to use. Device drivers are not loaded in conventional memory, as they are in DOS. They do not use up valuable memory for applications. Multiple windows are permitted, as well as multiple versions of DOS, eliminating the RAM cram problem. Different memory-hungry applications can run in their own windows, rather than competing for resources in one session. Terminal emulation does not have to coexist with a word processor; just run them in separate windows. In addition to performing DOS program functions, these windows support cut and paste. Fonts as well as the window itself are sizable.

Windows programs, too, can run in a simulated Windows environment within OS/2. Win-OS/2 is a Windows emulator built into the OS/2 operating system. It can be configured to replicate an existing Windows Program Manager desktop. Just as OS/2 can run DOS in an OS/2 window, it can run Windows in an OS/2 window. How about this—Microsoft Word running in Windows inside OS/2's Workplace Shell!

A feature called *Dual Boot* lets you use your computer as both an OS/2 platform and a DOS machine. The PC can be brought up in either environment, permitting both to be available on the same computer. Some DOS programs are problematic within the OS/2 DOS session environment, and running both is a way to get around that limitation. Further, a Boot Manager lets the user choose between multiple environments when booting the computer, including OS/2, DOS, and AIX (an IBM version of UNIX).

Using the above methods, it is possible to access features of diverse PC operating systems, all from within OS/2. DOS programs can run in VDMs. Windows programs run as well. And OS/2 programs can run, of course. OS/2 has both a GUI interface and a command-line interface.

11.8 File Systems

OS/2 offers two different file systems to access the files stored on the disk drives:

- *High-performance file system (HPFS)* is native to OS/2. It is the faster of the two methods for accessing disk data, using optimized disk access and advanced caching. HPFS is downwardly compatible with DOS files named in the file allocation table (FAT) format. In addition, it supports much longer and therefore more meaningful filenames than FAT does. Filenames in HPFS can be up to 254 characters, as opposed to eight in FAT with an optional three more as an extension. A FAT file named CASA94Q4.TXT is obviously not as decipherable as an HPFS file called California_Sales_1994_Quarter_4. Using HPFS, OS/2 can handle enterprise-size databases on PCs and networks.

- *FAT* is the alternative to HPFS. It is from the DOS environment and is the default configuration for OS/2. It is not as fast as HPFS and does not have its capacity in terms of file and partition size.

11.9 Configuration Files

OS/2 uses files on the disk drive to indicate how it should be configured at startup (boot) time. These files are the following:

- CONFIG.SYS: Like DOS, OS/2 uses this file to indicate which device drivers to load at startup. There are many more entries in this file for OS/2, however, to accommodate the increased number of device drivers necessary for OS/2.

- STARTUP.CMD: OS/2 automatically executes programs listed here at startup time.

- AUTOEXEC.BAT: This file starts up DOS sessions within OS/2. Each virtual DOS machine (VDM) can have its own individualized AUTOEXEC.BAT.

11.10 Summary

OS/2 is a fully featured operating system for the PC. It has many built-in facilities that enable various types of client/server applications. OS/2 becomes a powerful platform for client/server development, especially when the Communications Manager is added. Terminal and printer emulation, remote SQL, APPN, and APPC are all supported by OS/2. DOS programs run as do Windows programs. These features permit a wide variety of client/server solutions.

Why hasn't OS/2 captured the PC multitasking market? The answer is a combination of insufficient marketing on the part of IBM, the high hardware requirements of OS/2, and the fact that all the major software vendors have thrown their lots in with Microsoft's Windows. Many of the most popular software packages are simply not available for OS/2. Whether they remain so is open to question.

12

UNIX

12.1 UNIX

UNIX is a multiuser, multitasking operating system. It can run multiple programs at the same time for a number of different users. It is simultaneously a network operating system as well as a workstation operating system. UNIX was the first environment to develop client/server applications. It does not belong to one type of hardware, or even one software developer, but runs on many different platforms, which is unlike the IBM world, where the operating system software is proprietary.

UNIX is mostly used as a command-line environment. Even though it has a windows-type interface, most systems still use the command line. Users generally connect to a UNIX server from remote terminals. It is less advanced in terms of GUI features than the IBM world, and certainly less than the Apple Macintosh world.

UNIX is scalable. It runs on differently sized platforms—PCs, midranges, and mainframes. These can be Sun SPARCstations, Hewlett Packards, IBM RS/6000s, or many other types of computer hardware. It can also run on IBM machines under OS/2 or Windows. It is a much more consistent and uniform environment than is the IBM world. It can connect with numerous platforms, many of which do not need to be running UNIX. Connections to the IBM world of operating systems and platforms are increasing. UNIX is written in the "C" language, which was developed at Bell Labs just for this purpose. Portability is a primary function of both the "C" language and of UNIX itself. *Portability* means that systems designed for UNIX using "C" can be "ported," or moved, from one hardware platform to another with relative ease. The term *relative* is important here. Certainly it can be said that UNIX systems port to a different UNIX platform more easily than DOS or OS/400 systems port to other systems.

UNIX is a more open environment than IBM operating systems. It has grown organically over the years in Bell Labs, as well as in the university and technical settings, which use it extensively. What it has gained in creative development, however, it lacks in standardization, for the same reasons. No one vendor controls its development. Many flavors of UNIX now exist, along with the applications and utilities that run under it. UNIX environments are very adaptable and can be tailored to specific needs with a multitude of software options. (Tailoring does require the presence and labor of several software designers, programmers, or engineers.) UNIX is a less packaged or integrated platform than IBM's offerings, and many businesses prefer to go with a system that provides tools for all their needs in a bundled software package. Technical and research settings often prefer the more flexible aspect of UNIX and are better equipped to handle the technical aspects of adapting UNIX to the purposes at hand. These distinctions are not exclusive, however, and many UNIX systems are found in the world of business. UNIX and its partner "C" are found especially in areas where a large volume of high-performance application development is required.

UNIX shell scripts and the shell programming language can be used to automate often-used operating system functions into batch processes. Thus, the user does not need to know some of the obscurities of the operating system. Shell commands and requisite cryptic parameters can be put into a shell script and executed with a more sensible command name that the user provides. These programs can have logic structures and can prompt the user for input and then react to it.

UNIX consists of several layers, described in the following subsections.

Kernel. At the lowest level, the kernel communicates with the computer hardware to provide memory, disk, printer, modem, and other hardware type services to programs. Any peripheral device or basic input/output request to the system is handled by the kernel.

Shell. The *shell* is the basic command interpreter of UNIX, containing the primary UNIX commands, such as 1s to list files in the current directory. The command-line interface, or shell, of UNIX is by far its most common form. The user types a command onto a screen and receives system responses; no pictures or point-and-click icons. The standard character-based shell is, however, replaceable with other shells that do perform such functions. Several forms of the standard UNIX shell are the C, Korn, and Bourne shells, all offering approximately the same functions, but the C shell has somewhat different syntax. UNIX commands and other system names are case-sensitive. Lowercase is generally required for commands.

Utilities. *Utilities* are the basic application packages for the user to perform activities such as text editing, print spooling, and e-mail.

Applications. At a level higher than the utilities, the applications are a group of programs that provide the main functions the user ultimately wants to perform. Word processing, database management, spreadsheets, and graphics packages are all applications.

12.2 Connecting

Telnet is a pervasive feature of UNIX that allows the user to connect to remote systems. Dialing into a UNIX server over telephone lines is very common in the UNIX world. Modems, at both ends of the telephone line connection, translate computer signals into telephone signals and back again. Configuration of the modem and communications software is required to make a compatible match at both ends of this scenario. This method of connecting offers much slower response times than direct, on-site connections through a network, yet it is a mainstay of the distributed, loosely organized UNIX communications scheme that is at the heart of, for instance, the Internet. Because telephone lines are everywhere, why not use them as network connections to create a global network? Nodes are wherever someone plugs a modem into a computer and telephone line—no assembly required.

Security is one of UNIX's strengths. UNIX implements security through user accounts and passwords administered at the server by the system administrator (also called *root user* or *superuser*). The user logs in, either locally through the network or remotely through telephone connections. After giving a correct account name and password, the user is placed into the home directory. This directory is for the personal use of that particular user, and contains files or projects. Files in directories, and directories themselves, have permissions associated with them. These permissions specify which users can access the files for various purposes. Who can read, execute, change, or delete these files is specified in the permissions attached to them. The owner of a file can decide what type of access control to attach to each file or directory.

There are three categories of user:

- User or owner
- Group
- Other

These types of users can access a file in three ways:

- Read
- Write
- Execute/search

In this way, specific users or groups can be given access to particular files. You can use the umask command to see how default permissions are granted by the system. You can also set a file creation mode mask with the umask command. You can allow yourself unlimited rights, your group read and execute rights, and everyone else no rights (which is usually desirable) with the following command:

```
umask 027
```

The preceding command is a good example of why UNIX at the command line is considered by some to be inscrutable and unfriendly to casual users.

File transfer protocol (FTP) is a file transfer utility for sharing files between systems. It can copy files from one computer to a remote location. Electronic mail and messaging is one of the advantages of using UNIX. It is possible for one user to contact another using the write command to place both terminals into conversational mode. Users can then type to each other and hold a small, character-based conference.

12.3 X-Windows

The standard UNIX interface has been the command prompt $ on the screen. The user types in somewhat cryptic commands that are case-sensitive and gets back system messages or nothing. You need to know program names and parameters, as in DOS. This method of communicating with the operating system requires a much higher level of computer knowledge than the graphical user interface (GUI), with its icons and point-and-click technique. *X-Windows* is the UNIX answer to this need. It provides the easy GUI interface many users have come to expect from their computers ever since the Apple Macintosh pioneered it. You point at a little picture or icon that represents what you want to do and click the mouse button. As with most window-type GUI interfaces, it is possible to bring up a character-based screen within the windows environment to access the $ prompt and issue commands. UNIX can run Windows and DOS applications, too, in their own X-Windows. It is possible to have several completely different operating systems up on the screen at the same time, each one processing concurrently with the others. The system clipboard provides cut-and-paste functionality between these diverse windows.

In keeping with the UNIX philosophy of open systems, no one standard window manager exists. Several, however, have gained popularity recently, including OSF/Motif and Sun's Open Look.

12.4 Connection Program/400

IBM offers a package to facilitate communications between UNIX platforms and the AS/400. Connection Program/400 allows connections between the AS/400 and the SUN SPARCstation, the IBM RS/6000, and the HP/9000 workstations. These platforms can access client/server utilities on the AS/400 through either SNA or TCP/IP. Connection Program/400 is designed to be used with UNIX GUI clients that access the AS/400 as a server. Although the reverse is possible, most functions work best with the AS/400 as a server sharing resources and data. The UNIX components can use their high-resolution graphics capabilities to display data that is served transparently by the AS/400 database.

Programs and features installed at both the AS/400 end and the UNIX end implement these functions. They are as follows:

- AS/400   OS/400 V3R1 or higher
  ~Token Ring, Ethernet, X.25, or SDLC (only SNA)
  ~PC Support (Client Access) for SNA connections
  ~TCP/IP Connectivity Utilities/400 for TCP/IP connections
  *Both PC Support and TCP/IP Utilities are bundled with OS/400 V3R1; they just need to be installed.

- RS/6000: AIX V3R2 or higher
  ~AIXwindows Environment/6000 V1R2 is required for x5250 terminal emulator
  ~AIX SNA Services/6000 for the SNA connection
- SUN SPARCstation
  ~Sun Operating System 5.1
  ~OpenWindows 3.0
- HP/9000   HPUX 9.0
  ~X-Windows System Release 4

The UNIX clients work best with at least 16Mb of RAM.

12.5 5250 Terminal Emulation

Both full-screen, character-based screens and X-Windows sessions are available to the UNIX client, which attaches to the AS/400 through Connection Program/400.

The e5250 terminal emulator can reproduce the AS/400 screen in full-screen mode on the UNIX ASCII display. The reproduction looks just like the AS/400 display—it is not windowed. The UNIX keyboard can easily be remapped to 5250 functionality. In this way, the user can sign on to the AS/400 and work just as if sitting at a local 5250 terminal.

The x5250 terminal emulator places an AS/400 session into an X-Windows session. GUI features such as cut and paste, window sizing and moving, pop-up menus, and hot spots are available through x5250. This environment is very close to the Windows look and functionality of Rumba. The EUI 5250 datastream is supported, providing X-Window compatibility with the AS/400 in terms of pushbuttons, scroll bars, and other GUI features. You can configure and define hot spots to combine the point-and-click functionality of the mouse with the AS/400 screen. The user can push a button to execute AS/400 commands within X-Windows running under UNIX.

12.6   Remote Printers

Connection Program/400 lets UNIX clients send print jobs to an AS/400 printer. Using PC Support technology, the UNIX print job is brought over through SNA (and is not supported by TCP/IP).

The AS/400 can also send print jobs to a UNIX-attached printer. Connecting through either SNA or TCP/IP, the UNIX client uses either e5250 or x5250 emulation to access the AS/400, along with Connection Program/400 remote printer functionality, which is associated with the terminal emulation to print the job on the UNIX side.

12.7   Data Access APIs

UNIX machines can submit remote SQL statements to the AS/400 for processing and data return. These are implemented through SQL APIs. Results can be downloaded to the UNIX client or simply viewed from the UNIX client, through X-Windows 5250 emulation. This remote SQL facility brings the powerful features of the AS/400 database manager into the UNIX environment. Once the data has been returned to the UNIX client, it is then available for further processing and can even be returned to the AS/400. Remote SQL is a very significant facility to be considered when developing client/server systems between the AS/400 and UNIX.

12.8   File Transfer

Files can be transferred to the UNIX client from the AS/400 server with SQL-like field-and-record selection. The UNIX client has file information from the AS/400 available when designing the transfer request. The AS/400 database manager (DB2/400) serves this request and returns the result of the query to the UNIX requester. Going in the other direction, only entire files can be transferred from UNIX to the AS/400, which is obviously a less useful facility because many applications that require a small excerpt from a server database cannot afford to bring in the whole database. Under this restraint, the UNIX machine makes a better client than server for the AS/400.

12.9 Remote Commands

The AS/400 can submit commands from a remote location to the UNIX system. The UNIX computer can remotely submit AS/400 commands and programs. Thus, each system can control processing on the other, enabling a number of client/server implementations and solutions. The UNIX client could initiate a process on the AS/400 side, wait for it to complete, download the results, and display them in its own native formats, for example. All of this functionality without even being signed on to the AS/400. The reverse is equally possible. A terminal emulation session is not required, just a correctly configured router session between the two platforms. Programs on the client can run programs on the server and vice versa. In fact, using this technique begins to blur the distinction between client and server.

12.10 SNA or TCP/IP

System network architecture (SNA) and system application architecture (SAA) provided a degree of uniformity and services between essentially different IBM platforms. Transmission control protocol/internet protocol (TCP/IP) is UNIX's counterpart to IBM's SNA. Using TCP/IP, connections are made between computers on networks and between networks, which is the foundation of the Internet, a loosely organized, extensive global network of smaller networks and information resources. Some believe that TCP/IP is becoming an accepted international communications standard to a degree that SNA is not.

12.11 Summary

Admirers of UNIX claim that UNIX is more open and flexible than alternative operating systems, and this question of open architecture is getting much attention because of client/server development. UNIX is probably more open than IBM systems, but IBM systems are becoming more open all the time. While UNIX gains in standardization, IBM gains in openness, and the two are beginning to converge. UNIX has gained a certain amount of respect in technical and scientific circles because of its versatility and adaptability to specific projects. There is even a certain amount of pride taken in the high learning curve of the "C" language. "UNIX 'C' is not for wimps," they like to say. This attitude is both an advantage and a drawback. An intelligent group of business analysts and programmers might have an easier and more productive time with other environments. If you need lightning response times from a system with superior graphics capabilities, universal connectivity, and excellent security, however, it is hard to beat UNIX. Combined with the powerful database-handling characteristics of the AS/400 as a server, UNIX is a powerful client.

Chapter
13

Apple

Apple and IBM formed a joint venture to provide ways of connecting their computers. As a result, you can connect a Macintosh to the AS/400 three different ways: SNA, TCP/IP, or AppleTalk. Once the communications link has been established, four application services are available. These are the 5250 terminal and printer emulation, data access language (DAL) Server for AS/400, and file transfer or storage. These services constitute the major components of client/server systems, enabling remote sign-on and data and file access across the platforms. Not all application services are available with all the connection methods. Table 13.1 summarizes which services go with which connection.

TABLE 13.1 Apple Connections and Associated Services

	5250 Terminal	5250 Printer	DAL	File Transfer	File Storage
SNA	X	X	X		X
TCP/IP	X		X	X	X
AppleTalk	X	X			

All three connections provide a terminal session. Printer emulation is not available with TCP/IP. The Macintosh DAL can be used to access AS/400 data through SNA or TCP/IP. File transfer, using file transfer protocol (FTP), can be implemented in TCP/IP. File storage and exchange is available using network file system (NFS) and TCP/IP or shared folders and

SNA. A connection method can be selected depending on which services are required.

13.1 SNA Gateway Connection

The Macintosh can run SNA.ps Gateway to provide a link between an AppleTalk network and the AS/400 (or System/390) on Token Ring or synchronous data link control (SDLC). One of the Macintosh computers acts as the gateway between the two unlike networks, translating protocols and routing traffic between the AppleTalk network and the IBM SNA LU6.2 network. The gateway does not need to be dedicated solely to this function. Mostly, the communications run at the card level, leaving the central processing unit (CPU) free for other tasks. This solution is attractive because not all the Macintoshes need communications adapter cards. The gateway has the card and configuration that provide the connection for the other Macintoshes to use in connecting to the AS/400. This solution is available for 10, 35, and 70 active users. An active user is a terminal emulation client or a DAL client. SNA.ps Gateway provides the widest range of application services to the AS/400. 5250 terminal and printer emulation, DAL, and shared folders are supported. The advanced program-to-program communications (APPC) APIs can be used with this option. If this rather complex and powerful feature is needed, SNA is best.

A Macintosh running the SNA.ps Gateway must have a long NuBus slot and 2.5Mb of memory. Macintosh IIxx, Centris 650, and most Quadras can run the Gateway function to the AS/400. The Apple Token Ring 4/16 card, the Apple TokenTalk NB card, or the Apple Serial NB card can be used for the network connection. The Apple Internet Router can be used in the Macintosh SNA.ps Gateway or on another Macintosh in the network to combine both LocalTalk and EtherTalk networks in the connection to the AS/400. This router allows configurations of TokenTalk, LocalTalk, and EtherTalk to coexist in the SNA connection to the AS/400. It also has add-ons for AppleTalk/IP Wide Area Extension for TCP/IP and AppleTalk/X.25 Wide Area Extension for Internet X.25.

13.2 TCP/IP Connection

Transmission control protocol/internet protocol (TCP/IP) is a widely used communications protocol. It can run on the AS/400, making this computer a node in a network of diverse TCP/IP devices. This type of connection does not use a Macintosh as a gateway as does the SNA connection. Because the AS/400 is running TCP/IP, it can field requests directly from each IP address out on the TCP/IP network. Some of these can be Macintoshes. If a TCP/IP network is already in place, this network can integrate the AS/400 right into it. It supports 5250 terminal emulation, DAL, and file serving and exchange.

There is no printer emulation on the Macintosh to make a locally attached printer behave like an AS/400 printer. It is also necessary to configure each Macintosh for the TCP/IP connection to the AS/400 because there is no gateway.

The TCP/IP connection requires TCP/IP Connection for the Macintosh and TCP/IP Connectivity Utility on the AS/400. Token Ring or Ethernet can form the direct physical link between the two platforms. LocalTalk connections require a LocalTalk/Ethernet gateway to furnish protocol conversions for the link over the Ethernet to the AS/400. It is possible to run more than one TCP/IP service at the same time, such as TELNET, mail transport (*SMTP*), file transfer (*FTP*) and network file system (*NFS*).

13.3   AppleTalk Connection

Macintoshes can connect to the AS/400 using AppleTalk, which is included with the Macintosh operating system by running SNA.ps 5250. No gateway exists, so each Macintosh connects directly to the AS/400 through TokenTalk for Token Ring, EtherTalk for Ethernet, or LocalTalk for Local-Talk. The AS/400 must have the appropriate adapter for Token Ring, Ethernet, or LocalTalk. This solution offers the least in the way of communications services, providing 5250 display and printer emulation. No file services or DAL are supported. One feature available using AppleTalk is the ability to use the Macintosh as the AS/400 system console, which cannot be done either through the SNA or TCP/IP connection. The AppleTalk connection is probably the easiest and least expensive to implement, as long as its limited emulation features are sufficient.

13.4   Terminal Emulation

5250 emulation lets Macintosh users access the AS/400 as though they were sitting at an AS/400 5250 terminal. In other words, it replicates the AS/400 screens in windows right on the Macintosh. Anything you can do from an AS/400 terminal is available to the 5250 emulation session. Apple and IBM cooperated to create the SNA.ps 5250 emulator that runs on all three connection methods discussed above—SNA, TCP/IP, and AppleTalk.

SNA.ps 5250 is very similar to Rumba/400 in functionality. It allows you to remap the keyboard to personal preferences, using a keyboard on the screen. You can also place keypads on the screen for executing AS/400 commands by clicking on the keypad. Hotspots are supported to allow the user to click on areas of the AS/400 display to execute options. Extensive online help is available. Cut and paste are supported to enable the pasting of data back and forth between the Macintosh screen and the AS/400 display. The AS/400 can display in a movable, sizable window with automatically adjusted font sizes.

13.5 Printer Emulation

SNA.ps Print is a feature that lets you use a locally or network-attached Macintosh printer to print jobs that originate on the AS/400. You can sign on to the AS/400 through the 5250 terminal emulation program and run a job that prints right on the Macintosh printer. The AS/400 thinks it is sending the printed output to one of its own printers (3812 Model 1), while SNA.ps Print intercepts it and routes it to one of the Macintosh printers. This feature is part of the SNA.ps 5250 package. It is available with SNA and AppleTalk connection to the AS/400, but not with TCP/IP. You can preview the data before it is actually printed, save it for later printing, and format it for either Macintosh or AS/400 conventions. The print performance is better when using an Ethernet connection rather than LocalTalk. Macintosh's Print Monitor handles the spooling of SNA.ps Print jobs just as it would for Macintosh native print jobs.

13.6 DAL and SQL

DAL is a way to access the AS/400 databases (and other remote databases) from Macintosh programs. Like Microsoft's Open Database Connectivity (ODBC) driver, DAL enables relatively simple remote data access. It is possible to set up a Lotus 123 or Excel spreadsheet, for example, that accesses AS/400 databases through the services of DAL. DataPrism is another application which can be used to query AS/400 data. The AS/400 runs a DAL server that processes these remote data queries. It is not necessary for the user to know how to access AS/400 data; the AS/400 DAL server takes care of all of that. To the user, the data appears to be local.

The DAL Client runs on the Macintosh. It consists of an API that can be used in client programs as a link to the remote data. It is not necessary to know the intricacies of the database languages and access methods on the AS/400. The client program just accesses the DAL API on the Macintosh, which takes care of the rest, such as knowing how to get to the desired data on the remote system using the SQL method (like ODBC). Many Macintosh programs are capable of using DAL in this way. They include DataPrism, Excel, Lotus 123, Andyne GQL, and ClearAccess. The application program submits an SQL request through DAL, which is routed over the network using SNA.ps Gateway or TCP/IP and received by the AS/400. The AS/400 then interprets the incoming SQL request and runs it. The resulting data set is then returned over the same pathway to the waiting Macintosh program, which accepts it and processes it further, according to its own internal program logic.

The DAL Server runs at the server end on the AS/400. It receives a remote SQL request, as mentioned above, from the DAL Client. The request is submitted to the AS/400 database manager, which is part of DB2/400. The database manager processes the request, and the resulting data is transferred back to the DAL Client on the Macintosh. Check which version of DAL Client is required to run with your connection scheme.

13.7   File Services

File storage and exchange allows Macintosh users to use files stored on the AS/400 as if they were stored on AppleShare volumes. Just as IBM PC workstations running DOS, Windows, or OS/2 can access files stored on the AS/400 in shared folders, so can Macintosh clients. This way, the AS/400 can function as a file server to a diverse network of clients, all sharing the same files. Shared Folders for Macintosh provides file exchange for Macintosh computers connected to the AS/400 through SNA. The Apple Chooser can be used to select files from the AS/400 shared folders and copy them to the Macintosh, using the AppleTalk Filing Protocol (AFP) for requesting and responding to Macintosh clients.

13.8   Other Connections

In addition to the tools described above, many third-party offerings can connect the Apple Macintosh to the AS/400. Some of these are the following:

- *Advanced Software Concepts (ASC) CTB Tools for AS/400*: communications utilities that can be used for 5250 terminal emulation and file transfer. These use TCP/IP or SNA.ps Gateway.

- *Advanced Software Concepts (ASC) 5PM Term*: 5250, 3270, and other emulation using TCP/IP or SNA.ps Gateway. Hot keys, scripting, hotspots, and tool bars are included.

- *Advanced Software Concepts (ASC) 5PM Pro*: a professional development tool for terminal emulation on the Macintosh used with 5PM Term. The development language is very similar to HyperTalk. Developers can place windows on the AS/400 display and create dialog boxes and drop-down lists. These lists and boxes can allow the Macintosh user to run AS/400 programs simply by clicking on GUI buttons and lists, eliminating the need to know anything about the AS/400.

- *Andrew ETU File Transfer Utility*: This program is installed on the AS/400. Once there, it allows an Andrew 5250 terminal emulation session to perform file transfers between the Macintosh and the AS/400 (as well as between numerous other platforms).

- *Andrew NetAxcess*: twinax gateway connection to the AS/400 for terminal and printer emulation as well as ETU file transfer to Macintosh on the AppleTalk network.

- *Andrew TCPAxcess*: TELNET 5250 client with MacTCP and ETU for file transfer.

- *Andrew TokenAxcess*: connects to the AS/400 using SNA.ps Gateway to provide 5250 terminal emulation. This product supports Apple Token Ring 4/16 NB and Serial NB cards.

- *Apple SNA.ps APPC Developers Kit*: hands-on access to APPC APIs from within Macintosh programs. These are rather complex to implement in C, Pascal, or assembler, but are very powerful.

- *Brio Technology Data Prism*: offers access to remote databases of various types, including the AS/400's DB2/400. GUI tools enable point-and-click access to the remote data. The connecting software is DAL or SequeLink.

- *CEL Blacksmith*: a GUI toolkit for developing windowed front-ends for AS/400 terminal emulators. It can be used with SNA.ps 5250 and Andrew TokenAxcess.

- *Connectivite Both*: a GUI toolkit for developing windowed front-ends for AS/400 terminal emulators. Can be used with SNA.ps 5250 and Andrew TokenAxcess. In addition, it provides access to both the AS/400 and the IBM mainframe from within the same window.

- *InterCon NFS/Share*: runs on the Macintosh to provide access to file transfers to and from the AS/400. The AS/400 must be running TCP/IP File Server Support/400 and TCP/IP.

- *Legent XCOM-Macintosh*: APPC file transfer, remote job entry, and a query tool for reports. Requires SNA.ps Gateway.

- *Miramar MACLAN Connect*: an IBM PC running DOS or OS/2 that has two network cards and functions as a file-sharing gateway between the AS/400's shared folders and the Macintosh. One card connects the PC to the AS/400 network and the other to the AppleTalk network. To the AppleTalk network, this IBM PC's access to the AS/400 shared folder file appears to be an AppleShare Server.

- *TechGnosis SequeLink*: AS/400 application that provides SQL access to the AS/400 database. Connects to Macintosh as well as Windows, OS/2, and UNIX. These clients must be running DAL-type applications such as Excel or DataPrism.

13.9 Summary

Connectivity is possible between IBM and Apple Macintoshes as a result of a joint venture between these two companies to develop communications software. SNA, TCP/IP, and AppleTalk connections are supported. Using these three connection methods, four communications services are available. 5250 terminal and printer emulation, DAL Server for AS/400, and file transfer or storage facilitate client/server processing between these distributed and divergent platforms.

14

Networks

It is important when discussing client/server applications and development to understand networks. Because client/server depends on the merging of services from different computer platforms, these platforms must be tied together or integrated. Only then are client/server systems enabled; they depend both on the physical and logical links between systems. Mostly, the smaller computers on the network, such as PCs, function as clients to the more powerful database machines or servers, such as the AS/400. A mainframe could be a client requesting data from a PC server, but this situation is not the norm. Client/server systems generally consist of PC GUI front-ends for the server database on the back-end. They allow users to access otherwise hidden data from the platform in a way most comfortable and productive to them. To understand how to provide these easy and seamless data interfaces, let us consider some types of networks that can bind together these services.

Networks are the connections between computers, devices, and services. They can be as simple as two office computers sharing files, or as complex and diverse as the Internet. Different types of computers can be connected through interface cards, cabling schemes, telephone lines, microwave transmissions, or satellite links. Once the physical layer is in place, the network operating system provides connectivity services over it. Each device on the network must contain an interface card that speaks the communications language (protocol) of the network. Networks comprise these three components: the computers, the physical links, and the network services.

Redirection is the key to understanding networks. Programs residing on the PC or network device redirect data or requests for file services from the local device to the file server. A PC program might think it is printing to a locally attached printer, but the resident network software on the PC has intercepted this request and directed it to a network printer in a different city. Or a PC program wants to read data from a file and sends out a typical DOS file request, but the redirector intercepts it and sends the request out to the network file server. The PC runs the redirection software, while the server runs the network operating system software. Working together, these programs form an integrated network out of diverse parts. The file server can be any of a vast array of computers, as long as the PC is running the correctly configured redirector. The AS/400 can be a file server for a PC file request. Typically, a server provides file maintenance, file sharing, file transfer, shared printers, security, systematic backup, and other administrative functions. Their capacity to integrate organizational tasks is significant.

Because many possible choices at each level of the network exist, the combinations are numerous. It is important to select components that work well with each other. We will look at how some of them relate to AS/400 client/server application development.

14.1 Protocols

Standards exist to implement network procedures and devices. The Open System Interconnection (OSI) model from the International Standards Organization (ISO) is the basis for most standards. The concept of the OSI model is that network protocols should be modular, or divided into discrete layers. Changes to one layer should be transparent to the other layers. Thus, you could substitute one network card for another, for example, without upsetting the operation of the OSI model. There are seven layers in the OSI model:

- *Physical*: the cabling and electrical transmission.
- *Data Link*: packaging the data and putting it on the physical layer.
- *Network*: the logical connections to devices and the server.
- *Transport*: integrity of transmission.
- *Session*: communications conversations between participants.
- *Presentation*: translations and conversions of data for network.
- *Application*: network functionality, such as terminal emulation and file transfer.

IBM's SNA protocol stack follows the OSI model, as does TCP/IP and most others. Advanced program-to-program communications (APPC) is IBM's transport protocol. It allows programs to communicate with one another over the network, as the name suggests. A significant component of systems application architecture (SAA), APPC is the glue that ties together IBM communications running over their advanced peer-to-peer network (APPN) devices. APPN lets computers communicate as peers. A PC can talk directly to a mainframe or an AS/400 without an intervening controller. It is a peer relationship, rather than master-slave. This situation is very useful for client/server applications. APPC is also known as LU6.2.

Network basic input/output system (NetBIOS) is not OSI-compliant, but it is a very common and useful protocol for connecting PCs. It is a session layer protocol that connects the network to PC programs. PCs can be connected through NetBIOS and a gateway to the AS/400, although the services thus established are not as comprehensive or robust as the native APPC connection for IBM devices.

14.2 LAN/WAN

Local area networks (LANs) consist of devices attached to each other through a physical layer and are generally at one site. Cables can be coaxial, twisted pair, or fiber:

Coaxial cable is used for cable TV, and varies in thickness from a finger to a pencil. Coax can handle a lot of traffic on multiple channels. To add a station, you need a tap or T-connector to the main line.

Twisted pair telephone cable, also known as unshielded twisted pair (UTP), is inexpensive and easy to work with. Modular cabling provides cable runs from wall panels at the user locations to a patch panel in the computer room. To add a station, you just plug it in to the wall panel (RJ-45). Twisted pair is by far the most prevalent solution.

Fiber has a very large bandwidth and can carry voice and data at the same time. It is good for long distances and very high traffic and is not susceptible to interference or noise; however, its cost is expensive. Fiber is often used for a backbone.

A *wide area network* (WAN) uses the connectivity of long distance telephone services or microwave or satellite transmissions. Usually, it is the various phone lines that provide remote connections.

Synchronous data link control (SDLC) is a method for connecting devices over an ordinary telephone line. It uses a card or emulator at the PC end, a modem, and a modem with a corresponding line description at the AS/400. SDLC is not the easiest type of remote connectivity to configure. Even though it is an APPC-type connection, it often cannot make use of the invaluable APPN feature of autoconfiguration, where the AS/400 sees a session coming in and automatically configures line, controller, and device descriptions for it. SDLC does enable you to hook up to an AS/400 through the telephone system, however, without any other network topology in place.

T-1 is a dedicated telephone company line for businesses to use in connecting voice and data. It can be divided into channels, some dedicated to voice and some to data. The T-1 carries up to 1.5Mb per second of information. It is always there, providing a reliable, dedicated connection between points.

Integrated services digital network (ISDN) offers switched conditioned lines for data communications. These lines are highly reliable for digital protocols. They are somewhat expensive, but offer an attractive alternative, especially if the line is not in constant use. For applications that require short bursts of lots of traffic (like video conferencing), ISDN works well.

A *bridge* is a device that connects similar networks together. Two Token Ring networks can be joined by the use of a bridge. The bridge could be a card residing in a PC dedicated to connecting the two networks. The bridge is connected to both networks, while the other devices on the networks are attached only to their own rings. The bridge decides when an information packet should be routed to the other network, which is a function of the medium access control (MAC) layer of the OSI model. Only packets destined for the other network segment are switched over to it. Bridges can divide networks into more manageable segments. Instead of having all devices circulate traffic across the entire network, only local traffic and bridged traffic from the other segment travel on a given segment. Remote bridges can connect two similar networks over a link such as a T-1 or other telecommunications line.

A *router* connects devices or networks that are dissimilar but share the same transport protocol, like SNA. An example of a router is the PC Support or Client Access Router, which connects the PC client to the AS/400 server. It is a protocol translator that sits between the two devices and translates the language of one into the language of the other. In this way, what started out as a PC DOS command can be sent to the AS/400 as a remote command to initiate an RPG program.

A *gateway* translates between networks that have unlike protocols, like SNA to TCP/IP. They are often used to connect a PC LAN to a larger server, like the AS/400. A PC on the network could have a gateway card in it and be dedicated to the task of translating incoming network traffic to the protocol of the server. Only packets with the server address are sent to the server. A gateway can provide emulation sessions and other functions for a number of PCs on the LAN.

14.3 Token Ring

Token Ring is a physical network layer comprising network interface cards in the computers or devices, cabling, and multiple access units (MAUs). It is the IBM-sanctioned network scheme. Token Ring has a 4- or 16-Mbps transfer rate, which is reliable and sufficient for most applications. Token Ring is the IEEE 802.5 standard; a baseband priority token-passing arrangement. Only one token is allowed in the ring at a given time—which is a very polite arrangement. Each station regenerates and transmits the token, providing a high degree of reliability. Each station waits its turn on the ring, as opposed to Ethernet, which transmits simultaneously and then manages collisions. Token Ring is easy to install and manage. It is actually cabled like a star, but creates a logical ring. All cables run to a central location and are plugged into an MAU (or some variant of MAU, such as CAUs or LAMBs). The MAUs are linked together to form a ring, and each device on the ring can pass the token when plugged in.

The MAUs used in Token Ring are often intelligent enough to isolate a defective member of the ring and remove it or bypass it, providing a very resilient and dependable environment. Token Ring is named for the token-passing method that characterizes it. Each station on the ring receives all the information circulating through the ring. It regenerates the information and passes it through the MAU to the next station. This process continues around the ring until the destination station is reached. The destination station recognizes this information as its own because all information traveling the ring is stamped with the destination address, much like a letter in the mail. The destination station removes the information from the ring and processes it locally. Token Ring supports up to 260 devices or users on a single ring. You can use bridges to connect networks to increase this limit.

IBM recommends Type 1 cable, which is quite thick and shielded. This cable is expensive and difficult to work with, but very bulletproof. More and more installations, however, are using unshielded twisted-pair cabling (UTP or Type 3). Type 3, level 4 carries up to 20 Mbps, while Type 3, level 5 carries up to 100 Mbps. This type of cable is very similar to ordinary telephone cable. It is inexpensive and easy to install and work with. Unless interference or line noise is very high in the immediate environment, UTP should be fine.

As a LAN solution, Token Ring is very appealing. It offers ease of installation, high reliability, and IBM standards. It supports SNA, NetBIOS, and APPC. Token Ring has high data transmission rates at all traffic levels and supports a large number of users without slowing down. If network traffic is expected to be heavy or have consistent spikes, Token Ring provides a good solution. It is not the most cost-effective solution, however, which brings us to the next and most popular network physical layer.

14.4 Ethernet

Ethernet is the most widely used physical network layer partly because it is much less expensive than Token Ring. Each Ethernet card is about four or five times less expensive than a corresponding Token Ring card for a PC. Multiply this by the number of PCs in an organization and the difference mounts quickly.

Ethernet represents the IEEE 802.3 standard. It uses carrier sense multiple access with collision detection (CSMA/CD) for determining how to transmit data. Under this scheme, the transmitting device listens for a clear channel on the Ethernet. It will not transmit until it hears a clear channel. Once a clear channel is detected, the device transmits. If more than one device transmits at the same time, collision detection comes into play. Each colliding device waits a random interval before transmitting again. This method can create bottlenecks at high-usage levels, as more and more collisions are detected and transmissions retried, although it is quite adequate at lower levels. Generally, Ethernet is good for smaller networks of 50 or so stations. The usual 10BaseT Ethernet provides a transfer rate of 10 Mbps, although a more expensive 100-Mbps version is now available.

Ethernet uses a variety of cabling types, although it is trending toward UTP, as is Token Ring. 10Base5 is the RG-8 coax cable known as *thick Ethernet*. 10Base2 is RG-58 coax also called *thin Ethernet*. 10BaseT is essentially the same as UTP. 10BaseF is *optical fiber*. The more usual approach these days is 10BaseT or 10BaseF.

Typically, Ethernet has a bus topology, constructed of a backbone, or trunk cable, with transceivers hanging off it as stations. Repeaters can be used to extend the length of a line. The ends of the Ethernet cable must be terminated with a 50-ohm terminator. A star topology can be used with 10baseT, giving it the same cabling scheme as Token Ring. Ethernet networks can be bridged to other networks to reduce the collision factor on each of the networks by not allowing traffic from one onto the other. Each network only has to process its own addressed packets. Ethernet is usually faster than Token Ring in situations where traffic is not too heavy and where it is intermittent (like offices). If utilization approaches 40 percent, however, the Ethernet segment maxes out and causes jamming on the network. Forty percent is probably sufficient, however, because many office environments operate at an average of 5 percent of network capacity.

14.5 Novell NetWare

Novell NetWare is the network file server operating system of choice for over 70 percent of LAN installations. Its popularity is based on good performance, ease of use, excellent security, and interfaces to many clients. NetWare is open and scalable; it can be adapted to a variety of technologies and platforms. DOS, Windows, OS/2, OS/400, Macintosh, and UNIX all connect to the Novell file server and can share peripherals attached to the network. Up to 1,000 of these devices can be connected. GUI interfaces let network managers see the entire network represented graphically and point and click their way to system administration. Just double-click on a network resource to access its properties and security features.

Simple network management protocol (SNMP) provides the ability to monitor and troubleshoot network resources from a central location. NetWare Management System (NMS) can use this protocol to control network functions. Through NetWare for SAA, Novell network data is made available to the AS/400 and other larger IBM systems running NetView. The RUNCMD command can be used in the AS/400 NetView environment to manage NetWare file servers from the host. The RCONSOLE utility allows network supervisors to control remote servers from any workstation on the network. It is not necessary to have network personnel at a remote location to perform server operations such as loading and unloading NLMs, as well as downing and rebooting the server.

The whole enterprise network can be made transparently available to authorized users. A single login is sufficient to access information on all the authorized servers in the network through NetWare Directory Services (NDS). NDS knows about all objects and services existing on the network and can organize these graphically in a tree structure, regardless of physical location. Users who are authorized can then access these compound resources as if they were all local. For example, a single user in New York could access related databases in Chicago and Atlanta and print a report in France without even knowing how the connection takes place. A single login can accomplish all of this. Because NDS knows all the various properties of network objects, the user does not need to. Just say, for example, "Fax this to Mary," and the network takes care of the distributed routing, assuming it knows what *this* is and who and where Mary is. NDS supports the mirroring of network partitions on remote servers to ensure availability and enhance response. Message Handling Service (MHS) provides store-and-forward messaging functions that can be used to support many third-party messaging packages. MHS integrates with NDS to allow easy configuration and maintenance.

Novell has an automatic file compression utility that runs in the background, which can save a lot of disk space. When a user requests a compressed file, NetWare automatically decompresses it. Network supervisors can designate which files, directories, and volumes are to be compressed. Disk mirroring protects data by automatically creating a duplicate image of it on another disk. If the first disk goes down, or its controller fails, the second is activated. Users would not even know a failure had occurred, but the supervisor would be notified. This redundancy is useful in real-time situations where downtime is unacceptable.

In a distributed network, security becomes even more important. NetWare now offers improved security and auditing features that can determine who can access network servers, resources, and objects. Users can be charged for network access on a variable rate scale.

Printer services are supported by PCONSOLE, with a Quick Setup option that eases printer configuration, print queues, and print servers. These are also defined to NDS to make them available system-wide for all users. A user in one office can easily send a print job to a printer in another office.

Internetwork packet exchange/sequenced packet exchange (IPX/SPX) is the protocol standard of Novell. It establishes a connection over the physical layer to the file server, using network drivers. At this point, a connection exists to the file server and the user can log in. In addition to IPX/SPX, NetWare supports TCP/IP and AppleTalk protocol routing.

Connections between devices on the network can be through Ethernet, Token Ring, and Arcnet. New versions of NetWare are optimized for WAN performance. Packet-burst technology enables devices to send data over communications lines without waiting for verification or acknowledgment, thus reducing remote traffic. Largest-packet negotiating lets both devices in a remote conversation use the largest packet size they can manage, further reducing transmissions. SAP Restrict cuts down on the advertising of services over the network between servers. NetWare link services protocol (NLSP) optimizes bandwidth usage, reducing overhead and providing enhanced management tools.

The Novell network requires the following:

- Server
  ~IBM or compatible 386 or better
  ~Minimum 8Mb RAM
  ~Hard disk big enough to accommodate all users and growth
  ~CD-ROM drive to install from (much easier, but not required)
  ~Network adapter
  ~Network backup device, such as tape
- Workstations
  ~IBM or compatible, or Macintosh
  ~Network adapter and drivers
  ~MS DOS 3.1 or better
  ~Optional NetWare Client for Windows (included with NetWare 4.1)
  ~UnixWare for UNIXOS/2 Standard Edition and NetWare Client for OS/2
  ~Macintosh System 6 or 7
  ~NetWare Client for Macintosh

14.6 Windows NT

Because Microsoft Windows has become such a popular operating system for PCs, its new NT version with network server capabilities is being used more frequently. NT is gaining market share at an impressive rate. This new version eliminates many of the problems inherent in Microsoft 3.x. It does not rely on DOS for file access, printer, or other services. It does not lock up with general protection faults (which is when Windows 3.x programs crash into each other's memory spaces). In short, it is a preemptive multitasker similar to OS/2. It manages concurrent jobs vying for processor attention in a civilized fashion. It is stable, robust, and full-featured. It can run on the workstation and the file server, providing one consistent operating system across the network. Workstations can also run Windows 3.1 in conjunction with NT on the server. NT allows users to access local and remote data seamlessly, without knowing how to navigate the network. It supports many useful desktop client/server development tools, such as PowerBuilder and SQL Server.

NT Server resources and data can be accessed from any client running Windows 3.x or better, MS-DOS, OS/2, UNIX, and Macintosh. One logon provides the authorized user with integrated access to the whole network. Many different types of hardware platforms are supported by NT, including IBM and compatibles 386 or better, MIPS, and Digital Alpha AXP. Open integration is provided for connecting to NetWare, UNIX, SNA, Macintosh, LAN Manager, and other networks.

NT supports multiple communications protocols such as IPX/SPX (Novell), TCP/IP, NetBEU, and others. WAN connections can be made through ISDN, X.25, and phone lines. TCP/IP support includes automatic addressing and name resolution of TCP/IP nodes.

Express Setup eases configuration chores while Plug-and-Play makes hardware upgrades and additions simple. Just plug in a peripheral and NT automatically configures it. It's about time the PC world caught up to the AS/400's `autoconfig` utility. Using CD-ROM for installation speeds and eases the process. Clients are configured using the configuration utilities. Upgrade utilities help migrate from Novell.

The Performance Monitor graphically represents system information. A dynamic chart on the desktop shows usage of server resources and databases to help manage system devices and identify bottlenecks. Network administrators can perform management tasks from any Windows client on the network, 3.x or better. Remote Access Service provides for remote network management.

The User Manager offers point-and-click access to configuring users. Security and rights can be easily set up, as well as access to distributed resources. Disk Administrator provides access to such network functions as usage information, partitioning volumes, and disk mirroring. Disk striping, mirroring, and RAID 5 support provide data redundancy for uninterrupted data access, even through disasters.

Windows NT has the advantage of being fully compatible with other Microsoft products such as Excel and Word, encouraging seamless integration of diverse or distributed network objects into the Windows desktop. Microsoft SNA Server integrates the Windows desktop and network with the AS/400 and IBM mainframes. Remote AS/400 and mainframe data can easily be brought into an Excel spreadsheet for further analysis.

Microsoft SQL Server can be used to provide the database functionality in a Windows NT network. Client/Server, developed with SQL Server, offers transaction processing and high performance and reliability. System Management Server centralizes network management for the diverse distributed network. Inventory, distribution, maintenance, and troubleshooting can be accomplished from one location using SMS. Microsoft Mail for PC Networks supports messaging across the network. Users can manage their own information-sharing requirements.

Windows NT requirements are the following:

- Server
  ~386 or higher PC (higher is much better) or RISC system
  ~16Mb RAM
  ~CD-ROM drive for installation
  ~90Mb disk space for operating system
  ~Network adapter
- Workstations
  ~386 or higher PC
  ~8Mb RAM for Windows 3.x
  ~16Mb RAM for NT350
  ~540Mb hard drive
  ~Network adapter

14.7 Summary

Networks connect individual users with other computers, servers, printers, devices, and services. They can be local area networks, where users in one location share files and resources or wide area networks, which connect users who are spread out geographically. Some networks are worldwide and consist of local area networks and single users connected over wide area networks. Many different types of hardware platforms, operating systems, and communications protocols can be connected in this diverse type of network. Increasingly, computers are being designed with openness in mind, to allow connections and services between diverse remote platforms. Computers and devices connected to a network need an interface card to enable them to plug into the cabling of the network and speak with other connected devices. This cabling can be coaxial, twinax, unshielded twisted pair, fiber optics, or telephone lines. The connection might not even be cable at all, such as in microwave and satellite link networks.

ISO offers the OSI protocol standard, consisting of seven layers of communications functions. Most prevalent communications protocols follow the OSI standard, such as IBM's SNA and TCP/IP. APPC and APPN are IBM's way of connecting computers as peers so they can talk together not as host and terminal or master and slave but as peers. APPN offers autoconfiguration, which is very helpful in setting up the sometimes complex configurations and parameters necessary to implement remote communications lines, controllers, and devices. Bridges, routers, and gateways form connections between network segments or different types of systems.

Token Ring and Ethernet are the two dominant protocol standards for setting up networks. Ethernet is becoming the more prevalent of the two. These protocols are generated by the interface cards used in the devices on the network. Devices that contain the same type of interface card can communicate with each other. Token Ring is the IBM offering. It uses a token passing scheme to avoid conflicts. One token is out on the ring at a time; all other devices wait their turn. With Ethernet, collision detection is used to recover from contention on the network. Token Ring is more reliable at very high traffic volumes. Ethernet is less expensive and probably faster at lower traffic levels. Both can use a star topology in which cables run from the devices to a central computer room, where they plug into MAUs or concentrators to connect them into a network.

Network file servers can run a variety of operating systems. Novell's NetWare is by far the most popular, with good reason. It offers excellent security and ease of management. Users can be presented with a monolithic network image instead of fragmented and distributed servers. One login can connect them to a logical collection of services which might reside on many different networks. Windows NT is becoming more popular as an integrated network and workstation operating system. This solution has the advantage of bringing the same technology to both the server and the desktop and of being integrated with so many of the popular desktop tools from Microsoft.

It is clear that a plethora of alternatives confronts the network designer. It is important to look at the big picture and to select an array of devices, cards, cabling, and operating systems compatible with each other and with the purposes of the network. Standardization is desirable in selecting PCs of the same type, with the same type of interface cards to reduce configuration complications. If the network is planned correctly, a whole range of client/server functions can be implemented seamlessly and effectively.

PC Client Applications

Now that we have the AS/400 and the PCs on a LAN with a file server, what do we do with them? Many applications exist for immediately implementing client/server functionality, while others allow the programmer to develop in-house custom solutions. Rumba and ShowCase VISTA both allow the user to start using data and services from the server immediately. Once Rumba is configured, the user has features such as terminal emulation and file transfer available without further ado. VISTA gives the user instant access to AS/400 databases through its GUI query designer. Other tools, such as PowerBuilder and Visual Basic, require system development, coding, testing, and implementation to provide the user with the requisite functionality. Rumba terminal emulation can even be invoked from within a Windows programming language, integrating the features of the two.

Wall Data's Rumba is one of the preeminent terminal emulation programs for the AS/400. Rumba also has some other features, including Shared Printers, but terminal emulation is how it is most often used. File Transfer allows files to go back and forth between the AS/400 and the client PC, which has its obvious uses in client/server systems. Hotspots allow the user to click on AS/400 screens to execute options, while macros enable commands to be recorded and replayed. Quick Step lets the user or programmer create custom pushbutton groups to place on the AS/400 screen for macro execution. This application is fairly close to running the

AS/400 like a Windows application. Cut and Paste permits areas of screens to be transferred into other applications, which is very handy for code excerpts and data examples between the AS/400 and the PC. Rumba Tools for APPC provide valuable interfaces to other Windows programming languages. Rumba for Database Access is a direct method of retrieving the data stored on the AS/400 from the Windows desktop.

If you want a quick and easy way to retrieve AS/400 data from the PC, ShowCase Vista is a good choice. Its query allows you to define and refine queries that run against the AS/400 data through the router. You can view the data within ShowCase Vista, or you can name Lotus or Excel as the data viewer. These options let you reformat and massage the data before presenting it. The Query Timer allows queries to be set up to run at predetermined intervals. This package is very popular with accountants who want to get up-to-the-minute information from the AS/400 but do not want to learn to navigate the machine's menus and commands.

The real client/server development tools for PCs are Visual Basic, PowerBuilder, Visual C++, and VRPG, which let the programmer design entire systems and programs to provide the user with point-and-click access to the AS/400. Whatever functions the user requires can be customized through these tools. If you want a screen to do input to an AS/400 database, with pop-up windows for edits, menus for database selection, and data saving mechanisms, or you want an inquiry into a product that has information stored in 15 different AS/400 databases, it's no problem with these tools. All these tools allow you to develop systems that present the user with a strictly Windows-like desktop, but that access the AS/400 behind the scenes. The user does not even need to know an AS/400 exists. You create the pipeline inside these programs.

Visual Basic from Microsoft is one of the most popular languages for developing client/server systems in Windows. It has project management for controlling the development of the application. The programmer places controls on the form to begin the design process. Some of these controls are capable of data access and are called bound controls. *Their properties are defined in such a way that a connection is made through an ODBC driver to the AS/400. The programmer can add menus and controls that execute the underlying Basic code. A debugger aids in locating problems. DDE and OLE can also be used within Visual Basic. Crystal Reports provides a reporting tool that can be used inside the Visual Basic program.*

The other prevalent desktop design tool for a Windows client/server is, of course, PowerBuilder. It comes in different versions, depending on the extent of the user's needs. Both desktop and enterprise versions are available. Because we are looking at AS/400 connectivity, we are interested in the enterprise version, which is more expensive. This version has two ways of connecting to the AS/400—ODBC and a native interface. PowerBuilder uses painters to create the various pieces of the application. The Window Painter allows controls to be placed on the desktop. Event-handling with PowerScript determines what happens in relation to these controls and user actions. The Query Painter lets the user define criteria for data access, limiting the scope of the data returned. This access uses embedded SQL, which can also be used explicitly in the code. DataWindows is one of the most popular features of PowerBuilder, probably accounting for its continuing popularity. It gives the programmer a fast, easy way to connect to the remote data from the AS/400.

PowerBuilder and Visual Basic are PC tools designed to access the AS/400 as a remote data server, but what about an IBM AS/400 tool? VRPG is just that. It has a host component that runs on the AS/400 and a PC component that runs under OS/2. These cooperate to provide RPG code on the client, which runs on the host. VRPG is perhaps the most direct method of accessing the AS/400 databases, consisting, as it does, of actual native RPG running on the AS/400. Its GUI Designer provides for easy placement of controls or parts on the application workspace. The Project Window controls the overall view of the development. You must define the server, after which the data on the AS/400 is available to the VRPG project on the PC as if it were right there on the `C:` *drive. There is even a utility for converting existing AS/400 displays in VRPG for the GUI look. This function is very nice for converting existing AS/400 functions to the PC GUI idiom. Action Links ties the parts to code fragments in the usual way for GUI design tools. Action Links is perhaps the tightest binding available between the PC and the AS/400.*

If you want to get closer to the bare metal, Visual C++ is the tool for you. In the tradition of the "C" language, it is a bit more involved and complex than the other tools described. It is also more powerful and flexible. Visual C++ uses the object-oriented programming paradigm, with its encapsulation of objects and polymorphism. It is a different way of thinking about program development. Basically, objects are derived from parent classes of objects, inheriting their characteristics

*and changing or adding more. The Visual Workbench is the
platform for system generation.*

    *Many excellent tools can be used to manage the numerous
objects involved in a Visual C++ application. The App Wizard
helps generate applications. Class Wizard aids in navigating
the thicket of classes and their derivations. App Studio
generates all the visual objects, including pushbuttons and
text boxes. Once these controls are placed on the desktop,
event-handling proceeds very much like it does in any other
visual design tool. OLE integration lets the developer place
objects in the application that are linked to external
programs. QuickWin facilitates the conversion of DOS
programs to rudimentary Visual C++ programs. This
environment is labor-intensive, but if you have the staff, some
of the most responsive performance is available from Visual
C++.*

    *Other client tools worthy of mention are included in the last
chapter of this section. I have described the most prevalent
ones. Oracle is an SQL-based relational database whose
transparent gateway for SQL/400 can make the AS/400
database a server for an Oracle-distributed database. Gupta
SQLWindows is a Windows programming tool for designing
client/server systems. Its QuickObjects helps paint the
application and link in code, written in SQLWindows
Application Language (SAL). LANSA presents AS/400 data
graphically on the PC through the Co-Operative Enabler.
SYNON is a CASE tool for application development that writes
the application code for you, in RPG or COBOL, and creates
the Windows interface, all automatically. VisualAge is an IBM
client/server development tool using the Smalltalk
programming language and a prototyping approach to
system development. PROGRESS/400 is a development tool
that connects to an impressive array of data servers,
including PROGRESS, Oracle, Sybase, OS/400, DB/2, and
ODBC. These tools are more high-end than the ones we
described in detail.*

    *The right tool for the job is the aphorism that covers most
project development, from plumbing to GUI programs: you
don't want to put in carpet tacks with a sledge hammer and
you don't want to use a tack hammer on a field post. The GUI
development tools we have looked at are all sufficient for most
projects. PowerBuilder and Visual Basic are both admirably
suited for light to medium tasks, such as looking up and
massaging data from the AS/400 on the PC. VRPG has the
advantage of being more native and integrated to the AS/400*

because it uses native RPG code on that platform. It requires OS/2 and has the added advantage of leveraging existing RPG skills into GUI development. Visual C++ is the most powerful and efficient language described, but also the most difficult to master. How important is speed in your application? The other tools mentioned, such as Oracle and LANSA, offer more industrial strength solutions, but at a considerably higher price. It should also be mentioned that less expensive and more popular tools like PowerBuilder and Visual Basic are becoming more efficient and capable with each release, along with new releases of the AS/400 operating system, which is continually optimized for client/server projects.

Chapter

15

Rumba

Rumba is a Windows application that enables terminal and printer emulation, file transfer, and a number of other PC Support operations from within the Windows environment. It connects between Windows or OS/2 on the PC to the AS/400 or mainframe. The terminal emulation session is integrated right into the window, and cut and paste is active for Rumba sessions. You can thus select a section of an AS/400 screen and paste it into another application, such as Microsoft Word or Lotus. This ability is very handy for documentation or for including AS/400 data in spreadsheets. Macros can be created to record AS/400 commands and assigned to pushbuttons within the session. The mouse can be used to navigate the AS/400 displays for those more comfortable with the Windows interface. Additional tools, such as Rumba Tools for APPC and Rumba for Database Access, provide additional development activities for PC Windows to remote data server access.

15.1 Terminal Emulation

The main feature of Rumba is probably its terminal emulation, which allows the AS/400 session to run in a window like any other Windows application. No special terminal is necessary to access the AS/400; the PC functions as both PC and AS/400 5250 terminal. You can switch between this window and other applications as well as cut and paste between them. The Rumba window is sizable and movable, similar to other application windows. The mouse is active in the Rumba window, performing various functions, described in the hotspots and macros sections.

The Windows Rumba session can communicate with the AS/400 via different communications interfaces, such as PC Support, gateways, etc. To choose an interface, you select it from the Options menu, Interface submenu. You then choose the appropriate interface from the list box and click OK. For example, if the interface is through PC Support (ClientAccess/400), select that from the list. This interface requires no further configuration. PC Support connects the PC and AS/400 together through the services of the PC Support router. This connection can work over SDLC, TWINAX, Ethernet, ASYNC, or Token Ring.

It might be desirable to autoconnect your session when opened to save a step when you start a session profile. The Rumba session is automatically started up with a terminal-emulation session active. To turn this feature on, select Autoconnect from the Session menu. Autoconnect starts a connection to the AS/400 through the communications interface in the session profile.

The Rumba menu bar can be shown at the top of the screen (the default), or it can be turned off. To toggle it on or off, click on the menu control box at the upper left of the screen and select Hide/Show Menu Bar.

The keyboard can be mapped to rearrange key assignments. Select Keyboard from the Options menu to get the Keyboard dialog box (Figure 15.1). The top is the PC computer keyboard, and the bottom is the special

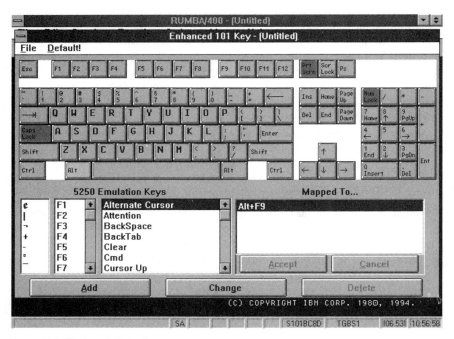

Figure 15.1 Keyboard dialog box.

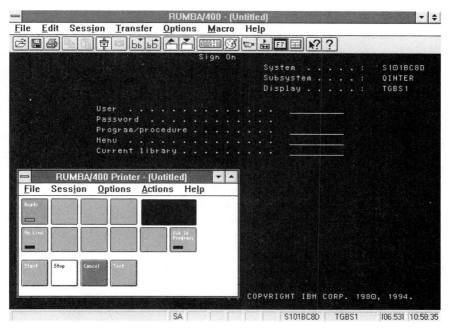

Figure 15.2 Both terminal emulation and printer sessions can be open at the same time.

additional keys found on 5250 (AS/400) keyboards. Click on one of these to see which PC key currently is mapped to that 5250 key, in the Mapped To text box. The assigned key on the keyboard at the top of the screen is also highlighted in green. Click on Add, Change, or Delete, depending on what you want to do to that key assignment. The Add button assigns the chosen 5250 key to an additional PC key. The Change button changes the highlighted PC key. The Delete button deletes the highlighted PC key assignment. After assigning keys, click the key combination on the keyboard at the top of the screen to assign them. Remember to click the Shift key first if the 5250 key is being assigned to a Shift-key combination. At this point, you can click Accept or Cancel. Save the keyboard mapping in a .MAP file. Default from the menu bar returns all keys to their default settings.

15.2 Printers

Rumba can emulate IBM's 3812 printer. Thus, a print job, initiated on the AS/400, can be routed to your local PC printer instead of to the usual AS/400 printer. Both terminal emulation and printer sessions can be open at the same time, in different windows (Figure 15.2). A Rumba printer emulation session is set up at the PC end, in Rumba. When the connection is made to the AS/400, the AS/400 sees the printer definition in Rumba as a local AS/400 printer and autoconfigures it. It then shows up on the AS/400 WRKWTR screen as just another AS/400 printer. When a print job is sent to that AS/400 printer, Rumba intercepts it and routes it over to the PC side for printing on the local printer. The job can even be directed to the PC network printer to which the PC has been spooled. This last option means that a PC networked printer can function simultaneously as a network printer and an AS/400 printer. It does not care where the data originated. All it knows is that a PC has routed a print job to it. The print job in this case originated on the AS/400 and was directed through Rumba to the network.

To configure a printer session, select File New from the Rumba menu and press the Open New 3812 printer session radio button. Then click OK. The printer session panel opens up (Figure 15.3). Choose Session Configuration from the Session menu on the printer session display. Use the drop-down box labeled System name to select the name of the AS/400 to which you want to connect this printer session. Enter a device name for the printer session in the Device Name box. This is the name by which the printer session will be known when configured on the AS/400. Choose a name in keeping with the printer naming convention on the AS/400 and one that does not conflict with an existing printer assignment (you cannot have two PRT01s,

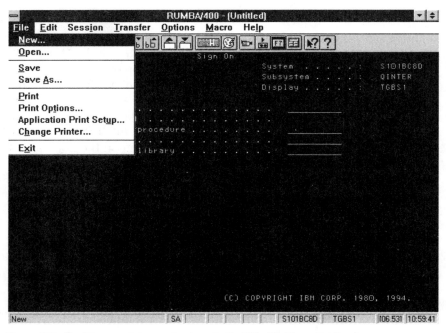

Figure 15.3 Configure a printer session by selecting File New from the Rumba menu.

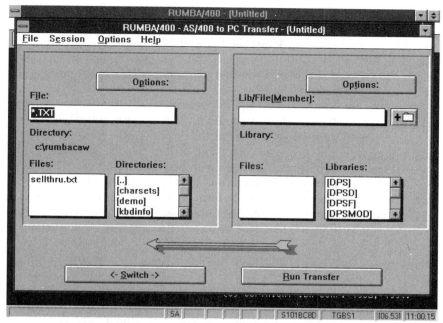

Figure 15.4   PC-to-AS/400 Transfer Window or AS/400-to-PC Transfer Window.

for example). Now, any print job sent to that printer on the AS/400 will be routed by this particular Rumba session to the appropriate PC printer, as long as the Rumba printer session has been started.

Parameters can be set for the PC printer by going to the File menu, selecting Change Printer, and then Setup. You can then select paper size, page orientation, fonts, and more. When the session is started and connected, the Ready light should be lit on the printer emulation panel, as well as the On Line light. This panel can be used to control the printer, just like the buttons on an AS/400 printer. Start, Stop, Cancel, and Test are all available. Autoconnect can be turned on from the Session menu here, just as with the terminal emulation session, to save a step.

15.3   File Transfer

The Transfer menu enables files to be transferred between the PC and the AS/400. You can Send a file to the AS/400 or Receive a file from the AS/400. These transfers can be accomplished from an AS/400 during a 5250 session. You can also pass through the AS/400 to a System/370 mainframe, so you can transfer mainframe files to and from the PC. For 5250 session file transfer, select Send or Receive from the Transfer menu. You see the PC-to-AS/400 Transfer Window or AS/400-to-PC Transfer Window (Figure 15.4).

To send a PC file to the AS/400, select the PC file you want to send and the host file you want it copied to. Use the drop-down boxes on the screen to select a PC file and an AS/400 library and file for the source and target files. Use the Options button to specify transfer options such as what type of file it is on the PC side and whether you want to create or replace a file or member on the AS/400 side.

To receive an AS/400 file on the PC, select the AS/400 file you want to send and the PC file you want it copied to. The Options button allows you to specify whether the file goes to a file, the display, or the printer on the PC end. If it goes to a file, you can select Join or Replace. On the AS/400 side, the Options button produces a screen with text boxes. You can fill in these boxes with criteria to select records and fields (rows and columns) for the download. These are put together to form an SQL statement that is passed to the AS/400 for servicing by the Database Manager (DB2/400). Be careful, however, because AS/400 files tend to be much larger than PC files and can easily fill up a disk drive. The Where clause of the Select statement is responsible for selecting which records are returned. Use the drop-down arrow button and the Ellipses button (...) to build the query syntax by selecting field names and operators from lists. Click the Run Transfer button to execute the file transfer.

For a 3270 file transfer, make sure that you have a mainframe connection active to the AS/400, then sign on to the AS/400. At the command line, type STREML3270 CTRLNAME where CTRLNAME is the controller name of the mainframe that the AS/400 knows about. Click the Configure menu item on the Transfer menu. Set up the file transfer. Select Send or Receive on the Transfer menu. To send a PC file to the mainframe, choose the PC file you want to send and the host file you want to receive it. To transfer a file from the mainframe to the PC, select the mainframe file you want to receive and the PC file you want to place it in. Click OK to execute the file transfer.

15.4 Hotspots

Hotspots are a way to execute AS/400 commands by clicking the right mouse button on specially designated screen areas or hotspot text. Rumba has default hotspot areas as well as the ability to designate user-defined hotspots and associated functions.

The AS/400 has special keys that function uniformly throughout the system, including the Enter key, Home, and the Function keys, such as F12 to cancel or F4 to prompt. Rumba allows the user to use hotspots to invoke these keys with their related procedures. Default hotspots need to be enabled by selecting Enable Hotspots from the Macro menu. The right mouse button is used by Rumba to execute functions or options shown on the screen. Double-click on a menu choice with the right mouse button to execute that menu choice. Also, clicking the right mouse button on More...

(when there is more information to scroll on a display), Function keys, or the Enter key executes those commands. Clicking the right button on the II (input inhibited) symbol on the status line is the same as pressing Enter. You can click the right mouse button on an option number shown above the display, hold down the button, and drag the option number into an input field (although this process is often more easily accomplished by simply typing the option number into the field).

In addition to the default hotspots, Rumba allows the user to set up user-defined hotspots with their own functions. The hotspot text and its related macro script must be defined. The macro must be defined first for Rumba to see it in the Macro script list box before the hotspot can be defined. Macro scripts are defined through Macro Record or the Macro Script Editor. Select Configure Hotspots from the Macro menu. Click on Add button. Rumba responds with the Hotspots Configuration dialog box (Figure 15.5). Enter the hotspot text without intervening spaces. Choose a macro script from the Macro Script list box. Click OK, which associates the macro with the hotspot text you entered. User hotspots must be enabled to use them. They are then run like any other macro by pressing the right mouse button on the hotspot screen location. Once defined, hotspots (.HSP) and macros (.MAC) can be copied for other users. Click on Show Hotspots on the Macro menu to highlight the hotspots on the screen.

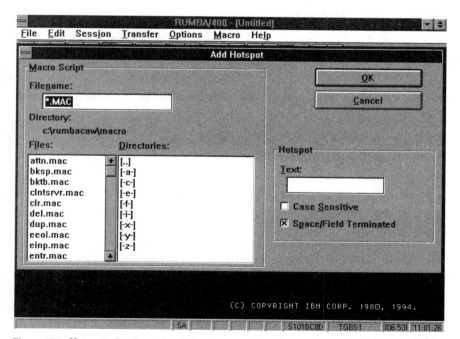

Figure 15.5 Hotspots Configuration dialog box.

15.5 Macros

A *macro* is a file that contains AS/400 commands and keystrokes. These can be recorded and executed as a unit rather than keying each command of the macro in every time. You can define a macro by using the Macro Editor to create a macro file, or you can turn on the Macro Recorder to record whatever keys you hit in a macro file. These two methods can be combined, so you can record keystrokes and then use the Macro Editor to edit the result. Macros are executed by assigning them to a QuickStep button. Click the button to execute the macro.

Select Record from the Macro menu to turn on the keystroke recorder for the macro. Perform whatever keystroke sequence you want to save as a macro. When finished entering keystrokes, select Record again from the macro menu. The Macro Script Editor appears. Enter a name (up to four letters) for the macro key name, with the file extension (.MAC). Enter a description for the key. Note the actual macro script commands that have been constructed by the recorder. You can place the cursor right into these commands and edit them.

To start the Macro Script Editor, choose Editor from the Macro menu and then choose an existing macro from the list box or type its name in the text box (.MAC). Note the choices available in the box to the right of the macro text. These items can be double-clicked to insert values into the macro script. They are the following:

- *Type* simulates the typing of characters in the script.
- *5250 key* simulates the pressing of special 5250 keys that you choose from a list, such as Enter.
- *Receive* waits for the appearance of a character at a specified screen location.
- *Prompt* gets input from the user for use in the macro.
- *Run* executes DOS commands on the PC end.
- *Label* inserts a label as the target of a Goto.
- *Goto* transfers macro flow to a label location.
- *Exit* terminates the macro.

To delete a line, select it and click Delete! on the menu bar. To move a line, highlight it by clicking it with the mouse. Place the mouse cursor between the two lines where you want to move the highlighted line. You will see a black bar, which shows where the insertion will occur. Click the left mouse button to move the text. To change an existing line, double-click it. Text can also be designated in the Type command as Hidden Field Text to send your password, for example.

Select Save to save the macro file and Exit to get back to the Rumba session. Go into QuickStep to assign the macro to a button.

15.6 QuickStep

QuickStep is a Rumba feature that places pushbuttons on the AS/400 screen. You can click these to run macros, just like any other Windows pushbutton. The difference with these is that the pushbutton runs AS/400 commands. You need to define the macro and then assign it to a pushbutton on a QuickStep pad (Figure 15.6). These QuickStep pads can be shown on the Macro menu. Click on one to open the terminal emulation window, further reducing the need for the end user to know AS/400 navigation techniques. Point and click can accomplish any task that has been recorded as a macro.

The QuickStep buttons show four-character labels, which are usually sufficient to describe what they do. The left mouse button runs the macro while the right mouse button displays the script (up to 32 characters) describing what the macro does.

Select QuickStep from the Macro menu to start it (Figure 15.7). From here, you can define and configure QuickStep pushbutton pads and list a QuickStep pad on the Macro menu. QuickStep pads can be configured with

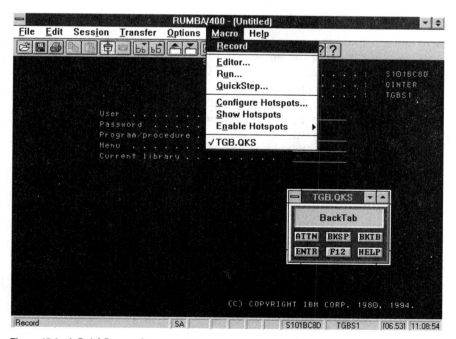

Figure 15.6 A QuickStep pad.

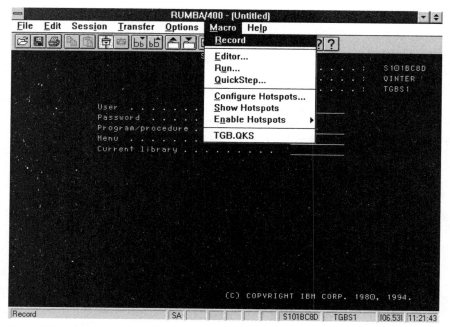

Figure 15.7 Select QuickStep from the Macro menu to start it.

6 to 48 buttons. In the lower left of the QuickStep Editor are two list boxes that contain values for the number of rows and columns. As you move the cursor around, you can see the actual QuickStep pad change in size and shape to reflect your choices.

Associating a macro with a QuickStep button is simple. Click on a macro from the macro list box, and it becomes highlighted. Then click on the QuickStep button you want to associate with this macro. The name of the macro appears on the QuickStep button. To delete a QuickStep macro key, select the QuickStep key with the mouse and press Delete. Colors can be changed by selecting an item from the QuickStep Colors list box and sliding the color controls at the lower right of the QuickStep Editor. Select Save from the File menu to save the QuickStep configuration. The QuickStep pad can be listed on the Macro menu by selecting List on Menu from the QuickStep Editor File menu. The QuickStep pad, once opened in the session, can be closed by double-clicking on the control menu box at the upper left of the pad.

15.7 Cut and Paste

Cut and Paste is a feature that allows the user to highlight a section of text in a Rumba terminal emulation screen (or any other cut-and-paste enabled application). This marked block can then be copied to the Windows system clipboard to be pasted into another application. In this way, sections of data or the results of a query on the AS/400 can be copied into other applications, such as a spreadsheet or word processor. This technique is called *cut and paste*, but it is much more commonly used as copy and paste. *Cut* means that the source text block is deleted as it is copied to the system clipboard. *Copy* means that a copy of the selected text is placed in the clipboard. A copy of the text is generally used because protected areas of the AS/400 screens cannot be cut.

You can use either the keyboard or the mouse to select the text to be copied, although the mouse is usually more adept at it. To use the keyboard, use the arrow keys to place the cursor at the upper left corner of the desired text. Press and hold the Shift key and use the arrow or PageDown/PageUp keys to move the cursor to the lower right corner of the text you want to copy, then release the Shift key. To select a section of the screen with the mouse, place the mouse pointer at the upper left corner of the text you want to copy. Hold down the left mouse button and move the mouse pointer to the lower right corner of the text you want to select. Both the keyboard and mouse method of selecting text draw a rectangle around the text so you can see what will be copied to the clipboard.

From the Edit menu, select Copy (or press Ctrl-Ins) to place a copy of the selected screen area on the clipboard, which also replaces any previous contents of the clipboard. Because we used Copy, the original text is unchanged on the AS/400 screen. Select Undo from the Edit menu to reverse the copy if no other operation has intervened.

The copied information is automatically parsed and can be imported or pasted into any Windows application that supports cut-and-paste operations. To change how this data is parsed, select Options from the Edit menu and select the type of parsing you want. Parse Data on Field Boundaries separates AS/400 data by fields when pasting it into a Windows application. If pasting AS/400 data into a spreadsheet, this command will place each AS/400 field into an individual spreadsheet cell. This capability is useful for pasting numbers or columns of numbers into a spreadsheet. The parsing option only applies to target applications that contain multiple fields, such as a spreadsheet. If you are pasting the data into an application with only one field or text area, such as a word processing application, the data cannot be parsed. The parsing option you choose is saved in the current session's profile.

The other side of cut and paste, after the data is placed into the clipboard, is pasting the data into the target application. To paste data, go to the location in the application where you want the data inserted. Select Paste from the Edit menu or press Shift-Ins to insert the data at the current cursor location. This procedure can be reversed with the Edit/Undo command if you make a mistake. The data is still in the Windows clipboard after a paste operation until you cut or copy something else to the clipboard. While the data is still there, it can be copied repeatedly into various applications. If there is too much data to paste it into one window, use Continue Paste from the Edit menu. If the data lines to be pasted are too long for the destination, Rumba asks you if you want to wrap the data around to the following line. If you do not, the data is truncated.

15.8   Rumba Tools for APPC

Rumba Tools for APPC is a programmer or developer utility that eases many of the problems in getting a direct connection between a PC application and an AS/400 database. Advanced program-to-program communications (APPC) is a feature of PC-to-AS/400 communications that offers the fastest method of accessing data across platforms. It is faster than ODBC, file transfer, or any other method. It is difficult, however, to write the required transaction programs (TP) and router APIs. Rumba Tools for APPC implements this type of communication through an easy, interactive interface that helps build TPs.

Using this communications scenario, programs must be written on both platforms that talk to each other through the use of APPC conversation verbs. The PC might have a Visual Basic application running in Windows, which communicates through Rumba APPC Tools dynamic link libraries (DLL) to the AS/400, which is running an RPG program. These two programs cooperate in tandem, providing a distributed functionality. The complexity of this arrangement, although eased by Rumba Tools for APPC, is more than that of an ODBC connection. The payoff, however, is in the response times and overall performance. Check the AS/400's QUSRTOOLS for APPC source programs that can be adapted to your purposes.

VerbTalk is a macro scripting utility that lets you work through menus to set up conversations between the PC and AS/400. VerbTalk presents lists of APPC verbs to choose from in building macros. It also prompts for parameters to complete the APPC conversation verb syntax. Communications verbs are invoked interactively, so you can see immediate results and correct errors. When you have your program right, you save the macro script for later execution, or even for inclusion into application programs. Sample programs for Visual Basic and Visual C++ help show how to implement these verb conversations. These scripts can be called from Visual Basic, Visual C++, or PowerBuilder using calls to DLLs provided with APPC Tools.

The Trace utility helps locate and fix problems anywhere in the complex flow of communications between the various platforms. The Configuration Utility helps define and save session configurations quickly. A FastPath feature can guide you through the required parameters. It is necessary to run Rumba's APPC Engine for Windows rather than the IBM version of Rumba to implement APPC Tools. The APPC Engine has all the APPC functions necessary to develop fully featured programs between the AS/400 and PC. It is a native Windows program, so it does not run as a terminate and stay resident (TSR) program, which eats up valuable DOS memory. It is also more fully featured than PC Support. It does not support twinax connections, shared folders, PC Support DOS, or Windows APIs. It does not come with APPC Tools, either, but you can purchase it separately.

Rumba also provides Tools for PowerBuilder and Visual Basic. These tools offer emulator high-level language application program interface (EHLLAPI) functions. They are a method for accessing the AS/400 from a program as if the program were an operator at a console. Functions first enable the program to establish a connection with the AS/400. The program can then sign on to and navigate the AS/400. Your program can look at the resulting AS/400 screens to see what is occurring. It can wait for the system to respond. It can issue any command-line OS/400 statements or CL commands, passing them parameters, just as if you were typing at a terminal. It can then sign off and terminate the connection. All these steps can happen visibly, in the Windows environment, or invisibly, hidden in a minimized icon. This method is one of the simpler ones to access the AS/400 from a PC program. The section on sample applications gives details of this method.

15.9   Rumba for Database Access

Rumba for Database Access is an end-user tool that enables PC programs to query and access AS/400 and IBM mainframe databases. It uses open database connectivity (ODBC), advanced program-to-program (APPC), and distributed relational database architecture (DRDA) technology to provide links between PC applications and host data. It is possible to set up a dynamic link between a PC spreadsheet and DB2- or SQL-based data servers on the host so that the spreadsheet automatically queries current host data and shows it in a color graph, for example. The server data is thus much more accessible to end users, while the computer maintains the processing power of other server databases and legacy systems. End users just point and click at fields and selections from server data to create queries and links to PC applications.

There are four editions of Rumba for Database Access:

- *Rumba for Database Access*: DRDA connectivity to mainframe and AS/400. DB2/MVS and SQL/DS are supported. ODBC connection to mainframe, AS/400, and LAN DBMS.

- *Rumba for Database Access (Administrator Edition)*: DRDA connectivity to mainframe and AS/400. DB2/MVS and SQL/DS are supported. ODBC connection to mainframe, AS/400, and LAN DBMS. With query packages to distribute to users and security features.

- *Rumba for Database Access (AS/400 Edition)*: DRDA connectivity to AS/400. ODBC connection to AS/400 and LAN DBMS.

- *Rumba for Database Access (Mainframe Edition)*: DRDA connectivity to mainframe. DB2/MVS and SQL/DS are supported. ODBC connection to mainframe and LAN DBMS.

These packages allow the user to point and click at remote server data for inclusion in PC applications and queries. PC platforms that can access these connections include the following:

- Microsoft Excel 4.0

- Lotus 1-2-3 4.0

- Visual Basic 3.0

- Crystal Reports

Rumba for Database Access has the following features:

- *Query Builder*: point and click at remote (DRDA) database fields and criteria to create queries.

- *Excel Macros*: packaged macros for instant Rumba for Database Access.

- *ODBC/DRDA Driver*: SQL connection to the server's SQL data engine.

- *Rumba for Database Access Guardian*: a run-time monitor for queries to control the queries and cancel them if necessary.

- *Rumba APPC Engine*: a router that replaces the PC Support router to enable all other Rumba features.

Rumba for Database Access can be given to end users to provide easy and efficient reporting tools on remote databases at the click of a mouse button.

15.10 Summary

Rumba offers several features that enable Windows access to the AS/400 session. Terminal and printer emulation in sizable, switchable, and movable windows are the most used elements. These bring AS/400 operations onto the Windows desktop. Rumba also offers hotspots, macros, and QuickStep to allow the user to use the mouse to click on screen locations and push-buttons in a session to execute streams of prerecorded AS/400 commands. Cut and paste implements the transfer of data or information between AS/400 sessions to other applications. File Transfer is a windowed interface for copying files to and from the AS/400, using an SQL query capability when downloading. Rumba Tools for APPC provides programmers direct access of AS/400 and other remote databases from the PC Windows platform. Rumba for Database Access is a PC query tool that offers point-and-click access to remote data. These features make Rumba a versatile and attractive choice for integrating the AS/400 quickly with the Windows environment. It is a powerful set of components for client/server connectivity and development.

16

ShowCase VISTA

ShowCase VISTA is a query tool and data viewer with capabilities for accessing the AS/400 remotely. With ShowCase VISTA, you can easily design queries using Windows GUI tools to report on AS/400 databases. Thus, end users can write their own queries into the AS/400 without knowing anything about the AS/400. Simply by using tool bars and menus and picking fields from lists, complex reports can be constructed. Using ShowCase VISTA is one of the fastest ways to realize a benefit from client/server computing with the AS/400. Development time is negligible, and results are virtually immediate. Programmers are not required to implement this package.

VISTA can also be used as a dynamic data exchange (DDE) link between Windows programs such as Excel or Lotus, providing live data links between spreadsheets and the AS/400 databases. It is possible to create a spreadsheet which, when retrieved, automatically displays a color graph showing the current state of AS/400 data. SQL statements are supported by ShowCase VISTA as a client request to the AS/400 server. When the AS/400 returns the data requested, it can be displayed on the screen, printed, or sent to a file for further use. The data access is one way. You can retrieve and view it from the AS/400, but you cannot update it. ShowCase VISTA also has a facility called Query Timer for storing queries and running them at a set time (such as at night, when resource contention is low).

ShowCase VISTA requires not only Windows, but also the AS/400 PC Support (now Client Access/400) router. This router must be started before ShowCase VISTA. It is then available for remote data access to the AS/400. It is not necessary to have a terminal emulation session up and running, only the router. The router is started with the STARTRTR command, assuming that PC Support is installed, or the Client Access connect icon.

16.1   The ToolBar and Menus

To start ShowCase VISTA, double-click on its icon in the Windows Program Manager desktop, opening the ShowCase VISTA main window (Figure 16.1). From here, you can access the various functions and features of the package. Note the presence of both a menu at the top of the window and a toolbar right under the menu. The functions can be reached via either of these, in keeping with Windows practices. You can follow the menu levels to the desired function or just click on its picture on the toolbar.

The Options menu choice allows you to set the type of menu interface you want to use. Basic provides a less extensive and simpler selection of options when designing queries. Advanced ensures that all options and dialog boxes are presented to the user when navigating the system. This type of interface option makes the navigation a bit more complex, but the choices are more flexible and complete.

ShowCase VISTA provides two distinct types of data servers for the user. ShowCase SQL is the fully functional AS/400 SQL language. It is flexible and can define result fields (as in Query/400) as well as complex selection criteria. AS/400 File Transfer server is a subset of the full SQL implementation. This server type is easier to use, especially for those users familiar with the AS/400 syntax. Each query can have either server defined. Once defined,

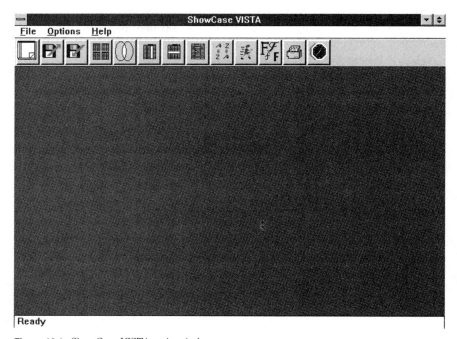

Figure 16.1 ShowCase VISTA main window.

the ShowCase VISTA system alters its displays and dialog boxes to accommodate the chosen server type. Do not change the server type once a query has been defined; it could corrupt the query because unsupported functions might get included from the other server type.

The ShowCase VISTA toolbar is used for fast and easy access to the more commonly used functions. To see a description of what each toolbar icon does, place the mouse pointer on the icon and hold down the left mouse button. A description appears in the status bar at the bottom of the window. If you do not want to execute that toolbar icon, move the mouse pointer off the icon before releasing the button. The toolbar contains the following choices:

- *File New*: create a new query.
- *File Open*: open an existing query for edit or execution.
- *File Save*: save the query.
- *Query Select*: select tables, views, or files.
- *Query Join*: join tables or files together for the query.
- *Query Select*: select columns or fields for the query.
- *Query Select*: select rows or records for the query.
- *Query Select*: select summary rows or records for the query.
- *Query Order*: order (sort) rows or records for the query.
- *Run*: run the query.
- *Format*: format fonts for the query.
- *Print*: print the query.
- *Timer*: set a time for the query to run.

If you do not want to use the toolbar, you can turn it off. Select Hide Tool Bar from the Options menu. It can be turned on again by selecting Show toolbar. ShowCase VISTA has a guided user interface to lead you through all the steps necessary to create a query. It brings up the screens or dialog boxes that require entries. This feature can be toggled on and off through the Options selection on the Preferences menu.

16.2 Defining a Query

To define a query (assuming that the guides user interface is not on), follow these steps:

1. Open an application file.
2. Select File New to create an empty window for the new application. The number of menu selections increases to accommodate the choices involved in defining a query (Figure 16.2).

3. Select AS/400 file(s) as the data source for the query. Read access is required for VISTA to query these files on the AS/400.

4. Select files from the Query menu to produce the Select files dialog box (Figure 16.3). In this dialog box, you type in values for the Library and File names you want to query. You can also use the down arrows next to the drop-down boxes provided to select from lists. If you know the names, however, it is much faster to type them in rather than select them from the lists. You can generally ignore the Member option on this screen.

5. ShowCase VISTA is now connected to an AS/400 database, ready for query criteria.

It is possible to join files together to devise reports from multiple sources. A customer header file containing a name and address can be joined to a transaction file to show details of each purchase. These two files would contain a field in common, probably the customer number, which can be used to link the two files together. Thus, files are joined on a common field. To accomplish this function, select Join from the Query menu to bring up the Join Files (or Tables) dialog box (Figure 16.4). Here, you can specify fields from each file, along with conditions or operators that relate them, such as

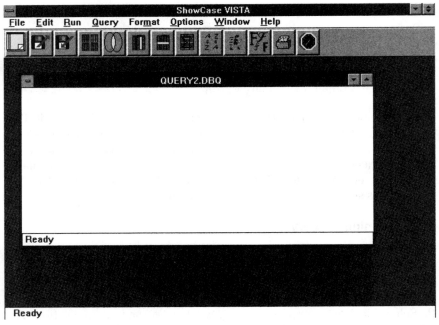

Figure 16.2 The number of menu selections increases to accommodate the choices involved in defining a query.

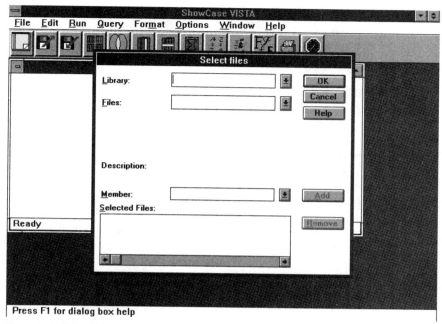

Figure 16.3 Select Files dialog box.

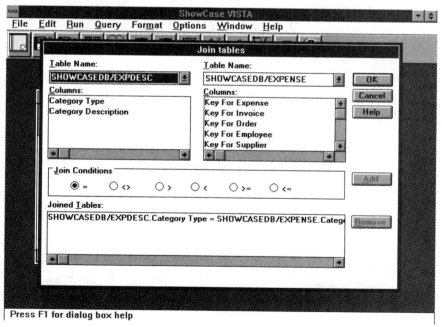

Figure 16.4 The Join Files dialog box.

`File1 Customer Number = File2 Customer Number`, which creates a relationship between the two files such that, when `File1` is positioned to a particular customer, `File2` is automatically positioned to the same customer. Now, fields from both joined files can be selected to create a query. Using the Files drop-down list boxes, select files to join. Using the Fields drop-down list boxes, select two fields that join the files. Select a comparison operator (=, >, etc.) from the Join Conditions box. (More than one field can be used to join files.) When finished with the join conditions, click Add to add the join specification to the Joined Files list box. Select OK to save these join specifications. This join relationship is now available for defining queries against the multiple files defined, along with all their fields.

Select fields to show on the query. These fields can be either the existing field or a summary level of the existing field. This way, you can get a summary for each unique field value. If there are 10 different records in the database for a given customer number, you get back only one record, summarizing the data for the customer number. Click on Select fields on the Query menu to produce the Select fields (columns) display (Figure 16.5). Enter the file you want to query. Fields from this file appear in the Fields list box. Select them in the order you want them to appear on the query results. To select fields, you click on the one you want to include. It becomes highlighted. Click on a button in the

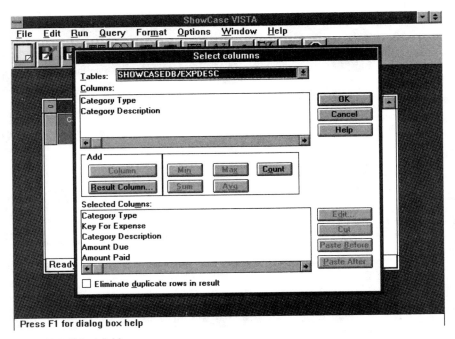

Figure 16.5 Select fields.

Add list box to indicate how you want the field included. You can show the field in detail by clicking on Field or in summary by clicking one of the summary buttons to the right. They appear in the Selected Fields list box. When all selections have been made, click OK.

You have now specified a database and the fields to be included for the query. It is necessary to provide criteria for selecting records (unless you want the whole database). Choose Select records (rows) from the Query menu to bring up the Select records (rows) dialog box (Figure 16.6). Here, you can select fields from the database you have selected and apply selection criteria to them. Use <All selected fields>, which is the default value for Files. Select a field from the Fields list box, a comparison operator from the Compare box, and enter an expression in the Expression text box to create a condition that can select records from the AS/400 database when it evaluates a given record to be true. All other records, which evaluate to false, will not be returned as query results. Note the And/Or pushbutton at the lower right of the Select records dialog box. This button allows you to create compound criteria for record selection like the following:

```
Year = 94 And Month Between 1 and 6
```

which provides only records for the first six months of 1994.

To sort (or order) the returned record set, select Order records from the Query menu. The Order records (rows) dialog box appears (Figure 16.7). Click on a field or fields in the Selected Fields list box. Use the Add buttons to specify Ascending or Descending sort order. The sort field entry appears in the Ordering list box at the bottom of the screen. Click OK.

Records can be selected by a specified summary field value. For instance, if you only want to see data where monthly subtotals are greater than $5,000, specify month as a group selection value by clicking on Select summary groups on the Query menu. The Select summary records dialog box appears. Click on a summary field value in the Fields box, choose a Compare operator, and enter a value. In this case we would say Sum (Amount) > 5000 (where Amount had been defined as a summary field breaking at the month level). Select Add. Click OK.

Save the file by selecting Close from the File menu. You are prompted whether you want to save the file. Click Yes. Enter a name for the file if it has not yet been named (if it is new). The default filename extension for a ShowCase VISTA query is .DBQ. In the Directories list box, select a directory for the query to be saved into. Click OK.

To run the query, open the application file. Make sure it is active by clicking on the window (Figure 16.8). Click the running figure on the toolbar. ShowCase VISTA connects to the AS/400, submits the query criteria, and receives a result set back. It then displays these results in the ShowCase VISTA viewer. Other viewers can be used, such as Excel or Lotus.

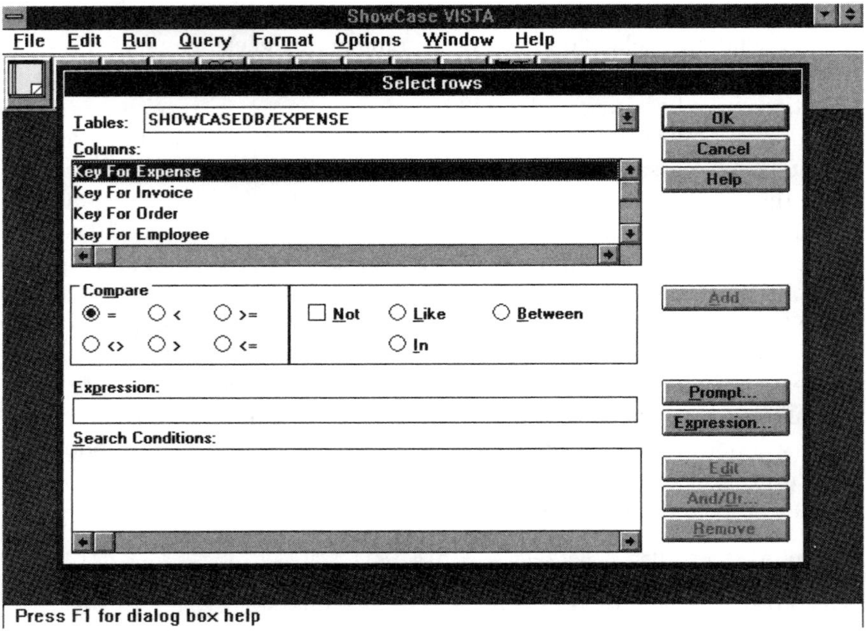

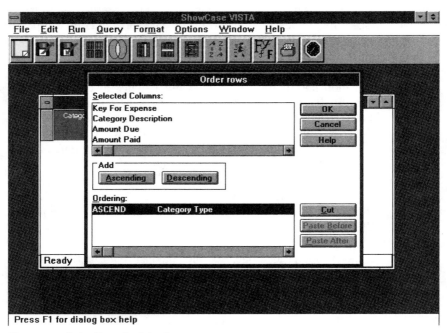

Figure 16.6 Select Records dialog box.

Figure 16.7 Order Records dialog box appears.

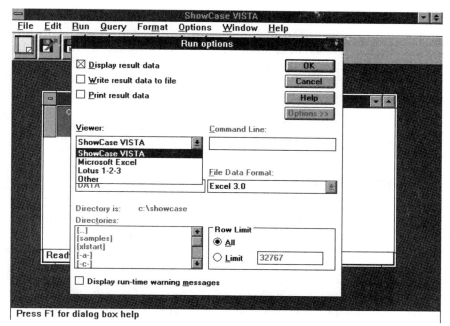

Figure 16.8   The Run options dialog box opens up.

16.3   Data Viewer (Lotus and Excel)

ShowCase VISTA has its own viewer built in for displaying data returned from the AS/400, which is usually sufficient for seeing the results of a query and printing it. If you want to format the data further, for presentation or analytical purposes, download it to a spreadsheet. One of the most powerful features of this package is its ability to use Lotus or Excel or even a word processor such as WordPerfect as the data viewer. ShowCase VISTA can run a query, retrieve data from the AS/400, and then start a Windows spreadsheet to receive the data. AS/400 data fields and records are automatically placed into spreadsheet columns and rows. It can be rearranged, and formulas and charts can be added as desired. This link between the server database functionality and the PC's high-level presentation functions is flexible and productive.

To select Lotus or Excel as the data viewer, choose Run options from the Run menu. Then click on the Options button. The Run options dialog box opens up. Make sure that the Display result data box is checked. Click on the down arrow attached to the Viewer list box to display a list of viewer choices. If your viewer of preference is in the current path, select it. If it is not in the path, select Other from the bottom of the list. Then, in the Command Line text box, enter a full path to the spreadsheet (for example, C:\MSOF

FICE\EXCEL\EXCEL.EXE). Use the File Date Format list box to select the correct file type for this spreadsheet to save the data into. In the Directories box, select a directory where you want the resulting spreadsheets to be saved. It is a good idea to check Row Limit and provide a numeric limit for the number of records returned by the AS/400. Remember that it is not unusual for the AS/400 to have hundreds of thousands or even millions of records in a database. You do not want to try downloading this to your PC or network spreadsheet. Row Limit provides a safeguard against that. Click OK to save your designation of data viewer along with the query definition.

16.4 Dynamic Data Exchange

ShowCase VISTA can be used as a pipeline to connect AS/400 data to other Windows applications. This feature is known as dynamic data exchange (DDE). The ShowCase VISTA SQL server is the intermediary between the other Windows applications and the AS/400 data. A connection is made between ShowCase VISTA and the AS/400 over the PC Support router. This connection can be used to return AS/400 data to ShowCase VISTA. Another connection is made between ShowCase VISTA and Microsoft Excel, for example, to funnel the data further. The features of Excel can then be used to format the data obtained by ShowCase VISTA from the AS/400. This facility provides a very flexible approach to presenting server data on the client.

This approach is more integrated than simply selecting Excel as the viewer for ShowCase VISTA. When a DDE link exists between another Windows application and ShowCase VISTA, the data is automatically pumped from the AS/400, through ShowCase VISTA, to the application program, whenever the application program is activated. You do not have to run VISTA explicitly. It runs in the background because of the DDE link. Also, any formatting done on the application program is saved, which is not true when you use the spreadsheet as a viewer from VISTA.

You can link to ShowCase VISTA two ways. First, you can create a paste link from ShowCase VISTA through the clipboard to the receiving application. Second, you can call ShowCase VISTA and run the application from a macro or program.

To create a paste link for ShowCase VISTA data into a Windows application, select the ShowCase VISTA data. Select Copy from the Edit menu. Activate the target application window (Excel or Lotus). Place the cursor where you want the pasted data to appear. Highlight a spreadsheet range for the data. Select Paste Link from the Edit menu. It appears in the active application window. Whenever this application is opened, it will retrieve this paste link data from ShowCase VISTA. Whatever is in VISTA will appear in Excel or Lotus.

The second method of using a macro or program is preferable for creating a DDE link between ShowCase VISTA and a Windows application. It is better because you do not need to know the extent of the range of the selected data for the paste operation. We will use Microsoft Excel as an example. When installing ShowCase VISTA, you can choose to add menu selections to Excel to enable this option, which allows Excel to adjust automatically to the size of the data being pasted from ShowCase VISTA. Also, the ShowCase VISTA application can be invoked from within Excel to refresh the data. These paste links are dynamic with the ShowCase VISTA query.

You can use these additional menu items to create dynamic paste links between ShowCase VISTA and a spreadsheet. Make sure that ShowCase VISTA viewer is selected. Select Query from the Excel Data menu. You see the Select Query dialog box. Choose a defined query as the source for this DDE paste link. Click on Add. Click OK. Select Paste Data Reference from the Excel Data menu. ShowCase VISTA is then started (if not already started). The Paste Query Reference dialog box is presented. Select columns and click on Allow Extend to ensure that the spreadsheet will extend the range to accommodate more data. Double-click in the Reference text box. Enter a range that is two consecutive cells in a column ($A$1:$A$2). Click on the Paste button. Select any additional columns you want to include in the spreadsheet. When finished, click OK, and you have a dynamic paste link between ShowCase VISTA and Excel.

To refresh the data in the spreadsheet, click on Refresh Query Data from the Excel Data menu. ShowCase VISTA then goes to the AS/400 for fresh data, reruns the query, and transfers the new data to the spreadsheet. If you have formulas in columns in the spreadsheet relating to imported columns from ShowCase VISTA, you need to specify that these are to be dynamically extended along with the imported data from the paste link by selecting Define Extendible Area from the Excel Data menu. Double-click on the Reference text box. Enter the spreadsheet column cells you want to extend along with the ShowCase VISTA data paste link. Click Add and OK when finished.

You now have a dynamic paste link between ShowCase VISTA and the Excel spreadsheet. The ShowCase VISTA query can be run from within the Excel spreadsheet to run the query, refresh the data from the AS/400, and import the results through the paste link. You can even show the results as a color graph if you want.

Follow a similar approach to include a dynamic paste link from ShowCase VISTA to Lotus 123.

16.5 Formatting

Once the data is returned to ShowCase VISTA by the AS/400, it can be formatted. The following formatting functions apply only to the ShowCase VISTA Data Viewer. If you are using another data viewer, you need to use its features to format the data.

You can provide more descriptive field headings, align them with the data, and make them bold and underlined. ShowCase VISTA uses the field headings defined on the AS/400 by default. To change them, select the field, select Heading Text from the Format menu, and enter the new text you want to use as the field heading. You can enter up to three lines of heading text. Click OK. To align headings, select Heading alignment from the Format menu. Click Left, Center, or Right to align the heading. Click OK. To change the heading fonts, select the field, and choose Heading font from the Format menu (Figure 16.9). You can choose from a list of Windows fonts, sizes, styles (regular, bold, italic, bold italic), effects (underline), and colors. Click OK.

The data in the fields can be formatted to display better. Select a field and choose Edit masks from the Format menu to produce the Edit masks dialog box (Figure 16.10) where you can select from a list of standard edit masks to show data with commas, dollar signs, and such. You can also use a custom format, described in the ShowCase VISTA manual.

Field widths can be adjusted and field fonts can be assigned to highlight important data. To set field width, select the field, choose Width from the Format menu, and type in the width. Click OK. To set fonts, select the field and choose Font from the Format menu. Select a font and size as well as effect and styles from the Font dialog box. Click OK.

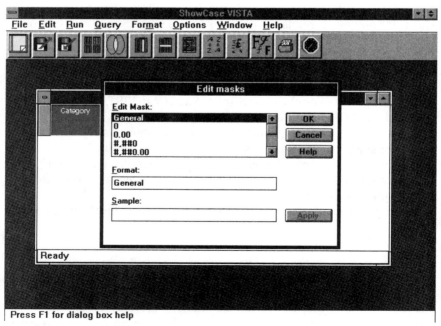

Figure 16.9 Edit masks dialog box.

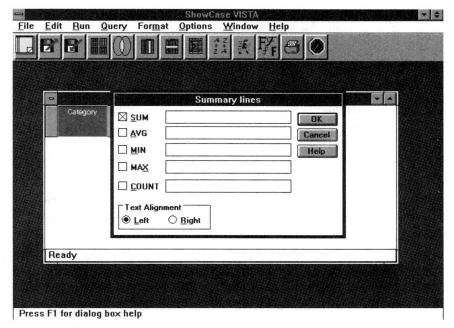

Figure 16.10 Summary lines dialog box.

Breaks can be inserted to show groupings of data, making it easier to view the data in subdivisions. Select the field you want to use to trigger the break. Choose Breaks from the Format menu and check off Break on this field. If you also want a page break at that point, check off Issue page eject after each break.

Totals and subtotals can also be inserted. Select the field you want to total. Select Summary lines from the Format menu to produce the Summary lines dialog box (Figure 16.10). Check off the types of summary you want to perform on this field (SUM, AVG, MIN, MAX, COUNT). Enter text to appear at that summary type. Click OK.

16.6 Printing

Results of queries can be printed either within ShowCase VISTA or by the data viewer you have chosen. To print within ShowCase VISTA Viewer, select Print from the File menu. The Print dialog box comes up (Figure 16.11). Make sure that the Windows default printer shown at the top of the dialog box is correct. You can print all the data or select a range to print by clicking on one of the buttons in the Print Range box. In addition, you can set print quality and number of copies. You can change the default printer

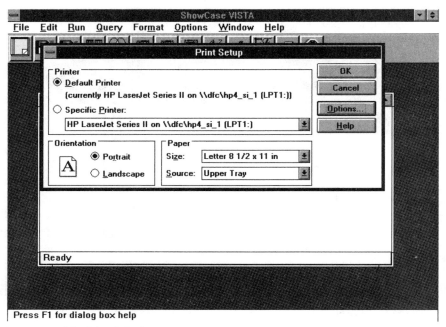

Figure 16.11 The Print dialog box comes up.

by clicking on Setup in the Print dialog box to bring up the Print Setup dialog box, where you can select any printer known to Windows.

If you want the results to print automatically, select Run options from the Run menu. Click on Print result data to check it off. Click on OK. Now, when you run the application, it will be sent to the default Windows printer.

If you want to print the results into a file, select Print from the File menu (assuming that the query has already been run using ShowCase VISTA's native data viewer). Check off the Print to File check box. Click OK. Enter the destination file into the Print To File dialog box. Click OK.

If you are using a data viewer other than ShowCase VISTA, such as Excel or Lotus, you can use the print functions of that application to send output to a printer or file.

16.7 Query Timer

ShowCase VISTA allows you to specify preset times to run a query automatically to avoid resource contention on the AS/400 if traffic is heavy. You can set a query to run at a specific date and time, or at a specified interval. You could have a query run in the middle of the night and print a report that is waiting on your desk in the morning. Click on the timer (clock icon) to get to the Timer setup dialog box (Figure 16.12). Here, you specify when the active ShowCase VISTA query is to be run. You can set it up to run at a certain date and time, a given time on a day of the week, or at a specified hourly, daily, weekly, or monthly interval. This dialog box shows currently set run times for the active ShowCase VISTA query. Set the run time you want to use. Choose Add. When finished setting up timers for the current query, click OK. Note that a query that contains a user prompt for row selection cannot be timed.

16.8 Charts

Charts can be created to display the data returned to ShowCase VISTA by the AS/400 in an attractive format. To create charts, you need to select one of the spreadsheet packages enabled for ShowCase VISTA as a data viewer function. When the data is displayed in that application, it is available for graphing. For instance, if Excel is used as the data viewer, you can create a chart with the data once it appears in the Excel spreadsheet. Create a chart by clicking on the Chart Wizard in Excel once the data has come in from ShowCase VISTA. Chart Wizard can guide you through the steps necessary to select a data range, a chart style, and chart format.

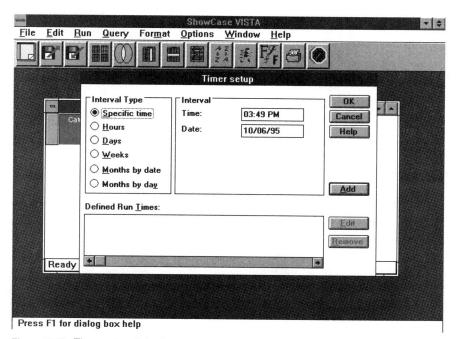

Figure 16.12 Timer setup dialog box.

16.9 Summary

ShowCase VISTA is a very useful and flexible tool for realizing a quick productivity boost in the client/server arena. It lets you design queries in Windows that run against the AS/400 database and return data to the PC. Data returned by the query can be formatted for appearance. The query can be timed to run automatically at preset intervals or times. The results can be printed from the built-in ShowCase VISTA data viewer or saved to a PC file. The data can be set to print automatically when run. The user can choose data viewers, such as ShowCase VISTA data viewer or Lotus or Excel, which allows further analysis and formatting. This option allows for the Accounting department to get an incisive analytical tool for reports and presentations. The server data becomes accessible to the end user, often without the intervention of the MIS department.

17

Visual Basic

Visual Basic makes Windows programming accessible to a wide range of programmers. The intricacies of managing the graphical user interface (GUI) are vastly simplified by the Visual Basic collection of utilities and tools. Creating windows for user interaction, once a daunting task, is now a matter of click and drag. This product is brought to us by Microsoft, the creators of DOS, Windows, and the BASIC language. It owns the Windows desktop and has now given us a tool for designing our own Windows applications. What was once a language used mostly by students learning programming has now become a state-of-the-art development platform for Windows.

Event-driven programming is the heart of the Visual Basic paradigm. The program responds to mouse events. The user clicks on something, and the system responds. Visual Basic provides easy tools for placing objects on the desktop and managing mouse actions regarding the objects. Generally, a visual object, called a control, has several possible valid actions. You might place a pushbutton, used as a control, in a window. You can select its properties from a list to set colors, fonts, visibility, and other parameters without writing code. Visual Basic handles these steps for you. You can select its designated action from a list to write a section of code specifying what happens if the user clicks on that pushbutton. Visual Basic associates the control with the event with the code and executes it when appropriate. These tasks, once extremely labor-intensive, are now quite simple. You only write the code that responds to mouse actions, not the code for Windows screen management.

Visual Basic comes in two editions, standard and professional. The standard edition contains most of what you need to create desktop systems. It has the following:

- *Visual Basic*: the actual compiler for creating Windows applications.
- *Help*: online manual to answer questions about the product.
- *Data Access*: drivers for access to common PC databases from within Visual Basic, including dBASE, FoxPro, Btrieve, and ODBC.
- *OLE*: object linking and embedding control to place an object from another application (such as a spreadsheet) within the Visual Basic application.
- *Icon Library*: an extensive group of icons for creating applications.
- *Sample Applications*: examples of Visual Basic code to be used in developing your applications.
- *Learning Visual Basic*: an online tutorial that guides you through creating a Visual Basic application.

The professional edition has all of the above, as well as the following:

- *Help Compiler*: to create Windows-like help facilities for your applications.
- *Custom Controls*: additional controls for use in Windows development.
- *Clipart*: bitmaps that can be incorporated into the application.
- *Control Development Kit*: a utility for creating your own controls.
- *Windows API Reference*: online reference for the actual routines that Windows uses to manage the desktop and environment.
- *Knowledge Base*: answers for frequently asked Visual Basic questions.
- *Visual Design Aid*: a description and guide for creating Windows standard interfaces.
- *Crystal Reports*: a utility for creating reports to run from within Visual Basic, or as a standalone report writer.

17.1 Projects

Visual Basic has a concept called the *project*, which associates all the resources and code constituting an application into one unit. Visual Basic maintains the project file for you when you work on the various pieces of an application. This file has a .MAK extension and is a listing of all the Visual Basic components of the application. A project contains forms (.FRM), controls (.VBX) and code modules (.BAS) attached to events for the controls.

You don't need to manage these project files; in fact, they are handled automatically by Visual Basic for you when you save a project or application. You do not want to touch them, but it helps to know about them to understand how Visual Basic works and how you work with it.

Forms are the basic concept of Visual Basic. They correspond to the idea of a window. A form is a window that contains controls, such as command buttons. These controls react to mouse actions (events) by executing code. More than one form can exist in an application; these applications are called *multiple-form applications*. Generally, there is a parent form and child forms activated from the parent in response to mouse events. The child forms are invisible until invoked. Visibility can be set along with many other properties by using the property window for a form or control.

As with any visual tool for Windows, Visual Basic is based on event-handling. The user is presented with a window or form that contains menus, controls, and text. Mouse actions relating to the controls on the form are captured and processed by pieces of code attached to the controls. Controls are the link between the form and the code. They consist of the command buttons, list boxes, and other Windows gadgets used to interact with the user. You place a control on a form and then write code to associate with an event for that particular control.

Code modules are the actual program code with which programmers are familiar from other programming environments. Here is where the logic of event-handling takes place. The visual objects are handled by the Visual Basic tools for placing and handling forms and controls on the desktop, along with their related properties. The logic of event-handling is found in the code modules attached to a control's events. The modules hold the variable declarations, subroutines, and all the traditional features of programming languages. Some code modules do not respond to mouse events; instead, they might be invoked as a form initialization or a subroutine call from another code module.

To open a new project, click on New Project from the File menu. You get a blank form for the new project and the Visual Basic design environment (Figure 17.1). This screen can be a little cluttered or confusing. You have the project window, the form window, the properties window associated with the form, and the controls toolbar used to place controls on the form. All these are superimposed on top of any existing Windows applications that were started before. All these windows are movable, and all but the toolbar are sizable. You can place them where you want on the desktop to make a more sensible working environment. Because it is easy to lose one window behind another (for example, the project window behind the form) it is a good idea to move the form to the middle of the screen and the others to the edges. Ensure that at least a corner of each window is visible at all times so you can click on it to bring it to the foreground and make it active. You also can activate a window by clicking on the Window menu item

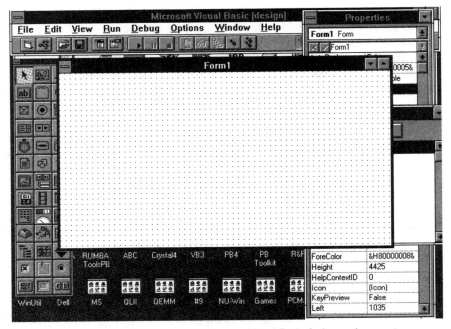

Figure 17.1 Blank form for the new project and the Visual Basic design environment.

at the top of the screen and selecting the name of the window you want to activate.

We have not yet assigned any controls or written any code, but we actually already have an executable form. Select the Run menu and then Start to execute the new form. You see it appear on the desktop. It is, of course, still blank and doesn't do anything, but look at how much Windows functionality has been provided simply by clicking on New Project. You have an executable window on the desktop which is sizable, movable, and switchable with other windows. Imagine writing the code to handle all of this in Windows—one pixel at a time!

17.2 Controls

Controls are the mechanisms used to execute code with the mouse. You place a control on the form by double-clicking on a control from the toolbar, such as a command button. It then appears on the form and is movable and sizable. It says *Command1* on it. Let's make this a Quit button. The properties window is now active for the command button. Note the little black boxes around the command button. They indicate that it is the active, or selected, control. They can be used to size the button by placing the cursor on top of them and dragging them. The properties window applies to the selected control. Go to the Properties window and click on Caption. The caption for the button appears in the text box near the top of the window. Type in "Quit" to change it. Then click on Name to change the name of the command button to something more meaningful than `Command1` when writing code. Type `Cmd_Quit`. Now you can use this name in your code to refer to this button. You can also set other properties such as font style, labels, and visibility using the properties window.

To add some code for the Quit button, place the mouse pointer over the Quit button and double-click, which opens the code window. Note that you see the object (control) you just created in the Object list box at the top of the window. This list box can be used to select the object that needs code. To the right of that is the Proc: list box. Click on the down arrow to the right of this list box to select an event for which you want to write code (the Quit button). Select Click. Note that Visual Basic creates a subroutine in the code window called `Sub Cmd_Quit_Click()`. You now have a subroutine associated with the mouse click event for the command button you just placed on the screen. Now just write code to handle the mouse click on the Quit button. The code is simply

```
Sub Cmd_Quit_Click ()
  End
End Sub
```

Visual Basic has provided the `Sub` and `End Sub` lines. We just insert `End` between them, and we have a functioning Quit button. Click on the right arrow icon from the toolbar at the top of the Visual Basic screen (under the menu bar) to run the form. Click the Quit button to see the code take effect and close the window. This procedure is the Visual Basic design paradigm in microcosm. Open a form, place controls, select events for the controls, and write code.

The standard controls in the Visual Basic Toolbox, in order of their appearance in the Toolbox from left to right and top to bottom, are the following:

- *Pointer*: to size or move a control after it's been placed on a form.

- *Picture Box*: display a graphic image on the form.

- *Label*: for informational text the user cannot change.

- *Text Box*: for user input.

- *Frame*: to draw a rectangle around a group of related controls.

- *Command Button*: a button the user can click to execute code.

- *Check Box*: a box for checking off choices. Click it to select (X) it.

- *Option Button*: buttons for choosing only one of multiple choices.

- *Combo Box*: combination text box and list box where the user can either enter text into the text box or choose text from a drop-down list.
- *List Box*: drop-down box to display and possibly scroll a list of items. The user can select one by clicking on it.
- *Horizontal Scroll Bar*: to scroll right and left through a number of choices.
- *Vertical Scroll Bar*: to scroll up and down through a list of items.
- *Timer*: invisible control to trap timer events.
- *Drive List Box*: to show list of disk drives.
- *Directory List Box*: to show list of directories.
- *File List Box*: to show list of files.
- *Shape*: to draw shapes like rectangles or circles on the form.
- *Line*: to draw lines on the form.
- *Image display*: graphic bitmap, icon, or metafile on the form.
- *Grid*: spreadsheet-like grid with columns and rows.
- *OLE Control*: object linking and embedding from an OLE server into the form.
- *Data Control*: to access database fields through bound controls on the form.
- *Common Dialog*: dialog boxes for common tasks.

This group of standard Visual Basic controls is usually sufficient to create simple desktop applications. More advanced controls are available with the professional edition, and third-party vendors provide enhanced functionality not found in either edition.

17.3   Data Access Using Bound Controls

Visual Basic offers a convenient method for accessing data contained in external databases, such as Microsoft Access, dBASE, or the AS/400's DB2 ODBC driver. The *data control* is a control from the Toolbox that creates a connection to a database without writing any code. Double-click on the data control (it looks like four arrows) to place it on the form. Now you can place other controls like text boxes on the form that are connected through their properties to the database named in the data control. These controls are called *bound controls* because they are bound or connected to the data control. The data control is the connecting link between the text box (the bound control), which shows the field on the Visual Basic form, and the database field. When the application is initiated, the data control opens the database to which it refers. It creates what is known in Visual Basic as a *Dynaset*, or dynamic record set. This data is accessible to other controls placed on the form. Five types of controls can be bound to a data control:

- Text box
- Label
- Image
- Check box
- Picture box

Because these controls can display and manipulate data from the data control, they are said to be *data aware*. Changes made to them are reflected in the Dynaset created by the data control and consequently in the connected database.

Visual Basic by default uses the Microsoft Access database as the local database. Open database connectivity (ODBC) is the default connection for remote databases. If connecting to a database other than Microsoft Access, you need to specify which one it is in the Connect property of the data control. To connect to an AS/400 file, you enter the ODBC driver information as configured in Appendix A, separated by a semicolon, in the Connect property of the data control:

```
Connect:            ODBC;DSN=MYDATA;UID=ME;PWD=XXX
```

In the RecordSource property, enter the path of the database:

```
DatabaseName:       MYLIB.MYFILE
```

You now have a connection to the database from within Visual Basic (see Chapter 23 for more details). Other controls, like text boxes, can be placed on the form to reference the database fields through the data control's Dynaset. Changes made to the text boxes are saved to the database fields when the record pointer is moved. Fields from the new record are automatically shown in the text boxes when the record pointer is moved in the database. You can place text boxes on the form to display fields from the database and accept input. Double-click on a text box in the Toolbox, and it appears on the form. Click on the properties window to make the form active (or press F4). Set properties as follows:

```
DataSource:         pcdata
DataField:          field1
```

Once you have specified the DataSource property for the bound control, the fields in the database become available to the properties window. You can type in the name of the DataField property or select it from a list.

To use a list, click the down arrow to the right of the `DataField` property to open a drop-down list of fields in the `DataSource`. Select one of these fields to specify the field for the bound control. Repeat this process to place all desired fields on the form.

You can set the Visible property of the bound control to False if you don't want to see it on the form. In this case, you would have to handle record movement through the database yourself by writing code attached to control events. You can leave the bound control there to use the arrow keys on it for navigating the database.

17.4 Menus

Most Windows programs contain menu bars at the top of the screen. The user is accustomed to this interface from other Windows programs. It ensures that the user can adapt quickly to the new application and it provides an intuitive method for navigating the features of the application. Menus can be created using the Menu Design window. With a form open, choose Menu Design from the Window menu to open the Menu Design window (Figure 17.2).

In the Caption text box, enter a name for the menu item. This name appears on the menu bar. If you want to put a separator bar in the menu, type a hyphen (-) in this text box.

Place an ampersand (&) before a letter for the user to execute a menu choice by pressing the Alt key and that letter. The letter after the & is underlined in the menu.

In the Name text box, enter a control name for the menu item. This control name can be used in code to manipulate the menu object. It does not affect the menu bar.

The following are the rest of the menu design items:

- *Index*: a text box in which you enter a number for the menu control's array position, not the screen position.

- *Short Cut*: a drop-down list box where you select a shortcut key for the menu item.

- *Window List*: a box you check if you want the menu to show a list of open child forms in an MDI application.

- *Help Context ID*: a text box in which you enter a number to be used in finding the relevant Help topic in the Help file.

- *Checked*: a check box used if you want a check mark to appear to the left of a menu item to show whether the option is toggled on or off.

- *Enabled*: a check box used to determine whether the menu item is active or inactive.

- *Visible*: a check box that determines whether the menu item appears on the menu.

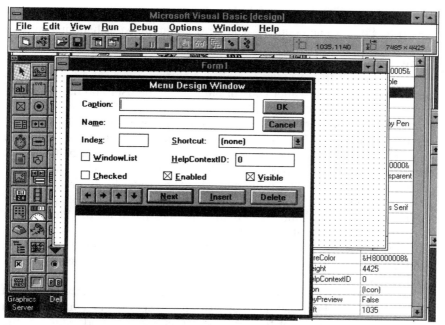

Figure 17.2 Menu Design window.

At the bottom of the Menu Design window is a list box that contains a tree view of the menu structure you are creating. Use the arrow keys to move around the menu levels. The left and right arrow keys change menu levels from a higher level to a lower level. It is possible to create up to four levels of submenus. The up and down arrow keys change the position of a menu item in its level. In the list box are menu items in a hierarchy or tree structure. Submenu items are indented. The Next button moves to the next line. The Insert button inserts a line before the current line. The Delete button deletes the current line. Click OK to close and save the menu.

The menu now appears at the top of the form. It cannot be executed in the form designer, but only when the application is run, either from within Visual Basic or when compiled. To attach code to menu items, double-click on the menu item to open the code window, just like attaching code to a pushbutton or other control. Select the event for the menu item (usually Click). Then write the code you want to respond to that menu item in the resulting subroutine (for example, Sub MyMenu_Click ()).

17.5 Coding Fundamentals

Visual Basic is derived from the BASIC language. It is a complete coding language coupled with visual design tools. After the controls are placed on the form using the Toolbox, code must be written for any events you want to respond to, i.e., for each control. The most common event-handling routine specifies what happens when the user clicks on a command button.

We will use an example that shows the use of a command button and a text box. We will design a form to look up a customer in a database. It is thus necessary to get a customer code or name from the user and find that customer in the database, moving to the correct record. This step can be accomplished by placing a command button called *Find* on the form. When the user clicks on the Find button, a text box, previously invisible, opens up next to the Find button. The user enters the customer code or name to look for in the text box, and presses Enter. The program recognizes whether the user entered a name or a numeric code. The Visual Basic program then finds that value in the appropriate database field.

The events we are handling here are the Click event for the Find button and the KeyPress event for the text box. Visual Basic monitors these actions or events automatically. All we have to do is attach some code to the appropriate events for the controls. When the selected event occurs, Visual Basic will execute its code segment.

Place a command button on the form by double-clicking on the command button in the Toolbox. Use the Properties list to set the label on the button to Find, and to rename it to Cmd_Find (it is easier to understand in the code than Command1). Double-click on the command button on the form to open a window for writing code for this control. Click the down arrow to the right of the Proc: text box to open up a drop-down list of possible events for this control. Visual Basic knows which events apply to which types of controls, so you always get the relevant list. Select the Click event from the list. Visual Basic creates an empty subroutine in the code window for the event you specified. The code for the Find button is very simple. It just makes the text box visible and then sets the focus to it:

```
Sub cmd_find_Click ()
  findtext.Visible = True
  findtext.SetFocus
End Sub
```

The text box is the control that gets input from the user and finds the correct record in the database. Place a text box on the form by double-clicking on the text box icon in the Toolbox. Using the Properties window, change the name of the text box to FindText. Double-click on the text box on the form to open its code window. Select the KeyPress event from the list of available events for this control. Visual Basic first creates a blank FindText_KeyPress subroutine, initializing the keyascii variable as required. Every time the user presses a key, Visual Basic executes this code, determining what to do next. If the user types in letters or numbers, the code for the KeyPress event does nothing except wait for the user to press the next key. In this routine, we are only interested in one key press, the Enter key. When that key is pressed, we take the contents of the text box and look it up in the CUSTOMER database. The program will be smart enough to look up the customer by name if a name is entered, or the customer number if a number is entered. We will use a Select Case structure, even though we are only looking for one possibility, just to demonstrate this structure. Although this code excerpt is not long, it demonstrates many different features of the Visual Basic language. Enter the code as follows (note that comments are inserted after an apostrophe):

```
Sub findtext_KeyPress (keyascii As Integer)  'begin subroutine

Select Case (keyascii)                        'top of case structure

  Case 13                                     'if Enter was pressed (13)
    n = Len(Trim(findtext.Text))              'how long is findtext?
    seekcust = Trim(UCase(findtext.Text))     'make it uppercase
    isnum = "True"                            'see if it is a number

    For textloop = 1 To n                     'for next loop tests for char
      If Not InStr("1234567890", Mid(seekcust, n, 1)) = 0 Then
        isnum = "False"
      End If
    Next
    If isnum = "False" Then                   'look up name or number
      Customer.Recordset.FindFirst "left$(num," & n & ") = '" & seekcust
        &"'"
    Else
        Customer.Recordset.FindFirst "left$(name," & n & ") = '" &
seek cust&"'"
    End If

    findtext.Text = ""                        'make textbox invisible again
    findtext.Visible = False                  'make textbox invisible again

    If Customer.Recordset.NoMatch Then        'error message if not found
      MsgBox ("Not Found...")
    End If

  Case Else

    '''
End Select                                    'end of Select Case

End Sub                                       'end of subroutine
```

String handling functions are plentiful in Visual Basic. Note the Len(), Trim(), Ucase, Instr(), Mid(), and Left$() functions that manipulate the string variables. Visual Basic is rich in functions. Consult the manuals for a listing of functions with descriptions and examples of usage.

Note the `Customer.Recordset.FindFirst` construct. Visual Basic uses this type of compound name often. It consists of an object name with property or function names concatenated to it using periods. This construct says to execute the `FindFirst` function on the recordset of the CUSTOMER database, looking up the value that follows it (in the double quotes). Assume that the user entered a name instead of a number. The value in the double quotes takes the left n characters out of the name field and compares them to the `SeekCust` value entered in the text box by the user. The ampersand is used to concatenate the variable called n as the second parameter in the left function. Note the use of double and single quotes in this line. If the user typed in "SMITH," this line would evaluate to:

```
Customer.Recordset.FindFirst "left$(name,5) = 'SMITH' "
```

Including or concatenating variable names into this type of syntax, within double quotes, can become complex, as you can see. Using this routine as an example, you should be able to construct others.

Another example of compound name usage is the line `Findtext.Visible = False`. This statement is very common in Visual Basic. It uses the period to connect a control name to a property and sets the property of the control from inside the code at run time, as opposed to using the property window at design time. Thus, controls can be managed dynamically at run time. They can appear and disappear; get and lose the focus; and change color, fonts, or other attributes as needed.

17.6 Debugging

Very few applications run correctly on the first attempt. Compiler errors can result from syntax errors. Typos and mismatched data types come under this category. Forgotten syntax elements, like a missing `End If`, also generate compiler errors. If the syntax is OK and the program compiles cleanly, there might still be run-time errors when the application executes, including dividing by zero or referencing a nonexistent file or one not in the path. Finally, even if the compile is fine and no run-time errors exist, flaws might still exist in the logic of the program. The program runs, but the results are incorrect.

To run the program once compiled, select Start from the Run menu. Visual Basic provides a useful debugger to aid in isolating bugs or errors. You can set breakpoints to stop the program at a given line of code to inspect variables and results. You can add a watch expression to watch its value change as the program progresses. You can single-step (F8) line-by-line or procedure-step (Shift + F8) through the program to test the effects of lines or sections of code.

Click on the Debug menu option at the top of the screen to set debug options such as breakpoints, single-step, and watch expressions. The Debug window allows you to test the program code and to see and change values. Select single-step from the Debug menu, then open the Debug window by selecting Debug from the Window menu (Figure 17.3).

The Debug window has a Watch pane, which is directly under the title bar. This area shows the contents of any watch expression you have defined. Below this is the Immediate pane for entering code you want to execute immediately. Type or paste a line of code and then press Enter to run it. Type `print` x to show the value of a variable called x.

Select Restart from the Run menu or press Shift + F5 to reset all variables and restart the program. To close the Debug window, double-click its Control menu (the little square at the upper left corner).

17.7 Dynamic Data Exchange

Dynamic data exchange (DDE) allows applications to share data directly between themselves. Each application must be DDE-capable. The client application requests data from the server application. The server application receives this request and satisfies it by returning a data stream. The client

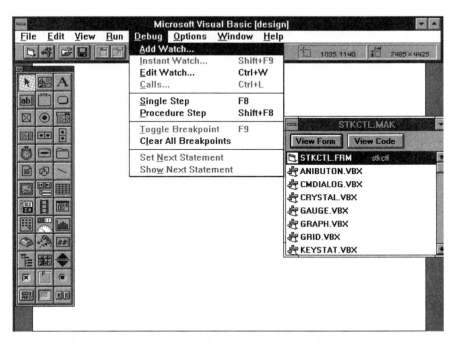

Figure 17.3 Open the Debug window by selecting Debug from the Window menu.

application receives this data back from the client and formats it for presentation. This exchange is cooperative processing between two or more (but usually two) Windows programs. Because Windows can switch tasks, it can accomplish the give and take necessary to achieve this effect. A DDE conversation is initiated, creating a link between the two applications. Data is transmitted back and forth, through the Windows environment, and the link is terminated. This procedure is the essence of DDE, and in fact, of client/server systems in general.

Visual Basic can be both the client or server in DDE exchanges. It can request and provide data links. A link is established in tiers, as follows:

- *Application*: the server application, accessed by name (e.g., Excel).

- *Topic*: the desired file for the server application.

- *Item*: the actual data, maybe a range of cells or a block of text.

These link parameters are specified to Visual Basic as properties of controls. The Application and Topic are included together in the `LinkTopic` property of the control, separated by the long bar character. The Item is specified in the `LinkItem` property. For instance, you might place a text box on the form named `Text1`. Set the link properties for the control as follows:

```
LinkTopic      "Excelsheet1"
LinkItem       "r1c1"
LinkMode       1
```

Possible `LinkMode` values are:

- 0 (None), which means no link is established.

- 1 (Automatic), which means an automatic link is established, and any changes to the server data are automatically reflected in the container (client).

- 2 (Manual), a manual link is established, and the program must get the data explicitly (with `LinkRequest`).

- 3 (Notify), the server notifies the container when the data is changed.

The text box displays the value contained in the Excel spreadsheet called Sheet1 (the default start-up worksheet name) at r1c1 (row 1, column 1). Excel must be active at the time the program is run to serve the DDE link request. It can be opened before the Visual Basic program is started or by a Shell statement in the `Form_Load` event of the form:

```
Dim excel As Integer
excel = Shell("c:\msoffice\excel\excel", 6)
```

This statement tells the form at run time to start Excel from its full path name. The 6 tells Windows to run Excel minimized and without the focus. But it is there, ready to supply DDE links.

17.8   Object Linking and Embedding

Object linking and embedding (OLE) is a technique whereby data from another application, or another application itself, is included on the form. The data can be completely formatted by the server application, unlike DDE, which merely passes the data. You could, for instance, run a Microsoft Excel spreadsheet graph in a window from a command button on the form. Objects from one application are thus embedded into another. Visual Basic has an OLE control in the Toolbox, which can be used to perform this function. Once placed on the form, the control acts as a link to another application. You can show the results of the latest changes to a spreadsheet right in the Visual Basic form if you wish. This client/server system is a form in which both the client and the server are Windows applications. The OLE control requests a data object from the server, which responds by supplying the object. Both applications in this scenario must be OLE-capable.

If data is linked, it is kept in the server application and only sent to the requesting client application on demand. If it is actually embedded, however, the data is kept in both places. Each one contains a physical copy of the embedded data. An OLE object is either linked or embedded, but cannot be both simultaneously. Linking is accomplished by means of a reference to the external object. Embedding is an actual copy of the external object.

OLE automation takes this one step further in that the client application can request that the server application perform an action on the returned object. In effect, the client runs the server application remotely, even though it might be on the same computer. The client application that contains the linked or embedded OLE object is called the *container application.*

Visual Basic gives you a control that enables OLE. This control is not one of the standard ones, but a custom control. If you did not install custom controls when installing Visual Basic, you need to put it on the Toolbox now. Select Add File from the File menu. Select MSOLE2.VBX from the list (it's in C:\WINDOWS\SYSTEM). Click OK.

The terminate and stay resident (TSR) program SHARE.EXE must be loaded for OLE to work. Add a line to your AUTOEXEC.BAT file that says:

```
C:\DOS\SHARE.EXE
```

This line automatically loads the SHARE program when you start your computer, enabling different applications to share the same data.

To place an OLE control on the form, we first need the object to embed. We can use an existing Excel spreadsheet (as an example) or create one on the form. Double-click on the OLE control in the Toolbox. This opens a window from which to select an OLE-capable application to be embedded on the form. Select Microsoft Excel from the list. Note the radio buttons on the upper left of the Insert Object window. Create New is the default; it lets you create a new worksheet. Click Create from File if you want to specify an existing Excel spreadsheet to embed in the form. If you select Create from File, a Browse button appears that you can use to find the spreadsheet for inclusion. Click the Browse button. Locate and select your spreadsheet from the resulting list box. Click OK.

You now have an Excel spreadsheet embedded in the Visual Basic form. Click the Run icon to see it in operation. The right mouse button can be used to bring up a pop-up menu allowing you to perform the following functions on the embedded OLE object in the design window:

- *Insert Object*: insert another object into the form.

- *Paste Special*: paste an OLE object from the clipboard into the form.

- *Delete Embedded Object*: delete the OLE object.

- *Edit*: edit the current OLE object in the container, using server application.

- *Open*: open the OLE object.

Edit and Open are also available by clicking the right mouse button on the OLE object at run time.

17.9 Crystal Reports

Visual Basic bundles an excellent report writer along with the rest of the application. Crystal Reports can be used as a standalone report writer, or it can be linked to Visual Basic programs to generate reports from the form. It is easy to design and format reports for the Visual Basic environment with Crystal Reports.

To start Crystal Reports, select Report Designer from the Window menu. Select New Report from the File menu. Select a database from the Choose Database File dialog box. Alternatively, you can click on the SQL Table button to select a database from external ODBC connections, such as the Client Access/400 ODBC driver for the AS/400. Click OK.

The Crystal Reports report editor appears (Figure 17.4). It contains Page Header, Details, and Page Footer sections on the report template. The Insert Database Field dialog box is superimposed on the Report Editor. Click on a field you want to include in the report and then click the Insert button. The mouse pointer becomes a rectangle representing the field you

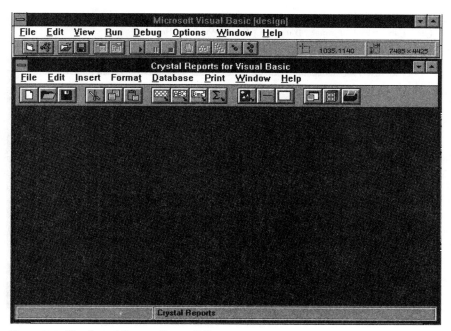

Figure 17.4 The Crystal Reports Report Editor appears.

selected. Place it in the Details section on the report where you want it and click again. The field is placed on the report. Note that the field brings its header as defined in its database along with it and places the header in the Header section of the report template. Continue in this manner until all the fields you want are placed on the report.

Select Text Field from the Insert menu and enter a title for the report. Click Accept and position the rectangular field pointer where you want it in the Page Header section. Note that you can insert a number of items from the Insert menu, including database fields; formulas; or calculated fields, date, page numbers, and graphics. Select Font from the Format menu to make the title large and bold.

You can drag fields around with the mouse by holding down the left mouse key on the field and moving the pointer. Change the width of the field by dragging the little black boxes or handles on the field when selected. To format a field or create a subtotal for it, click the right mouse button on the field. A pop-up menu shows formatting and total options (Figure 17.5). From here, you can change the font and print characteristics of the field. You can also change the format and alignment within the field. Select Insert Subtotal and define the subtotal criteria in the Subtotal dialog box when it appears. Select group break fields. Crystal Reports automatically

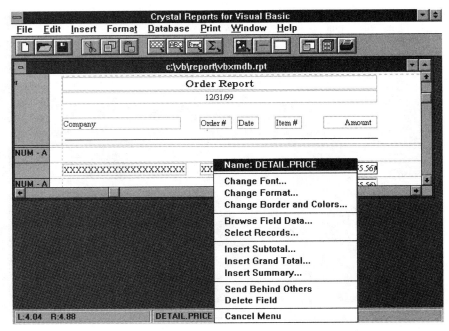

Figure 17.5   A pop-up menu shows formatting and total options.

sorts the database on the break fields. To insert a grand total, choose Insert Grand Total. To change the sort order, choose Record Sort Order from the print menu. To change group by field, select Group Section from the Edit menu.

Select Formula from the Insert menu to create calculated fields. Enter a name for the formula in the Insert Formula dialog box. Then enter the formula itself in the Formula Editor. You can select fields, operators, and functions by their list boxes. Click the Accept button to place the formula on the report. To select a subset of the records in the report, click the field(s) that you want to use as selection criteria. Click the right mouse button to get the pop-up menu for field definition. Click Select Records to get the dialog box (Figure 17.6). Define the record selection criteria using the drop-down list under the field name. Click OK.

Select Print To Window from the Print menu to preview what the report looks like. Select Print To Printer from the Print menu to print it.

17.10   Summary

Visual Basic is a powerful tool for developing Windows applications. It was adapted from the BASIC language for PCs by Microsoft to provide a much more accessible environment for Windows development than previously available. Most PC programmers would have little trouble adapting to this set of tools. It provides a set of prepackaged GUI visual toolbox controls including command buttons, drop-down lists, and text boxes. Just click on them in the Toolbox and they appear on the form, ready to use. Each control has a group of properties, such as font type and color, which can easily be set in the Properties window. You can even connect a text box to a database field through the use of bound controls and data controls. ODBC drivers enable data connection to remote databases, like DB2/400. This object-oriented visual toolbox greatly reduces the headaches and work inherent in maintaining a Windows environment. Once the controls are in place on the form, it is simple to choose relevant events for each one and attach a segment of code to them. The control is ready to be executed by the actions of the user and the mouse. The user clicks on one of the controls, and the attached code segment is executed. Event-handling made simple with visual tools is the core idea of the Visual Basic application development.

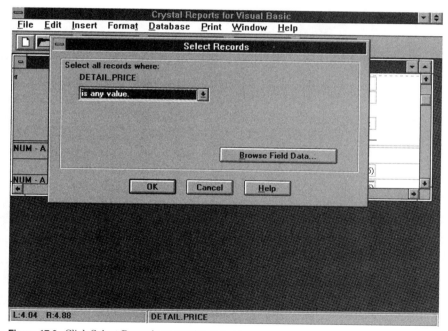

Figure 17.6 Click Select Records to get the dialog box.

18

Powerbuilder

PowerBuilder is one of the most useful and productive tools for developing client/server applications on the PC. It is used to create Windows systems with full functionality, including pushbuttons, list boxes, and menus. DataWindows are quickly built for data access, complete with scrolling and update features. A visual programming environment facilitates intuitive system creation using predesigned building blocks. PowerBuilder supports functions of the integrated desktop such as dynamic data exchange (DDE), object linking and embedding (OLE), and dynamic link libraries (DLL). Many of the features of object-oriented programming such as classes, inheritance, encapsulation, and polymorphism are incorporated into the PowerBuilder design paradigm. PowerBuilder offers connectivity to a multitude of platforms and remote databases. The client/server open development environment (CODE) is an open technology standard developed by Powersoft. Through CODE, interfaces are available between PowerBuilder and over 200 major products from other vendors, including database servers, network operating systems, CASE tools, connectivity tools, and application management tools.

Several methods of remote connection to the AS/400 are offered. The Client Access ODBC driver can be used, as well as native APPC interfaces like the third-party tool Easy Access. Client Access also has several APIs that can be used within PowerBuilder to access AS/400 data. The section on sample applications describes this ability.

18.1   Desktop and Enterprise Versions

PowerBuilder is a product from the Powersoft company, which offers the product in several configurations. PowerBuilder comes in two versions—the desktop version and the enterprise version. The desktop version has all the functionality of the enterprise version except for the extensive native connectivity to remote platforms and databases, as well as some of the more advanced deployment tools. Many connections are still possible, however, and the extreme difference in price makes the desktop version attractive for learning, as well as local database usage. Powersoft bundles the WATCOM SQL database with PowerBuilder, which is the easiest, although not the most popular, desktop database to access from PowerBuilder Desktop. Desktop PowerBuilder can be upgraded with the PowerBuilder Enhanced Database Kit and Application Library. PowerBuilder Desktop supports desktop ODBC drivers for:

- dBASE III, IV
- Btrieve 5.x, 6.x
- FoxPro 1.x, 2.x
- ASCII
- Microsoft Access
- Clipper Summer 87, 5.x
- Microsoft Excel
- NetWare SQL
- Paradox 3.x, 4.x

The enterprise version offers extensive additional remote database connectivity through API and remote ODBC. Native access is provided for many industry-standard databases, including the AS/400, for optimal performance. ODBC access is provided for many other databases, at a somewhat lower performance rating, although the Client Access ODBC driver provided with version 3, release 1 of OS/400 is much faster than before. The enterprise version is much more expensive than the desktop version because of this native database access, but it provides a tool to connect to the major databases and build industrial-strength applications. The Enterprise version connects to the following:

- ALLBASE/SQL ORACLE
- DB2 DEC Rdb (ODBC)
- DB2/400
- SQLBase
- DB2/2 (OS/2)

2

- SQL Server (Microsoft, Sybase)
- INFORMIX WATCOM SQL ODBC XDB

PowerViewer and PowerMaker are basically PowerBuilder's DataWindow Painter feature sold separately as a data viewer. They enable quick data views and reports for users but do not have the capability for designing entire applications.

18.2 Painters

PowerBuilder offers several types of painters or tools to accomplish the various tasks that constitute application development. These tools are GUI point-and-click facilities for designing the different parts of the system. Several types of painters allow the user to easily create databases, window types, reports, and whatever else is required. These painters are well integrated on the desktop; it is easy to move from one to another. The PowerBar at the top of the screen contains icons representing each painter (Figure 18.1). They include the following:

- *Application Painter*: define applications with global defaults and data sources.
- *Window Painter*: set up GUI windows and controls with event scripts.
- *Database Painter*: set up databases, tables, and views.
- *DataWindow Painter*: define a data access window with scrolling and update.
- *PowerScript Painter*: write executable code triggered by controls and events.
- *Menu Painter*: define pop-up menus attached to executable scripts.
- *Library Painter*: check objects in and out and organize the project.
- *Structure Painter*: define data structures to be used in event scripts.
- *Query Painter*: dialog to design SQL instructions for database access.

This collection of painters and other utilities can be accessed three ways. First, you can see them all on the PowerBar as small icons. These icons are quite small, however, and it is difficult for beginners to know what the utilities do without any text attached. Second, you can make the icons larger and see them with labels attached underneath. Unfortunately, they do not all fit across the screen this way. These two views can be toggled by placing the mouse pointer on the PowerBar, right-clicking, and turning on and off the Show Text in the pop-up menu by left-clicking on it. Third, you can choose the PowerPanel as opposed to the PowerBar to show the icons enlarged and

Figure 18.1   The Power Bar at the top of the screen contains icons representing each painter.

with labels in a floating, movable panel in the workspace, but this panel tends to get in the way. Place the mouse pointer on the PowerBar and right click. Turn off PowerBar by left clicking on it. If you have the PowerPanel up and want to change it to the PowerBar, left click on the box at the upper left-hand corner of the PowerPanel and choose PowerBar from the resulting pop-up menu. At first, it is probably desirable to view the icons with attached labels to understand what they do. It is quite easy to switch these views, depending on what you are doing and how you want to see them.

18.3   Event-Handling with PowerScript

PowerBuilder has its own built-in language for writing code that can be attached to controls and events. These typically small code segments are invoked in response to a user action, such as clicking on a pushbutton or menu selection. PowerScript is a BASIC-like language with hundreds of useful built-in functions as well as user-defined functions and external function calls. PowerBuilder does much of the work for you in the form of the available visual objects. Mostly, scripts are written to handle user events. The PowerBuilder design philosophy is object-oriented, which means that you can use predefined building blocks to assemble the system. It provides standard objects for dealing with the user interface, without the need for reprogramming. The objects can be modified by defining their attributes and writing event scripts for them. Much of the power of PowerBuilder applications is provided automatically by the built-in functions of the visual objects themselves, together with their defined attributes.

The PowerScript language is not difficult. It combines structured form with a rich set of event-handling functions and easily embedded SQL statements for data access. There is not room in this chapter for a complete description of PowerScript, but some of its salient features can be described to get a feeling for it and to get started. Examples are included throughout the chapter as they apply to specific instances. See the excellent PowerBuilder manuals and online help for full documentation. Generally, scripts are attached to controls—pushbuttons or menu options—to handle what the user might do. Scripts can test what a user has typed into a text box, which button has been clicked, and whether a control has focus or not. Consider the following for closing a window if the named control is clicked by the user:

```
If Control1.Clicked() Then
      Close(Parent)
End If
```

This block of code contains the familiar If/Then/End If construct. The named Control is associated with an event-handling function by the period (Control.Clicked()). If you had to program what the user was doing with the mouse by yourself without these event-handling functions to paint the pixels and locate the mouse, it would be much more difficult. A Close function is used to close the parent window and any subordinate windows and controls attached to it. All this functionality is accomplished with three easy lines of script. We would expect to see this type of structured code if coming from a third generation language (3GL) top-down programming environment such as RPG or COBOL or "C." All logic is handled by the program code in control blocks, such as IF and DO WHILE. The functionality of this small block of code, efficient as it is, however, can be invoked even more easily by attaching it directly to the control in question. Double-click on the control in the Window Painter (maybe a Quit pushbutton). A dialog window appears that allows you to set attributes for the control, as well as attach scripts to it. Choose the Clicked event of the control button from the Select Event drop-down list (Figure 18.2). Write the code:

```
Close(Parent)
```

How much simpler could this code be? It all can be accomplished from the command button's dialog box. The point here is that it is often unnecessary to write much code; just get into the appropriate painter and attach scripts to events for controls. This process is the essence of visual programming—scripts attached to events for controls.

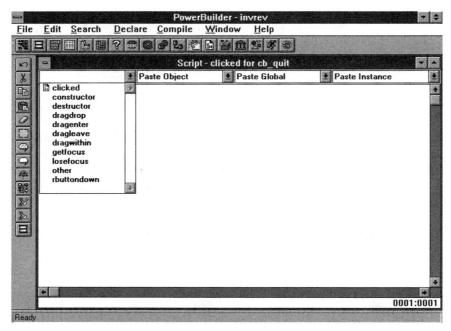

Figure 18.2 Select Event drop-down list.

Other controls and windows can be opened in scripts, and attributes of controls can be set in scripts. For instance, to disable pushbutton `Control2` when `Control1` is pressed, attach this code to `Control1`'s Clicked event:

```
Control2.Enabled = False
```

This syntax is standard for this type of visual programming. It is seen not only here but also in Visual Basic. A control or object name is concatenated with an attribute name for that object, using a period. Then a value is assigned to it. The visual object in question handles the rest; it is smart. It is an encapsulated object and only needs to be sent a simple message to know what to do. This behavior is also typical of visual programming. We send the appropriate message to an encapsulated object.

PowerBuilder supports the usual data types such as character, integer, decimal, long, Boolean, date, and string. Variables can be simultaneously declared and assigned as follows:

```
decimal x{2} = 4.25
string s = "Four and a quarter"
```

The first line declares x to be a variable of type decimal with two digits after the decimal point. It further assigns the value 4.25 to x. The second line defines variable s as a character string and assigns the value "Four and a quarter" to it.

Comments are inserted in the code with the double slash:

```
// This is a comment
```

Line continuation is done with the ampersand, &.

18.4 Query Painter

Query Painter is a GUI dialog for creating SQL SELECT statements to access local or remote databases. You do not need to know SQL syntax; just pick items from lists of options. It is much better to be conversant with SQL, however, to use PowerBuilder. These statements, once defined, can be saved with a name and reused for various purposes as a data source. The SQL statements actually return a subset of a specified database. Click the Query icon in the PowerBar to produce the Select Query window (Figure 18.3). Select one from the list or click New to create a new one. This action responds with the Select Tables window (Figure 18.4). Here, you can point and click to choose tables, fields, sort groups, calculated or computed fields, and other parameters of SQL statements. Click the Preview icon in

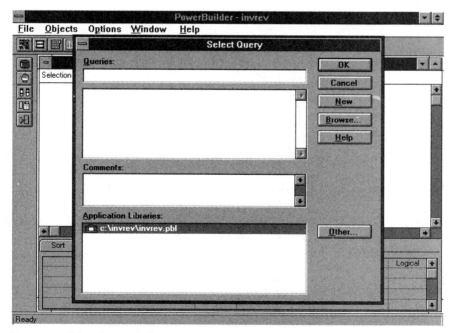

Figure 18.3 Select Query window.

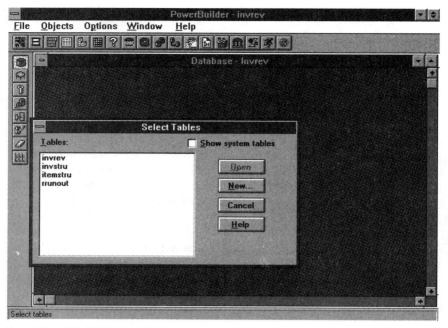

Figure 18.4 Select Tables window.

the Query Painter toolbar to see the results of the query just defined. Save the query by choosing Save Query from the File menu. Note that this process is very similar to that of defining an SQL Select data source for the DataWindow Painter.

18.5 Embedded SQL

SQL can be used within PowerScript code to create or process a subset of a database. This process is called *embedded SQL*. Following is an example that updates an entire database, giving a raise to just the MIS department.

```
decimal Increase{2} = 1.20
UPDATE EmpTable
    SET Salary = Salary * :Increase
    WHERE EmpTable.Dept = 'MIS';
```

The variable `Increase` is initialized with two decimal places to 1.20. Note the use of the colon before the variable name `:Increase` in the SQL syntax. The colon tells PowerBuilder that it is a host variable as opposed to a table column value (database field). Note also the required semicolon at the end of the SQL statement. See the SQL chapter for more on SQL syntax.

18.6   Sample Application

We can now develop a sample application. Many of the above features and more can be demonstrated while actually designing something, and this activity will give you the feel of working in the PowerBuilder visual object environment. Let's design an employee database, with department, name, date of birth, and salary. We will need the database or table itself, with data definitions and extended field attributes, including validation. We first need an application object and a window launched by it. This window should have some pushbuttons and menu options for Update, Print, and Quit. Then we will need a way to manipulate the data from within the window. We want the finished application to look like Figure 18.5.

Create the database

The Database Painter allows you to point and click to create tables, indexes, and views. You can define primary and foreign keys to relate tables. Security and referential integrity can be applied easily, as well as extended field attributes. A convenient feature is how the right mouse button is used to bring up lists of attributes to be defined for objects. Left click on the Database Painter icon in the PowerBar. Any database icon shown here can

ABC Inventory Review

Product	Jan	Feb	Mar	Apr	May	Jun	Jul	Aug	Sep	Oct
01119	2000	2046	1650	1800	1800	0	0	0	0	1100
01120	0	0	0	0	0	0	0	0	0	1
01129	9000	10032	7200	9000	9000	0	0	0	0	5235
01219	1100	1254	1254	0	0	0	0	0	0	869
01220	0	0	0	0	0	0	0	0	0	1
01229	4020	4008	4008	4000	4000	0	0	0	0	3562
01305	0	0	0	0	0	0	0	0	0	2
01306	0	0	0	0	0	0	0	0	0	4
01365	0	0	0	0	0	0	0	0	0	10
01403	0	0	0	0	0	0	0	0	0	
01404	0	0	0	0	0	0	0	0	0	
01519	360	5580	4185	1300	3500	3500	0	0	0	1230
01619	1215	3510	3375	1800	3500	3500	0	0	0	1564
01719	1080	1305	1080	1300	1500	1500	0	0	0	721
01819	950	1100	1000	1300	1700	1700	0	0	0	711
01919	0	1600	1600	1600	2000	2000	0	0	0	946
05119	2500	2508	2046	2400	2400	2400	0	0	0	1412
05129	10020	12504	12480	10750	10750	10750	0	0	0	7544
05219	2400	2046	2046	2000	2000	2000	0	0	0	1113

Update	DownLoad	Edit	SaveData	Print	Quit

Figure 18.5   Finished application.

be expanded by clicking the arrow in the upper right-hand corner, making it show a list of fields and keys. Right click and a pop-up menu appears to provide several choices for data definition (Figure 18.6). Select Definition from this menu and the Alter Table window opens up (Figure 18.7). This window is one of the better features of PowerBuilder. It allows extensive definition of tables with field attributes, validation parameters, and initialization values.

Click on the Database Painter in the PowerBar to start it up (Figure 18.8). Click on Cancel because we do not want to select an existing database from the list; we want to create a new one. From the File menu at the top of the screen, select Create Database. Input a full path to the database and the database name. Click OK. The database is created for you in the format of the DBMS you are connected to. (We are using the default WATCOM SQL database for simplicity. See the vendor manuals for connections to other data sources.)

Click on the Table icon from the Database Painter toolbar to display the Create Table window (Figure 18.9). Supply a name for the table in the upper left-hand corner of the window. Under Table is a blank space labeled Name, which is for the name of the first field or column in the table. Enter "Dept." Type of field, width, number of decimal places if applicable, and accept null value are to the right of the field name. We will let these remain

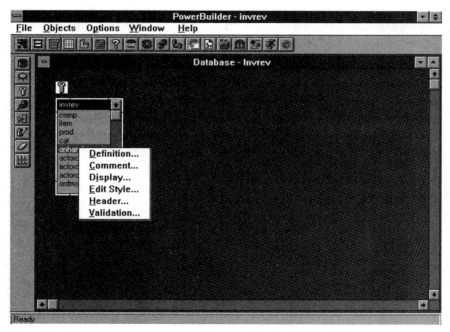

Figure 18.6 Pop-up menu appears to provide several choices for data definition.

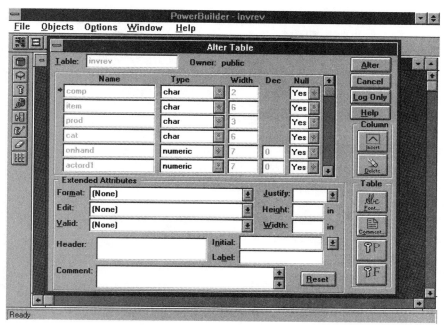

Figure 18.7 Alter Table window opens up.

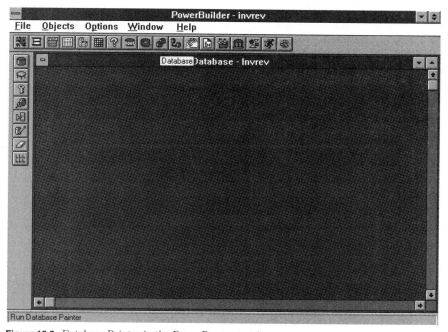

Figure 18.8 Database Painter in the PowerBar to start it up .

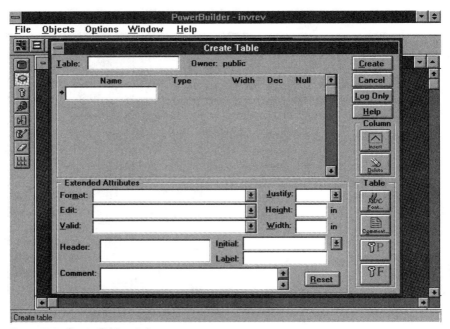

Figure 18.9   Create Table window.

the default values. Note that at the bottom of the screen several fields are used to define Extended Attributes such as format, valid, edit, header, etc. These can be used to define how the field will behave in all subsequent usages. This feature is very useful in that edits are defined once in the actual database and automatically applied by PowerBuilder after that. It encourages thinking out the data definitions at the beginning. The extended attributes can be changed later.

Press the down arrow or use the mouse to place the cursor in the next field name definition box. Enter "Name" and accept the defaults for the other values. Press the down arrow or use the mouse to next place the cursor in the next field name definition box. Enter "DOB" for date of birth. Tab to the Type field and press the scroll bar to select the "date" type. Now we can use some extended attributes. Using the mouse, place the cursor in the box at the bottom of the window that says Header and delete the default column header, which is "dob." Type in "Date of." Then press Ctrl-Enter to move to the second line of the header and type in "Birth." This two-line header can now be used by the system whenever a header is called for. Go to the "Label" box, delete "dob," and type in "Date of Birth:." This label will be shown to the left of the field when in an edit window. In the "Edit" box, click the down arrow scroll bar to select the "MM/DD/YY" format from the list.

Move the cursor up to the fourth box and enter "Salary." Tab to the Type field and select "numeric" as the data type. Enter "10" as the field width and 0 as the number of decimal places. In Extended Attributes, we can leave the default for the field header and label, but let's validate the input so that nothing under 10,000 can be entered. This rule will help avoid input typos. We first need to define a valid clause. Click "Create" to create the table and return to the Database Painter. Point to the table name and right click to open a pop-up menu from which you select "Definition." Press "New" to create a new validation rule, which can be applied to more than one field, if desired. Call the new rule goodsal and then define it. Note that many functions are available at the bottom of the screen. Our rule is fairly simple, so we will just type it.

```
@salary > 10000
```

The Input Validation window has syntax checking. If errors exist, it tells you. Go down to the Validation Error Message box and change the word "Item" to "Salary" to display the message "Salary 5,000 does not pass validation test" should the user enter 5,000. This validation rule can now be applied to the salary field. Press OK in the Column Validation screen. Right-click on the salary field in the expanded EmpTable database to open the pop-up window. Select Definition. Move the cursor to the salary field and then down to the Valid box. Select goodsal from the list of validation rules. Click Alter to change the table definition, and it is done. Field attributes can be changed at any time. Right-click to define a table's validation rules. Then right-click the field on the expanded database icon to add the validation rule to the extended field attributes.

We now need to add data to our new database. Open the Database Painter. Click on EmpTable on the list of tables to select it. Click on Open. You see the icon for the EmpTable database on the screen. From the Objects menu at the top of the screen, select Data Manipulation and then Tabular. You see the field headers, defined earlier. From the Data Manipulation toolbar, select Insert Row to place the cursor in the Dept field of the first record. Fill in values for several records. Try entering a value less than 10,000 for salary to see the validation rule and message. Click Updt Db on the Data Manipulation toolbar to save the entries to the database (they are not automatically saved). This procedure can be used at any time to make entries to a database. We now have a database, loaded with data.

Create an application

The Application Painter is control central for development. It defines defaults for the entire application, including global values, fonts, colors, and databases. It is the launcher for the initial window and performs any setup script (code) associated with it. The Application Navigator is a feature that lets you right-click on the application icon in the Application Painter to expand it into a tree view that contains the various components of the system being designed. These can also be expanded until the whole application is represented as labeled icons hanging from a graphical tree. Left-click on these objects to open their appropriate painters.

To create a new application, click the Application icon in the PowerBar to open the Application Painter. Select the File menu from the top of the screen and then New from the submenu. Give the application a name. Click Icon on the Application Painter toolbar to select a run icon for the application. Choose Emp.Ico and click OK. This step selects an icon to be used when the application is distributed, although you can select any icon available in your system.

The Application Script is code that executes to initialize the application when it is run. We need to add code to open the database for use. Click on Script on the Application Painter to open the Application Script window. Using the mouse, click on the scroll bar to the right of Select Event and select Open. We are defining a process to be executed when the application starts up. Type in the following code exactly:

```
SQLCA.DBMS=ProfileString("PB.INI","Database","DBMS"," ")
SQLCA.DbParm=ProfileString("PB.INI","Database","DbParm"," ")
//Open(w_emp)
```

PowerBuilder provides a default mechanism for accessing database information from within a window. It is called *SQLCA* (SQL communications area). This object is global. Its parameters are contained in PB.INI or APPL.INI. SQLCA handles transfer of all data from the database to the window and back to the database. The first line in the application script names this SQLCA as the data mechanism. The second line specifies parameters for it. The third line opens the main window for our application, which we can design next. Actually, PowerBuilder does not like undefined objects in the code. W_emp is such an object, so we will just comment it out (using the double slash // until we have this window defined). Later, we can uncomment it.

Create the window

Now we are ready to create a main window for the application through the Window Painter. Launch it by clicking on it in the PowerBar. Click the New button. You are now in the Window Painter (Figure 18.10). The gray rectangle in the painter is the sizable, blank form for the window we are about to create. Place the mouse pointer at the lower right corner of the window so that the cursor appears as a double-headed arrow. Press the left mouse button and, holding it down, drag the corner of the window down and to the right to enlarge the window.

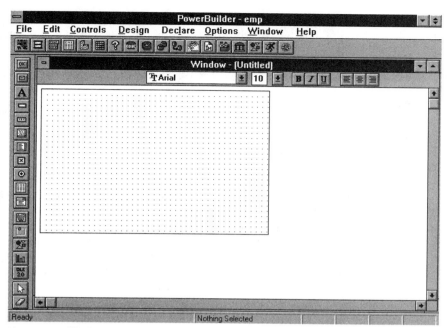

Figure 18.10 Window Painter.

Note the toolbar of controls at the left of the screen (this location is the default, and it can be moved). What we need to do is choose controls from the toolbar and place them on the window, then write PowerScript code for their events. We place buttons for New, Update, Print, and Quit to allow us to manage the employee database. Place controls into the window by clicking on the desired control in the toolbar, moving the cursor to where you want the control and then clicking one more time. The control appears at that spot. You can use Ctrl-T to duplicate controls that have been selected or repeat the process of placing them from the toolbar. Place four Command buttons into the window, along the top or the right, leaving room for the actual data window to be placed as well. Note that these buttons are also movable and sizable.

We select each button in turn and set its attributes and script. Use the text box at the upper left of the Window Painter to enter text you want to appear on the button. Right click on the Quit button to bring up a pop-up menu of attributes to be set for this control. Click on Name and change the name of the button to something more meaningful than the default cb_1 or whatever number it is. I suggest cb_quit. Note that here you can also set attributes, such as whether the button is visible and enabled. Click on Script to bring up the Script Window for the "Quit" control button (Figure 18.11). Click the scroll bar to the right of the Event text box to expand a list of suitable events for this control. Select Clicked. Write the script:

```
Close(Parent)
```

This statement closes the window that is the parent of this control, along with any of its other subordinate controls or windows. Click on Return (the bottom icon on the control toolbar), or on the box at the upper left of the script window and select Close. Answer Yes to save the script. You now have an operational command button in a window. It can be used to end the session. Because the other three controls on the window involve data manipulation, we wait until the data window is designed to implement their scripts. For now, set their names and texts by right-clicking on them. Give the window a title by right-clicking on a blank spot. Choose Title from the pop-up menu. Enter a title for the Title bar of the window we are designing—Employees. Click OK. Then choose File from the top menu bar and then Save. Name the window as w_emp. This name illustrates a good convention to follow; name main windows as w_xxx, data windows as d_xxx, and menu controls as m_xxx. When you develop a multitude of controls, this practice helps sort them out. We now have a main window and can add data to it. We

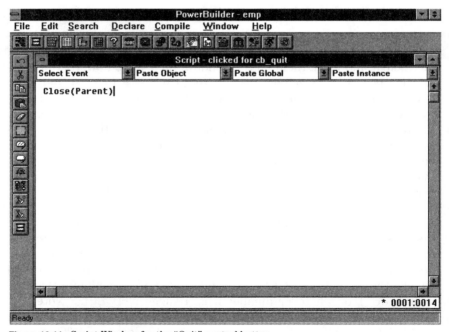

Figure 18.11 Script Window for the "Quit" control button.

can also remove the comment in the application script where we referenced w_emp.

Arrange data

The DataWindow Painter is a tool for manipulating data in a tabular format. As in a spreadsheet or database browse, data can be viewed, scrolled, panned, and updated in place. Dynamically changing group and final totals can be shown along with the data rows. DataWindow is smart enough to know how to access, format, and update data from a variety of sources through SQL. You do not have to code the SQL data access; it comes along for the ride with the DataWindow. Thus, once a DataWindow data source is defined, you can manipulate it quite easily. The DataWindow takes care of the behind-the-scenes transactions with each individually supported back-end database, whether it resides in the same directory on the PC or in a different location on the AS/400. A pop-up DataWindow automatically retrieves database fields and values without any programming or even knowledge of the particular database's access methods.

Click the DataWnd icon in the PowerBar to produce the Select Data Window dialog box (Figure 18.12). Because we have not yet defined it, click on New, opening the New Data Window display (Figure 18.13). Choose Quick Select for Data Source and Tabular for Presentation Style. Make sure the Preview-when-built option is not checked. We could set window colors by clicking Options but let's skip that for now, accepting the defaults. Click OK. When the Quick Select window comes up, select EmpTable from the list to produce a list of the fields from EmpTable. Click on Add All to take all the fields for the Data Window. Go down to the Sort label at the bottom of the window and click on Dept and then Name to sort the incoming data by these two fields. Select Ascending when prompted. Click OK to get into the Data Window designer or painter.

You now see the format for designing the Data Window. In this painter, you can toggle between Design and Preview to see what the data will look like and then return to designing the window. Try it. Press Preview at the left of the Data Window toolbar to see the data retrieved from EmpTable. Then click Design to return to formatting the data window.

To create group breaks in the Data Window, select the Rows menu at the top of the screen. Then click on Create Group. The Specify Group window opens (Figure 18.14). Where it says Group Item Expressions, click on the scroll bar to reveal a list of fields. Select Dept to identify this field as the one to break on. Click OK. You will notice when you get back to the Data Window Painter that header and trailer bands have been added to the format for the group just defined. They say *Header Group dept* and *Trailer Group dept*. You can drag these header and trailer bands with the mouse by placing the mouse cursor on them. When the mouse pointer becomes a double-headed

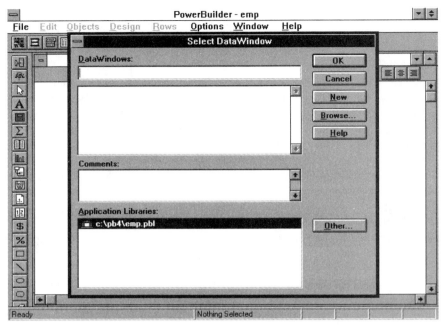

Figure 18.12 Select Data Window dialog box.

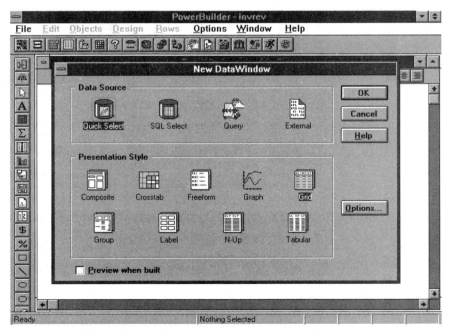

Figure 18.13 New Data Window display.

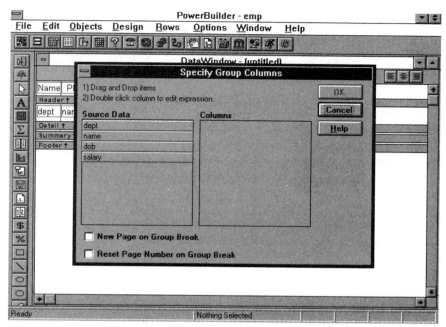

Figure 18.14 Specify Group window opens.

arrow, hold down the left mouse button and move the band to open the amount of space you want to appear between groups. In this space, you can type text or embed fields. To enter text, click the Text icon in the Data Window toolbar. Place the mouse cursor where you want the text to be, and click again. This puts a text box at that location. The text box can be sized by dragging the edges with the mouse. To edit the text in the text box, select the box and type the desired text into the edit box in the upper left of the Data Window Painter (not the text box). Key fields can be moved from the detail line to a header or trailer line so they only print on breaks.

To add calculated fields, or computed fields as PowerBuilder calls them, select the Objects menu at the top of the screen. From the drop-down menu select Computed Field. Click on the Data Window where you want the computed field to go to open the Computed Field Definition dialog box. Here, you can assign a name to the computed field. In the box below that, enter the definition for the computed field. Note that you can select lists of functions and database fields from list boxes to build the computed field. When finished with the definition, press OK and the computed field appears where you indicated. It is sizable and movable. The results of the computed field appear when you run or preview the Data Window. The definition appears in the computed field when in the Data Window Painter in Design mode.

To save the Data Window, choose File from the menu at the top of the screen. Click on Save from there. Enter the name as d_emp. The letter d identifies this object as a Data Window. Press OK and we have a Data Window that can be launched from the main window in the application.

DataWindow can be used to generate reports as well as interactive data manipulation windows. Because it provides facilities for grouping, summing, and calculated fields, it is well suited for the task of reporting. Graphs and pictures can be included. You just set up a DataWindow as usual. Then use the built-in Print() function as a script attached to a control, such as a print pushbutton or menu choice. This action sends the DataWindow to the printer, using the Windows printer drivers. The syntax is the following:

```
dw_name.Print()
```

Add a data window to the main window

We have now defined the main objects in a windowed application. We have the application object, the main window with controls, and the data window. We need to glue them together. First, we add the data window to the main window.

Open the Window Painter. Click Data Window in the painter bar (not in the PowerBar), then click into a blank spot in the workspace. A blank data window appears. Place the mouse cursor on the lower right corner of the blank data window so that the mouse cursor turns into a double-headed arrow. Drag the corner down and to the right to enlarge the window. When the window is larger, double-click in the blank data window control. The Select Data Window display opens. Select the data window we created for this application (d_emp). Set the Vscroll Bar on (click it) to give the data window a vertical scroll bar for moving through the data. Click OK.

We now have a data window associated with the main window, but we need to write a script to enable SQL I/O between them. This script goes in the open event for the main window, not in the data window because we want all the data to be loaded automatically when the main window is opened. Place the pointer over a blank spot in the main window and right-click. Click Script on the pop-up menu to place us into the script painter. Click on Select Event and choose Open from the list. We are now defining code for what happens when the main window is opened. Type in the following code:

```
connect;
d_emp.settransobject(SQLCA)
d_emp.retrieve()
```

The retrieve function is what actually loads the data into the data window. Click on the Return icon, or the box in the upper left-hand corner of the Script Painter and choose Close from the pop-up menu. The script to load the data into the main window's data window is now complete. While we are here, we can write scripts for the rest of the data window behavior—for the other three command buttons.

Right-click the command button that says New and choose Script. In Select Event select Clicked. Write the script:

```
d_emp.InsertRow(0)
```

Right-click the command button that says Delete and choose Script. In Select Event select Clicked. Write the script:

```
d_emp.DeleteRow(0)
```

Right-click the command button that says Update and choose Script. In Select Event select Clicked. Write the script:

```
if d_emp.update() = 1 then
    commit;
else
    rollback;
end if
```

Now save the main window by selecting File from the top menu bar and then Save. We are ready to run our program. Choose the Run icon from the PowerBar or the Run selection from the File menu. The main window opens with the data window in it. You can scroll the data, edit the data, add records, delete records, print a report, and quit. Press the Quit pushbutton to close it. Note how little code we have actually written and how much functionality is included.

Define menu bar

Most Windows applications have a top menu bar, which provides a standard look and feel. Users can navigate new applications with relative ease. They know where to look for desired functions and how to invoke them.

Click on Menu in the PowerBar to open the Menu Painter. Click New. In the next screen, type in File, which is the first menu choice on most Windows menus. Use the scroll bar labeled Menu Bar Items to get to the next blank and enter Edit, and do it again for Quit. We now have a standard Windows menu bar defined and need only add pop-up submenus. Actually, we will add a pop-up submenu only to File because this exercise is only a walk-through. Other menu options can be handled in a similar fashion. Using the Menu Bar Item scroll bar, you can move through the defined menu choices and add submenu choices in the boxes underneath, labeled Menu For:. Go over to File and add two submenu choices: Save and Exit. Click Design Preview from the PowerBar to see what the menu will look like. Click on File to see it expand into our two choices.

To add the scripts to the menu items, select Script from the menu painter bar, which will add code to these menu items. Select the Save item under File and then click on the Script icon in the Menu Painter toolbar. Select Event is Clicked. Type in the code

```
commit;
```

to save the current data window to the database. Click return on the toolbar. select the Exit submenu choice and click Script. Enter the code:

```
close(w_emp)
```

This line closes the main window when selected from the menu. Select File Save from the PowerBuilder menu and name the menu m_emp.

Now we can add the menu to the main window. Go to the Window Painter. Select w_emp. Select Design from the top menu, then select Window Style from that. Click the box that says Menu and select the menu you just designed from the list (m_emp). Click OK. That's it. The menu is attached to the window. Select Design Preview to see it. You can also run the application from the File menu's Run option, or click the Run icon in the PowerBar.

Create the .EXE file

We now have an application that can be run from within the PowerBuilder development environment. It can be compiled into a standalone application that runs off the Windows Program Manager desktop, like any other Windows application, by clicking an icon. Click on the Application Painter. From its toolbar select Create .EXE and give the application a name (or accept the default). You now have an executable Windows program that can be associated with a Windows icon. Select File New and then Program Item from the Windows Program Manager menu to make the association. A Deployment Kit (included in the enterprise edition) is available from PowerSoft to aid in the distribution of applications to users who do not have PowerBuilder.

18.7 Library Painter

This feature controls objects in shared-object libraries. Projects can be managed by using the check-in/check-out facility to determine who is working on what for development integrity. The open library API allows developers to import and export objects from third-party sources. This facility enables a controlled development environment when a number of people are working on a project at the same time.

18.8 Summary

PowerBuilder is one of the best development tools available for Windows. With it, you can select from predesigned visual objects to construct GUI applications. There is no need to handle all the nasty internal API intricacies of Windows graphical objects. PowerBuilder provides encapsulated objects that can be easily adapted to individual purposes with a minimum of code. Object orientation provides a wealth of dependable, pretested modules for system development. You use various painters to design windows and place controls such as pushbuttons or data windows in them. Place a menu bar at the top of the window for the standard Windows look, and then associate scripts and a rich function library with events for these controls. Bring them all together as an application, and create the executable file. It is hard to imagine working more easily or productively than this method.

Chapter

19

VRPG

Many client/server tools or application development packages offer the ability to design graphical user interface (GUI) systems that communicate with the AS/400, using a windowed front-end and an ODBC driver for data connection. Visual RPG (VRPG) Client/2 has the advantage of being specifically designed to work with the AS/400's main language, RPG. It runs on the PC in OS/2 and provides a GUI front-end for the AS/400 RPG back-end using an APPC connection, which is faster and more efficient than the prevalent ODBC method of connecting between Windows programs and the AS/400. It uses RPG as the AS/400 database processing language. The resulting system runs faster, using the native interface features of RPG to access the AS/400 database. Existing RPG programming skills in the MIS department are thus leveraged, adding PC GUI functionality to an existing skill set. Of course, a considerable learning curve exists for the conversion from straight RPG coding on the AS/400 to VRPG, but it is still less than going from RPG to one of the other GUI tools, such as Visual Basic.

VRPG Client/2 has several components. WorkFrame/2 is a development platform that allows the developer to organize projects and the components used in them. The GUI Designer consists of the Project Window and the Palette. These are used to design the PC GUI front-end of the system, with all the pushbuttons, list boxes, and other graphical interfaces for the user. LPEX is the editor used to write the actual RPG program code, using GUI editing features such as token highlighting and syntax checking. IPMD is the debugger that helps the developer isolate and fix problems with the system. It offers breakpoints, a variable monitor window, and run features to aid in debugging.

WorkFrame/2 is control central for the VRPG project. Components of the VRPG system are organized into projects, and these are organized into composite projects or applications.

19.1 GUI Designer

The GUI Designer is the tool used to place and configure the graphical objects that constitute the application and attach program code to them. It has a Project Window used for the placement of GUI objects like pushbuttons or list boxes. These graphical objects are called *window parts*. It also has a Parts Palette, which contains the actual GUI objects themselves. These can be placed in the Project Window. Place the cursor on a window part in the Parts Palette. Hold down the left mouse button. While holding it down, move the mouse pointer to the position in the Project Window where you want to place the window part. Release the left mouse button to drop it at that location. This process is called *drag and drop*.

19.2 Project Window

The Project Window has several parts. The Client Area, the Menu Bar, the Toolbar, and the Information Area all combine to provide a graphical tree (or icon) structured view of the project and its constituent parts.

The Client Area shows a tree or icon view of the project. The tree view shows a hierarchical branching of icons, which represent the windows and parts of windows in the project. The various windows and window parts that compose the project are shown here with their interrelationships. The objects seen in the Project Window bear a child-parent relationship to each other. A window part belongs to a parent window which, in turn, might be part of another window. The icon view shows only the parent window level of the project. All these dependencies or relationships can be seen in the Client Area of the Project Window.

The Menu Bar is a typical window-type menu that leads to all the functions of the system through various levels of pull-down submenus. Move the mouse pointer to one of the main choices on the Menu Bar, such as Project. Click the left mouse button. A drop-down menu appears, from which further choices can be made. In this way, all the features of the VRPG system can be reached. The main menu choices of the VRPG Menu Bar are the following:

- Project
- View
- Define
- Customize

- Windows

- Help

Pop-up menus are those that can be accessed by using the right mouse button, also called the *manipulation button*. These menus are generally used to define parts of windows. To define a pushbutton, place the cursor on the pushbutton and press the right mouse button. The pop-up menu appears. This step can be performed in the client area, the Parts Palette, or the Parts Catalog.

The Toolbar is a quick way to access common functions from the Menu Bar. Simply by clicking on one of the icons in the Toolbar, you execute that option. This saves you the trouble of stepping through the various levels of menus and submenus to access a given function. Saving a file is performed often and can be accomplished quickly by clicking on the Save icon in the Toolbar. When the mouse pointer is positioned over one of the icons in the Toolbar, the Information Area shows a short description of that icon. After a while, you recognize the icons in the Toolbar, but this feature is helpful, especially in the beginning. The position of the Toolbar can be changed using the View menu.

The Information Area is at the bottom of the Project Window, although it can be moved. It shows a short description of icons and objects that happen to be under the mouse pointer. Move the mouse pointer to a Toolbar icon or Parts Palette icon, and a brief description of it appears in the Information Area.

19.3 Creating the Project

Let us walk through the steps for creating an entire VRPG application. Click on the VRPG Client/2 folder to open it. Click on the VRPG GUI Designer icon. A window opens for the application. Enter a name for the application and select New. Select a folder in which to create the application from the Open Folders list box. Enter a file name for the project files in the Source file field or accept the default provided by VRPG (the first eight characters of the application name you input). VRPG will create several files with the name you supplied and various extensions for managing the application development. In the Source directory field, enter the name of the directory where you want VRPG to create and store all the files that constitute the project or application. It defaults to the same name as what you put in the application name field, but you can change it. Click OK.

VRPG creates a composite project folder in the folder you named above. This project folder has the same name as the application. A relationship now exists between the new folder on the desktop and all the files that VRPG has created in the directory you specified. VRPG creates a subdirectory of your application directory. This subdirectory is named RT_OS2. It contains objects compiled by VRPG for your application. You are now ready to design the actual application.

To work on an existing project, drag the project component icon in the VRPG Client/2 folder over to, and drop it on, the VRPG GUI Designer icon. VRPG opens up the Project window.

VRPG allows for composite projects to contain other projects, as an application might. To add a new component to the project, select New component from the VRPG Client/2 Application window. Enter a name for the component in the Component field. Select one of the composite projects from the Open composite projects list box. Click OK.

VRPG does much of the work for you, creating and naming files, folders, objects, and directories, and it makes certain assumptions about these. It is not a good idea to fool around with any of these files. Do not rename them, delete them, or edit them in any way except using those methods provided through VRPG and the WorkFrame/2 environment.

19.4   Parts Palette and Catalog

The Parts Palette is a group of objects or parts of windows that you can choose and place in the client area of the project window. These parts are used to create the various GUI interfaces of the application like pushbuttons, text boxes, and list boxes. You just drag and drop parts from the Palette to the project window. You can then write code for what happens when the user interacts with these parts, clicking the mouse or entering text or whatever. This process is called *event-handling*—specifying what happens in a GUI application when the user invokes a certain action.

The Parts Palette contains these components:

- Audio
- Menu item
- Check box
- Message subfile
- Combination box
- Multiline edit
- DDE client
- Radio button
- Entry field
- Slider
- Graphic pushbutton
- Spin button

- Group box
- Static text
- Image
- Subfile
- List box
- Submenu
- Media panel
- Timer
- Menu bar
- Window

Most of these components correspond to the Visual Basic concept of controls, such as the Graphic pushbutton and the List box. Others are peculiar to the RPG setting, like the Subfiles. Full descriptions of these components and their functions and usages can be found in the IBM Parts Reference manual.

The contents of the Parts Palette can be changed using the Catalog. The Catalog contains all the parts available in VRPG. Not all of them are shown on the Parts Palette for space reasons. Keep the parts you need on the Palette. Lesser-used parts can be kept in the Catalog for reference as needed. The user can define new parts for the Catalog, and from there place them on the Palette. Switch between the Catalog view and the Palette view by clicking on the icon on the title bar or using the View menu.

19.5 Using the GUI Designer

The purpose of the GUI Designer is to allow the user to select windows and their parts from the Parts Palette and place them in the Project Window client area or design window. Applications are thus built up. Parts are placed and then code is written for them. To place a part within the design window, place the cursor over it in the Parts Palette. Holding down the left mouse button, drag it over to the desired position in the design window. Release the left mouse button. The part stays at that location. It is that simple. Just drag and drop the parts of the application from the Parts Palette to the design window.

The first thing you probably want to put in the project is its own window for it to run in. Then you can add various types of parts like pushbuttons and text boxes within that window for interacting with the user. These items are the typical components of most windowed applications.

Menus can be added to the application window the same way. Drag and drop the menu bar part from the Palette to the design window. To add a submenu item to an existing menu bar in the design window, drag and drop the menu item icon to an empty spot in the menu bar. In this way, menu bars with levels of submenus and menu items can be built up for the application. If you want a separator bar in the menu to differentiate areas, select Add Separator from the Edit menu.

It is easy to change the settings for a part once placed in the design window. Place the cursor over the part and double-click the left mouse button to produce the part's settings notebook. This notebook follows the customary format for all OS/2 settings notebooks. It consists of several pages of different types of settings, with tabs at the right-hand edge. Click on the tabs to change the page. Within a given page, you can set the page parameters. For instance, on the Data page of a part's settings notebook, you can set the data type and length for the part. If it is an entry field, you could specify it as a numeric data type of length 11 and two decimal positions. Other tabs in the settings notebook allow you to set the color, font, style, and other settings for the window part. When finished editing the settings, double-click on the box at the upper left-hand corner of the settings notebook (the system menu) to close it.

Once placed in the Project Window, a part can be sized, moved, and copied. To change the size of a part, click on it. It is now selected. Then, use the mouse to drag one of the sides of the part to make it wider or taller. Or, you can drag a corner to make it wider and taller simultaneously. To move a part, select it and drag it to the new location, then drop it by releasing the mouse button. To copy a part, select it and move it to the new location by holding down the Ctrl key while dragging it. Alternatively, you can copy it to the clipboard using the Edit selection of the part's pop-up menu (remember, right click the part to get its pop-up menu). Once the part is in the OS/2 clipboard, it can be pasted into any location within the VRPG system where a part can be used, including another application or project. Pasting is done using the Edit/Paste option of the pop-up menu for the window where you want to place the part. To remove a part from a window, select Edit/Clear from its pop-up menu.

To change the labels or text that appears on the various window parts, hold down the Alt key and select the part. This action produces a text box where you can type in the new label you want to use for that part. Place the mouse pointer in an empty section of the screen and press the left mouse button. Fonts can be changed for the text in window parts. Select View/Font from the GUI designer menu. Drag a font from the resulting Palette to the part in question and drop it there. Change colors of parts in a similar manner. Select View/Color and drag and drop the desired color on a part. You can edit the colors on the Palette by clicking the Edit Color pushbutton. Using the color wheel, mix the particular color you want.

When placing parts manually with the mouse, the grid aids in placement. The grid is similar to graph paper, but is on the screen. When moving or sizing parts with the mouse, they snap to positions in the grid. This function is available when the grid is turned on from the Grid option of the Design window's pop-up menu. The size of grid coordinates is adjustable. Parts can also be automatically aligned, sized, and spaced within the window as opposed to manual placement to produce a professional look. To automatically arrange parts, select a group of parts with the mouse. Select the pop-up menu of the part you want to use as the anchor, or the example for the placement of the others. Choose the Alignment option, which produces a group of pictures that show different options for aligning the parts. They show alignments from left to right and top to bottom. Select the one you want and the system automatically lines them up accordingly. Spacing and sizing work similarly. You select a group of parts and then select one to act as the anchor or example. Produce its pop-up menu with the right mouse button. Select a template for the sizing or spacing option you require.

When changing the format of the parts in the window, you might make a mistake. VRPG provides the Undo option to get you out of any undesirable change that has occurred. Select Edit/Undo to reverse the most recent change (or one of the most recent changes).

19.6 Defining the Server

VRPG relies on a connection to the AS/400 for many of its functions. This connection is a behind-the-scenes communications session between OS/2 running locally on your PC and OS/400 running on the AS/400. It needs to be configured by the user before VRPG can take advantage of the features that operate across the platform boundaries.

Communications Manager must have already been set up for a connection between the PC and the AS/400. Refer to the PLU alias name used in the Communications Manager configuration, as it will be used in configuring VRPG for the AS/400 server connection. This connection actually relies on the underlying services provided by Communications Manager.

Select Define/Servers from the menu bar of the GUI designer. Enter the PLU alias name of the server that you looked up in Communications Manager. Select Auto start. Click on OK to complete the definition of the server. Now VRPG can give this server definition to Communications Manager for processing when a connection is required.

If you don't want to enter the user name and password every time VRPG needs to access the AS/400, you can define the sign-on information once and use it automatically after that, whenever a connection is invoked. Select Define/Servers logon from the Design window menu. Enter user name and password as required. Remember, however, that this action means that anyone trying to access the AS/400 from your terminal through VRPG will automatically have your name and password. If you don't define logon information for the server, the system prompts you for user name and password for attempted connections to the AS/400 in your VRPG sessions if the connection is not already made.

File access authority is defined for the user by the system administrator on the AS/400. A minimum of *USE authority is required to access AS/400 files from VRPG.

19.7   Accessing AS/400 Data

AS/400 databases are directly accessible from VRPG. VRPG was designed by IBM specifically to access AS/400 data from the PC. A host program on the AS/400 cooperates with the PC portion of the program to provide highly integrated data access. This facility uses an APPC connection that is more efficient than the traditional ODBC type of connection often used with visual PC tools. It is not based on remote SQL, but uses the native interface of the AS/400 database. To access AS/400 database fields, the server must first be defined to VRPG (see the section on defining the server). The AS/400 must also be able to find some special functions and the intersystem communications function (ICF) file called EVFICFF. The library that contains these files must be part of the initial library list for the job description of the user specified when defining the server.

Once all setup chores are completed, you can place AS/400 data fields in the design window by creating a part to contain the AS/400 data field. Select Reference fields from the Define menu to produce the Define Database Reference Fields window. Click Always Refresh to build a current list of AS/400 paths and files. Enter a full path to the AS/400 database field as:

```
Library/File/Record/Field
```

Or, you can point to the various components of the path, using the mouse. If you know the path, it is much easier and faster just to type it in. Once you have the field, you can drag and drop it into the design window to create a part for the data field.

Another method is to work through the part's notebook settings. To put the field in a project, place an entry field in the design window. Open its notebook settings by double-clicking on it. Select the Reference tab to open up that page. Click on Reference to produce the Define Reference Field window. Select Always Refresh. Enter the full path name to the data field as above. Select a field from the field list. Click OK.

The type of VRPG part created for the design window depends on the field usage specified in the AS/400 data description specifications (DDS) for the field. VRPG automatically converts these parameters for its own use. It retains AS/400 specifications such as COMP, EDTCDE, RANGE, and VALUES to define how the field is used and what can be input to it. Once the AS/400 data field is placed within the design window, it can be formatted in a number of ways by changing its attributes.

19.8 Using AS/400 Displays in VRPG

You can import a screen definition from a preexisting RPG program (written in DDS) for use in the VRPG system. VRPG can convert this screen definition along with its keywords, if applicable to the VRPG environment, to its own format for you.

Select Project/Import from the Designer menu. Enter the full name of the display file you want to import in the form `Server/Library/File/Record`, or you can look for them in lists. Because you are attached to the AS/400, VRPG can give you lists of servers, libraries, files, and records from which to select the correct item. Enter a part name to the Part name field for the VRPG name of the converted AS/400 display file. Select whether you want to add the new part to the Catalog only or to both the Catalog and the Palette. Click on Import. VRPG converts the display format from the AS/400 and makes it available as a user-defined part in the Catalog and Palette. From there, it can be dragged to the Client area of the Designer window. Refer to the IBM Parts Reference manual for details of how AS/400 display formats are converted to VRPG parts or windows.

19.9 LPEX Editor

VRPG contains its own text editor for writing the underlying RPG code connected to the various parts in the project window. This editor is called *LPEX*. It offers such GUI features as token highlighting, prompting, and syntax checking. Like SEU, the main editor used on the AS/400, it knows when you have made a syntax error in the code. Unlike SEU, but similar to CODE/400, it highlights various parts of the RPG code line in different colors. Especially with RPG, which is so run-on and column-oriented, the different colors help differentiate the components of the syntax. Variables might be in red, while operating system codes or verbs are in green and comments are in black. RPG is rendered much more readable by this feature. The colors are configurable by the user.

19.10 Program Code

Like all visual design tools (Visual Basic, PowerBuilder, etc.) VRPG uses the event-handling paradigm. You first place objects in the design window, such as pushbuttons and entry fields. You then attach sections of code, or subroutines, to the various visual components of the system. When the user activates these graphical objects by clicking on them or whatever, the system responds with a piece of code. Instead of a top-to-bottom program, as seen in traditional RPG programming, you have a kaleidoscopic collection of code fragments attached to visual objects. Instead of using function keys and indicators to interact with the user, you use pushbuttons, menus, and windows. These visual objects can create other visual objects when activated. Clicking on a pushbutton might open a new window.

Apart from the visual aspects of VRPG, the underlying RPG language has not changed that much. VRPG is an implementation of the ILE RPGIV language. There are still the various types of specs:

- H   Header specs to describe the program
- F   File specs for defining and accessing files
- I   Input specs to define input fields and data structures
- D   Definition specs for data
- C   Calc specs
- O   Output specs for defining output to printer

The method for editing the lines of VRPG has changed considerably from the familiar interface of SEU on the AS/400. The Define menu contains selections for entering lines of code in the different types of specification formats. Select one of these formats and enter the spec in the resulting prompt screen. Templates are provided as in SEU to help with the syntax in the different types of specs. You choose a spec type from the Define menu, enter code for it, and save it. The Define menu allows the following:

- Program specs H, F, I, D
- Output specs O
- Table and Array **
- User Subroutines BEGSR

19.11   Action Links

Relationships are defined between the subroutines and the window parts. It is necessary to create a link between the part and event and the code. In other words, you might specify what happens (subroutine) when the user clicks (event) on a pushbutton (part). These are known as action links. To create an action link between a subroutine and a window part, place the cursor on the window part in question. Click the right mouse button to produce the pop-up menu for the part. Select Events from the pop-up menu to get a list of appropriate events for that type of part. Click on an event in the list to produce the action subroutine template window that allows you to enter code. The name of the action subroutine defaults to the name of the part, the event, and the window. It is contained in Factor 1, Factor 2, and the Result field as, for example, `QuitClickWin1` (the click event for the button named Quit in `Window1`). This name is the compound name by which the action subroutine is known. Enter the code for this subroutine to specify what happens for the event and the part, and save it. VRPG takes care of executing this code whenever the user invokes the related event for the window part.

Often, invoking an event for one part causes a change of attributes in another part. For example, a window might become visible when a pushbutton is clicked, and become invisible when a certain menu item is selected. VRPG supports these links between parts with the `AddLink` and `AllowLink` attributes. The part that initiates a change in another part is called the *source part*, while the affected part is the *target part*. Use the `AddLink` and `AllowLink` attributes of the source part to change the attributes of the target.

The Define menu has a submenu called *Action links*. From here, you can browse, create, edit, copy, or delete action links.

You can work with the source code all in one piece, instead of in the fragments associated with the action links to window parts. After the action links have been created, select Full RPG Source from the Define menu to get the complete source code in the edit window. You can then work with it in a manner similar to coding RPG on the AS/400 with SEU. This method is only used as an afterthought, however. It is necessary to create the action links first through the part's pop-up menu or the Define menu.

19.12 Debugger

VRPG has a debugger to aid in the resolution of application problems. You can set breakpoints, execute the application, and watch variables. When compiling the application, if debug is to be used, you must specify the debug option. Once this option has been specified, the debugger can be activated to investigate the state of the application as it is running.

Select Debug from the Project window to start the Debugger and bring up the Debug Session Control window. The Components box shows the program and link files that are running in the application. To single-step through the program source code, select View from the Debug Session Control window. Then, select the type of view you want to use for the debugging. Options are Source, Disassemble, or Mixed. Next, select the type of stepping to use: Step over, Step into, Step debug, or Step return.

It is often necessary to locate a particular position in the source code for debugging. To find that position, VRPG provides a function that searches the source code for a given string. Select View from the File menu of the Debug Session Control window. Indicate which program view you want: Source, Disassembly, or Mixed. Then select Edit and Search. Enter the desired string. If you want the search to be case-sensitive, select it. Click OK. VRPG then finds the correct place in the code for you.

Breakpoints are one of the most useful features of a debugging tool. You can select a place in the code where there seems to be a problem and set a breakpoint to make the system stop when it gets to that line. You can then look at the contents of variables to determine how the system is behaving. This process is called *monitoring variables*. Select Run from the title bar in the program view window to begin the program. The program stops at the breakpoint and the program view window opens. You see variables and their values in the Program Monitor window. You can add variables to the Program Monitor by selecting Variables from the Program View window. You can change the contents of variables in the Program monitor by double-clicking on them.

Many of the parameters of the Debugger can be changed to suit user preferences, including window placement, fonts, view window properties, animation rate, and debugging mode. They are accessed by selecting Options from the Debug Session Control window.

19.13   Building and Compiling

Once the parts have been placed in the window and action links created between them and the RPG subroutines, it is necessary to compile the program into an executable module and distribute it to the users. Select Build from the Project menu to produce the Compiler Options window. Select Find to select an appropriate icon for the application, if one has not yet been selected. Enter the compiler options you require for this application and then click OK. VRPG takes care of compiling the application for you. If there are any problems with the compile, an error message is displayed informing you of what they are. Click OK to open up the Error list window. From here, you can select errors, find the place in the source code where they occurred, correct them, and save the changes. Once all is corrected, you can build the application again. When it compiles cleanly, you have an application that can be run and deployed to users.

Many of the system files generated by VRPG and used for running the application are located in a subdirectory of your application directory called RT_OS2. Do not remove or otherwise tamper with these files, as it will probably cause run-time problems. To run the application, select Run from the Project menu.

Once the application is designed, debugged, and built satisfactorily, it must be installed on the individual user's workstations. Each workstation that is to run the VRPG application must have the same kind of access to the AS/400 that the development computer had. That is, a router connection needs to be in place, and the server needs to be defined. The run-time code for the application as well as the application itself then must be installed on the workstation.

VRPG provides the Package function for creating an installable version of the run-time code. Select Tools from the Project menu and then Package from there to open the Package window. Click on Run-Time and then OK to open the Package Run-Time window. VRPG asks for the target directory for the run-time package. You probably want to create an installable version on a floppy in the A: drive. Click OK. VRPG creates an installable package for you on the target drive.

To package the application, select Tools from the Project menu and Package from there to open the Package window. Click on Application and then OK. This opens the Find window. Select the application and click on Package. Enter target directory, title of application, and number and version of the application. Click OK. When the process is complete, you have a disk suitable for installing the application to a workstation.

It is necessary to install the run-time code before the application. Place the packaged installation diskette in drive A: of the workstation. Type at the OS/2 command line A:\VRRINST. Follow directions. Reboot the computer. Then install the application itself by typing A:\VRAINST at the OS/2 command line. Follow directions. When this process is finished, you are asked if you want to configure the AS/400 connection. Select the name of the workstation's Communications Manager configuration file that will be used by VRPG to communicate with the AS/400. Click OK. That's it. The application is ready for use.

19.14 Summary

VRPG is IBM's answer to visual development. Running in OS/2, it provides an efficient link between the database-handling capabilities of the AS/400 and the GUI features of the PC. It uses an APPC connection to the AS/400, as opposed to the more usual ODBC link, which is more efficient and improves performance. VRPG leverages existing RPG skills from the AS/400 MIS shop into an advanced GUI type of client/server development environment. While the event-driven paradigm of visual programming must be learned, many of the existing functions of the RPG language are still valid, minimizing the learning curve associated with the transition to a visual programming environment. Action links provide the mechanism for invoking RPG code from visual objects such as entry fields or pushbuttons. These are easily managed from the menu bar.

VRPG provides many tools that ease the task of creating GUI client/server systems. The Parts Palette allows you to drag and drop graphical interfaces into the project design window. The LPEX editor offers help and syntax checking. The Debugger aids in isolating and correcting program errors. Taken together, the VRPG features constitute a powerful and productive platform for client/server systems development.

Chapter

20

Visual C++

20.1 Overview

Visual programming has become a prevalent method of systems development in the Windows environment. Visual Basic and PowerBuilder are two examples of fairly easy-to-use, object-oriented visual tools. Visual C++ remains the most powerful visual tool available for the Windows desktop. It is an extremely flexible language and the source of many objects used in the other visual tools. It is considerably more difficult to learn than Visual Basic or PowerBuilder, but it cannot be surpassed for custom tailoring objects and systems using the object-oriented programming model. It provides visual tools for handling the complex tasks inherent in Windows graphical user interface (GUI) programming, which traditionally had to be written from scratch by C programmers using the Windows APIs. It is now easier to learn to program with the Windows Visual C++ tools. It combines the visual ease of use seen in Visual Basic with the full functionality of the C language. Don't forget that this product is brought to you by the same people who developed both Windows and Visual Basic—Microsoft. It is, in fact, the underlying development language of those two. It is now available to us as a visual programming tool, complete with encapsulated visual objects.

Visual C++ can generate much of your application for you and provide entry points for tailoring the result to your specific needs. Obviously, this chapter cannot provide an exhaustive view of Visual C++. This product is very deep. A description of its main features is presented here to give an idea of what is possible with this language—the most powerful and flexible

263

of all PC Windows tools. You must refer to the Visual C++ manuals for implementation details.

20.2 Object-Oriented Programming

Visual C++ makes extensive use of object-oriented programming (OOP) to simplify the task of managing the visual GUI. The objects that compose this environment are extremely complex internally. OOP provides prepared objects that can perform Windows functionality with a fairly simple user interface. They can be tailored to your specific needs. Most of the fundamental operations of, say, a data browsing window, can be prepackaged. It is not necessary to code each element of every system from scratch. Objects provide tested, generic components that can be combined to form systems. The emphasis is on selecting objects and inheriting characteristics into related cloned objects. Developers, familiar with the object libraries, can think in terms of the objects when analyzing the system. Before coding, they associate objects to provide a framework of the system. Entities in the real world are reflected in objects that constitute the system. These objects provide access via messages sent to them. They are responsible for figuring out how to satisfy the message. They also have access points for modifications to the code.

An object is a synthesis of data structures and procedures that operate on that data, bundled together. Objects are adaptable to various situations. Their simple exterior can mask a complex interior. In most cases, we do not need intimate knowledge of the inner workings to use the object. Our environment is full of objects we do not understand, but still use constantly and productively, such as the computer or the automobile. Objects contain methods, or subroutines, that define their behavior in various circumstances. The class defines the highest form of an object. It is a template from which specific objects are created or inherited to provide more specific solutions. The object is an instantiation of the class.

Objects inherit data structures and methods from their parent classes. Alterations and additions are allowed. A generic class is adaptable to various applications. Altered inherited subclasses are more specifically useful than their parent classes. An extensive class library enables the rapid development of sophisticated objects through inheritance. These objects are invoked by sending messages to them requesting they perform their interior methods on the relevant data. If the message and the result are known, it is not necessary to know the internal mechanism of an object.

Encapsulation is the property of enclosing the inner workings of the object in a "black box." It performs a function reliably, in response to a message. Thus, objects are extremely adaptable and time-saving. Polymorphism is the ability to send the same or similar messages to a variety of objects derived from the same class. They share a common message interface. These are the fundamentals of object-oriented programming, and the GUI chapter provides more information.

20.3 Visual Workbench

Various features of the Visual C++ environment simplify the working interface and the handling and modification of objects. Studios, Wizards, and Workbenches aid in project development. The Visual Workbench is where most of the work is done. It assists in writing code, running the application, and then debugging it. In keeping with the Microsoft standard of coding tools, the syntax of Visual C++ statements in the Visual Workbench is differentiated by color. Different colors make it much easier to understand the code, finding variables and keywords more rapidly. Visual Workbench is used to write the code of the application contained in .CPP program files and .H header files.

The Visual Workbench can be navigated through the use of the toolbar. By pressing the icons on the toolbar, the following functions are available:

- *Project Files*: see constituent files in the project.
- *Open*: edit a program.
- *Save*: save a program.
- *Find Text Box*: search for text in a program.
- *Find Next*: search for next instance of text.
- *Compile File*: compile the program.
- *Build*: build the application, compile files that have changed since last build.
- *Rebuild All*: build the application, compile all files.
- *Toggle Breakpoint*: debug breakpoints.
- *Quick Watch*: change contents of Watch Window.
- *Run*: run the application from Visual Workbench.
- *Step Into*: run one line of code.
- *Step Over*: run one line of function.
- *Step Out*: run to end of function.

These toolbar utilities provide most of the functionality required to write and debug Visual C++ programs. It is somewhat similar to the Visual Basic design environment.

Visual Workbench builds the application, compiling and linking all necessary parts of the project into an executable file, .EXE, including programs and resources. Visual Workbench has kept track of how you have designed and created the parts of the application using the system utilities, so it knows how to build it. It displays any errors it encounters along the way. Visual C++ maintains a number of files to manage the environment so painlessly. Mostly, you do not have to know much about these files. They include project files, precompiled headers, configurations, and link libraries. Some of these might appear at times in various places in the environment. Do not change them.

Visual Workbench has a Browser function that facilitates navigation of the Visual C++ environment, which can sometimes get a little confusing. Browser helps you find controls, events, and classes, along with their definitions and reference points in the code. It needs to be invoked if you want to use it. To activate Browser, select Project from the Options menu. Then choose Compile, Listing File, and Browser to enable it. These actions create an entry in a .BSC database for Browser to use to track the various bits and pieces of the application. When you want to use Browser, just press Shift-F11 or use the Browse menu. The item at the current cursor location is used for the Browse. Click on Display Result to see the Browse result. Browser can show several types of graphic trees to illustrate the structure of your application. You can see class, function, and symbol trees with parent/child relations, where applicable.

Visual Workbench contains a very useful debugger with breakpoints, a call stack, and a watch window, among other features, to aid in isolating and fixing problems. Extensive online help is available from any point in the Visual Workbench to answer questions.

20.4 App Wizard

App Wizard is a feature of Visual Workbench that generates generic window applications, ready for customization. These windows have existing menus and toolbars. You just add code to tailor them to specific needs. It is actually possible to create an entire windowed application in Visual C++ without knowing anything about writing visual objects. This application generator takes care of declarations, includes, and standard subroutines and programs to create a window with the usual Windows functionality.

Select App Wizard from the Project menu. Enter a name for the project. Parameters can be set when generating an application with App Wizard to influence the type of window to be created by clicking the Options button. Select Options, Initial Toolbar, and Medium Memory Model. Click OK and then Create. That's it. App Wizard creates a standard Windows application, ready for customization. Note the information on the New Application Information screen after you pressed OK. It indicates which techniques and classes underlie this deceptively simple interface.

20.5   Class Wizard

Features can be selected when using App Wizard to generate an application that can bring the output as close as possible to the desired result. To implement options not provided by App Wizard, changes can be made to the source code App Wizard generates using Class Wizard. Class Wizard simplifies the task of managing classes and their inherited objects. You can browse through a list of classes and their messages. Class Wizard pops you right into the place in the internal code that handles that message for that class without searching for it. This function is extremely convenient and time-saving. Many projects can be managed entirely through the use of App Wizard and Class Wizard.

Start Class Wizard by selecting it from the Browse Menu in Visual Workbench or by pressing Ctrl-W. Class Wizard uses a tabbed page interface. Click on a tab to bring up a page of commands and features to see what is available and to switch between groups of functions. Functions are the following:

- *Message Maps*: relate class resources to their message handlers.

- *Member Variables*: list of variables that belong to controls such as dialog boxes and forms.

- *OLE Automation*: list of methods and properties for linked or embedded objects.

- *Class Info*: general class information.

Message Maps is the default mode for Class Wizard. It allows you to browse through a list of applicable messages for a given class and add or select one. Messages currently being used in the class are shown with a little hand to the left. Double-click on a message in the member function list box to see or edit its code using Visual Workbench. Typically, you use App Wizard to generate an application as close as possible to what you need, and then use Class Wizard to find mapped sections of the application. You then select the ones that need modification and double-click on them for editing in Visual Workbench.

Class Wizard also allows you to add or import a class, add a message handler, and add member variables for controls. It then generates the required declarations, code, and message maps for the event or object you specified.

20.6   App Studio

App Studio is a visual design center for the controls found in windows applications. Graphics tools enable the creation of pushbuttons, icons, dialog boxes, menus, etc. These features become available to the Visual Workbench for inclusion in projects. It is quite easy to move around the environment, creating a visual control in App Studio and then using it in an application through Visual Workbench. These visual controls are implemented through resource files with the extension .rc. A resource file manages all the relevant bitmaps, icons, cursors, and other visual objects for the application. Generally, you do not work directly with the resource file; you work in the visual tools, and Visual C++ manages the .rc for you. The compiler compiles these resources and binds them to the executable at build time.

The App Studio toolbar is launched from the Tools menu and contains the following icons:

- *New Script*: open a new resource file.
- *Open*: edit an existing resource file.
- *Save*: save the resource file.
- *Undo*: reverse the most recent change.
- *Redo*: undo the undo.
- *New Dialog*: create a dialog box.
- *New Menu*: create a new menu.
- *New Cursor*: create new cursor.
- *New Icon*: create new icon.
- *New Bitmap*: create new bitmap.
- *New String Table*: create new string table.
- *New Accelerator Table*: create new accelerator table.
- *Symbol Browser*: list resources.
- *Class Wizard*: go to Class Wizard.
- *Help*: go to help text.

In addition, many of the above toolbar selections open their own toolbars to aid in the designing of other visual controls. Some of these toolbars allow you to align and size controls.

20.7 Event-Handling

Windows programs are driven by the actions of the user. When the mouse is moved somewhere on the screen and clicked, for example, the programmer must respond to the action with an event handler. An event handler is a section of code invoked by the action of the mouse. Start Class Wizard and create an OnLButtonDown event handler. Select CMsappView from the Object ID list box and WM_LBUTTONDOWN from the Message list box to form a relationship between the window and the left mouse button click. This action declares and creates a member function called CMsappView::OnLButtonDown in the

Member Function box below. Double-click on this box to add the code for what you want to happen in this event (user clicks left mouse button).

Visual C++ offers the `Invalidate` and `InvalidateRect` functions, which can be used to clear the screen or a known section of the screen in response to mouse actions. You can handle subsequent screen painting chores by calling the `OnDraw` function. The need to draw and maintain screens is one of the major tasks of programming with Visual C++.

20.8 OLE

Object linking and embedding (OLE) is a mechanism whereby one application can contain information from another application. For example, a pushbutton on a form could activate a spreadsheet graph within the form or could call in data from a spreadsheet. The possible combinations are extensive—OLE simply means that you do not need to leave one application to access an object or data in another; it can be included or embedded right in the current application.

Select OLE Options from App Wizard. Choices for types of OLE are the following:

- *No Compound Documents*: no OLE container or server generated.

- *Container*: OLE container (client) generated, can open an OLE server within the client application.

- *Mini-Server*: a smaller OLE implementation that can only be run from within the client.

- *Full-Server*: OLE server that can run on its own or be opened from within another client.

- *Container-Server*: OLE implementation that can function fully in both modes, as the client (container) and server.

Automation support is also available to automate your code for OLE access. The user does not need to do anything to retrieve the OLE object; everything is handled by the client or container macro code for OLE. Automation servers are objects registered with the Windows system and thus available for use in other applications. They can be accessed through their properties, methods, or the interface macro language.

20.9 QuickWin

The full power of Visual C++ is implemented in the Windows environment, but it can also convert DOS applications using the character-based idiom as a starting point to generate the GUI application. QuickWin creates Windows applications from DOS applications. They might run in a window with some

Windows characteristics, such as menus and toolbars, but are essentially DOS applications. The full Windows characteristics would need to be addressed at a later stage to convert the applications fully to Windows.

Select New from the File menu and enter the source code for your QuickWin application. This code takes the form of DOS-based C and does not have all the advanced Windows classes available to it. Save it. Select New from the Project menu. Enter a name for the project and select QuickWin from the drop-down list. Enter a directory for the application and a .mak file name. Double-click the name of the source file to enter it to the Project Edit dialog box.

20.10   Build

Once appropriate changes have been made to adapt App Wizard's creation to your purposes, the application needs to be built (or actually rebuilt). Click the Build icon on the Visual Workbench toolbar, or select Build from the Project menu at the top of the screen. Visual C++ then compiles and links the application into an executable file. The application can now be run by selecting the Run command from the Project menu or by pressing Ctrl-F5, if, of course, there are no errors. If there are, it will inform you of what and where they are in the Output window, and you can proceed with debugging. Use the F4 key to move to consecutive error locations in the source code.

20.11   Classes and Objects

Much of the benefit in working with Visual C++ is derived through the use of classes. Remember that a class is similar to a data structure definition bundled together with the methods that operate on this data. Thus, an object type is formed from the class. Many useful and complex classes are provided by Visual C++ in the class library for developing applications. Classes must be defined, like any other data type. Their data members must be defined, as well as their member functions. The class has member data and functions that belong to it. Following is a simple class definition for a class named new_dialog, derived from the CDialog dialog box class, found in a header file (.h):

```
CDialog New_dialog;
```

Member functions of classes can be accessed through the context operator (::). The double colon means that the named function is a member of a class as follows:

```
Class::member
```

Classes are implemented through inheritance. A base class is developed into a derived class, which shares (inherits) the data and function members of the base class. Thus, new classes can be easily adapted to current purposes using the preconstructed features of an appropriate base class, saving a lot of work. A class is derived from a base class with the following syntax:

```
class NewClass:public BaseClass
```

The above class definition indicates that a new class is to be derived from the base class and that all the member data and functions of `BaseClass` will be available. Further, the members of `NewClass` will now have public access rights. Only the relevant elements or members of `BaseClass` need to be changed for our purposes. These are changed by redefining functions or adding new ones within the derived class.

Classes are instantiated into objects. Through the use of a constructor function, bearing the same name as the class itself, the class creates an object when called. Constructors initialize the class, and destructors clean up after them. These are parts of the code typically altered when inheriting characteristics from a class and creating an object from it. Constructors and destructors cause the compiler to create and destroy memory storage for variables. The constructor function has the same name as the class:

```
Class1::Class1 (float var1, float var2) {
       m_var1 = var1;
       m_var2 = var2;
}
```

Constructor functions are explicit and coded by the programmer, while destructors can be explicit or implicit. They can be handled automatically by the compiler when the class or object is removed from memory or goes out of scope. They can also be used to perform additional specified clean-up routines such as file I/O and memory management. The destructor, like the constructor, bears the same name as the class, with an added prefix tilde (~):

```
Class1::~Class1()
```

Some of the more useful classes containing member functions in the Visual C++ class library are the following:

- `CArchive`: file I/O for documents.
- `CBitmap`: for managing bitmaps or pictures in memory and on the screen.
- `CBrush`: creates a brush object for drawing on the screen.
- `CDC`: creates text, graphics, and screen management such as color.

- CDialog: creates Windows dialog boxes.
- CDocument: used by App Wizard to create documents as application platforms.
- CEditView: enables editing of text in windows.
- CFont: manages fonts for printing in conjunction with CDC.
- CFrameWnd: creates a main application window and manages its interfaces such as menus, icons, toolbars, etc.
- CMDIFrameWnd: creates a multiple document interface parent window.
- CMDIChildWnd: creates a multiple document interface child window.
- CListBox: creates a list box object.
- CRect: manages the rectangles that form the window borders.
- CScrollView: creates a scrollbar from CView for data viewing in a window.
- CString: character string-handling functions.
- CVBControl: incorporates Visual Basic controls into the Visual C++ application.
- CView: manages the client area of the window for graphics and user input.
- CWinApp: created by App Wizard as the application framework object.
- CWnd: provides handles for managing windows.
- CWnd: the base class for many other types of windows.

20.12   Language Elements

Visual C++ retains most features of the C language. It adds many new ones, most notably the Visual Workbench, App Wizard, Class Wizard, App Studio, and extensive use of objects and classes. The following is not intended as a full compendium of C++ syntax (which is beyond our scope), but as a summary of the underlying language syntax.

Preprocessor directives

It is necessary to tell C which data and function definitions will be included in the code you are writing. These directions are called *preprocessor directives* and are found at the beginning of any C program. All preprocessor directives are preceded by the # character in the code. Visual C++ and App Wizard handle much of this task for you.

Includes.   The Include is the most common form of preprocessor directive. It tells the C compiler to look for header files to import to your code, defining certain data elements for functions or operations you intend to perform. `Include` files all have `.h` as their file extension. Without the `Include`, the program will not compile. It is therefore necessary to know in advance which functions you will be using and to incorporate the appropriate `Includes` in your program. Again, these are handled by App Wizard and Class Wizard in Visual C++. They take the following form:

```
#include <filename.h>
```

Defines. Defines are another type of preprocessor directive and are used to set up special data names for use by your program. For instance, if you want to specify that the data name SUCCESS indicates a successful read of a record, you need to define SUCCESS as being equivalent to the return code for a successful read.

```
#define SUCCESS 1
```

Defines take the form of macro substitution, so that any time the program encounters a `Defined` term, it substitutes the characters indicated in the preprocessor definition. In the above example, the program substitutes the character 1 for the term SUCCESS.

Preprocessor directives can have logical constructs just like program code.

- `#ifdef` is used to evaluate whether an identifier has already been defined elsewhere.
- `#ifndef` evaluates if the identifier has not been defined.
- `#endif` marks the end of the conditional directive block.
- `#include` brings in preprocessor directives from another file, so they do not need to be entered again if already defined elsewhere.

Variables

C has only a few data types, which need to be declared to the program before they are used. Data items must be explicitly declared before they are referenced in the C program. You must provide the data type and name. Following are C data types:

- *char*: one-byte character
- *int*: integer
- *float*: single-precision floating point numeric
- *double*: double-precision floating point numeric
- *short*: short integer
- *long*: long integer
- *unsigned*: unsigned integer, no negatives, therefore twice as large as int

The most common forms of data type are char, int, and float. Following is a declaration for character variable name and an integer variable x that will be used in the program:

```
char name;int x;
```

Multiple variables can be declared in one line:

```
int x,y,z;
```

Variables can be initialized in the declaration:

```
char name = "A";int x = 1;
```

Arrays are declared like any other data type, along with an additional parameter in square brackets indicating array length:

```
char name[25];
```

Note the use of the semicolon (;) which is used in C to denote the end of a statement. By far the most common bug in C is forgetting the semicolon at the end of a statement.

C is case sensitive, so that X and x are two different variable names. Lowercase is the standard for writing C code. White space or blanks in the code can be used freely in most situations to make the code more readable in terms of indentation and blank lines.

Keywords

There are only 28 inherent keywords in C. Everything else is either user-defined or imported through Includes or external link library functions. The C keywords are the following:

auto	extern	sizeof
break	float	static
case	for	structure
char	goto	switch
continue	if	typedef
default	int	union
do	long	unsigned
double	register	while
else	return	
entry	short	

Notice that the C keywords are concerned with variable declarations of various types and control of logic flow. C provides logic control in the form of the following:

```
if          switch
else        case
for         break
while       goto
```

Mathematical operators

C's mathematical operators are very straightforward and can be used to write algebraic-like expressions:

```
+   add
-   subtract
*   multiply
/   divide
%   modulus
```

Parentheses are used to group operations in an expression. An expression such as this is possible in "C":

```
a = ((b*c)/r) - 1;
```

Of course, all these variables must have been declared previously to the expression. There is no exponential operator. You must use a function for this expression.

Assignment and comparison

As we have seen, assigning values to "C" variables is easily accomplished as in the following:

```
x = 1;name = "Fred";
```

Comparing data items for logic flow requires the use of these operators:

```
==   equals
!=   does not equal
>    is greater than
>=   is greater than or equal to
<    is less than
<=   is less than or equal to
```

Note that the comparison for *is equal to* requires the double equal sign ==. It is a common mistake to use a single equal sign for comparison purposes. Correct syntax is as follows:

```
if(a == b)
```

These comparison operators are found within the parentheses associated with flow of control words like if, while, for, or, switch, and case.

Functions

Most of the power of C is available through classes with their member functions. These functions are of two types—library functions that are provided with the compiler and user functions that you write yourself. More libraries of classes and functions for C are available all the time to handle whatever special tasks you might have, from event-handling to file I/O. It is therefore necessary to become familiar with the function and class libraries available for C.

Functions are called in C in the form funcname(arg1, arg2) where funcname is the name of the C function and arg1 and arg2 are the parameters passed to it. (Not all functions have two arguments.)

User-defined functions

In addition to the functions that come with your C compiler, you can create your own functions in C. To write a function, you must identify it, declare variables used inside it, write the code in it, and return a value to the function call:

```
userfunc(a,b)
int a,b;
{
        int c;
        c = a + b;
        return(c);
}
```

This example is a user-defined function called userfunc that receives two variables (*a* and *b*) from the calling routine. It will add *a* to *b* giving *c*, all three of which are declared in the function. It will then return the value of c (not the variable name *c*) to the calling routine.

Parameter passing to functions

The above example is a user-defined function that returns the result of *a* + *b* as the value of variable *c* when called by the program. The return value of the function simply substitutes for the function after it is called. So the function call

```
x = userfunc(q,r)
```

passes the integer variables *q* and *r* to the function, receives them into variables *a* and *b*, adds them together into variable *c*, and returns that to the calling statement as variable *x*. Assuming that variables *q* and *r* have been previously declared as int and have the values of 1 and 2 respectively, the function call evaluates to $x = 3$. You must pass the function the same type of variable that it declares in its variable declarations.

Flow of control

C provides keywords for handling the flow of control logic. You can test variables and branch to other parts of the program depending on the results of the test.

If is the most common form of logic testing. It has this syntax

```
if(x == 1) funcname();
```

The above If statement says to perform the function funcname() if x is equal to 1. Note the double equal sign (==) used for comparison testing.

C also has an else:

```
if(x == 1)
  funcnam1();
else
  funcnam2();
```

The While statement in C iterates a loop until the While condition is met:

```
while(x <= 10)
{
  x = x + 1;
}
```

The above While loop adds 1 to x until x becomes greater than 10.

Note the use of the curly brackets to enclose the body of the while loop. This practice tells the compiler where the While loop ends.

The For statement provides a compact method for performing an iteration. The above While loop could be written as a For:

```
For(x = 1; x <<= 10; x++)
```

This For loop says that beginning with $x = 1$, and continuing while $x <<=$ 10, increment x. Note the shorthand notation for incrementing x (x = x + 1 is expressed as x++).

Switch is C's case statement. It tests a succession of possible cases, executing the correct one.

```
switch(x)
{
  case 1:
    func1();
    break;

  case 2:
    func2();
    break;

  default:
    break;
}
```

The above will test variable x. If it is 1, func1() is called; if it is 2, func2() is called. The Default statement, last of the Case statements, executes if no previous case has been matched. The Break statement is required in the Switch syntax. It causes flow to leave the loop after its associated Case or Default has been met and executed.

C has a Goto statement for purposes of branching. It has this form:

```
if(x == 1)
  goto label;
```

where label is a name in the program followed by a colon:

```
label:
```

If the condition in the test is matched, the program branches to label: and continues processing with the line after it.

Of course, in a structured language such as C, Gotos are frowned on, with structured control being the preferred method. Sometimes, however, they are the easiest and clearest method of directing the flow of control.

20.13 Summary

Visual C++ is the most powerful and flexible development tool for the Windows environment. It has, consequently, the highest learning curve of any language discussed. The use of true object-oriented procedures such as inheritance and encapsulation take some getting used to. Other tools such as PowerBuilder and Visual Basic are much easier to learn but do not offer the extensive features of the "C" language. If direct communication with API functions is necessary for a Windows application, or if it is necessary to access the operating system functions, Visual C++ is a good choice. Visual Workbench, App Wizard, and Class Wizard save a lot of time and work when developing systems.

21

More Client Tools

In addition to the tools discussed in individual chapters in this book, many others are worthy of note. Client/server systems can be created with any of these. More of them are coming on the market continually, as the demand for client/server systems grows. It is important to select the tool or development platform that best suits your requirements and current skills.

21.1 Oracle

Oracle is an SQL-based relational database that resides on an Oracle Server. Its Transparent Gateway for SQL/400 can make the AS/400 database appear to be part of the Oracle distributed database. Open Gateway Technology makes all of the data in the distributed Oracle network look like local data to the Oracle client. DB2/400 can be accessed through remote SQL. The user only needs to know the name of the table being accessed, not where it is or what type of network it is on. Oracle's Open Gateway Technology takes care of these details. A single SQL request can locate data on diverse systems.

Oracle graphical client tools are used as the front-end to access AS/400 data on the back-end through remote SQL. These Oracle tools are easy to implement—no programming is needed. Transparent Gateway services include SQL statement-parsing for distribution, PL/SQL processing, two-phase commit processing, database link processing, data dictionary support, and datatype conversions. Multisite queries and updates, subqueries, joins, and views can all be accomplished with a single SQL statement that parses to remote locations. ANSI-standard SQL, which is also used on the AS/400, is the basis of these Oracle procedures.

Oracle's SQL*Net is the key to remote AS/400 connectivity. The Transparent Gateway for SQL/400 supports both APPC and TCP/IP protocols, which means that clients can be as diverse as the RS/6000 workstation using TCP/IP or an OS/2 with APPC. More than 85 platforms can be used as clients to the AS/400 database through SQL*Net and Transparent Gateway. Both Oracle's security system and the AS/400's native security apply to remote access, protecting AS/400 data from unauthorized access or update. Data resident on the AS/400 can easily be copied to the Oracle platform for further processing or analysis.

Oracle Transparent Gateway requires the following:

- AS/400: OS/400, V2R2 or higher
- Oracle Transparent GatewayIBM TCP/IP (product 5738-TC1)
- Oracle7 Server: Oracle7 Server

21.2   Gupta SQLWindows

SQLWindows is a full-featured GUI Windows-based development tool for designing client/server systems. Many features of object-oriented programming make this a productive platform. *QuickObjects* is the SQLWindows term for the collection of object tools that can be adapted fairly easily for your particular needs.

Using QuickObjects, the developer can paint the application, placing visual objects such as pushbuttons and list boxes on the desktop, as with PowerBuilder or Visual Basic. Then, scripts or pockets of code, written in SQLWindows application language (SAL), are associated with these objects to handle user events like a mouse clicking on a pushbutton. Connections to remote data sources as well as sophisticated data manipulation are available literally at the touch of a button. QuickObjects provides a group of reusable visual objects with generic functions, reducing the time required for the developer to create an application. Obviously, the more a QuickObject requires in the way of customization, the more involved it gets. QuickObject classes can be manipulated through the object-oriented techniques of inheritance, encapsulation, and polymorphism. The SQLWindows compiler creates high-performance executables.

QuickObjects come in three categories. The Data Source is an object that performs a connection to a remote data source and links it into the SQLWindows application. Data is transparently pumped in from the remote database, and any user changes can be updated back to the remote database. These remote databases can take the form of DB2/400 as well as many other relational databases.

The Visualizer handles the graphical user interface. They are the graphical objects or controls placed on the desktop application to interact with the user. List boxes, combo boxes, edit fields, and radio buttons can be used to manipulate the data source. Visualizers are associated with Data Sources through the services of the Quest Window or the Table Window.

The Commander handles the processing logic of the application. For instance, if the user clicks on a pushbutton, the underlying SAL handles the data tasks like connect and update. Commanders are prewritten, ready for use on typical generic applications. They can, of course, be adapted to individual needs.

QuickForms is a guided path for developing an application. It takes the user through all the steps required to build a desktop form. Data source controls are chosen, along with visualizers and commanders associated with them.

21.3 LANSA

Aspect Computer's LANSA is a tool that presents AS/400 data graphically on PCs. The LANSA Co-Operative Enabler is the link between the AS/400 data and the PC platform. It provides a current view of the data from the server. Event triggers, data validation, security, and efficient data access methods make LANSA a viable choice for developing client/server systems.

The LANSA/Server is middleware that connects the AS/400 back-end databases to the PC front-end. It does not use the universally accepted but slower ODBC or remote SQL method of data access. Instead, LANSA uses its own custom-made interface for bringing AS/400 data to the PC platform, using the AS/400 native RPG data interface. It is faster than the SQL interface. Random access to AS/400 records using access paths is much more efficient than remote SQL. Cut and paste of AS/400 data to the PC for spreadsheets is easily performed. PC applications can submit AS/400 programs and procedures remotely.

The PC client can run any of a large selection of GUI-based applications packages or can be developed using LANSA/Client. This package offers point-and-click development of PC applications with AS/400 data access through LANSA/Server. Its Query Tool lets users run ad hoc requests against AS/400 data. The Builder enables development of full PC GUI applications. The LANSA repository encapsulates data validation rules for remote updates.

Advanced Client/Server Environment (ACE) is a full development platform for modeling the database, prototyping applications, and constructing client systems. A central database manager protects data integrity while PC tools implement GUI presentation, text processing, spreadsheets, and on-line PC data entry. ACE application templates allow reuse of code, making the code you write generic through "soft linking." ACE generates Visual Basic code that allows you to test the application interactively, without compiling first. ACE can then ask you questions to automatically modify this soft-linked code for a new but similar purpose. ACE has the same technical requirements as PC Support.

LANSA is not the least expensive solution for AS/400 client/server application design, but it is certainly one of the most efficient and sophisticated.

21.4 SYNON/CSG

SYNON is an IBM business partner. It works closely with IBM in developing its fully featured CASE tool for application development. This product actually writes the application code for you, in RPG or COBOL, after the data model and business rules have been defined. Entities are the building blocks of the SYNON application. An *entity* is a unit of the business concept, like a client or an order. Once the components of the various entities are defined, in terms of data and processing logic, SYNON can create the databases and screens required for the application. Modifications are often necessary, but the bulk of the application is generated by the package. This approach has been proven to reduce time and expense of system development and maintenance.

SYNON has a client/server offering called the client server generator (CSG), which helps the developer automate the creation of client/server systems. As an add-on to the standard SYNON/2E package, CSG provides a way to distribute a SYNON system between the PC GUI platform and the AS/400 as the database server. It makes educated guesses about which processes or interfaces would run most efficiently on which platform. It then generates distributed client/server code. Prototyping is one of the strengths of this type of approach. Users can be involved in the design process at all stages, ensuring that their requirements are being met. They can review screens and report formats as they are developed, correcting any problems and keeping the project on track.

The base package is SYNON/2E. It helps design and generate applications with relational databases, menus, screens, and procedures. The developer defines and refines the data model, specifying fields, edits, relational databases, and the like. SYNON generates the code for the application.

SYNON/2G is the graphics part of the package. It runs on the PC and provides the typically more intuitive and responsive interface of that environment. Object orientation and ease of use are the main points of SYNON/2G. Like SYNON/2E, SYNON/2G generates RPG or COBOL code.

The real client/server features of SYNON are to be found in SYNON/CSG. This package generates true client/server systems that distribute the application between the AS/400 and the PC Windows or OS/2 environment using the IBM advanced program-to-program communications (APPC) protocol. The system is still designed using SYNON/2E, but CSG can offload some of the functionality of this system to the PC GUI interface. The language that implements this on the PC is Micro Focus COBOL/2. AS/400 terminal interfaces are translated by CSG to GUI interfaces, resulting in user convenience and productivity gains. The programmer or developer does not need to know how to program Windows-type interfaces. SYNON/CSG automatically converts the AS/400 5250 interfaces to the Windows (or OS/2) environment, complete with pushbuttons and pull-down menus.

The AS/400 acts as a database server for the PC, offering a remote SQL access or native RPG or COBOL. Distributed relational database architecture (DRDA) support is available in this solution. IBM recommends using Token Ring as the connection method, with SNA APPC and PC Support (Client Access) running at the workstation. On the PC, the OS/2 Communications Manager handles the communications requests.

SYNON/CSG requires the following:

- AS/400:   any AS/400 except 9402 Y10 and 9404 B10
  ~V2R2 or later
  ~RPG or COBOL
  ~PC Support or Client Access
- PC: 386 or better with at least 16Mb of RAM and 120Mb disk
  ~PC Support or Client Access
  ~OS/2 2.0 Base and 2.0 ES or DOS 6.0 and Windows 3.1
  ~Micro Focus COBOL/2

21.5 VisualAge

VisualAge is an IBM client/server development tool with many integrated features. Object orientation implements client/server distributed processing with Windows GUI user screens. Smalltalk is the programming language that underlies these features. Like SYNON, VisualAge encourages a prototyping approach to system development. As modules are cast by the designer, the user can review them for appropriateness, as the work is in progress. This collaborative effort results in systems that are much more responsive to user requirements. In addition, modular development allows the application to be built up in sections or pieces, which are easier to work with and can be assembled later.

The Visual Program Generator (VPG) helps in implementing the often intricate and difficult-to-code GUI front-end. A portable library of reusable GUI tools and objects makes this task much more manageable. The AS/400 Component Library contains objects and modules used to access AS/400 data remotely in a variety of different data types. Change and history management ensure that the ongoing application development proceeds in a well-controlled manner by those who are authorized to do so.

VisualAge's Smalltalk language runs on the PC in both Windows and OS/2. It is actually a superset of IBM Smalltalk, containing extra functions for the client/server environment. A class hierarchy browser simplifies navigating and working with the various classes that are the basis of this and all object-oriented languages. Classes, methods, and instances are presented in a readily accessible visual tree format. VisualAge saves your working environment at the end of each session as an image. This image is like a bookmark, which allows you to open the session at a later time and have the windows and various objects all opened at the same place where you left them.

VisualAge provides the developer with many of the standard GUI controls for designing windows. These include PushButton, Checkbox, Combobox, EntryField, Label, Container, and others. Controls can be selected from the Controls pull-down menu and just clicked onto the window design form. They are easily moved and sized. User events that relate to these objects, like clicking on a pushbutton, are automatically trapped by the objects themselves. You just write code, called methods, for what happens when the user clicks on the pushbutton.

Many specialized object classes exist to implement the interface to the AS/400 from the PC. Record-level keyed database access via distributed data management (DDM) is supported. You can create, read, write, update, open, and close the various AS/400 file types from the PC. DRDA SQL access is also available with tables and views, commitment control, and database authorization. Data queues can be used as a technique to communicate with the AS/400, and AS/400 programs can be executed from the remote platform. Remote access is provided to AS/400 system functions such as data areas, system values, DDS, stored procedures, network attributes, and more. Remote procedure calls are also included.

VisualAge can automatically create a PC Smalltalk object that replicates an existing AS/400 object and the reverse. This very useful feature eliminates the need to reinvent the wheel. If you have a program on the AS/400 that you want to convert to the PC environment, VisualAge does it for you.

APPC and APPN communications services are at the heart of the VisualAge application. These allow the PC to communicate with the AS/400 on a peer-to-peer basis. Conversations can be initiated in which the PC functions as an intelligent client to the AS/400 databases and network services. PC Support (Client Access) allows the Windows client to converse with APPC. With OS/2, it is the Communications Manager that implements these conversations.

VisualAge/Manager provides management tools for version control. A unified view of the objects in a VisualAge application exists because all the code is actually stored on the AS/400, in a repository. Even the PC objects are stored on the AS/400 in shared folders. The image created for each developer is used to form an overall view of the application. This image is used by VisualAge/Manager to control the project. Components, history, configuration, and changes are all tracked by the Manager.

VisualAge/Packager helps in the creation of distribution modules for the users. This utility automatically creates the `.EXE` and the `.DLL` files required to run the application on the PC desktop.

Requirements are the following:

- AS/400: VisualAge
  ~V2R2 or higher
  ~PC Support or Client Access
- PC: 486 33 MHz or higher
  ~32Mb RAM
  ~PC Support or Client Access
  ~OS/2 2.0 and OS/2 ES or Windows 3.1 and DOS 5.0
  ~VisualAge

21.6 PROGRESS/400

PROGRESS/400 is an application development tool that facilitates the implementation of distributed processing among a variety of platforms. These include PROGRESS, Oracle, Sybase, OS/400, DB/2, and ODBC. The resulting applications are portable and interoperable. A fourth generation language (4GL) development environment allows the creation of a data dictionary and GUI windows for user interaction.

On the server, PROGRESS/400 DataServer furnishes data sets to the requesting program or client. A number of middleware drivers enable the PROGRESS application to plug into various databases on the back-end. This process is transparent to the client. It addresses a standard interface for data access, and the details of the back-end communications and access are handled by the drivers. This feature provides an independence of application design and a flexibility in data location and access. The data dictionary contains what it calls *schemes*, which define the remote database fields and files. Schemes provide a very open type of enterprise data access requiring that the AS/400 files be defined using IDDU. SQL-defined tables or databases do not work with PROGRESS.

PROGRESS/400 4GL + DataServer enables the development of systems that run on the AS/400 host. It lets the user develop and deploy distributed systems through the use of a 4GL work environment, prototyping, and query tools. Applications that have been designed on the AS/400 using PROGRESS/400 can be easily ported over to the PC. The PROGRESS language, with its English-like syntax, completely eliminates the need for RPG or COBOL subroutines or programs. It is a self-contained production environment. On the client, there is PROGRESS Application Development Environment (ADE), which allows the programmer to develop applications that access and update AS/400 databases. The development is on the PC, while the data requested is served by PROGRESS/400 DataServer on the AS/400. This interactive set of tools enables database definitions, screen painting, and coding. Also included are a User Interface Builder, a Data Dictionary, a Procedure Editor, a Report Builder, a Debugger, and more integrated tools. You can click controls, or widgets as they are called, onto the desktop form and then handle events for those controls. Widget attributes like font and color are easily changed by using the pop-up attribute menus attached to them. Frames are used to display fields in the PROGRESS application, and PROGRESS automatically creates the frames for you. You can easily alter them. The data dictionary supports triggers, referential integrity, automatic data validation defined at the field level, and user permissions.

PROGRESS run time

PROGRESS Query/Report and PROGRESS RESULTS are GUI report generators that offer easy point-and-click report design for developers and end users. These interactive tools allow the developer to deliver fully implemented reports with the system. Users can develop their own ad-hoc queries and download the results for further analysis and presentation.

Connections to the AS/400 are accomplished through APPC running over Token Ring, Ethernet, SDLC, ISDN, twinax, or X.25 networks. The client can be a Windows 3.1, OS/2 or RS/6000 AIX.

PROGRESS requires the following:

- AS/400:   V2R2 or higher
  ~PC Support (Client Access)
  ~PROGRESS/400 DataServer or 4GL + DataServer
- PC: OS/2 1.2 EE or higher or DOS 3.3 and Windows 3.0 or higher or AIX 3.1 2006 or higher and SNA Services/6000
  ~PROGRESS client product

21.7 Summary

Many advanced and sophisticated tools are available for client/server development using PCs and the AS/400. These two platforms alone offer hundreds of different combinations of networking, connectivity, and services. This chapter, and in fact this entire book, comes nowhere near exhausting the products that can be used to design distributed systems using the AS/400. The ones described, however, are some of the most useful and popular development packages. They have proven abilities. Some of them offer connectivity to other platforms as well. The more sophistication, automation, and interoperability included in a development environment, the more it costs, both at the server and the client. With some careful thought, this mix of packages, interfaces, and connection methods can yield effective solutions for your business requirements.

Part

5

Sample Applications

This section demonstrates how to connect the AS/400 to Windows programs using various examples. Our overriding concern in developing these programs is the interface. It is the nature of client/server applications to care for the user. We shield the user from the AS/400. He or she does not need to know anything about the AS/400 to access data from it, even to run CL and RPG programs on it—not even that the AS/400 exists. Certainly, we should not expect users to know how to get around on it. We inform them all along of the progress of their job. We let them do other work while waiting for AS/400 jobs to finish. We show them the elapsed time for the AS/400 portion, so they can estimate the time required. We reassure, expedite, and entertain with visuals. Most Windows programs perform these functions. They do not just let the user sit there guessing at what is going on behind the scenes. They inform and involve the user. This functionality is very reassuring for the user who is not all that familiar with how the system works. We as developers might know that pressing a pushbutton is going to invoke Rumba Tools EHLLAPI functions to submit an RPG program on a remote platform. The users don't know this, don't want to know this, and shouldn't have to know this. It is our obligation in developing client/server systems to cradle the user in the comfort and familiarity of the Windows environment while all this arcane technical stuff occurs behind the scenes. This is really the power of client/server systems: they take the fear out of computers while at the same time increasing the information gathering power of the end user. We make the complex look easy, friendly, and simple.

At this point, we assume a familiarity with the preceding elements of client/server environments, including RPG, Windows, PowerBuilder, etc. Many different combinations of programs, running on different platforms, can be involved. It is a good idea to draw a map or flowchart of the project as the first step, as seen in Figure 22.12 for the PowerBuilder example. The PC can communicate with the AS/400 in different ways in a client/server application. First and foremost, there is the Client Access router itself, which establishes a connection between the PC and the AS/400 over which all the other functions can run. Beyond this, other functions like File Transfer, Rumba Tools with EHLLAPI functions, ODBC, and data queues enable running AS/400 programs and accessing the files. Some processes run across the platform boundaries, while others run on their native platform.

The PowerBuilder example is by far the most involved. It presents the user with a window from which several pushbuttons run AS/400 programs, download files, allow data editing in Windows, and print reports through an interface with R&R report writer. Many different aspects of client/server systems development can be seen in this example. Parts of it can easily be used in other applications as modules. For instance, the use of radio buttons to select reports and submit them to an external report program is useful in almost any application. Rumba EHLLAPI functions are used to connect to the AS/400 and submit a program to batch. A data queue is used to monitor the progress of the submission through the batch queue, active processing, and finished status. When it is finished, the user is notified that a download can proceed. All this functionality happens at the simple touch of a button. Data editing is accomplished on the PC side through PowerBuilder's very useful data window, providing the ability for users to massage data from the AS/400 without touching the actual data on the AS/400—a very common requirement.

The Visual Basic sample program shows how to use an ODBC connection for a simple data viewer on the PC. It uses Visual Basic bound controls to connect the Visual Basic form to the AS/400 data. Once the ODBC data source is defined, it is a simple matter to create a bound control and connect through it to text boxes for display. The bound data control also offers a convenient way for navigating through the data in the actual physical file on the AS/400.

Crystal Reports is used to demonstrate an ODBC connection to the AS/400. It is a very useful and powerful tool that is easily implemented. In this way, Windows reports can be designed, using the easy, intuitive methods of the Windows environment. Just point and click fields from the AS/400 database onto the Crystal report, using all the labor-saving Experts of the Crystal paradigm. Once the ODBC data source is connected, the rest of the development is just like designing a report on a database on your C: drive. Users as well as MIS personnel can easily learn how to design Crystal reports.

A Lotus ODBC connection is shown for accounting departments. Like so many other ODBC connections, a Lotus connection is fairly easily accomplished. A few entries to a configuration file, and the AS/400 data is ready to be accessed through Lotus' Tools/Database menu. Data can be rolled directly from the server into the spreadsheet, ready for further analysis and formatting.

Rumba is thought of as a terminal emulation program for 5250 access to the AS/400. And so it is. But it also provides the ability to design sessions for other uses. Here, we use it to design an automatic download function that can be run from an icon in Windows. Without even opening a terminal session on the AS/400, files can be transferred up or down at the touch of a button.

These sample applications demonstrate the range of possibilities in designing client/server systems for cooperative processing between the AS/400 and the PC. Really, almost anything is possible, although not all is desirable. Applications that rely heavily on presentation and formatting as well as ease of use for the user are likely candidates for the client/server model. Programs that are highly interactive with AS/400 databases, including intensive data editing or lengthy batch processes, are probably not. Careful selection of likely projects can yield satisfactory results for the designer and the user. As our underlying tools and connections become more powerful and efficient over coming years, more and more will become feasible for PC-to-AS/400 client/server development.

22

PowerBuilder Sample Application

In this chapter, we use PowerBuilder to develop a client/server application. I have selected an inventory system as a representative application. It accesses the AS/400 and submits an RPG program to batch. It reads data queues to determine the status of the job. It then downloads data to the PC for the user to manipulate or edit the data. Finally, reports are printed. All these events take place from a single Windows screen with pushbuttons for each function (Figure 22.1). We actually evoke four different operating systems from this one screen, executing programs or functions in each. These operating systems are DOS, Windows, Novell (if our system is placed on the network), and OS/400. We presume, of course, that all the configurations are in place for this interoperability (see the networks chapter and Appendix B). We access the data using PowerBuilder, Client Access, CL, RPG, Rumba Tools for PowerBuilder, EHLLAPI, Clipper, ODBC, and R&R. This example is the most complex client/server application we develop in this book. It demonstrates how to do a wide range of activities.

The first button allows the user to update or refresh the data on the AS/400. When it is pressed, it opens a window asking the user for the month and year of the run (Figure 22.2). The user keys these in and presses OK. Now the PowerBuilder program signs on to the AS/400 and submits a job stream to batch through a CL program, updating the data. This request is accomplished using Rumba Tools for PowerBuilder, available separately from Wall Data. They include extended high-level language application program interface (EHLLAPI) functions. These can run the AS/400 from a remote program as if it were a human operator sitting at a terminal. The PowerBuilder program, using Rumba Tools, actually connects to the AS/400

ABC Inventory Review

Product	Jan	Feb	Mar	Apr	May	Jun	Jul	Aug	Sep	Oct
01119	2000	2046	1650	1800	1800	0	0	0	0	1100
01120	0	0	0	0	0	0	0	0	0	1
01129	9000	10032	7200	9000	9000	0	0	0	0	5235
01219	1100	1254	1254	0	0	0	0	0	0	869
01220	0	0	0	0	0	0	0	0	0	1
01229	4020	4008	4008	4000	4000	0	0	0	0	3562
01305	0	0	0	0	0	0	0	0	0	2
01306	0	0	0	0	0	0	0	0	0	4
01365	0	0	0	0	0	0	0	0	0	10
01403	0	0	0	0	0	0	0	0	0	
01404	0	0	0	0	0	0	0	0	0	
01519	360	5580	4185	1300	3500	3500	0	0	0	1230
01619	1215	3510	3375	1800	3500	3500	0	0	0	1564
01719	1080	1305	1080	1300	1500	1500	0	0	0	721
01819	950	1100	1000	1300	1700	1700	0	0	0	711
01919	0	1600	1600	1600	2000	2000	0	0	0	946
05119	2500	2508	2046	2400	2400	2400	0	0	0	1412
05129	10020	12504	12480	10750	10750	10750	0	0	0	7544
05219	2400	2046	2046	2000	2000	2000	0	0	0	1113

Update	DownLoad	Edit	SaveData	Print	Quit

Figure 22.1 Windows screen.

ABC Inventory Review

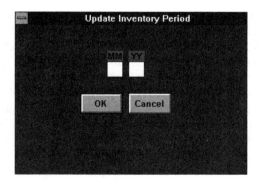

Figure 22.2 Window that asks for month and year.

and signs on as if it were a user. Then it looks around to make sure it is at the right screen. Next, it runs a CL program (which, of course, we also wrote). This CL program writes and reads data queues and monitors the progress of the RPG jobs through the batch queue and active status until finished. At each stage, the PowerBuilder program informs the user what is happening on the AS/400. The program signs on the AS/400 (Figure 22.3) and submits the job to the job queue (Figure 22.4). When the job becomes active on the AS/400, we notify the user of this fact (Figure 22.5). Finally, when the job is finished, we show a message saying so (Figure 22.6). We count off the elapsed time in a graphic window, like many Windows programs. The user can switch to another task, such as Excel or WordPerfect while the program is running. When the job is finished, the PC beeps, notifying the user that it has finished running the AS/400 job. He or she can then return to this application and continue with the download.

This procedure demonstrates how to run an AS/400 program from a Windows program. We do not require the user to deal with the AS/400 at all. The program takes care of the connection and the job submission. We inform the user all along of the progress of the job. We let the user perform other work while waiting, and check on the elapsed time for the AS/400 portion to estimate the time required. This elapsed time display is also for entertainment, being something active to look at on the screen while pro-

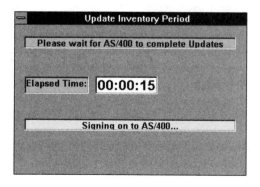

Figure 22.3 Signing on the AS/400.

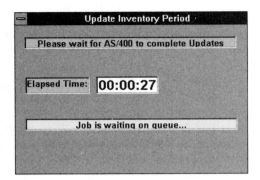

Figure 22.4 Submitting the job to queue.

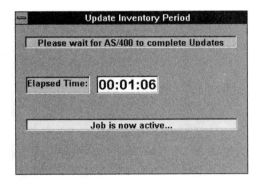

Figure 22.5 Notifying the user.

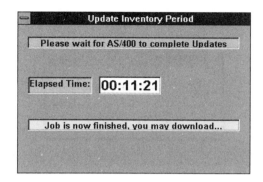

Figure 22.6 Completion message.

cessing is going on. We, the developers, know that the pushbutton is a graphic control event trapped into invoking Rumba Tools EHLLAPI functions to submit a stream of CL and RPG programs on the AS/400. The user probably has no use for this knowledge, and in fact, should be entirely insulated from the complexities of our client/server system. We deal in complexities so the user can work simply and easily.

The user clicks on the next pushbutton to execute the download, which brings up a response window that must be answered before proceeding (Figure 22.7). Because we want to make sure the user does not proceed to another step before the download is finished, and also just for demonstration purposes, we use the extended DOS version of the Client Access download function (Figure 22.8). It is possible to use the extended DOS functions of PC Support from within Windows programs. Because it is a DOS program, nothing else can run until it is finished. Using the PC Support File Transfer function, we design a download definition to be run in batch. Once the data has been brought down to the PC, it is imported to a PC-type database. I have selected the dBASE format to show how ODBC can access various types of databases. This section of the application shows how to run DOS programs from Windows. I use Clipper to manage the data in DOS and dBASE. Of course, we could have used the Client Access native interface, along with Rumba's file

Figure 22.7 Response window.

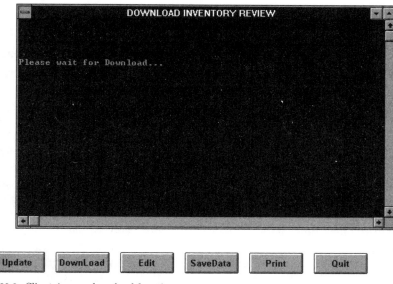

Figure 22.8 Client Access download function.

transfer, for a Windows download of the data. We take a look at how that is done, as well.

So far, we have run two remote functions from the PowerBuilder desktop—a remote AS/400 command and a DOS or Rumba file transfer. Now we come to the native PowerBuilder part of the application. The third button puts up a data window for editing the data we have brought over from the AS/400. This window shows the data in tabular format, much like a spreadsheet (Figure 22.9). Here, the user can scroll, pan, page up, and page down through the data. This navigation can occur via the arrow keys or the mouse, depending on preference. It is also possible to freeze the titles on the left, just like in Lotus, so that when panning right, we always see the item numbers on the left, and they do not roll off the screen. The fourth button saves the data. This, too, is native PowerBuilder and quite simple. It uses an SQL statement to save the edited data back to the database.

The fifth button runs the R&R reports from a user window (Figure 22.10). We do not need to go into the internals of the R&R report design. You could really use any report writer here that is compatible with your PC database that can run from PowerBuilder. Crystal Reports would be another good choice. It is bundled with Visual Basic or available separately as Crystal Pro. Here, we are running an external Windows program from within the PowerBuilder application, similar to using the Rumba download earlier.

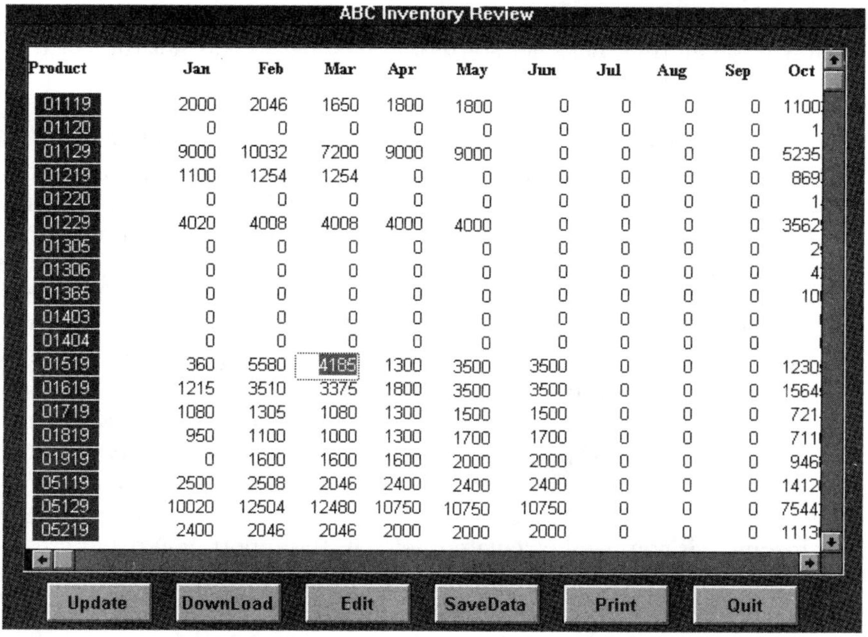

ABC Inventory Review

Product	Jan	Feb	Mar	Apr	May	Jun	Jul	Aug	Sep	Oct
01119	2000	2046	1650	1800	1800	0	0	0	0	1100
01120	0	0	0	0	0	0	0	0	0	1
01129	9000	10032	7200	9000	9000	0	0	0	0	5235
01219	1100	1254	1254	0	0	0	0	0	0	869
01220	0	0	0	0	0	0	0	0	0	1
01229	4020	4008	4008	4000	4000	0	0	0	0	3562
01305	0	0	0	0	0	0	0	0	0	2
01306	0	0	0	0	0	0	0	0	0	4
01365	0	0	0	0	0	0	0	0	0	10
01403	0	0	0	0	0	0	0	0	0	
01404	0	0	0	0	0	0	0	0	0	
01519	360	5580	4185	1300	3500	3500	0	0	0	1230
01619	1215	3510	3375	1800	3500	3500	0	0	0	1564
01719	1080	1305	1080	1300	1500	1500	0	0	0	721
01819	950	1100	1000	1300	1700	1700	0	0	0	711
01919	0	1600	1600	1600	2000	2000	0	0	0	946
05119	2500	2508	2046	2400	2400	2400	0	0	0	1412
05129	10020	12504	12480	10750	10750	10750	0	0	0	7544
05219	2400	2046	2046	2000	2000	2000	0	0	0	1113

Update   DownLoad   Edit   SaveData   Print   Quit

Figure 22.9 Spreadsheet format of data.

ABC Inventory Review

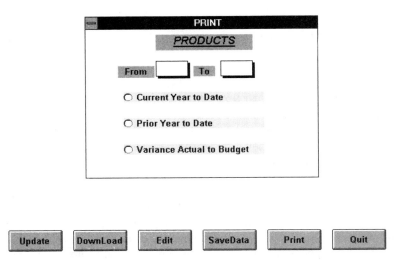

Figure 22.10   Button for R&R reports.

How to do all this? Let's get started. Remember, this is not the place to learn PowerBuilder. The PowerBuilder chapter is for that. We assume some familiarity with PowerBuilder for this application.

First, we need a database to store the download from the AS/400 and to be the source of editing and reporting. Create a dBASE database by typing dBASE at the DOS command prompt. Then, define fields as in Figure 22.11. Press Ctrl-End to save the database definition, and it is ready to receive a download from the AS/400.

The main interface for all of these procedures is the PowerBuilder application. From here, all other functions are executed. We are able to run programs on other platforms like the AS/400 as well as other Windows and DOS programs. All these are called from the PowerBuilder program itself. Because this is a distributed process, you have a choice of where to start. You could write the RPG program first or the PowerBuilder application. It is important to keep the big picture in mind while working on the pieces, because actions in RPG influence what happens later in PowerBuilder or R&R. For instance, if you need calculated fields in the report, you could create them in RPG, Clipper, PowerBuilder, or the R&R report itself. As with most client/server systems, all these options can get complicated and confusing, so I suggest drawing a map of the functions first, such as Figure 22.12. Note the levels of interaction between the PC and the AS/400. First, there is Client Access itself. Without this connection, none of the other distributed processes would be possible. Then there is the Rumba Tools interface for running the CL and RPG programs. Finally, there is the download. Apart from these, all processes run in their own environment. The RPG program runs in a batch queue on the AS/400 just like any other RPG program, except it was called from the PC.

Now let us create the PowerBuilder application—the base from which all other functions are launched. Start up PowerBuilder and click on the Application icon. Select File New and enter a name for the new application. Because we are doing a sample inventory review program, I suggest InvRev for the application name. Note that the extension for the Power-Builder application is .PBL, pronounced "pibble," which means Power-Builder Library. Click on No when PowerBuilder asks if you want to generate an application template. We will add all our functions ourselves. You see the application icon in the Application Painter (Figure 22.13). We now add windows and controls to it. After we have added these, you can right-click on the application icon to expand it into a graphical tree view of the entire application. Now click the Script icon for the application (on the left toolbar) and enter the code for the opening event of the application

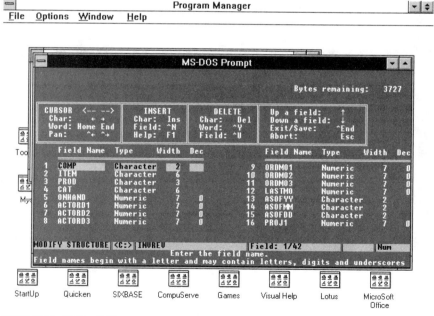

Figure 22.11 Define fields.

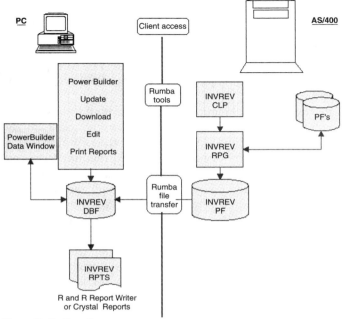

Figure 22.12 Function map.

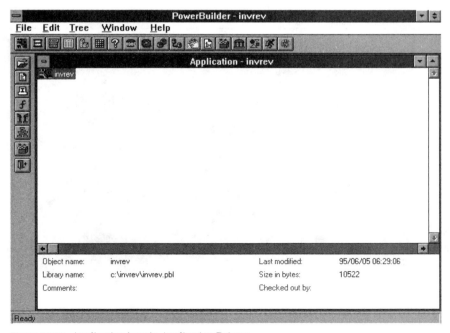

Figure 22.13 Application icon in Application Painter.

(Figure 22.14). These statements help define the ODBC data source for dBASE to the PowerBuilder application.

Actually, we are not using the ODBC connection to the AS/400 here, although we could (see the Visual Basic sample application for direct ODBC connection to AS/400). We are creating a file on the AS/400 and downloading it to a PC database. We are then accessing that database. We do this for two reasons. First, we do not want to update the data on the AS/400. We want to collect it and massage it for reporting purposes, leaving the original data unchanged. Second, we gain speed in editing by downloading the data and having a local database for the interactive process.

The open event for the application also opens the main window. Every application must have an opening script.

It is necessary to set up the ODBC connection to the data source so you can define any data source to PowerBuilder for which Windows has a registered (installed) ODBC driver. (See the ODBC appendix for how to set up the AS/400 ODBC driver.) We, however, are not taking that route. Click on the ODBC icon. Note that you might not have an ODBC icon. PowerBuilder has too many icons to show on the toolbar, so they are not all there. If you need one that is not there, close all painters and click on File/Toolbars/Customize (Figure 22.15). You now see the full collection of PowerBuilder icons (Figure 22.16). You can drag and drop the one you want into the cur-

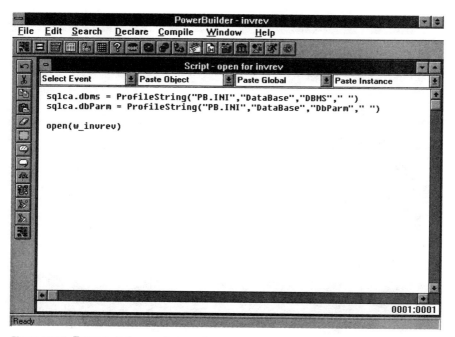

Figure 22.14 Enter code for opening event.

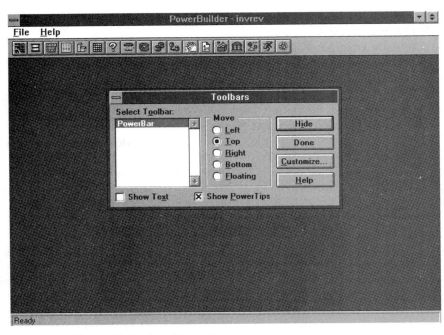

Figure 22.15 Click on File/Toolbars/Customize.

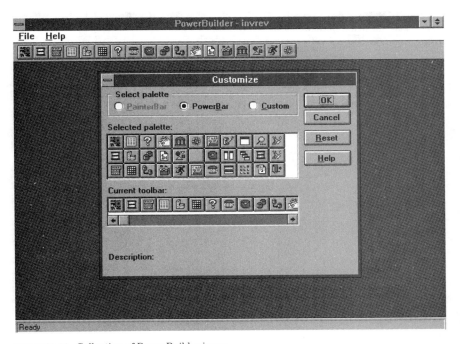

Figure 22.16 Collection of PowerBuilder icons.

rent toolbar. The ODBC icon looks like a green drum with ODBC on it. While you're at it, get the DataBase Profile icon, too. It's a green drum with a lightning flash. Once you have the correct icons on the toolbar, click on the ODBC icon.

The Configure ODBC window opens (Figure 22.17). Here, you select from the top list box the type of ODBC driver you want to use. Once selected, existing names of data sources using that ODBC driver are listed in the box at the bottom of the window. You can edit an existing one or create a new one. Press Create to reveal the ODBC dBASE Driver Setup window (Figure 22.18). Enter a descriptive name for your data source in the Data Source Name box. Enter the path of the dBASE file(s) in the Database Directory box. Select a Create Type (DBASE3). Press Define to get to the Define File window (Figure 22.19). Here, you just highlight a file and press OK. Next is the Define Table window (Figure 22.20). You can select an existing index file for the database specified earlier. Click OK and you have a data source defined for PowerBuilder using the ODBC driver.

It is a good idea to check out the newly created data source, just to make sure it is working correctly. Click on the Database Profiles icon on the toolbar to bring up the Database Profiles window (Figure 22.21). Here, you can select a database profile or data source that has been defined for PowerBuilder by highlighting it and pressing OK. PowerBuilder is now hooked up to that data

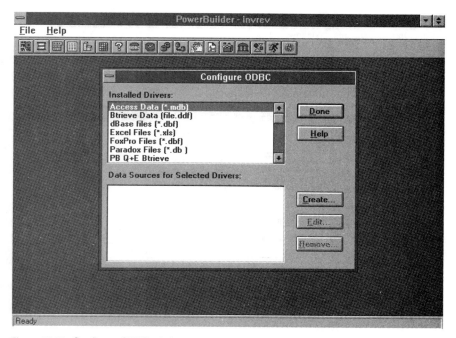

Figure 22.17 Configure ODBS window.

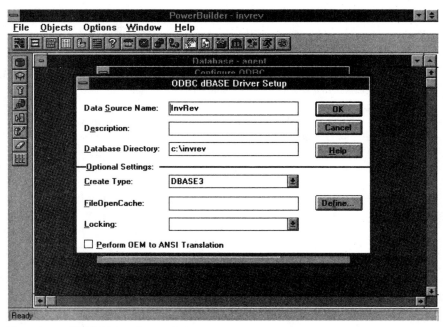

Figure 22.18 dBASE Driver Setup window.

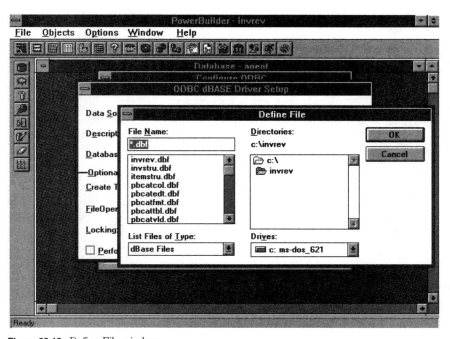

Figure 22.19 Define File window.

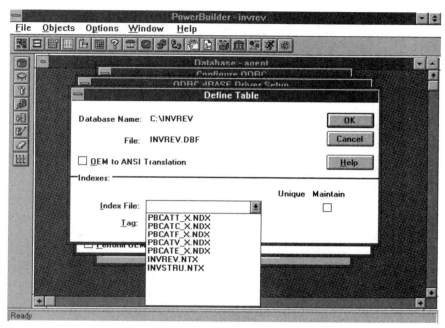

Figure 22.20   Define Table window.

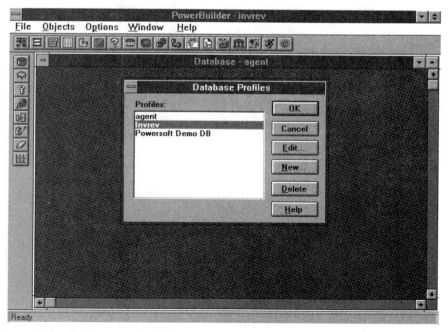

Figure 22.21   Database Profiles window.

source. Next, press the database icon in the toolbar. PowerBuilder shows you a list of databases in that data source. In this context, a data source is actually a directory. The ODBC driver can present any database in the specified directory or data source to the PowerBuilder application. You see a list of databases in the data source directory (Figure 22.22). Select one and press Open. PowerBuilder connects to it. Now you see the database represented as a list box of field names (Figure 22.23). Once you see this, you know you have a good data source. Note the key at the upper left of the database list box. The key means that the database is keyed, or has an index associated with it.

Now that we have the database defined and connected through an ODBC driver to PowerBuilder, we can set up the application. Open the Window Painter and place six pushbuttons across the bottom of the form as in Figure 22.24. These pushbuttons will run the entire application. We attach code to them to provide the gamut of services for the application from Update through DownLoad, Edit, SaveData, Print, and Quit. You can set the window style for this, the main window of the application, by right clicking on a blank spot on the window (Figure 22.25). The use of the right mouse button to access attributes of objects is a nice feature of PowerBuilder. Menus appear so you can set colors, styles, and attributes, such as visible and resizable. Also note the selection at the top of the menu for Script. This is how you attach code to the ob-

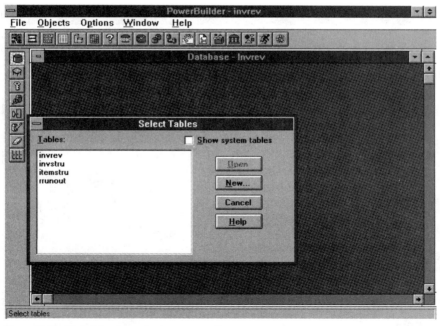

Figure 22.22 List of databases in data source directory.

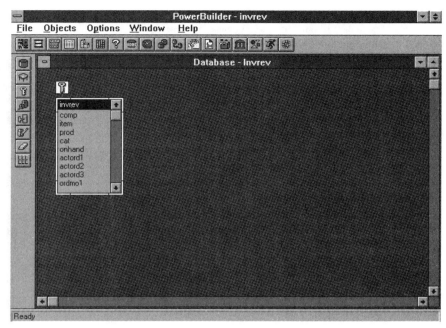

Figure 22.23 Database as list box of field names.

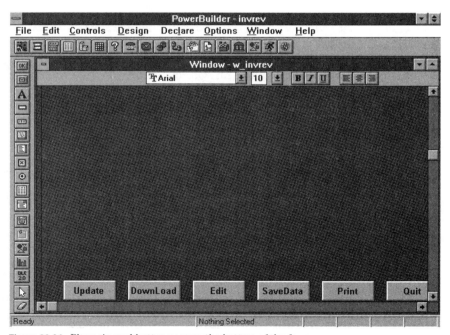

Figure 22.24 Place six pushbuttons across the bottom of the form.

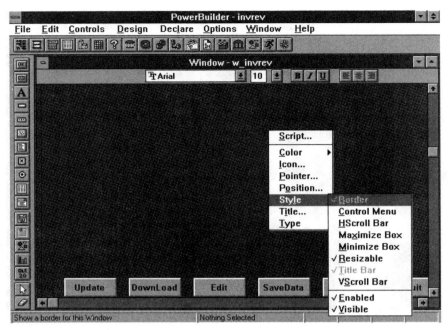

Figure 22.25   Right-click on blank spot.

ject. Click on that and a Script window opens up (Figure 22.26). Here, we select the event for the object. We are concerned with the open event for the
window. When the window is first opened by the application, we want to connect to the data source and set up a TransObject, or transaction object, for the
data. This is how PowerBuilder handles updates to the database through the
ODBC driver. Actually, dw_invrev refers to a data window that we have not
yet designed and will generate a compiler error. Objects referred to in the code
must be known to PowerBuilder.

So, we just comment out this line with the double slash // until the data
window is designed. We must remember to come back later, however, and
uncomment this line for the program to work. Open the Data Window
Painter to design the window for editing the data once downloaded from
the AS/400. Figure 22.27 shows the Select Data Window screen. Click New
to design a new one, which results in the next screen for New Data Window
(Figure 22.28). Here, we can specify the type of data window we want.
Quick Select for Data Source and Grid for Presentation Style will be our
choices. Press OK. Now we have the Quick Select window (Figure 22.29)
where we can pick a table and select fields from it. As columns are placed
at the bottom of the screen, it is possible to indicate sorts and selection criteria based on them. We will not do this now. Press OK. The next screen allows us to specify sort columns. Here, we drag and drop our sort columns

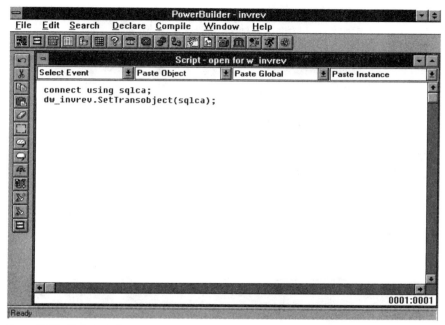

Figure 22.26 Script window opens.

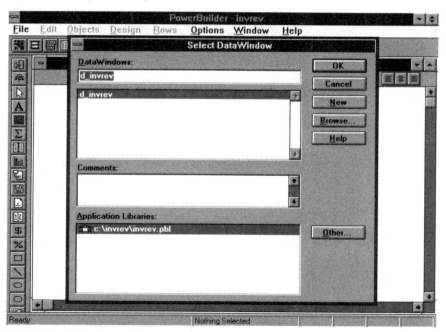

Figure 22.27 Select data window screen.

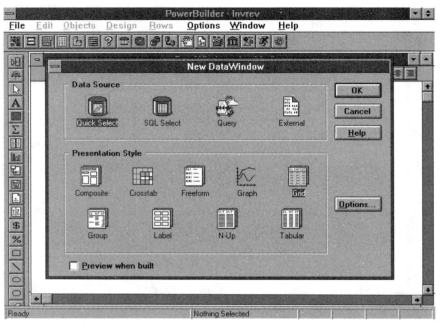

Figure 22.28   New Data window.

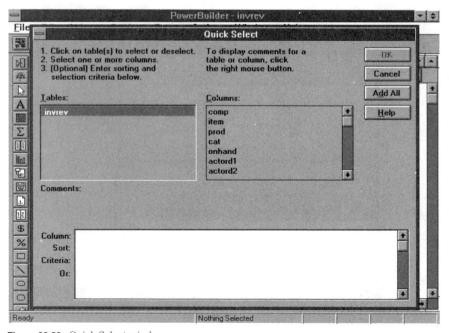

Figure 22.29   Quick Select window.

from the list at the left to the box at the right. We can also specify ascending or descending, as you can see. Finally, we come to the actual data window painter itself (Figure 22.30), which is where most of the work is performed for formatting data edits in PowerBuilder, and is one of the primary strengths of it. This data window painter makes it quite easy to custom design many different editing and input screens for the user. We include the fields we want and convert the numeric run date from the AS/400 into the character representations of the months you see across the top of the screen with computed fields (Figure 22.31).

Some properties of the data window need to be defined to implement data entry and editing. First, we need to specify tab order. Tab order is the order in which fields are accessed when the user presses the tab key. If a field does not have a tab order, it is not accessible. Note in Figure 22.30 the small numbers above each data column. These are the tab numbers specified by selecting Design/Tab Order from the menu. When finished with setting up the tab order, you must select Design/Tab Order again to get out of this function.

Next, we need to set up the Update properties of the data window. Select Rows/Update to get to this screen (Figure 22.32). Here, we need to select a table to update (use the down arrow). Then we must tell PowerBuilder to Allow Updates, select Updateable Columns, and select which of these

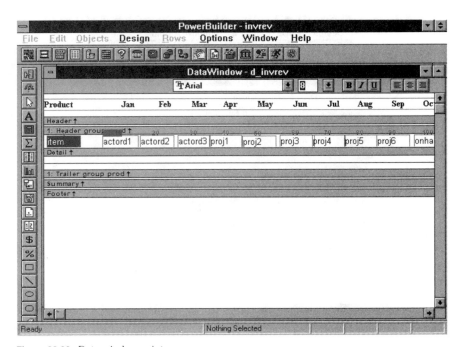

Figure 22.30 Data window painter.

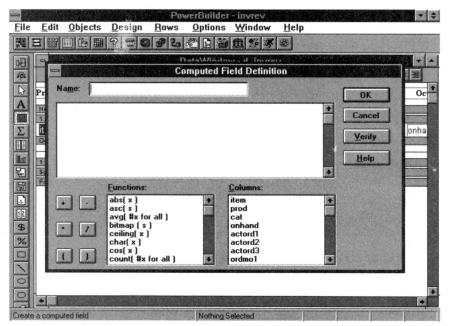

Figure 22.31 Using computed fields to create months.

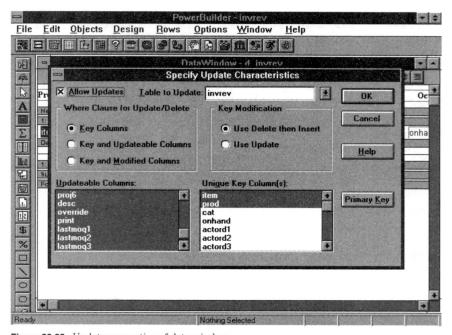

Figure 22.32 Update properties of data window.

columns are to be used as Unique Key Columns. PowerBuilder must have a unique key for the ODBC driver to find the correct record in the data source for update. The data window is now designed and enabled for updates. Click on the Preview icon at the top of the left toolbar to see what the window will look like when the user runs it (Figure 22.33). Cosmetic changes can be made to the window by pressing the right mouse key on a blank portion of the window (Figure 22.34), including color, fonts, position, border style, and the like.

OK, we now have a data window. Let's attach it to the Edit button in the main window. We also need to remember to uncomment the reference to the data window in the open event of the main window. Go to the Window Painter (not the Data Window Painter). Right-click to bring up the Script Painter for the open event of the main window. Take out the double slash from the line that says:

```
//dw_invrev.SetTransobject(sqlca);
```

Save the file. Now we can click on the data window icon in the toolbar at the left of the screen to place a blank data window in the main window, which appears as a small blank rectangle. Use the mouse to drag the corners of this data window to the approximate size you want. Right-click on the

Product	Jan	Feb	Mar	Apr	May	Jun	Jul	Aug	Sep	Oc
01119	2000	2046	1650	1800	1800	0	0	0	0	110
01120	0	0	0	0	0	0	0	0	0	
01129	9000	10032	7200	9000	9000	0	0	0	0	523
01219	1100	1254	1254	0	0	0	0	0	0	86
01220	0	0	0	0	0	0	0	0	0	
01229	4020	4008	4008	4000	4000	0	0	0	0	356
01305	0	0	0	0	0	0	0	0	0	
01306	0	0	0	0	0	0	0	0	0	
01365	0	0	0	0	0	0	0	0	0	1
01403	0	0	0	0	0	0	0	0	0	
01404	0	0	0	0	0	0	0	0	0	
01519	360	5580	4185	1300	3500	3500	0	0	0	123
01619	1215	3510	3375	1800	3500	3500	0	0	0	156
01719	1080	1305	1080	1300	1500	1500	0	0	0	72
01819	950	1100	1000	1300	1700	1700	0	0	0	71
01919	0	1600	1600	1600	2000	2000	0	0	0	94
05119	2500	2508	2046	2400	2400	2400	0	0	0	141

PowerBuilder - invrev
File   Edit   Display   Rows   Window   Help

DataWindow - d_invrev

Hit Cancel to stop retrieval. Rows retrieved: 125   No rows

Figure 22.33 Using the preview icon.

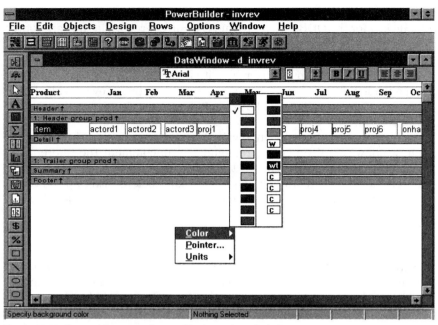

Figure 22.34 Press right mouse key on blank portion of window.

data window to open the menu for specifying which data window you want to place here (Figure 22.35). This is the reason we had to design the data window first—to have it available for placing here. Select your data window from the list and press OK. The data window is placed in the main window. You must adjust it for dimension and position above the pushbuttons.

Now, right-click on the Edit pushbutton and add the code that opens the data window for editing when the user clicks on the button (Figure 22.36). We make the data window visible and enabled and set the focus to it. This raises the question as to whether we want the data window visible before the user clicks the Edit button. Perhaps we do not. Right-click on the data window to bring up the usual attributes menu (Figure 22.37) and select Style. Turn on HScroll Bar for horizontal scrolling, and Vscroll Bar for vertical scrolling. Turn off the Maximize and Minimize boxes because we don't want the user changing or losing the edit screen. Also turn off Resizable, Enabled, and Visible. These determine the defaults for the data window, when the application is started. Note that we change their attributes later from within the code attached to the pushbuttons. Click on the icon of the running man on the toolbar at the top of the screen to run the application and test it.

Now for the tricky part—running an AS/400 program from a PowerBuilder button. We are using Rumba Tools for PowerBuilder, which provides several

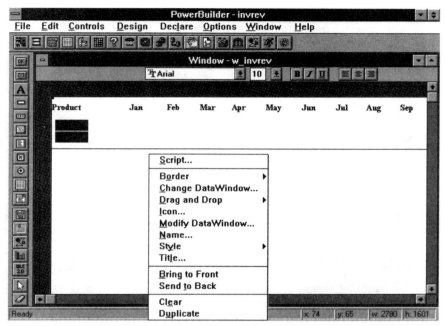

Figure 22.35 Open menu to specify which data window you want.

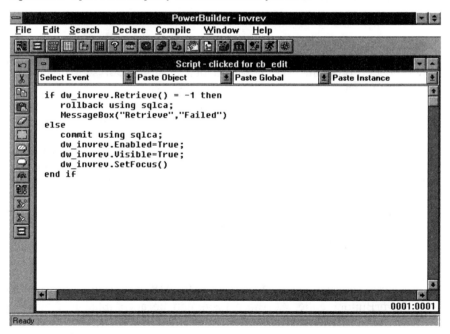

Figure 22.36 Data window for editing.

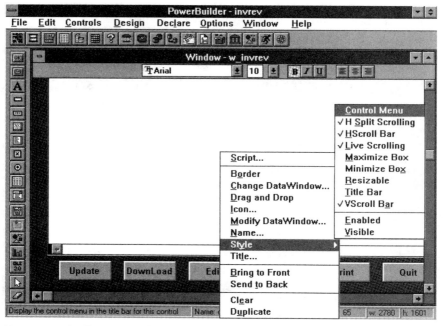

Figure 22.37 Attributes menu.

useful tools. The easiest to use is EHLLAPI. These functions allow the programmer to build a robot-like remote control for the AS/400 into the PowerBuilder program. The PowerBuilder program can sign on to the AS/400 and ensure it is in the right place, just like we do. It can then type commands at the command line, adding parameters that the user provided on the PC side. It checks on the status of the job as it is running, as a user might. Finally, when the job has finished, it signs off.

We need to enable several things to pull this off. First, we need a Rumba session to be used for this purpose. This session is designed just like any other Rumba session, with a few differences. We want it to sign on automatically when it is invoked, so it needs an automacro for this. The user profile fed into automatic sign-on determines many characteristics of the session, such as file authorities and start-up screen. We need to think about this carefully, because we want the user profile for the EHLLAPI session to have adequate authority for the necessary AS/400 objects without being able to do any damage. Also, it needs to have EHLLAPI enabled and to be given a short (one character) EHLLAPI name to be used later in the PowerBuilder code. All these tasks can be accomplished from the Rumba menu. Click on the Session icon in the Rumba group. (See the Rumba sample application chapter for details.)

We need Rumba Tools for PowerBuilder, available separately from Wall Data. Once this is installed, we need to define its functions to the Power-Builder application, which is done by selecting Declare Global External Functions from the Main window menu (Figure 22.38). You then import the text file WDHLLAPI.TXT, which comes with Rumba Tools, to this window using cut and paste. This file is probably in the C:\PB4\RUMBA directory. We now have an EHLLAPI-enabled Rumba session with autosign-on and Rumba Tools functions defined for PowerBuilder. We are ready.

The Update pushbutton opens a new window from which to get user input, submit the command to the AS/400, and show the user the progress of the submitted job. When the user clicks on the Update button, it simply opens up the new window. Design this window by using the Window Painter. It has several features. Two long text boxes (single-line edits, or SLE) for messages, two text boxes for the user to input month and year, a text box to count off elapsed time, and three pushbuttons (Figure 22.39). The OK button runs the entire procedure. Another OK button appears at the end to inform the user that all is finished and to proceed to download. It simply says:

```
close(parent)
```

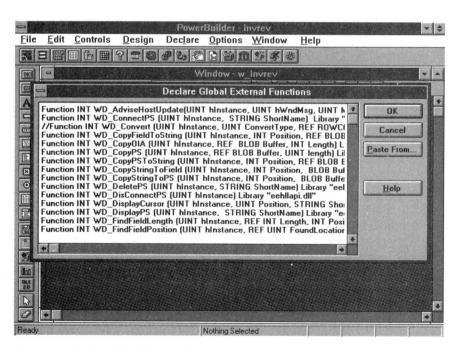

Figure 22.38 Declare Global External Functions from Main window menu.

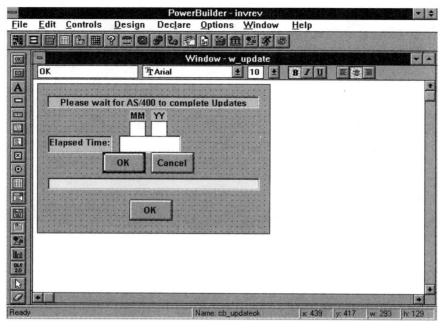

Figure 22.39 Proceed to download button.

in its Clicked event. Not all these controls are visible at the same time when the program is running.

First, we should design the new window, then reference it in the Update button, to avoid the undefined variable problem we had with the data window (we had this problem for instructive purposes). Open the Window Painter and create this small window. When the user clicks on Update, the window opens to get the month and year. Then, the user clicks OK, and it is this button that implements the connection with the AS/400. Figure 22.3 showed the system counting off the elapsed time and what was occurring on the AS/400.

A CL program called INVREVCL is used to submit the job stream on the AS/400 (Figure 22.40), which is what is actually called from the Power-Builder program. It receives command-line parameters. Then it clears the data queue INVREV and writes a value '(ACTIVE!!)' to the data queue. Because all this is submitted to a batch queue, we know the job has gone to active status when we see the word '(ACTIVE)' in the data queue. While the entire job stream is waiting on the batch queue behind other jobs, the data queue is empty. A CL program called DQCHK (Figure 22.41) is run by the PowerBuilder application at set intervals to look in the data queue, thus monitoring the progress of the job. If the data queue is empty, the job is on the queue. If it says '(ACTIVE!!)' the job is active. When it says '(OK**Done)', the job is

```
Columns  . . .  :    1  71            Browse                    DPSMOD/QCLSRC
SEU==>                                                          INVREVCL
*************** Beginning of data ***************************************
0001.00 PGM   (&MMYY)
0002.00
0003.00  DCL   VAR(&MMYY) TYPE(*CHAR) LEN(4)
0004.00  DCL   VAR(&MM) TYPE(*CHAR) LEN(2)
0005.00  DCL   VAR(&YY) TYPE(*CHAR) LEN(2)
0006.00  CHGVAR     VAR(&MM) VALUE(%SST(&MMYY 1 2))
0007.00  CHGVAR     VAR(&YY) VALUE(%SST(&MMYY 3 2))
0008.00
0009.00  CALL QCLRDTAQ (INVREV QGPL)
0010.00  SBMJOB CMD(CALL QSNDDTAQ (INVREV QGPL x'00010f' '(ACTIVE!!)'))
0011.00  SBMJOB CMD(CALL INVREVPC (&MM &YY))
0012.00  SBMJOB CMD(CALL QSNDDTAQ (INVREV QGPL x'00010f' '(OK**Done)'))
0013.00
0014.00  ENDPGM
***************** End of data *******************************************
```

Figure 22.40 Submitting the job stream on the AS/400. ® Copyright IBM Corp. 1981, 1994.

```
Columns. . . :  1  71     Browse            CLNTSRVR/QCLSRC
SEU==>                                      DQCHK
*************** Beginning of data ****************************************
0001.00PGM
0002.00
0003.00 DCLF  FILE(CLNTSRVR/DQSCR)
0004.00 DCL  VAR(&DQDONE)TYPE(*CHAR)LEN(10)
0005.00 CHGVAR VAR(&DQDONE) VALUE('    ')
0006.00
0007.00 CALL QRCVTAQ (INVREV QGPLx'00010F'&DQDONEx'0000f')
0008.00 SNDRCVF RCDFMT(DQ1)
0009.00ENDPGM
***************** End of data *******************************************
```

Figure 22.41 DQCHK program.

finished and the PowerBuilder program can continue (Figure 22.42). This DQCHK CL program uses a display to show the contents of the data queue. The PowerBuilder application can read the display looking for values in the data queue (actually in this display, the CL program reads the data queue). When the job is finished, the data queue contains the value '(OK**Done)'. When the PowerBuilder application sees this on the AS/400 display, it knows the job has finished. The CL program INVREVCL, in addition to reading and writing data queues, submits the RPG program INVREVPC to collect data from various AS/400 databases into physical file INVREV. This is the file to be downloaded to the PC.

Right-click on the Update button to add the code to the Clicked event to open the Update window. It is very simple: Open(w_update). The open event for this update window contains the following code to make invisible or hide controls we don't want to see yet:

```
st_pleasewait.hide()
st_complete.hide()
```

```
st_elapsed.hide()
st_elapse_label.hide()
cb_okfinished.hide()
```

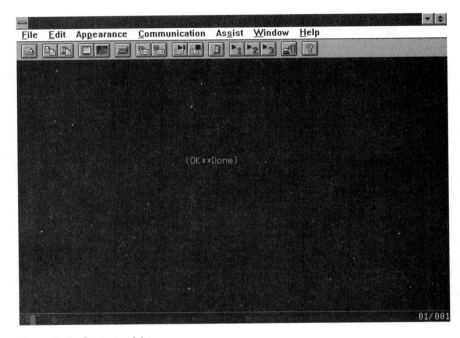

Figure 22.42 Contents of data queue.

When the user clicks OK to run the submission, we will show and hide other controls. Right click on the OK button in the Update window to add this script. Figure 22.43 is the full PowerBuilder code that submits the job to the AS/400 through the Rumba session:

Figure 22.43 Full PowerBuilder code.

```
//_____
// edit date: this is a comment, beginning with the double slash
//_____

if sle_MM.text < '01' or sle_MM.text > '12' &
or sle_YY.text < '94' or sle_YY.text > '99' then
    beep(1 )
    MessageBox("EDIT","Date not Valid, e.g. 03 95")
    sle_MM.setfocus()
    goto badmmyy;
end if

//_____
// This section hides and shows the various window devices we want now
// cb_ is command button, sle_ is single line edit, st_ is static text
//_____

cb_UpdateOK.hide()
cb_UpdateCancel.hide()
```

Figure 22.43 Continued.

```
sle_mm.hide()
sle_yy.hide()
st _mm.hide()
st_yy.hide()
st_elapsed.show()
st_elapse_label.show()

//_____
// Define variables needed in the functions
//_____

char active;
active = ' ';
int result;
uint location;
uint location2;
ulong ssp_lwait;
//_____
// build the string to be submitted to the AS/400 as a command
// note the use of double and single quotes and concatenation to construct the line:
// call invrevcl ('12' '95')
// or whatever the date is
//_____
string command;
command = "call invrevcl ('" + sle_MM.text + sle_YY.text + "')";

//_____
// declare an unsigned integer called hwnd to be the handle of the window for
// program reference
//_____

uint hwnd;
hwnd = handle(this);

//_____
// load a text box with a message for the user and show it
//_____

st_complete.text='Signing on to AS/400...';
st_complete.show()

//_____
// Connect the PowerBuilder window to a Rumba session for EHLLAPI functions.

// We can make the window visible or shrink it to an icon while it is running.
//_____

WD_RunProfile("c:\rumba\as400\clntsrvr.wsf",7) // 9 is visible 7 is icon
WD_ConnectPS(Hwnd,"R")

//_____
// Look for the PDM screen when the session signs on. Wait for it.
// The user profile says to start on the PDM screen.
//_____

location = 0;
location2 = 0;
do while location = 0
        WD_SearchPS(Hwnd,location,1,"(PDM)")
loop
```

Figure 22.43 Continued.

```
//_____
// Send the command, and then the Enter key
//_____

WD_SendKey(Hwnd,command)
WD_SendKey(Hwnd,"@E")

//_____
// look at data queue to see where the job is
//_____

WD_SendKey(Hwnd,"call clntsrvr/dqchk")
WD_SendKey(Hwnd,"@E")
WD_wait(Hwnd)
WD_Pause(Hwnd,6)
WD_SearchPS(Hwnd,location2,1,"(ACTIVE!!)")
WD_wait(Hwnd)
WD_Send Key(Hwnd,"@E")
if location2 <> 0 or active = 'Y' then
        st_complete.text='Job is now Active...';
        active = 'Y';
else
        st_complete.text='Job is waiting on Queue...';
end if
st_complete.show()

//_____
// wait until INVREVCL is finished processing
// count of elapsed time in HH:MM:SS to amuse and inform user
//_____

dec n;
dec start_time;
dec restart_time;
dec this_time;
dec dif_time;
dec hhmmss;
dec hh;
dec mm;
dec ss;
char done;
done = 'n';

start_time = (Hour(Now()) * 3600) + (Minute(Now()) * 60) + Second(Now());

do while done <> 'y'

    restart_time = (Hour(Now()) * 3600) + (Minute(Now()) * 60) + Second(Now());
    dif_time = 0;

    // sleep number of seconds, then check AS/400 data queue
    do while dif_time < 180

            yield()
            this_time = (Hour(Now()) * 3600) + (Minute(Now()) * 60) +
Second(Now());
            dif_time = this_time - restart_time;
            WD_Pause(Hwnd,1)

            // show elapsed time in text box
            hhmmss = this_time - start_time;
            hh = Int(hhmmss / 3600);
```

Figure 22.43 Continued.

```
        if hh > 0 then
                hhmmss = hhmmss - (hh * 3600);
        end if
        mm = Int(hhmmss / 60);
        if mm > 0 then
                hhmmss = hhmmss - (mm * 60);
        end if
        ss = hhmmss;
        st_elapsed.text = string(hh,"00") + ':' + string(mm,"00") +':' +
string(ss,"00");
        loop

        // look at data queue
        WD_SendKey(Hwnd,"call clntsrvr/dqchk")
        WD_SendKey(Hwnd,"@E")
        WD_wait(Hwnd)
        WD_SearchPS(Hwnd,location,1," (OK**Done)")
        WD_SearchPS(Hwnd,location2,1,"( ACTIVE!!)")
        WD_wait(Hwnd)
        WD_SendKey(Hwnd,"@E ")

        if location <> 0 then
                done = 'y';
        end if

        if location2 <> 0 or active = 'Y' then
                st_complete.text='Job is now Active...';
                active = 'Y';
        else
                st_complete.text='Job is waiting on Queue...';
        end if

        st_complete.show()

loop

//_____
// job is finished. Beep and display message
//_____

beep(1)
st_complete.text='Job is now finished, you may Download';
st_complete.show()
cb_okfinished.show()

//_____
// SignOff
//_____

WD_SendKey(Hwnd,"SIGNOFF")
WD_SendKey(Hwnd,"@E")
WD_wait(Hwnd)

//WD_DisConnectPS(Hwnd)
WD_DeletePS(Hwnd,"R")

//_____
// This is the label where the program goes if the user date edit fails
//_____

badmmyy:
```

The RPG program, which is called in the above PowerBuilder script, is shown in Figure 22.44.

The user now has run the updates on the AS/400, creating a file for download. The next step is to download it by pressing the DownLoad button. Before we can execute the download, we need to define a batch download procedure, using the RTOPC.EXE program found on the I: drive in shared folders. Run this from the DOS prompt. If you can't run the extended DOS interface because you are completely migrated to Client Access, you will have to use the Rumba file transfer. This might even be preferable, because it is native Windows. We want to look at both. To continue with the DOS example, after running RTOPC.EXE, you get the screen in Figure 22.45. Press enter and the next screen (Figure 22.46) allows you to create a transfer request. Press F10 and select Create. Fill in the screen for Create an AS/400 System-to-PC Transfer Request as shown in Figure 22.47, substituting your own system name and filenames. Press Enter when complete. Then press F3 to exit. You must name the file that contains the batch transfer request definitions as shown in Figure 22.48. Now that this file exists, you can run the request in batch.

Figure 22.44 RPG program.

INVREVPC RPG

```
FITEMMASTIF   E         K         DISK
FITEMDETLIF   E         K         DISK
FINVREV  O    E         K         DISK
**
C             *ENTRY    PLIST
C                       PARM            MM      2
C                       PARM            YY      2
**
**
C             TOP       TAG
**-----------------------------------------------------------------
** READ A PRODUCT RETAIL RECORD
**-----------------------------------------------------------------
C                       READ ITEMMAST                      99
C                       MOVELITNAM      IRNAM
C                       MOVELITMNUM     IRITM
C             *IN99     IFEQ *ON
C                       GOTO END
C                       ENDIF
**-----------------------------------------------------------------
** GET THE DETAIL
**-----------------------------------------------------------------
C             ITMNUM    CHAINITEMDETL                      98
C             ITMNUM    DOWEQDTLITM
C             *IN98     ANDNE'1'
**
C             MM        IFEQ '01'
C                       ADD  TFJAN      IR01
C                       ADD  TFJAN      IRYTD
C                       ENDIF
**
```

Figure 22.44 Continued.

```
C           MM          IFEQ  '02'
C                       ADD   TFFEB     IR02
C                       ADD   TFFEB     IRYTD
C                       ENDIF
  **
C           MM          IFEQ  '03'
C                       ADD   TFMAR     IR03
C                       ADD   TFMAR     IRYTD
C                       ENDIF
 **
C           MM          IFEQ  '04'
C                       ADD   TFAPR     IR04
C                       ADD   TFAPR     IRYTD
C                       ENDIF
 **
C           MM          IFEQ  '05'
C                       ADD   TFMAY     IR05
C                       ADD   TFMAY     IRYTD
C                       ENDIF
 **
C           MM          IFEQ  '06'
C                       ADD   TFJUN     IR06
C                       ADD   TFJUN     IRYTD
C                       ENDIF
 **
C           MM          IFEQ  '07'
C                       ADD   TFJUL     IR07
C                       ADD   TFJUL     IRYTD
C                       ENDIF

C           MM          IFEQ  '08'
C                       ADD   TFAUG     IR08
C                       ADD   TFAUG     IRYTD
C                       ENDIF
 **
C           MM          IFEQ  '09'
C                       ADD   TFSEP     IR09
C                       ADD   TFSEP     IRYTD
C                       ENDIF
 **
C           MM          IFEQ  '10'
C                       ADD   TFOCT     IR10
C                       ADD   TFOCT     IRYTD
C                       ENDIF
 **
C           MM          IFEQ  '11'
C                       ADD   TFNOV     IR11
C                       ADD   TFNOV     IRYTD
C                       ENDIF
 **
C           MM          IFEQ  '12'
C                       ADD   TFDEC     IR12
C                       ADD   TFDEC     IRYTD
C                       ENDIF
 **
C                       READ ITEMDETL
 **
C                       ENDDO
 **
C                       WRITEIR
C                       GOTO TOP
 **-----------------------------------------------------
C           END         TAG
C                       SETON                   LR
```

326   Sample Applications

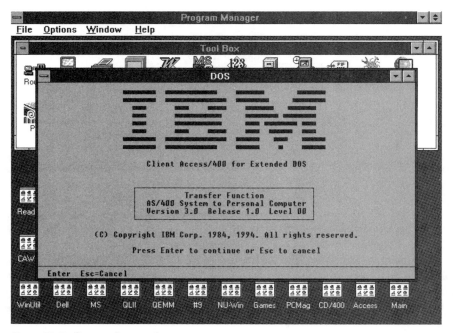

Figure 22.45 Screen after running RTOPC.EXE.

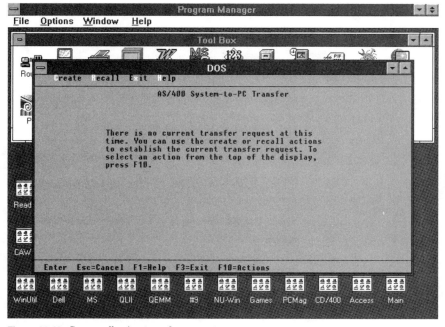

Figure 22.46 Screen allowing transfer request.

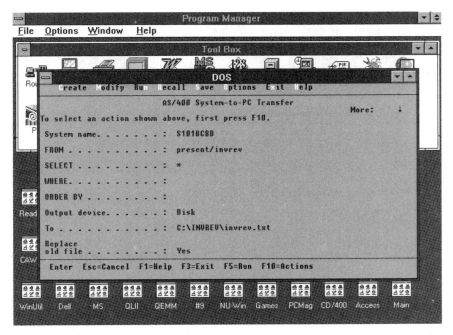

Figure 22.47   Creating transfer request.

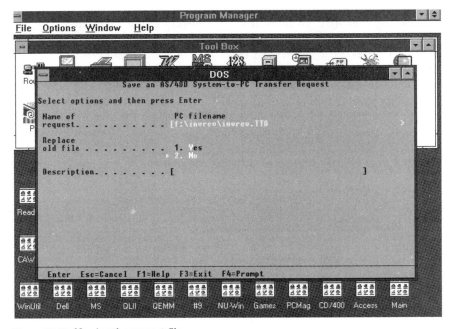

Figure 22.48   Naming the request file.

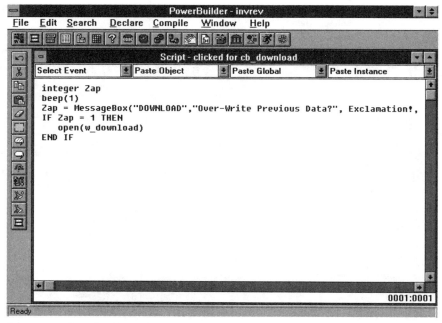

Figure 22.49 Download button's clicked event.

Again, we will open a window from the DownLoad button for managing the process. The DownLoad button's clicked event (Figure 22.49) displays a message and opens the `w_download` window (which we must design before referencing it here). The open event for the download window (Figure 22.50) actually invokes the download by calling a DOS PC support function. We did it this way not only to show how to call DOS programs from PowerBuilder, but also because the DOS session will seize the computer for its duration, not allowing the user to do anything else, which is what we want. We could have defined a Rumba download, saved it as an `.RTO` file (download definition), and run that from here just as easily with the command:

```
Run("c:\cawin\rumbafil.exe c:\invrev\invrev.rto")
```

We are running a DOS download, however, so let's stick with that. To execute a DOS command from within a Windows program, you need to define a program information file (`.PIF`) for it. You actually call the PIF, instead of the DOS program. It manages the running of the DOS program from Windows. The PIF Editor is found in the Main or Accessories group (Figure 22.51); open it (Figure 22.52). Here, you put in the name of the DOS program you want to run, a title for the window, the start-up directory, and the other run parameters as shown. Note that the windowed radio button is pressed to make the DOS session run in a window rather than in full-screen mode.

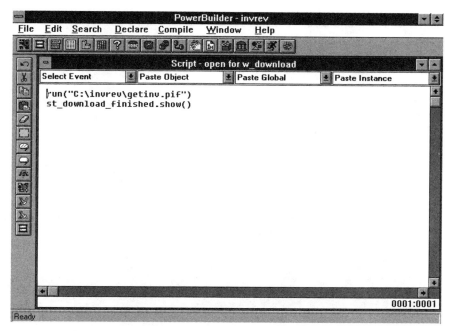

Figure 22.50 Open event for download window.

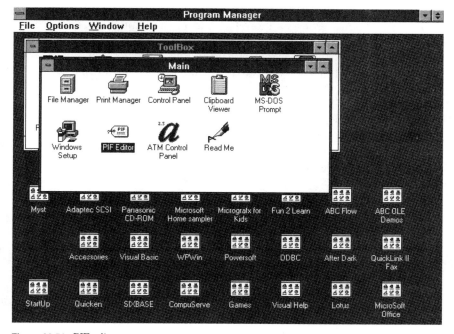

Figure 22.51 PIF editor.

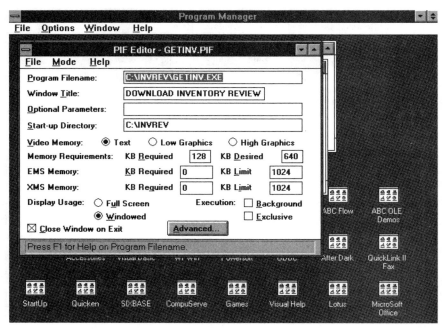

Figure 22.52 Opening PIF editor.

The window makes it look more like part of the Windows program. Save this file as INVREV.PIF, which is what we call from the DownLoad button. This INVREV.EXE that is called by the PIF is actually a clipper program (Figure 22.53), showing how the world of dBASE can be integrated to PowerBuilder client/server applications. This program loads the down-loaded file into a dBASE file and processes it. We could also have done all this with Windows programs like Rumba's download and the WATCOM SQL database, which is bundled with PowerBuilder.

Next is the SaveData pushbutton for the Edit window, which we have al-ready done. This is very simple. Its script can be seen in Figure 22.54. There is a COMMIT and then the data window is hidden.

The last major feature is the Print button. This button, too, opens another window (Figure 22.55). We need to design the Print window as in Figure 22.56. The user has two edit boxes in which to specify a range of products for the report. Three radio buttons determine which report is printed. Under the clicked event for the radio buttons is a simple script that sets the report number and closes the Print window (Figure 22.57). As it is closing, the Close event for the Print window actually runs the report, using the pa-rameter set by the radio button (Figure 22.58). This uses the PowerBuilder

Run command to execute a report designed in R&R, another Windows program. The report could actually be written in a number of other report writers, such as Crystal Reports.

Finally, there is the Quit button, which closes the main application window and everything dependent on it (Figure 22.59).

```
Clear
@5.0 say 'Please wait for download...'
!i:rtopch f:\invrev\invrev
use invrev
zap
append from invrev delimited
delete for item ='  '
pack
go top
mm=trim[aspf,,]
do case
case mm='1'.or.mm='4'.or.mm='7'.or.mm='10'
    num=3
case mm='2'.or.mm='5'.or.mm='8'.or.mm='11'
    num=2
case mm='3'.or.mm='6'.or.mm='9'.or.mm='12'
    num=1
endcase
replace all override with num
index on prod + item to invrev
close data
```

Figure 22.53 Clipper program.

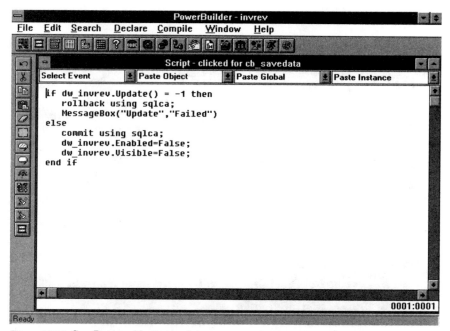

Figure 22.54 SaveData pushbutton script.

ABC Inventory Review

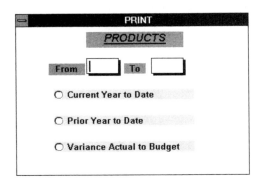

Figure 22.55 Window from Print button.

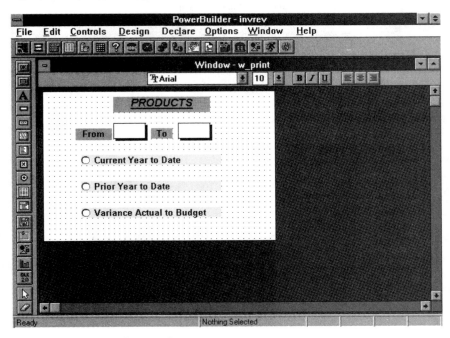

Figure 22.56 Designing Print window.

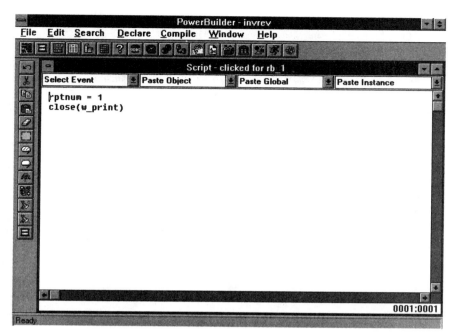

Figure 22.57 Script for Print window.

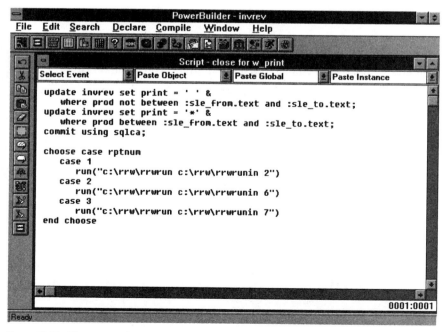

Figure 22.58 Close event that runs the script.

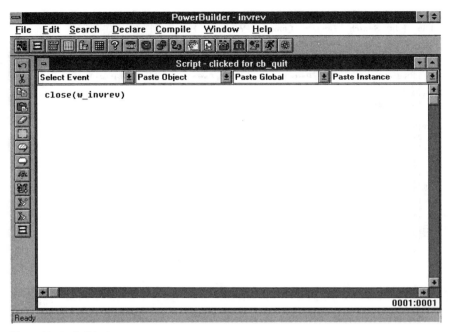

Figure 22.59 Quit button.

There you have it. That is the entire PowerBuilder client/server application. We have created a PowerBuilder application, run AS/400 commands, read data queues, downloaded data, edited it, saved it, and printed reports. These elements are applicable to a variety of applications, and they can be used to develop a range of client/server systems.

23

Visual Basic Sample Application

This sample application shows how to use Visual Basic with the AS/400 Client Access open database connectivity (ODBC) driver. We show live data from the AS/400 physical files in a window on the PC. It is a fairly simple application, just to show how to do it. The prerequisites for doing this are the following:

- Client Access
- Windows
- Visual Basic
- ODBC

During the Client Access installation process for the PC, which is going to run this application, specify that you want to load the ODBC portion. The ODBC driver is then copied and registered with Windows. Next, you must set up a data source, using the Client Access ODBC icon to connect the Client Access ODBC driver to AS/400 libraries and files. Appendix A shows how to do this. The following is a brief recap:

1. Install Client Access with the ODBC option.
2. Ensure the ADDRDBDIRE command has been run on the AS/400.
3. Set up a data source for the AS/400 physical files.

Once all these procedures are in place, it is a simple matter to access AS/400 data from a Visual Basic application.

Start Visual Basic. You get a blank form as in Figure 23.1. On this form, you can place controls and attach code to them to trap events. One of the specialized controls available in Visual Basic 3.0, Professional Edition, is the data control. This type of control links the form to an external data source, as in the case of our AS/400 ODBC data source. Once this control is created, you can create other controls such as text boxes that are bound to the data control. These are known as *bound controls.* They are bound to the data control, which is in turn linked to the ODBC driver, which is connected to the data source on the AS/400.

Visual Basic consists of different windows or panels visible on the desktop. One is the form on which controls are placed. Another is the toolbar of controls themselves. These are clicked onto the form. The third important panel on the Visual Basic desktop is the Properties window, which is used to define properties and attributes of selected controls. The Toolbar and Properties window can be seen on the desktop alongside the form in Figure 23.1. Left-click on a control on the form. It is highlighted. Click on the Properties window to activate it. Now you can select and set many different properties for that control. One of the properties you can set for a text box is the data source. Visual Basic makes this very easy for us to do.

To begin a new application, we need to define a new project to Visual Basic. A *project* is what Visual Basic calls a collection of forms and con-

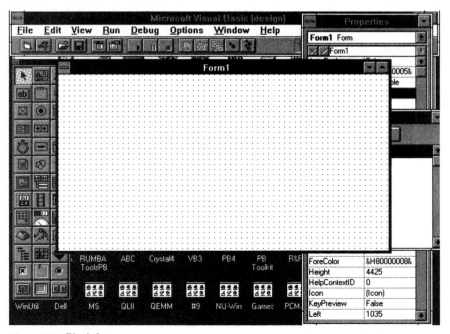

Figure 23.1 Blank form.

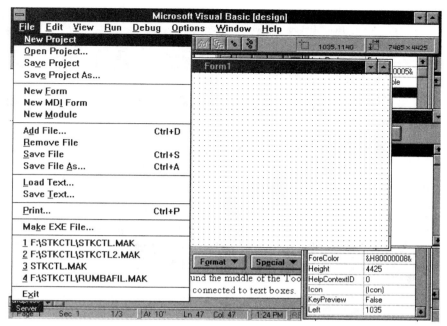

Figure 23.2 Bring up new project.

trols with their related properties and code. Click File/New Project (Figure 23.2) to bring up the new project. It appears as a blank form named Form1.

We can click several controls onto this form. The first control we need is the data control, which is the rectangle with four arrows pointing left and right at the upper right-hand corner of the form in Figure 23.3. This control is used to connect the form to the data source and also navigate the data source. Clicking on the right arrow moves the form one record down in the data source. The right arrow with the vertical line moves to the last record in the data source. The left arrows similarly move to records in the data source. You can make the data control invisible and handle navigation in the data source yourself, getting input from the user and finding records. This example is a simple demonstration, however, and we leave the data control visible and use it to move around in the AS/400 physical file.

Double-click on the data control icon in the Toolbar to place it on the form. This icon is generally found around the middle of the Toolbar. It looks like a left and right arrow with the left arrow connected to text boxes. This unassuming little widget is Visual Basic's connection to the external data sources, including the AS/400. We need to tell it that it is connecting to the AS/400 ODBC driver. Make sure the data control is highlighted. Click on the

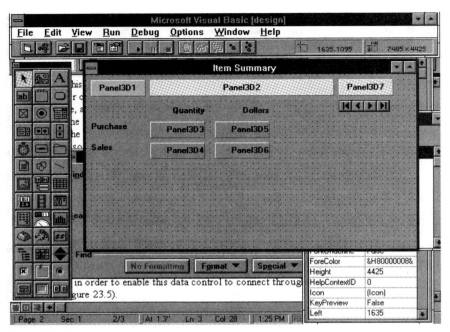

Figure 23.3 Data control.

Properties window. We only need to fill in two properties, to enable this data control to connect through ODBC to the AS/400 (Figure 23.4).

The Connect property should read

```
odbc; dsn=datasource; uid=username; pwd=xxx
```

where `datasource` is the name of the data source defined in the ODBC configuration, `username` is the name of the user, and `xxx` is the user's password.

The `RecordSource` property should be

```
Libname.Filename
```

where `Libname` is the name of the AS/400 library and `Filename` is the name of the physical file you want to access. The two are separated by a period. Note that the `DatabaseName` property is left blank. That's all you need to do. AS/400 data is now available to this Visual Basic application.

All that remains is to place text boxes on the form and link or bind them to the data control. Double-click on a text box. It appears on the form (Figure 23.5). We need to fill in two properties for this bound data control.

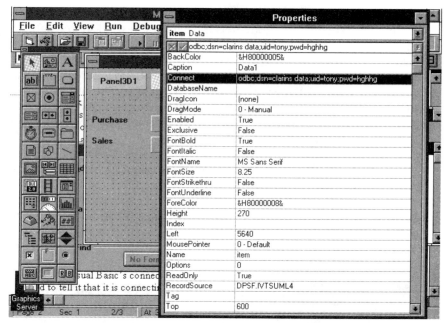

Figure 23.4 Filling in properties.

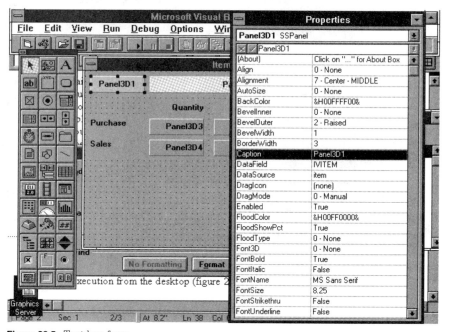

Figure 23.5 Text box form.

`DataField` is the name of the field in the AS/400 physical file you want to appear in this text box. `DataSource` is the name of the datasource defined for the ODBC driver when it was set up. This text box now shows the data in that field in the specified AS/400 database. Select Run from the menu at the top of the Visual Basic screen to test this assertion (Figure 23.6). The arrows on the data control (not the bound control) can be used to move through the AS/400 database, showing the data in consecutive records in the text box. We can enhance the form with colors and 3-D text boxes and such, but that's basically it.

Note that there is absolutely no code involved in this application. It is entirely accomplished with controls and properties, Client Access, and ODBC.

Select File and Save Project As to save the project and the form (Figure 23.7). Then select File/Make EXE File... to create an executable file for Windows (Figure 23.8). All that remains is to go to the Windows desktop and select File/New/Program Item to create an icon for execution from the desktop (Figure 23.9).

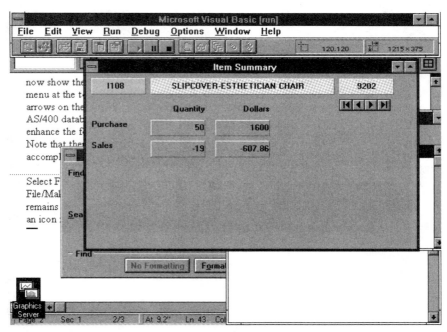

Figure 23.6 Running program.

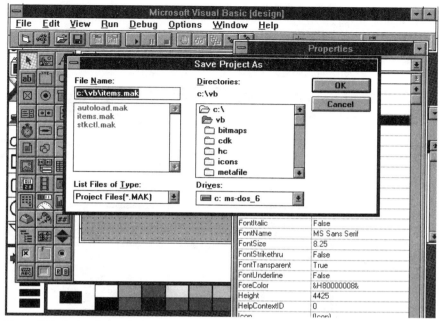

Figure 23.7 Saving the project.

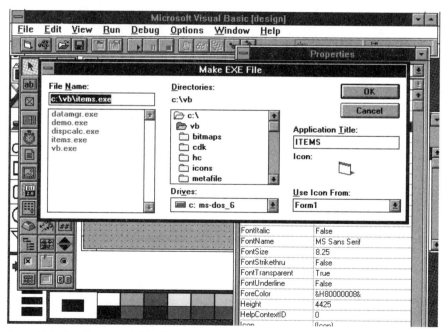

Figure 23.8 Creating executable file.

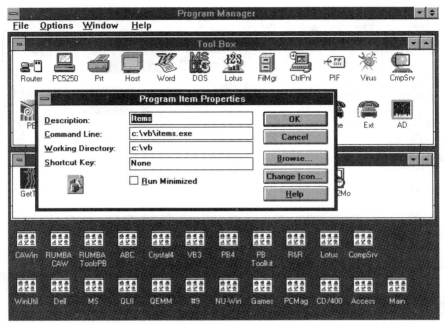

Figure 23.9   Creating icon for program execution.

Chapter

24

Crystal Reports
Sample Application

Crystal Reports is a report writer for Windows. It comes bundled with Visual Basic, or it can be purchased separately. Purchase the separate version, because you then get Crystal Reports Pro, which has more features. It provides a very easy and convenient way to access AS/400 databases from a Windows reporting front-end. As with most Windows programs, Crystal Reports is intuitive—easy to learn and use.

Once the ODBC driver has been installed and a data source has been defined (see Appendix A for ODBC configurations), it is simple to hook it up to Crystal Reports for querying the AS/400 databases. Click on the Crystal Reports icon in the Windows desktop. The main window opens up (Figure 24.1). Click on File New (Figure 24.2) to create a new report. Then select Standard Expert (Figure 24.3), which indicates that you want a sequence of screens which will guide you through the creation in a menu-driven process. To specify our AS/400 data source for Crystal Reports, select SQL/ODBC from the first screen in the Create Report Expert (Figure 24.4).

In Step 1, a list of servers appears (Figure 24.5). Select the ODBC data source, which was defined for this purpose. Press OK. A message appears, informing the user that the logon was successful. We are now connected to the ODBC data source and can continue with the report definition. From this point on, it is just as if the data were sitting right on the c: drive, while it might even be in a different state or country. A list of physical files included in the selected data source appears (Figure 24.6). Select the one you want and press Add. When finished, press Log On Server. Now press Next to get to the next step in the Create Report Expert.

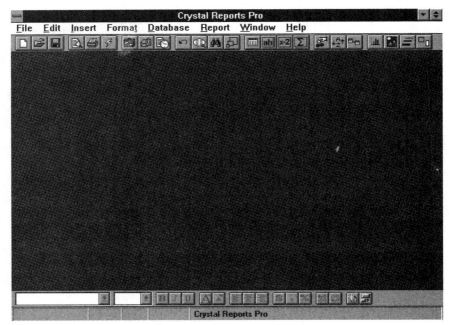

Figure 24.1   Main window.

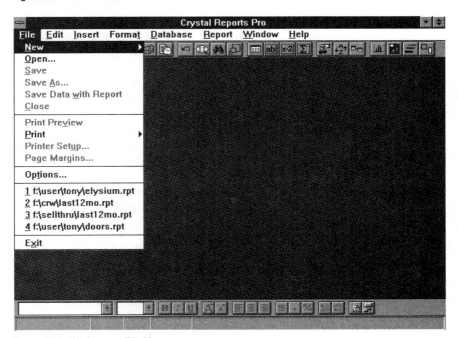

Figure 24.2   Clicking on File New.

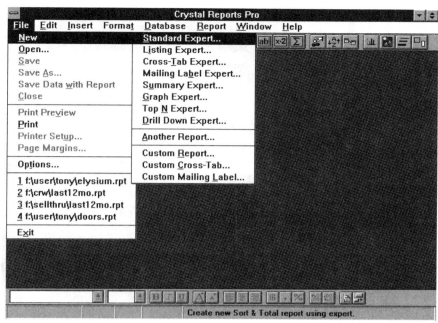

Figure 24.3 Selecting Standard Expert.

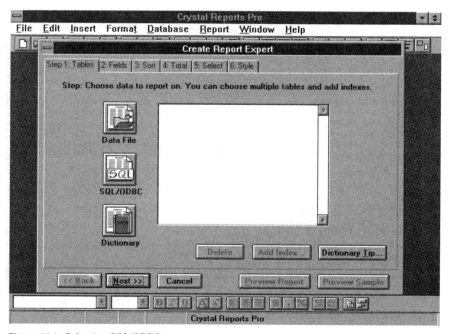

Figure 24.4 Selecting SQL/ODBC.

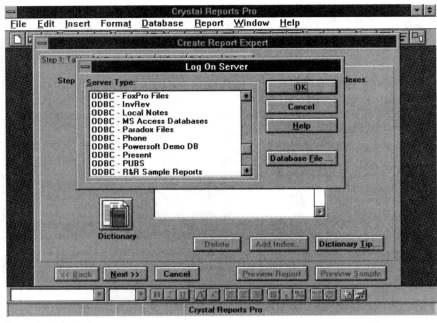

Figure 24.5 List of servers.

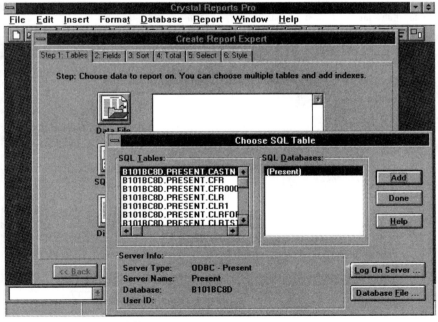

Figure 24.6 List of physical files.

In Step 2, you select fields from the selected database (Figure 24.7). Move the cursor to fields you want in the left-hand list box and click Add to move them to the right-hand list box for the report. You can enter column headings for each selected field in the Column Heading text box. The headings are automatically used in the report when the fields are placed. Note the Browse Data button, which lets you look through data in a selected field. Press Next when finished.

Step 3 (Figure 24.8) is to select group fields. These are automatically used by Crystal Reports to sort the data. Press Next.

In Step 4 (Figure 24.9) you select fields for which you require totals. Different types of totals can be specified, such as sum, average, and count. These total fields, once specified, appear automatically on the report at the specified break levels. Remember to click on Add Grand Totals to make these appear at the end of the report. Click Next.

Step 5 is to select records for the report (Figure 24.10). You just select a field name from the list box on the left, click on criteria and enter values. Note that you can preview the report to test the selection criteria with the Preview Report button underneath.

Step 6 (Figure 24.11) is where you select the style for the report. Using a combination of Create Report Experts and Styles, you can get a wide variety of automatic report formats, without further programming. We just select

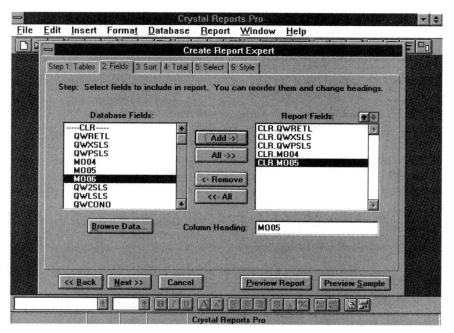

Figure 24.7 Selecting fields from database.

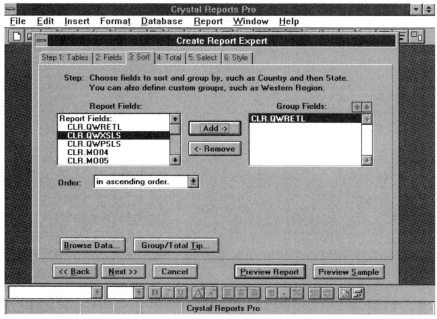

Figure 24.8 Selecting group fields.

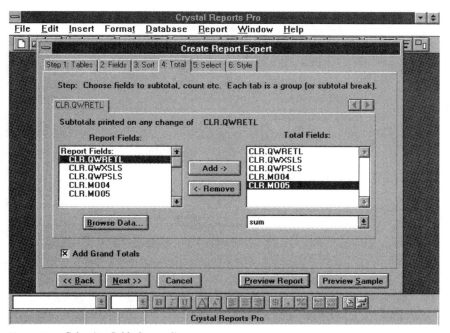

Figure 24.9 Selecting fields for totaling.

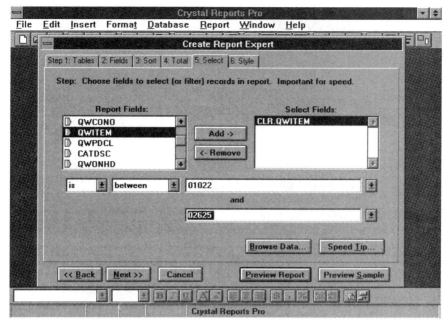

Figure 24.10 Selecting records.

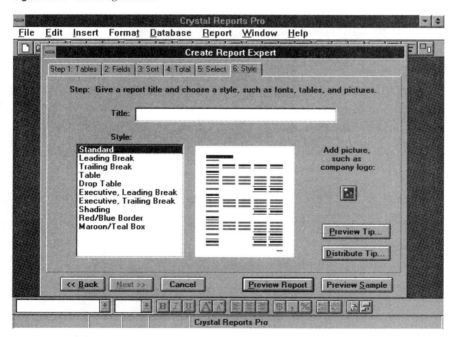

Figure 24.11 Selecting report style.

Standard, and we are finished with the basic report definition. It is that simple to define a basic report for ODBC connection to the AS/400 database.

Now for some enhancements. Let's not see the detail records, only the summary levels. Click on Edit, and then Show/Hide Sections... (Figure 24.12), which produces the screen in Figure 24.13 where you simply highlight a section and click the radio button for Show or Hide. Select Details and click Hide. Note the group levels we defined are shown here. We can show or hide them, as well.

Press Insert to place a Formula Field (Figure 24.14) on the report, which gives you the Edit Formula screen (Figure 24.15). Here, you can click on field names, functions, and operators and type into the Formula text box to construct the logic for formula fields. Press Check for Crystal Reports to check the validity of the formula you have entered. Press Accept to save it.

Highlight a field in the report and select Format/Field from the main menu (Figure 24.16) to alter the appearance of fields you have placed on the report. If you selected a numeric field, you see the Format Number screen (Figure 24.17). You can select many different display attributes of the field, as shown.

If you need more than one database for the report, select Database/Visual Linking Expert (Figure 24.18).

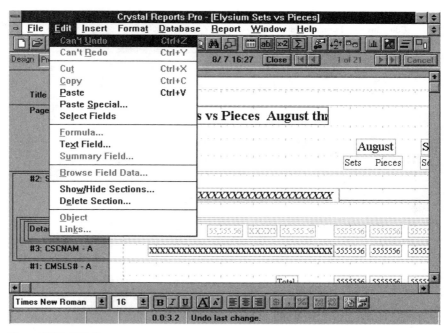

Figure 24.12 Edit the menu.

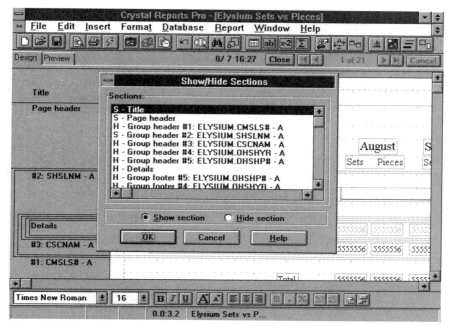

Figure 24.13 Show/hide sections.

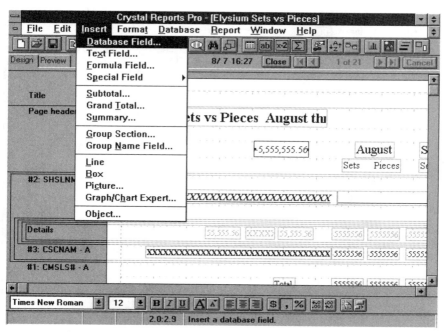

Figure 24.14 Placing Formula Field.

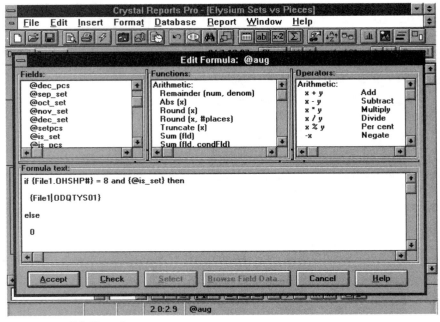

Figure 24.15 Edit Formula screen.

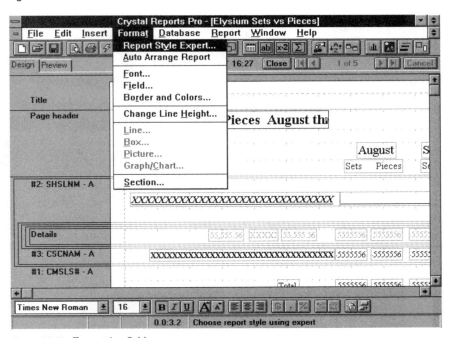

Figure 24.16 Formatting fields.

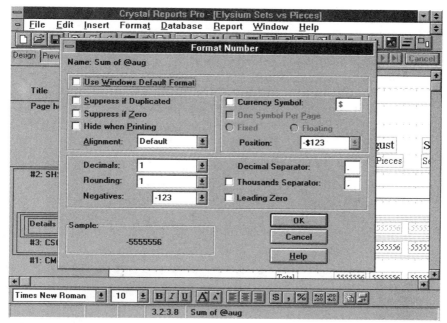

Figure 24.17 Format Number screen.

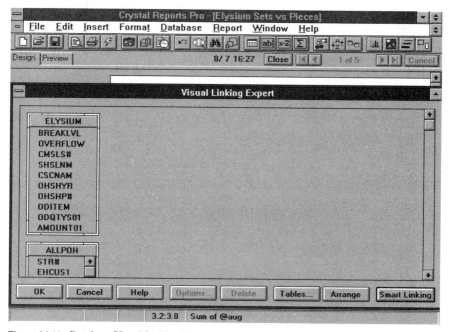

Figure 24.18 Database/Visual Linking Expert.

In the Report menu (Figure 24.19), you can define record selection. You can also specify that you only want to see records for which a group total meets specified criteria (Figure 24.20).

You can highlight a field on the report and use the right mouse button (a nice feature) to produce a pop-up menu for defining that field (Figure 24.21).

Our finished report is previewed in Figure 24.22.

Crystal Reports Pro is a very easy and powerful tool for connecting users to the databases on the AS/400. With some guidance from the MIS department, users can be given real-time access to data from the server. This method is perhaps the shortest path to client/server implementations for end users, if no other functions, such as data manipulation, are required. There is a performance hit on the AS/400 for these connections, so it is important to manage multiple simultaneous ODBC reports. End users are usually very impressed with this easy, transparent access to remote data.

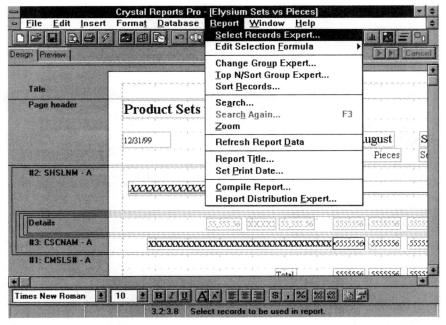

Figure 24.19   Report menu.

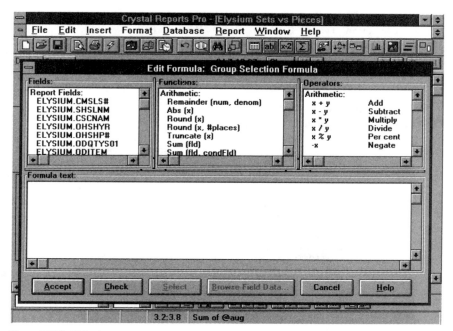

Figure 24.20 Criteria.

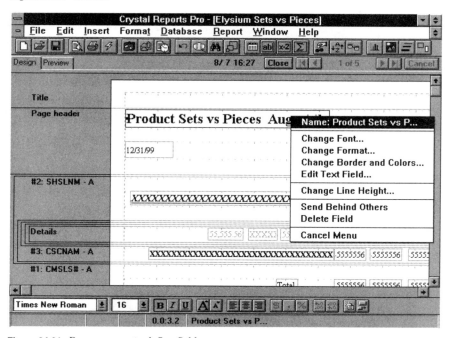

Figure 24.21 Pop-up menu to define field.

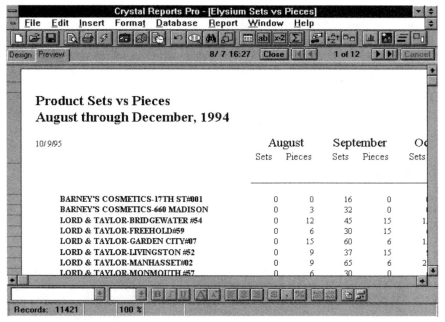

Figure 24.22 Finished report.

25

Lotus/ODBC Sample Application

Under the AS/400's operating system, an open database connectivity (ODBC) driver is implemented. This feature, included with OS/400, allows PC Windows applications to access AS/400 data remotely, but online. Your Lotus or Excel spreadsheet can be set up to pull data from the AS/400 for further analysis.

Before your spreadsheet can pull data, the ODBC driver for the AS/400 must be set up. Appendix A provides the details. It is a fairly straightforward procedure. Once the configuration is accomplished and data sources have been set up for the ODBC driver, PC applications can access the AS/400. As shown in Appendix A, there is a little setup required on the Lotus side, before the data can flow. Using a text editor, open up the LOTUS.BCF file in the LOTUSAPP/DATALENS directory (Figure 25.1). Whichever editor or word processor you use, make sure you leave this file in its original ASCII format. We click No Conversion as seen in Figure 25.2. Make the following entries at the top of the file:

```
DN="AS/400" DL="DLODBC"
DD="ODBC for the AS/400"
DC="driver=ehnodbc.dll";
```

as seen in Figure 25.3. These entries define for Lotus the type of connection to the AS/400. Once this connection is done, AS/400 data is available to Lotus spreadsheets.

Start Lotus. From the menu, select Tools and Database (Figure 25.4). Click on New Query to bring up the New Query Assistant (Figure 25.5). This window lets us connect to the ODBC driver and data sources. Press External. Now you see the Connect to External window (Figure 25.6).

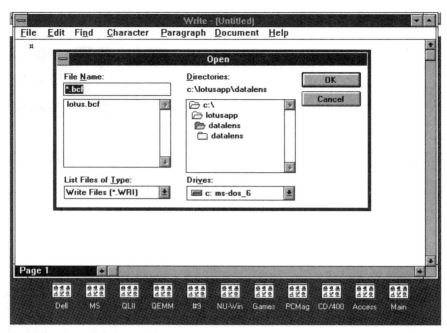

Figure 25.1 Opening file.

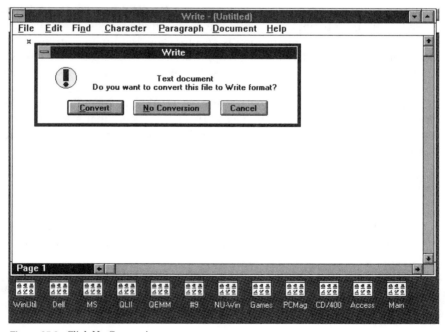

Figure 25.2 Click No Conversion.

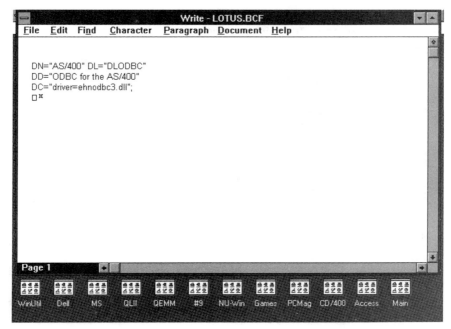

Figure 25.3 Adding code.

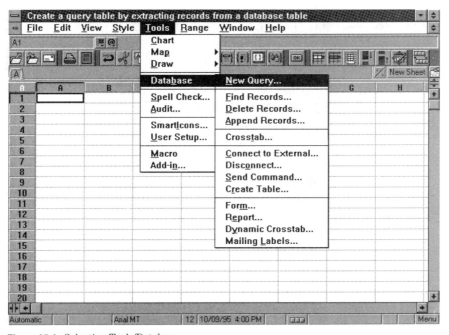

Figure 25.4 Selecting Tools/Database.

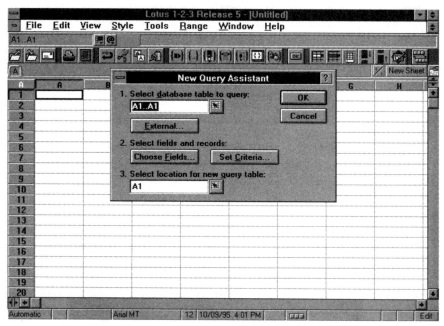

Figure 25.5 Bringing up New Query Assistant.

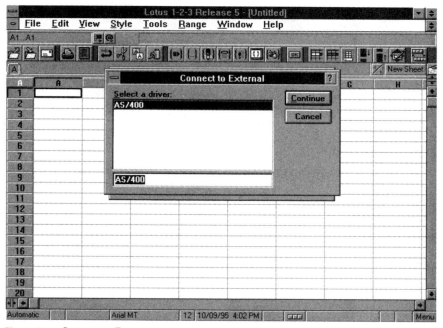

Figure 25.6 Connect to External window.

Select a driver from the list of drivers in the text window. These are the ODBC drivers defined to Lotus. Choose AS/400. Then press Continue.

Next, you see a list of databases defined for the data source when the ODBC driver was set up. Select the one(s) you want and press Continue (Figure 25.7), which takes you back to the New Query Assistant, with the name of your database in the first text box (Figure 25.8).

Now, you can press Choose Fields, Set Criteria, and Select location for new query table. These are available from the menu as well (Figure 25.9). Press OK. Select Query/Choose Fields... from the menu to select the fields from the AS/400 database that you want in your spreadsheet. Figure 25.10 shows the Choose Fields window. Highlight the ones you want and click OK. You can include Formulas from this window, as well.

Select Set Criteria from the Query menu to limit the records returned by the AS/400. This step is very important because it is unlikely that you would ever want to download an entire AS/400 database to Lotus, unless it was very small. AS/400 databases can get to be enormous—millions of records. Apart from the fact that they would not fit in a Lotus spreadsheet, the processing impact on the AS/400 must be considered. Figure 25.11 shows a record selection criteria defined, where only records that match the criteria are returned. Notice at the lower right of this window that you can limit the number of records Lotus will accept from the AS/400.

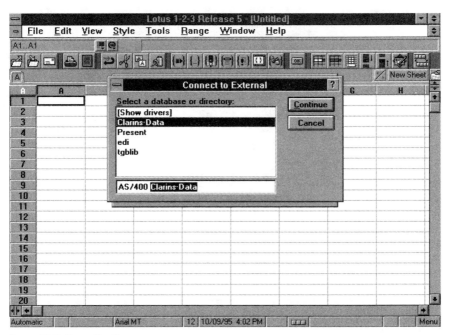

Figure 25.7 Press Continue.

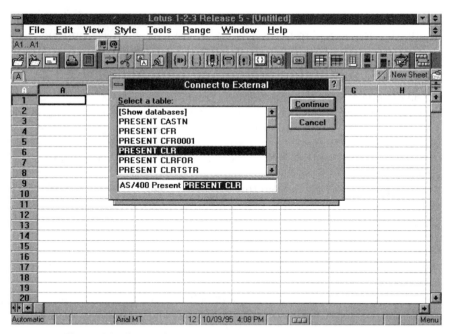

Figure 25.8 Name of database in first text box.

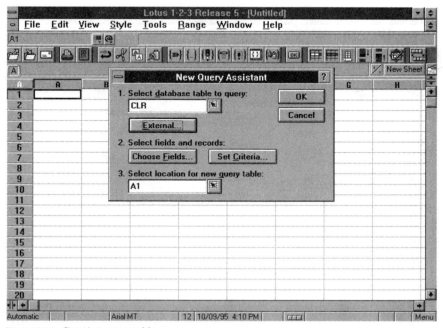

Figure 25.9 Creating query table.

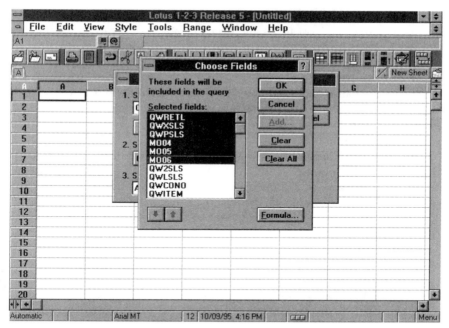

Figure 25.10 Choose Fields window.

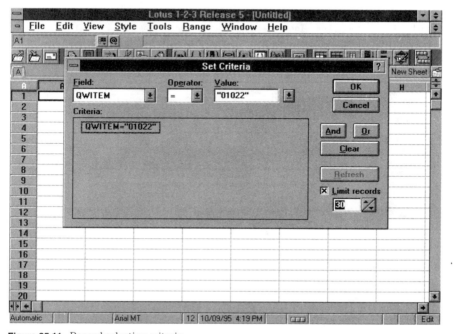

Figure 25.11 Record selection criteria.

Figure 25.12 shows how to set up a sort order for the data returned. Use the list box to select sort fields and check off Ascending or Descending order using the radio buttons.

Figure 25.13 shows some options that can be set for Lotus to AS/400 data access. Given the requisite authority to AS/400 objects, you can update the database. You can specify that you only want to see unique records, not duplicates. If you want to be able to see sample values in the filter, click that. Finally, you can specify auto refresh of the data in your spreadsheet (auto refresh, however, takes processing time on both ends).

The connection and data access implemented here is actually remote SQL. What is happening as you click on all the buttons and select items from lists is that an SQL statement is being constructed. When you are finished, this SQL statement is submitted to the AS/400 for processing by the DB2/400 database. If you want to see the actual SQL statement you have specified, select Query/Show SQL... (Figure 25.14). Select Query/Refresh Now to retrieve the AS/400 data into the spreadsheet (Figure 25.15).

Using these techniques, Lotus spreadsheets can be designed so that users can have up-to-the-minute access to AS/400 data.

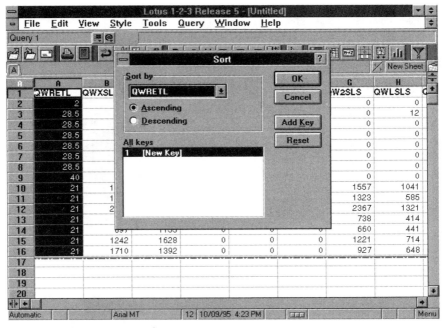

Figure 25.12 Setting up sort order.

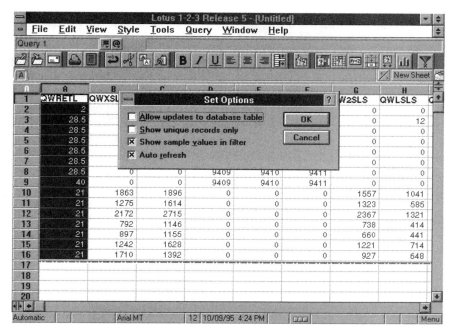

Figure 25.13 Options for Lotus.

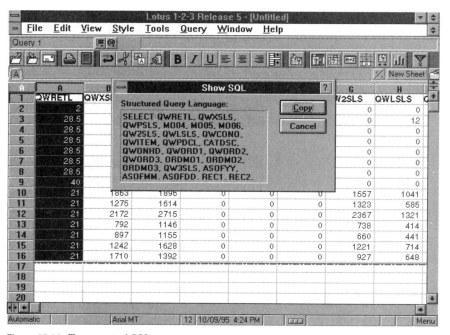

Figure 25.14 To see actual SQL statement.

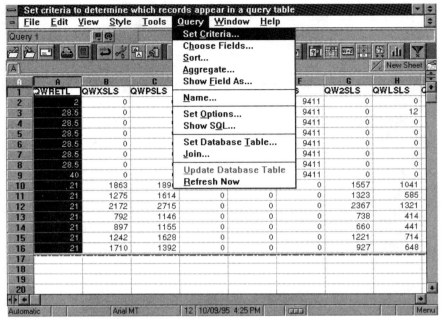

Figure 25.15 Retrieving AS/400 data.

26

Rumba Sample Application

26.1 Download

Sometimes, a full-blown client/server application is not necessary, and a simple download can suffice. Downloads are a very powerful and capable client/server solution. A power user could run a Query on the AS/400, create a file, and download it to the PC. In cases where the same database needs to be downloaded on a periodic basis, an automatic download could suffice. Just give the user an icon to click on to execute the transfer of data from the AS/400 to the PC (or from the PC to the AS/400, for that matter).

Downloads can be implemented in two steps. First, create a Rumba download definition file. Then, attach the download definition to an executable Windows icon. To create a Rumba download definition, click on the Terminal icon in the Rumba group (Figure 26.1), or from your own Rumba terminal emulation session menu. Click on Transfer in the Rumba menu (Figure 26.2) and highlight Receive (AS/400-to PC-transfer) to yield the transfer window as in Figure 26.3. Here, you specify the parameters of the download. On the right are the AS/400 library and filename, separated by a forward slash. On the left is the full path and name of the PC file you wish to receive the data from the AS/400. Click on Options on the left side of the screen to select where you want to place the downloaded data (Figure 26.4). Here, you specify that the data is going to a file. You can also select the type of PC file you want to create. We select CSV for a delimited file for import to dBASE. You could also select text or DIF for import to Lotus or another package. We can place an "X" in the box to Save Description File. Enter the name of the description file. On the right of the main Transfer screen, click Options to show

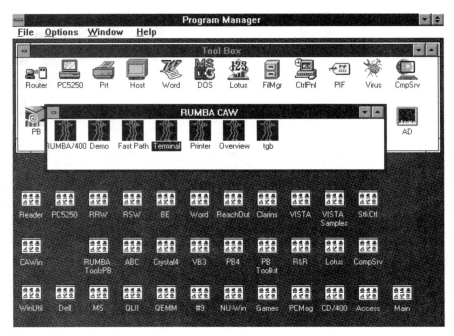

Figure 26.1 Terminal icon.

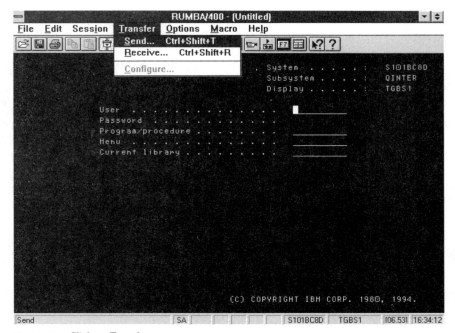

Figure 26.2 Click on Transfer.

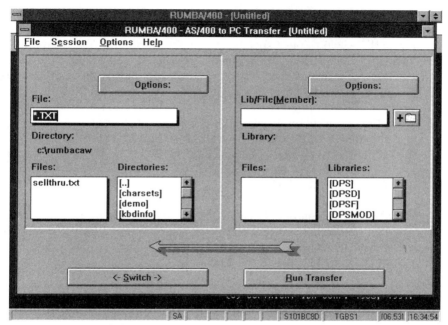

Figure 26.3 Transfer window.

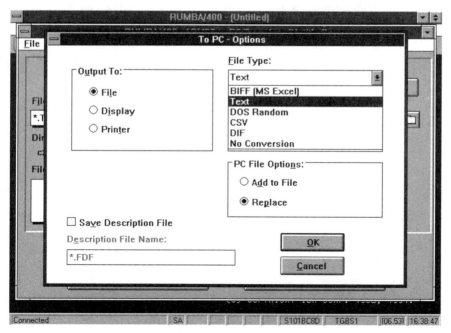

Figure 26.4 Where to place downloaded data.

the screen for data selection from the AS/400. The default is all fields and all records, but we can fill in values here to create an SQL statement to filter the data from the AS/400. Select specifies which fields we want. The drop-down box arrow provides a list of field names from the selected AS/400 database. The Where clause lets us specify which records we want, as in ITEM = 305. The Group By text box allows us to say how we want to group the data, while Order By is for a sort order. Join By defines a file join and Having allows selection at the group subtotal level. See the SQL chapter for more on these.

Once the download is defined, we can press Run Transfer to test it. We need to select a system. The transfer then runs. Select File/Save to give the download definition file a name (Figure 26.5). This name can now be used to call a Rumba download without having an active Rumba terminal emulation session. Exit Rumba.

In the Windows Program Manager, select File/New/Program Item to define an icon to execute our newly defined file transfer (Figure 26.6). The Description of the icon is Download. The Command Line, which actually executes the download is

```
C:\CAWIN\RUMBAFIL.EXE C:\path\filename
```

where path and filename point to the download definition we just created. This icon can now be placed on the desktop for the user to press to exe-

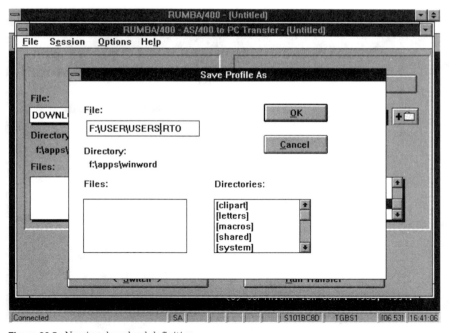

Figure 26.5 Naming download definition.

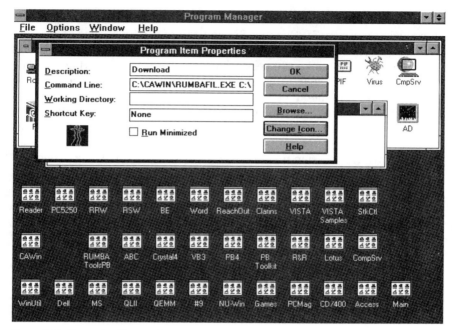

Figure 26.6 Executing file transfer.

cute an automated download, which can be used in numerous places in client/server systems.

26.2 EHLLAPI Session

Sometimes we need an actual session connection to the AS/400. We want to connect like a live user, but run the session in remote control, from a program such as PowerBuilder or Visual Basic. The functions that enable this are known as emulator high-level language application program interface (EHLLAPI). A Rumba session needs to be enabled for this purpose. Once enabled, the program can use EHLLAPI to connect to the AS/400 and to send any commands to it that you type at the command line. It can also look at AS/400 screens to see where it is or what they contain and respond to them.

Rumba Tools for PowerBuilder is one example of EHLLAPI functions. Visual Basic also has Rumba Tools. See the PowerBuilder sample application chapter for an example of how to incorporate EHLLAPI functions into a Windows program. Here, we are only concerned with how to enable a Rumba session for EHLLAPI access. You need a special terminal emulation session for this type of access.

First, start up a Rumba session from the Rumba group by clicking on Terminal (Figure 26.7). Click on Session to define the session. There are four things we need to define here (Figure 26.8). Click on Autoconnect and Autodisconnect to make the session behave in these ways when invoked and terminated, respectively, from the program. When you click on Autoconnect, the menu closes, so you must come back in again for Autodisconnect. Select Session Configuration to specify the remote AS/400 system, which produces the window seen in Figure 26.9. Use the down arrow on the AS/400 System Names text box to select the name of your AS/400. Give this session a name in the Device Name text box. Check off Auto Sign-on to make the session sign on automatically from a macro we will record. Click OK. Our last task in the Session menu is to click on EHLLAPI Configuration... (Figure 26.10). In the resulting screen, click on the check box for EHLLAPI SDK. Enter a one-character name for this session to be known by in your PowerBuilder or Visual Basic program. We could enter "R" for Rumba. Press OK.

Now go to the Macro menu (Figure 26.11). Click Record. Anything we do at the keyboard from this point on, until we press the Record button again, is recorded as a macro for later execution. Record is how we can set up an automatic sign-on sequence. Just type in the User profile name and password

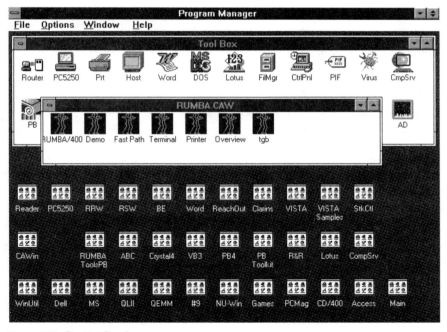

Figure 26.7 Starting Rumba.

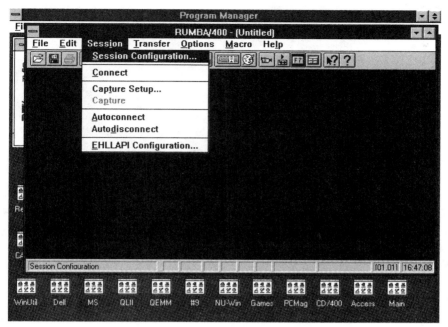

Figure 26.8 Defining session.

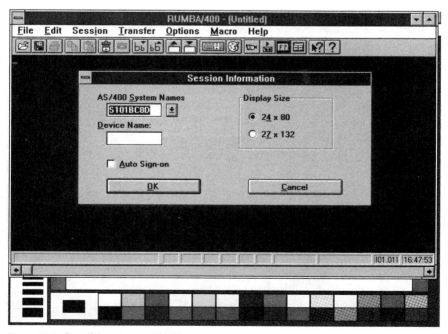

Figure 26.9 Specifying remote AS/400.

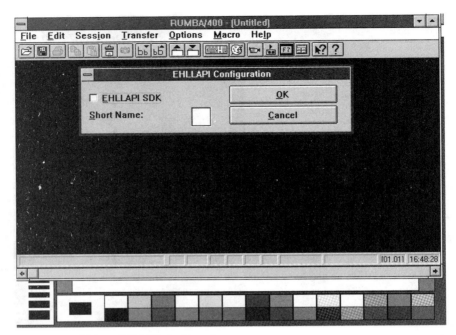

Figure 26.10 Click on EHLLAPI Configuration.

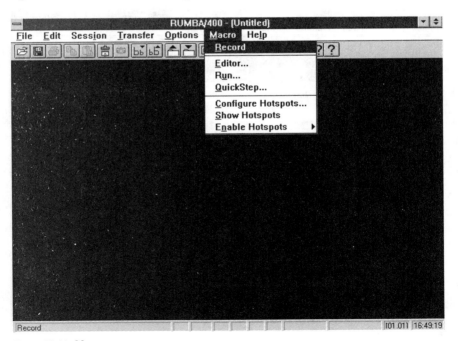

Figure 26.11 Macro menu.

you want to use for this session (consider authority carefully). Press the field exit and enter keys just as you would when actually signing on to the AS/400. When you reach wherever you want to be on the AS/400, press Macro/Record again to stop the recording of keystrokes and bring up the macro script editor (Figure 26.12). Here, you can see what you recorded, and you can edit it in the Macro Script window. When satisfied, select File/Save and give your new macro a name, such as SIGNON.MAC (Figure 26.13).

The only thing left to do is go to the Rumba File menu. Click Auto Macro to tell Rumba to execute this macro whenever this session is invoked (Figure 26.14). Save this session and name it (Figure 26.15). In conjunction with the automacro specification, our macro automatically signs this session onto the AS/400 from a PowerBuilder or Visual Basic program.

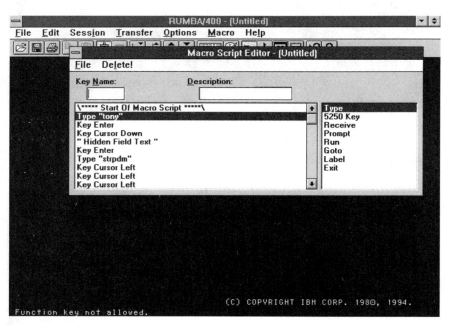

Figure 26.12 Macro script editor.

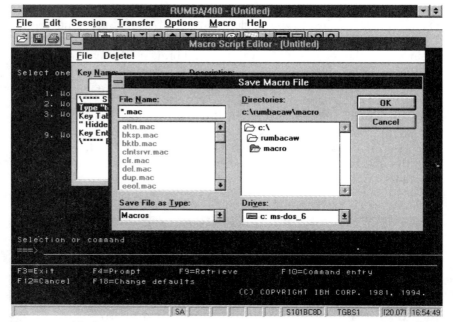

Figure 26.13   Naming macro.

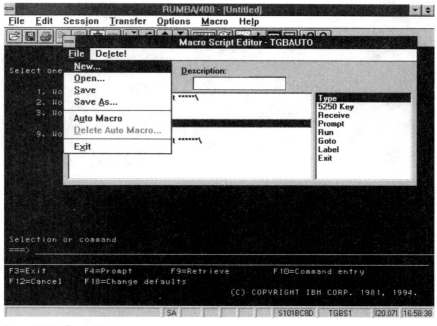

Figure 26.14   Executing macro.

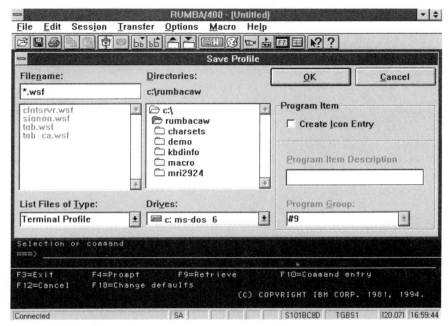

Figure 26.15 Naming session.

ODBC

Making the open database connectivity (ODBC) connection, a Microsoft standard way to access foreign databases, is probably the easiest way to get live AS/400 data into your PC programs. These databases can be on another machine like the AS/400, or just another PC format. If you are working in Visual Basic, you can as easily connect to a dBASE file as an AS/400 physical file (once the AS/400-to-PC configurations are in place). If you are running V3R1 or better of OS/400, Client Access provides an efficient ODBC connection to PC programs. ODBC is a form of middleware that translates file formats and access methods between two specific databases. One format is the PC Windows environment—generally a program running in Windows. The other format can be any of a number of other databases. Think of ODBC as an SQL pipeline that translates databases for Windows.

We are primarily concerned with ODBC connections for the AS/400. Many connections can be made, including the following:

- Client Access
- Database Access
- Visual Basic
- Crystal Reports
- PowerBuilder
- Lotus 1-2-3
- Microsoft Excel
- ShowCase VISTA

- Microsoft Access
- Brio Data Prism

These and other Windows platforms can be used to provide easy graphical user interface (GUI) access to AS/400 data in client/server applications. Once the ODBC connection is in place for the AS/400, PF data fields can be placed on a Windows program as easily as Microsoft Access fields, with some assembly. Up front, several things need to be configured to put the DB2/400 database on the Windows desktop.

First of all, V3R1 or better is highly recommended. Although an ODBC driver for the AS/400 is available as a PTF in V2R3, the performance and features are not really all that wonderful until you get to V3R1. Client Access, the renovated PC Support that comes with V3R1, includes the optimized ODBC driver. IBM believes in the future of client/server computing, so they put considerable time and resources into this effort. The result is an ODBC driver that really does behave like a local database on the PC.

Configuring the AS/400 for ODBC

Once V3R1 of the operating system is installed, there is very little to do on the AS/400 side of things to configure for ODBC. Most of the configuration is in Client Access on the PC side. The AS/400 must have a remote database directory entry, so that it can respond on the network to remote data requests. This entry is accomplished simply with the ADDRDBDIRE command (Figure A.1). Enter the serial number of your AS/400 as the *Relational* Database name, and *LOCAL as the remote location. That's it. The AS/400 is ready to furnish remote SQL data excerpts through Client Access.

Client Access

Client Access is the key to the ODBC connection between Windows and the AS/400. Actually, ODBC is a feature of Client Access. It is one of the programs in the integrated file services (IFS) QPWXCWN directory, which is the place where Client Access is stored on the AS/400. The driver is called EHNODBC3.DLL. It is installed to the PC during the Client Access installation process, if you select ODBC as an option.

The ODBC driver must be set up or registered with Windows, which can be done through the Microsoft ODBC Administrator window (Figure A.2). Click on the ODBC icon in the Client Access group to get to this window. In the bottom window in the screen you see the installed ODBC drivers. One of them should say Client Access/400 ODBC Driver. Highlight this and click on the Add New Name button, which allows you to name an ODBC pipeline to the AS/400 databases. In Windows programs, you can simply ac-

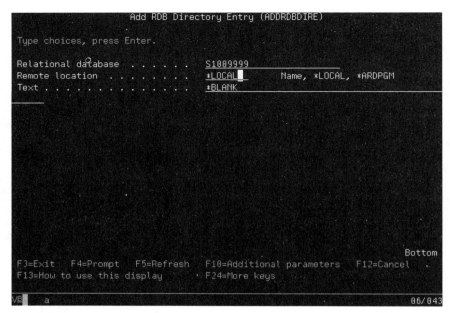

Figure A.1 Remote database directory entry.

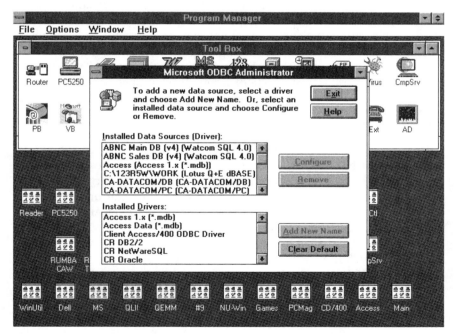

Figure A.2 ODBC Administrator window.

cess the data on the AS/400 by specifying that you want an ODBC driver by this name. The programs then look for it and follow the configurations to the AS/400 databases.

In the ClientAccess/400 ODBC Driver Setup screen (Figure A.3), enter a Data Source Name. Leave the description alone. Name your AS/400 system with the system name that you entered earlier in the ADDRDBDIRE command. You can enter which libraries you want to be made available to the ODBC driver. A data source is really a group of libraries, or as many files and libraries for which the user is authorized. You can leave this as *USRLIBL to let the user access the same libraries as he can on Sign On to the AS/400. When Client Access asks for common user ID on startup, it is the user profile that determines access rights. Leave the rest of the parameters as they are.

Once ODBC is configured, it might be instructive to look in the C: \WINDOWS\ODBC.INI file. This file contains specifications and syntax needed for Windows to make use of the various ODBC drivers. The Microsoft ODBC Driver Setup window actually places these parameters here. There are others here as well, that are used to optimize the performance of ODBC. They are initialized to values that set maximum optimization, so they should not ordinarily have to be changed. They are the following:

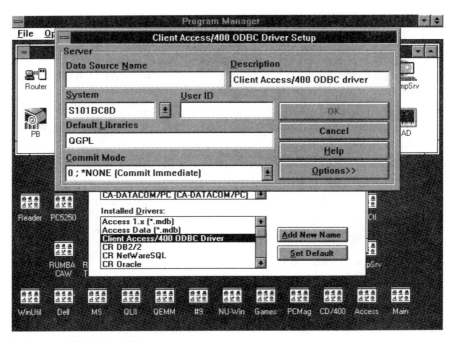

Figure A.3 ODBC Driver Setup screen.

- `ExtendedDynamic`: enables/disables package support on the AS/400. SQL statements that are run often can be stored on the AS/400 so they do not need to be transmitted and interpreted each time. Each application must be enabled and configured for extended dynamic package support, as well as the ODBC driver. If this is done, Client Access can save considerable time in submitting and running remote SQL commands. These commands are saved on the AS/400 in packages. When one of these is called in the application, Client Access searches for a matching AS/400 executable package statement, and can proceed right to it, very quickly. The first time you run an application that is set up for package support, the ODBC driver sets up the necessary entries in `ODBC.INI`. Packages are usually stored on the AS/400 in library `QGPL`. Users must have appropriate authority to the `CRTSQLPKG` command (`*USE`, `*ADD`, and `*CHG`) to take advantage of stored packages.

- `RecordBlocking`: determines when and how often the ODBC driver goes to the AS/400 for new data rows. The more it brings over at one time, and the fewer times it gets data, the more efficient it is. Default is 2 or enabled for all but `SELECT FOR UPDATE OF`.

- `BlockSizeKB`: determines how big the block is in kilobytes for data from the AS/400. The larger the block, the fewer number of transmissions. Defaults to 32K.

- `ODBCRemarks`: which value the ODBC catalog contains to describe the data source. Default is 0 or the *description* set by OS/400.

- `LazyClose`: if enabled, specifies that the `SQLFreeStmt` with `SQLClose` will not go to the AS/400 until the next request in invoked. Defaults to 1 or enabled.

- `AlwaysScrollable`: ensures that *record sets* returned from the AS/400 are scrollable, even if they only contain one record. Default is 0 or always scrollable.

- `ForceTranslation`: translates `CCSID 65535` columns from the AS/400 into ASCII data. Default is), or off.

- `LibraryView`: determines which libraries are returned to the SQL catalog. Default is 0 for the default library list.

Client Access Database Access GUI

Client Access contains a simple method for looking at the data provided through the ODBC driver called the *Client Access Database Access GUI*. Because we have installed Rumba, it is the Rumba for Database Access (Figure A.4). Click on the icon in the Client Access group to open this application up. Once in it, you can select an SQL data source in the pop-up

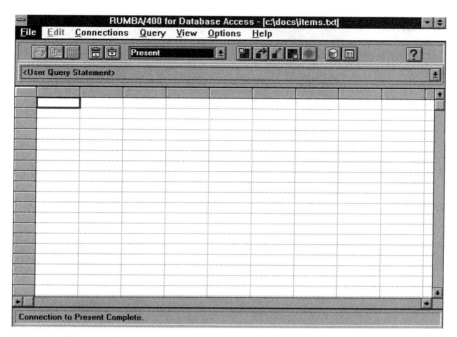

Figure A.4 Rumba for Database Access.

window. Then, the Query Builder window appears to guide you through library, file, field, and record selection (Figure A.5). Click on selections from these various windows to build up your SQL query. The Query Criteria button produces a screen for building up the Where clause of the SQL statement. Note the syntax used by Database Access Query. Periods are used to delimit the full path name to the data fields as: `Library.File.Field`. If you want to type in your own field names, you can observe this convention and enter them. Note that you can join files, order (sort) the records, and group them.

The Query can be run by pressing the Execute button at the bottom of the screen. It can also be saved for later retrieval. The *Execute* button sends the SQL statement to the AS/400 and returns a set of data to the spreadsheet-like viewer (Figure A.6). You then have an ODBC connection that can be used in a number of Windows programs for client/server application development.

Visual Basic

Microsoft's Visual Basic is one of the most popular Windows programming tools. It can connect to the AS/400 through an ODBC data source in several

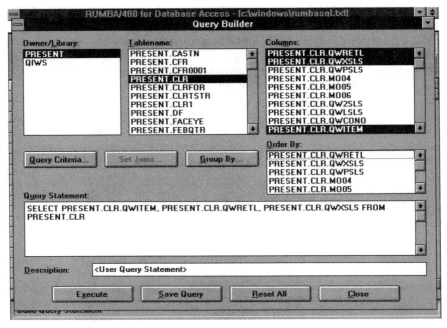

Figure A.5 Query Builder window.

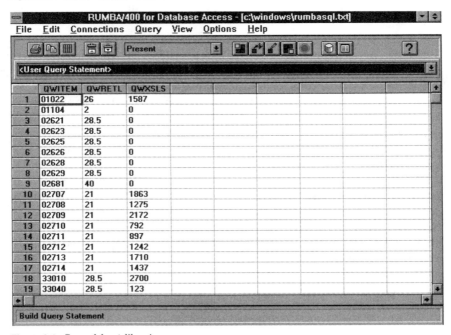

Figure A.6 Spreadsheet-like viewer.

ways. The simplest way is to place a data control on the form that is configured through its properties to connect to the ODBC data source. Then, bound controls can be placed on the form. These controls, like text boxes, are bound to the data control, so that they show fields from the current position of the database to which the data control is pointing through the ODBC driver.

Crystal Reports

Crystal Reports is a report writer bundled with Visual Basic. It can be directly connected to the AS/400 ODBC driver to provide a Windows-based query tool, which can also be integrated with Visual Basic applications. In Crystal Reports, click on New Query. In the Choose Database File window, click on the SQL Table button. Select the data source name you configured from the list of ODBC data sources and press OK. Now you see a list of tables from the ODBC data source. Select the one you want in the Choose SQL Table window. Click OK. Now you get the Insert Database Field window. Do so. Press Insert to point and click these fields onto the Crystal Report. When finished, press the Done button. This query can be viewed by clicking the Print to Window icon in the Crystal Reports toolbar.

PowerBuilder

PowerBuilder needs some configuration to work with ODBC. There is a file called PBODB030.INI or PBODB040.INI depending on the version of PowerBuilder you are using. This file is in the PB3 or PB4 directory. It contains statements that tell PowerBuilder how to configure available Windows ODBC drivers for its use in applications. You need to add a section for the AS/400 ODBC driver for DB2/400.

Make sure that the following syntax is exact:

```
[DB2/400 SQL]
DelimitIdentifier='YES'
PBCatalogOwner='AS/400 library name'
PBDateTime='ISO_TIMEDATE'
PBSyntax='DB24_SYNTAX'
IdentifierCase=3
```

Note: In the PBCatalogOwner entry, enter the name of an existing AS/400 library.

Now we need entries under pattern matching as follows:

```
[DB24_SYNTAX]
AlterForeignKey='ALTER TABLE &TableOwner.&TableName
     FOREIGN KEY &KeyName (&ColumnName,&ColumnName...)
     REFERENCES &RefTableName'
AlterPrimaryKey='ALTER TABLE &TableOwner.&TableName
     PRIMARY KEY (&ColumnName,&ColumnName...)
```

```
CreateTable='CREATE TABLE &TableOwner.&TableName
        (::ColumnElement,::ColumnElement)'
ColumnElement='&ColumnName & DataType & Not Null'
CreateIndex='CREATE &UNIQUE INDEX &IndexName ON &TableOwner.TableName
        (::ColumnIndex,::ColumnIndex...)'
DropTable='DROP TABLE &TableOwner.&TableName'
DropView='DROP VIEW &TableOwner.&TableName'
DropIndex='DROP INDEX &IndexName'
DropPrimaryKey='ALTER TABLE &TableOwner.&TableName
        DROP PRIMARY KEY
DropForeignKey='ALTER TABLE &TableOwner.&TableName
        DROP FOREIGN KEY &KeyName
```

The above entries set up PowerBuilder to use the Windows ODBC driver for the AS/400 DB2/400 database remote access. This data source, once defined as above, should be accessible through the Database Painter. Go to the Database Painter. Select the SQL data source you defined and hit OK. Select a table. Press the Open button and the Preview to see a scrollable excerpt of your defined data source from the AS/400.

Lotus 1-2-3

Lotus can access the AS/400 data, too. You need to make some entries to a configuration file to accomplish this remote link. In C:\WINDOWS\ LOTUSAPP\DATALENS\LOTUS.BCF, enter the following on one line:

```
DN = "AS/400 "DL = "DLODBC"DD = "ODBC for the AS/400"DC = "driver =
ehnodbc3.dll"
```

These entries should make DB2/400 data available to Lotus. To verify, go into Lotus. Click Tools/Database/New Query... and Press the External button. Select the AS/400 ODBC driver and hit Continue. Select the data source you defined and press Continue. Select the table you want and press Continue. Press OK to accept the default name Lotus suggests for the data range name (or you can change it). Use the New Query Assistant window to set fields and criteria for the Query. Click OK. The ODBC driver will return data into the Lotus spreadsheet.

Microsoft Excel

Excel has no extra setup to access the ODBC driver. Just start up Excel. Select Data/GetExternalData. Press the New Query icon on the toolbar. Press Other to define the data source. A list of ODBC data sources comes up. Highlight your data source and press OK. Press Use. In the Add Tables window, select the table you want and click Add and then Close to bring up the Microsoft Query screen. Here you can specify fields, joins, formats, criteria, and the like. The tables selected appear at the top of the screen. You can drag fields from these to the open result column. Select File/Return

Data to Excel to populate the Excel spreadsheet with up-to-the-minute data from the AS/400.

ShowCase VISTA

ShowCase VISTA was specifically designed to connect to the AS/400 and return data into a number of formats, including its own data viewer as well as Lotus and Excel. Start ShowCase VISTA and press the New Query icon on the toolbar. Select your data source and click Next. Expand the Library drop-down list box with the down arrow. Choose the library you want. Expand the File drop-down list box with the down arrow and select the file you want. Now click the Add button to add the file into the Query. Press Next when finished selecting databases. If you have *multiple* files, *ShowCase* VISTA will take you to the Join Tables window to join the files. Select the fields that are used to relate the files to one another. You see the Join Table Conditions window. Click Next. Now you have the Columns window. Here you can highlight column names and press Add to select the fields you want to include in the Query. There are function buttons available including Sum, Average, Min, Max, and Count. There is also a Result field button that allows you to create result or calculated fields for the Query. Finally, press the Run button when ready. The ShowCase VISTA data viewer shows the result set for the Query (unless you specify another data viewer, such as Lotus or Excel).

Microsoft Access

To get into Microsoft Access, double-click its icon. Select New Database on the toolbar. Enter the database name you want for Access. Select Attach Table on the toolbar. Then select < SQL *database* > from the list of available data servers and press OK to bring up a list of SQL Data Sources. Select the data source you configured for the AS/400 ODBC. Press OK to get Access to connect to the AS/400. It comes back with a list of available files or tables in the Attach Tables window. Make your selections and press Attach. Access provides a message box saying that the connection was successful. Press OK to acknowledge this. Select a table or file and hit Open. Access displays the data set from the AS/400 in a tabular format. This data is updatable. You can change records as well as add and delete if the file has a unique access path (index) defined on the AS/400. Otherwise, the ODBC driver does not know how to locate the record you are working with, back on the AS/400. In this event, the data is read-only.

Brio Data Prism

Open Brio Data Prism by double-clicking its icon to bring up the ODBC Logon window. Enter user name and password. Press the Change button to change the data source shown and bring up the Server Chooser window. Use the drop-down boxes in this window to select ODBC as both the Connection Software and the Database Software. Press OK to take you to the ODBC Host Logon window. You can enter the optional User and Password. Use the drop-down box for SQL Data Sources to select your data source. Press OK. Now you see a list of the files in the data source. Double-click the file(s) you want. Windows appear within the DataPrism window containing the fields for each file you selected. Click on columns to include them in the query. Press the Add button. When finished selecting columns of data, press the Process button. The data set from the AS/400 is displayed in a data grid window.

Performance

In general, remember that ODBC performance in client/server applications varies with many factors. Obviously you want to use the fastest processors possible. A 486 66-MHz or better (Pentium) is nice on the PC side, although a 486 33-MHz is possible. More memory is better, too. Use at least 8 or 12 RAM on the PC. Put as much as you can into QINTER on the AS/400. Also, ODBC is SQL-based, so it responds to many of the same factors as Query/400. Just like Query, ODBC will run much faster if it finds an existing access path it can use in its recordset construction. Extended dynamic package support can greatly increase performance. In general, try to reduce the communications traffic between the PC and the AS/400. Stored procedures and triggers are especially useful for this, as they are procedures that execute exclusively on the AS/400 without PC intervention. Record blocking can move larger chunks of data fewer times between the server and the client.

Ethernet Configuration

This appendix presents a sample configuration for a PC attached to an AS/400 through an Ethernet. As many sites are running Novell NetWare for a file server, it is also included. Coexistence between Ethernet, Novell, DOS, Windows, and Client Access is accommodated. When this many different drivers are loaded, conflicts are common. Novell wants to use the Ethernet card one way, while Client Access wants it another way. DOS runs out of conventional memory quickly. We need to run a memory management program to provide more memory in the lower 640K of RAM. Windows needs to be able to run several programs on different operating systems simultaneously, without locking up with the infamous general protection fault (GPF), where separate programs attempt to use the same memory area.

These are some of the considerations in setting up a PC for client/server access to the AS/400. This appendix recommends a sample configuration, but remember that all PCs are different. Memory, chip model, clock speed, disk space, and manufacturer as well as other factors can all influence the configuration requirements. Not all configurations work on all machines. We do not guarantee that the following will work for you, but it has worked for us.

To configure PCs for Ethernet, Novell, and Client Access, you need first to have a physical connection scheme in place. This usually consists of unshielded twisted pair (UTP) cabling. Most businesses these days are installing category 5 (cat 5) UTP, which is capable of up to 100Mb per second transfer rates. This is fast. Standard Ethernet 10BaseT runs at 10Mb, while Token Ring runs at 16Mb (if not 4). Cat 5 will handle fast Ethernet as well, at 100Mb. Cat 5 is basically fancy telephone wire, easy to install and use. It is terminated at the user end at a wall jack (RJ-45, which is a little bigger than a phone jack).

You just plug a cat 5 patch cord into the Ethernet card in the computer and into the wall. You are connected. It is wise to cable as many office locations as possible to allow future flexibility. In the computer room, there is a patch panel where all the cables from the user locations converge. Here, too, there are jacks. In the patch panel, you place Ethernet hubs (or Token Ring MAUs) to connect all the cables together into a network. You just plug a user's jack location in the patch panel into the hub, using another patch cord. In other words, there is a patch cord at the user's desk, and another at the patch panel to connect to the hub. All devices in the network can be plugged in this way, as long as they have an Ethernet (or Token Ring) card. Devices include PCs, the AS/400, printers, toasters, whatever. You need to get an Ethernet card for the AS/400 and configure it. You need a special gizmo to hook up the AS/400's Ethernet card with UTP, known as a *transceiver* or a *type 3 media filter*. It converts the female 15-pin AS/400 Ethernet card connection to female RJ-45, which is the standard UTP connection.

To get a PC onto this network, using Novell and Client Access, you need to perform the following steps:

Install the Ethernet card

1. Remove the cover from the PC.
2. Insert 3Com Ethernet card.
3. Replace the cover on PC. Plug an RJ-45 patch cable into the card and Ethernet hub.

Install the following drivers in the indicated directories.

Most of these drivers are installed automatically from disk when you install the software, like Novell or the Ethernet disk. Exceptions are PROTMAN.DOS, DXMA0MOD .SYS, DXME0MOD.SYS, and LANSUP.COM. Make sure that all drivers are current. Often, what comes in the box is not current. Check with vendors and bulletin boards for updated versions.

```
C:\LSP\PROTMAN.DOS                                    (protocol manager)
C:\LSP\ELNK3.DOS                                    (Ethernet card driver)
C:\LSP\DXMA0MOD.SYS          (AS/400 driver, created from Client Access)
C:\LSP\DXME0MOD.SYS                                      (AS/400 driver)

C:\LSP\NETBIND.EXE                                               Novell
C:\NWCLIENT\LSL.EXE                                              Novell
C:\NWCLIENT\LANSUP.COMIBMC:\NWCLIENT\IPXODI.EXE                  Novell
C:\NWCLIENT\VLM.EXE                                              Novell
```

Make the following entries to your CONFIG.SYS file

```
DEVICE=C:\DOS\HIMEM.SYS
BUFFERS=20,0
FILES=100
DOS=UMB
LASTDRIVE=Z
```

```
FCBS=4,0
DOS=HIGH

DEVICE=C:\DOS\SETVER.EXE
SHELL=C:\DOS\COMMAND.COM/P /E:1024
STACKS=9,256

DEVICE=C:\LSP\PROTMAN.DOS /I:C:\LSP
DEVICE=C:\LSP\ELNK3.DOS
DEVICE=C:\LSP\DXMA0MOD.SYS 001
DEVICE=C:\LSP\DXME0MOD.SYS N ,,,,6
```

Make the following entries to your AUTOEXEC.BAT file

```
PROMPT $P$G
C:\DOS\DOSKEY
MODE CON RATE=32 DELAY=1

PATH C:\;C:\DOS;C:\WINDOWS;C:\CAWIN;C:\RUMBACAW
SET MSINPUT=C:\MSINPUT
SET TEMP=C:\DOS
SET COMSPEC=C:\DOS\COMMAND.COM

C:\DOS\SMARTDRV
C:\LSP\NETBIND
CD\NWCLIENT
LSL
LANSUP
IPXODI
VLM

F:
LOGIN
C:
CD\

WIN
```

These entries load all the requisite drivers in DOS and start Windows at boot up time.

Set the alternate address on the Ethernet card. Setting the alternate address is so that the Novell drivers do not conflict with the Client Access drivers. Use the Ethernet configuration disk which came with the card (or set switches). Set the alternate address to 240h.

Run Memmaker's Express option. Running this option loads as many drivers as possible into high memory. Go to DOS and type "mem /c | more" to check that upper memory is working correctly.

Install Client Access. Place the Client Access installation disks in drive A:. In Windows, select File/Run. Type A:INSTALL. Follow the prompts to install Client Access (Figure B.1).

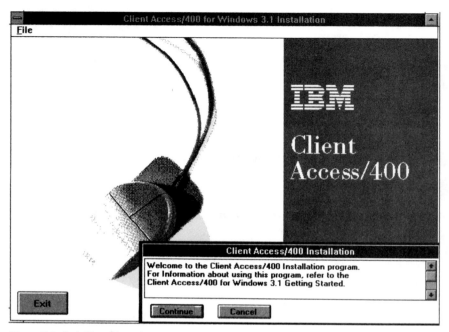

Figure B.1 Installing Client Access.

Place an x next to Update. Leave the installation directory as the default C:\CAWIN. Press Install. In Common Options, select LAN (Figure B.2). Enter the user's name for PC Location (must be unique).

```
PC Network = leave blank
AS/400 User ID = user's AS/400 profile
OK
Press Add (Figure B.3)
Enter your AS/400 System Name (S12345678, or whatever it is) as in Figure
B.4
Enter the LAN Address of your AS/400's Ethernet card (you need to know
this)
OK

OK
Restart = Yes
Enter user's password
Additional functions:
Network Printers (only if the user needs one)
Rumba
Replace Netware with AS/400 network? Yes
```

The Client Access group is created in Windows (Figure B.5).

Install Rumba. Because you indicated in the previous steps that you want to install Rumba, the installation process continues with the following:

```
Indicate single user
Press Install (files download from AS/400)
Run Rumba? Yes
Restart? Yes
Select Terminal from the Rumba group
On the Rumba menu, select:
   Session/ConnectSession/AutoConnectSession/AutoDisconnect

Map the keyboard with Options/Keyboard
   Map Enter & Field Exit functions to the usual AS/400 5250 keys

Save the profile as username.wsf

Place an icon on the desktop to run this Rumba session, using File/New/
Program Item in the Windows menu.

Command Line:
C:\RUMBACAW\RUMBAWSF.EXE username
Working Directory: C:\RUMBACAW
```

When this icon is double-clicked, it starts up a Rumba terminal emulation
session.

NSD.INI. As a result of the Client Access installation, a file is created
in the Windows directory called NSD.INI, which takes the place of

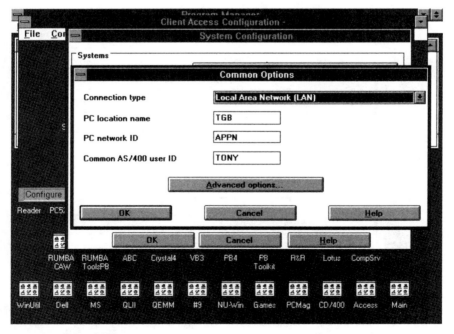

Figure B.2 Select LAN.

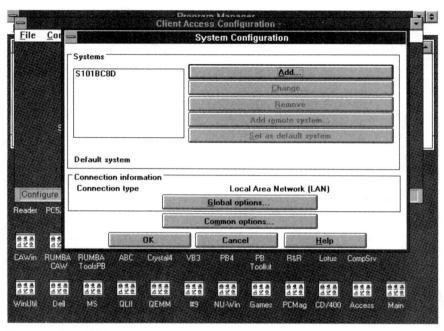

Figure B.3 Press Add.

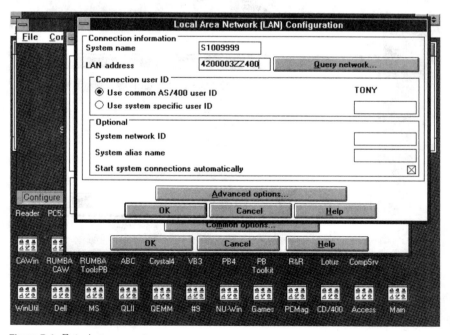

Figure B.4 Entering your system name.

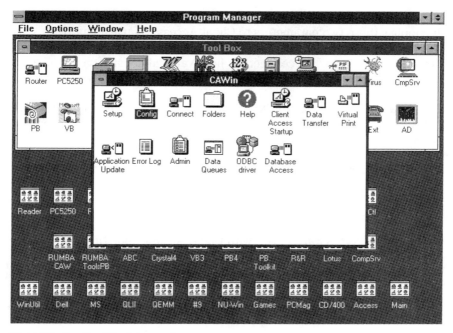

Figure B.5 Creating Client Access group.

CONFIG.PCS from PC Support. It contains many of the configuration parameters specified during installation. It looks something like this:

```
[Configuration]
LANGUAGE=2924
DIRECTORY=C:\CAWIN
COMMONUSERID=TONY
LOCALLUNAME=APPN.TGB
DLCTYPE=LAN
[MODES]
QPCSUPP=*, 7, 32, 16
QSERVER=*, 7, 32, 16
SNASVCMG=256, 1, 2, 1
BLANK=,2, 8, 4
#BATCH=256, 3, 8, 4
#INTER=, 7, 8, 4
[LAN]
TRLI1=S1041956,4200003CC300,,,,,,,,,,,
TRAN=0
TRSS=04
TRRL=5
TRAL =4
TRAS=5
TRMF=1496

[SIDEINFO]
S1041956=APPN.S1041956,QPCSUPP,*,SAME,TONY,XXXXX,S1041956,1
```

Note the user name and password (TONY, XXXXX) entered in the last line. It supplies these two parameters to Client Access when attempting to start the AS/400, relieving the user of the necessity to enter a password at this stage. This is only for the connection, however, and not sign on. If you want automatic sign on, you create a Rumba automacro.

NET.CFG. If you are running Novell NetWare, you must consider the NET .CFG file. It needs some changes to coexist with Client Access. Note the lines that say

```
LINK DRIVER 3C5X9LINK STATIONS 8SAPS 5
```

and

```
FRAME ETHERNET_802.3
```

These enable NetWare to run with Client Access. Your Novell file server needs to be configured for ETHERNET_802.3, as well.

NET.CFG looks like this:

```
; THIS SECTION IS FOR CONFIGURATION OF LINKWATCH MANAGEABLE END NODES.
;
Protocol DME
    BIND #1
; replace with your specific information for LinkWatch
    USER_NAME "Your Name"
    NODE_NAME "Your Node Name"
    NODE_LOCATION "Your Node Location"
; set password according to your network administrator's instructions
; NODE_PASSWORD "ABCDEFGH"
    PHONE_NUMBER "Your Phone Number"
    NOTES "Miscellaneous text"
    NOTES "and more text"

LINK DRIVER 3C5X9
LINK STATIONS 8
SAPS 5;
;
```

The following two parameters are required when using two or more EtherLink III adapters in a single machine. These parameters specify which specific EtherLink III adapter the driver is to attach itself to.

- PORT NNN, where NNN is the hex base address of the 3C509 ISA adapter
- SLOT NN, where NN is the slot number containing the 3C529, 3C579, or 3C509 configured as an EISA adapter
- PORT 200
- SLOT 3

The next line specifies the frame type. Because 3C5X9.COM is a 4.01 DOS ODI driver, the driver default frame type is 802.2. If attaching to a 3.11 server, the frame type is 802.3.

```
    FRAME ETHERNET_802.3
;
NetWare DOS Requester
    FIRST NETWORK DRIVE = F
    READ ONLY COMPATIBILITY = OFF
```

Summary

Configurations can be confusing, and no wonder. We are tying together OS/400, DOS, Windows, Client Access, Rumba and Netware through Ethernet (or Token Ring) to lay the physical and communications groundwork for client/server applications. Many different problems can and probably will arise during this process. Do not hesitate to call the various vendors and their help lines to resolve these problems. They will generally get back to you within a few hours or a day with answers to problems. Start early and configure just a few workstations to get the bugs worked out. Once you have a workable format, the rest of the PCs should go relatively easily.

Index

A

advanced client/server environment (ACE), 281

advanced peer-to-peer networking (APPN), 4, 11, 41-43, 136

advanced program-to-program communications (APPC), 11, 43, 156, 184

AppleTalk, 149, 151

application layer, 36, 156

application programming interface (API), 4, 11, 26, 43-44, 58-59, 136, 146

application services, 40, 44-46

applications, 287-289

  Lotus, 357-366

  PC client, 167-171

  PowerBuilder, 291-334

  Rumba, 367-377

  sample client/server, 12, 14, **13**

  Visual Basic, 335-342

  Crystal Reports, 343-356

architecture

  client/server, 35-48

  DIA, 40, 44

  DRDA, 40, 45-46, 68-70

  FDOCA, 39

  FOCA, 39

  GOCA, 39

  IOCA, 39

  PTOCA, 39

  SAA, 4, 38, 73-74, 147, 157

  SNA, 4, 40-41, 44-46, 147, 149, 150

  SNADS, 40, 44-45

  SNAMS, 40, 46

  WOSA, 58

AS/400 server, 4, 12, 49-51

  advanced server series, 91-97

  applications, 92

  Client Access/400 software, 53-60

  configuring for ODBC, 379

  DB2/400 database, 61-71

  distributed network features, 91-92

  file server input/output processor, 94-95

  models, 93

  performance enhancements, 94

AUTOEXEC.BAT, 108-110, 139

B

basic input/output system (BIOS), 31

batch files, 107-110

booting, dual, 139

bridges, 37, 158

  VM/MVS, 45

Brio Data Prism, 387-388

bus topology, 160

C

C programming language, 26

cable and cabling

  coaxial, 157

  Ethernet, 159-160, 389-397

  fiberoptic, 157

  T-1, 157-158

  unshielded twisted pair, 157

classes, 28-29

Client Access/400 software, 53-60

  API support, 58-59

  data queues, 57

  file transfer, 57

  installing, 54-55

  integrated file system, 57-58

  national language support, 58

  printers, 55-56

  requirements, 59

  submitting remote controls, 56

  terminal emulation, 55

Illustrations are indicated in **boldface**.

RAM, 104, 126
  upper, 106
memory management
  DOS, 105-107
  OS/2, 134-135
  Windows, 126-127
menus, 20, 22, **21**
message box, 25
message handling service (MHS), 161
messages, 29
messaging application program interface
  (MAPI), 58
methods, 28
Microsoft Access, ODBC and, 387
Microsoft Excel, ODBC and, 386-387
mouse systems, 22-24
  cursor placement, 23
  cut and paste, 23-24
  highlighting text, 23
  point and click, 22-23
multiple access unit (MAU), 158-159
multitasking, 104, 128
  preemptive, 133-134
multithreading, 128

N

name service, 37
named pipes, 134
NetBIOS, 157
NetWare, 160-162
NetWare link services protocol (NLSP),
  162
NetWare management system (NMS), 161
network driver interface specification
  (NDIS), 59
network drives, 59
network file system (NFS), 149
network layer, 36, 156
network node, 39
network redirector, 59
network transport services, 36
networks and networking, 11, 155-165
  APPN, 4, 11, 41-43, 136
  cabling (*see* cables and cabling)
  ISDN, 158
  LANs, 157-158
  LEN, 41
  protocols (*see* protocols)
  topologies,
    bus, 160
    Token Ring, 158-159
  WANs, 102, 157-158
node operating facility (NOF), 59

O

object linking and embedding (OLE), 124-
  125, 225

Visual Basic and, 219-220
Visual C++ and, 269
object-oriented programming (OOP), 27-30
  classes, 28-29
  encapsulation, 29
  inheritance, 29
  messages, 29
  methods, 28
  objects, 28
  polymorphism, 29-30
  Visual C++ and, 264-265
object-oriented programming (OOP), 27-30
objects, 28, 39
open database connectivity (ODBC), 5, 12,
  47, 58, 74, 105, 125-126, 357, 378-388
  Brio Data Prism and, 387-388
  Client Access, 379-382
    administrator window, **380**
    database access GUI, 382-383
    driver setup screen, **381**
  configuring AS/400 for, 379
  Lotus and, 386
  Microsoft Access and, 387
  Microsoft Excel and, 386-387
  possible connections, 378-379
  PowerBuilder and, 385-386
  ShowCase VISTA and, 387
  Visual Basic, 383-385
    Crystal Reports and, 385
Open Software Foundation (OSF), 4, 36-37
open systems interconnect (*see* OSI)
operating systems, 10-12
  DOS, 11, 31, 99-100, 103-111
  Network, 11
  OS/2, 4, 11, 32, 100-101, 131-140
  OS/400, 11, 91
  System 7, 4, 11, 32, 101-102
  UNIX, 4, 11, 32, 101, 141-148
  Windows, 4, 11, 31, 100, 113-130
  Windows 95, 127-130
  Windows NT, 100, 114-115, 162-164
  X-Windows, 11, 32, 101, 144-145
Oracle, 279-280
OS/2, 4, 11, 32, 100-101, 131-140
  AUTOEXEC.BAT, 139
  Communications Manager, 135-136
  CONFIG.SYS, 139
  configuration files, 139
  Database Manager, 136-138
  DOS and, 138-139
  Extended Services, 135
  file systems, 139
  folders, 132
  icons, 132
  memory management, 134-135
  preemptive multitasking, 133-134
  Presentation Manager, Workplace Shell,
    131-133

ABOUT THE AUTHOR

Tony Baritz is MIS director at Clarins, USA Inc. He has 15 years of experience as a systems analyst and computer consultant, designing and coding systems for major New York businesses. An adjunct lecturer at New York University, he is the author of *AS/400: Concepts and Facilities* (1990: McGraw-Hill).